DØ191369

Making Sense in
Life and Literature

Theory and History of Literature
Edited by Wlad Godzich and Jochen Schulte-Sasse

For other books in the series, see p. 348

Making Sense in Life and Literature

Hans Ulrich Gumbrecht

Translated by Glen Burns

Foreword by Wlad Godzich

Theory and History of Literature, Volume 79

University of Minnesota Press, Minneapolis

"Phoenix from the Ashes; Or, From Canon to Classic" originally appeared in *New Literary History*, 20.1 (1988). "Consequences of an Aesthetics of Reception" first appeared in *Poetica* 7 (1975): 388–413; "Metahistorical Historiography?" first appeared in Hans Ulrich Gumbrecht, Ursula Link-Heer, and Peter-Michael Spangenberg (eds.), *La littérature historiographique des origines a 1500. Grundriss der romanischen Literaturen des Mittelalters*, vol. 12, pt.1 (Heidelberg: Winter Verlag, 1986), 27–39; "The Role of Narration on Narrative Genres" first appeared in Eberhard Lämmert (ed.), *Erzählforschung* (Stuttgart: Metzler Verlag, 1982), 202–17; "Narrating the Past Just as if It Were Your Own Time" first appeared in Reinhart Koselleck and Jörn Rüsen (eds.), *Formen der Geschichtsschreibung, Theorie der Geschichte*, vol. 4 (Munich: Deutscher Taschenbuch-Verlag, 1982), 480–513; "A History of the Concept 'Modern' " first appeared in Otto Brunner, Werner Conze, and Reinhart Koselleck (eds.), *Geschichtliche Grundbegriffe: Historisches Lexikon zur politisch-sozialien Sprache in Deutschland*, vol. 4 (Stuttgart: Klett-Cotta, 1978), 93–131; "Laughter and Arbitrariness, Subjectivity and Seriousness" first appeared in *Wolfram-Studien* 7 (1982): 184–213; "Who Were the *Philosophes*?" first appeared in Rolf Reichardt and Eberhard Schmitt (eds.), *Handbuch politisch-sozialer Grundbegriffe in Frankreich, 1680*–1820, vol. 3 (Munich: Oldenbourg-Verlag, 1985), 7–88; "Outline of a Literary History of the French Revolution" first appeared in Jürgen von Stackelberg (ed.), *Die europäische Aufklärung III. Handbuch der Literaturewissenschaft*, vol 13 (Wiesbaden: Athinaion, 1981), 269–328; "Phoenix from the Ashes; or, From Canon to Classic" first appeared in Aleida Assman and Jan Assmann (eds.), *Kanon und Zensur: Archäologie der literarischen Kommunikation*, vol. 2 (Munich: Fink-Verlag, 1987), 284–99; "Pathologies in the System of Literature" first appeared in Dirk Baecker et al. (eds.), *Theorie als Passion: Festschrift für Niklas Luhmann* (Frankfurt: Suhrkamp-Verlag, 1987), 137–180; "It's Just a Game" first appeared in *Arete* [now *Aethlon*]: *The Journal of Sport Literature* 4 (1986): 24–43, by permission.

Published by the University of Minnesota Press
2037 University Avenue Southeast, Minneapolis, MN 55414
Printed in the United States of America on acid-free paper

Library of Congress Cataloging-in-Publication Data

Gumbrecht, Hans Ulrich.
    Making sense in life and literature / Hans Ulrich Gumbrecht ; translated by Glen Burns.
      p. cm. — (Theory and history of literature ; v. 79)
    Includes bibliographical references and index.
    ISBN 0-8166-1952-2 (HC)
    ISBN 0-8166-1954-9 (PB)
    1. Criticism. 2. Hermeneutics. 3. Aesthetics, Modern—20th century. 4. History—Philosophy. I. Title. II. Series.
    PN81.G86 1992
    801'.95—dc20   90-19965
                                                    CIP

Contents

Foreword
Figuring Out What Matters;
or, The Microphysics of History
Wlad Godzich

The idea for this collection arose during a brief visit by Hans Ulrich Gumbrecht to the University of Minnesota in the winter of 1983. I had read a number of his essays before his visit and was struck by what seemed to me then an interesting turn being taken within the German school of reception aesthetics, of which Gumbrecht was considered to be one of the younger luminaries. He had after all written his thesis at the University of Constance under the direction of Hans Robert Jauss, the acknowledged founder of the school and whose works, incidentally, we were just beginning to publish in English translation in this series. Gumbrecht himself had been described as the rising star of this school, achieving the extraordinary distinction of being named to a full professorship (*Ordinarius*) at the University of Bochum at the age of twenty-six. He had gone on from there to the University of Siegen, where he founded and directed the first graduate training program in literary and theoretical studies in Germany, a program marked by its openness to a wide variety of approaches, its active pursuit of interdisciplinariness, and an unheard of spirit of contentious though friendly disputation. All of these features were also very much in evidence in the soon-to-become legendary colloquia organized by Gumbrecht and his closest ally at Siegen, K. Ludwig Pfeiffer, in the Adriatic resort city of Dubrovnik, where scholars gathered from four continents and a dozen disciplines to examine notions or concepts that crossed or alternatively traced the boundaries between their fields.

When I first met him at Minnesota, Gumbrecht was the author of several books and over a hundred papers. My initial purpose in raising with him the possibility of drawing up a collection of his essays for this series was to explore what I had come to think of as the work of the second generation of practitioners of reception aesthetics. Instead of chafing at the restrictive way in which I was approaching him, Gumbrecht suggested very sensibly that I read as many of his essays as I cared to and suggest to him a possible table of contents. This volume is the result of this process, and, as the reader will soon realize, it is at some remove from the concerns and presuppositions of reception aesthetics, even though Gumbrecht's work has not abandoned one of its most important starting points.

This starting point is history, or perhaps more accurately, the nature of historical experience on the one hand, and the ability for our conceptual and scholarly apparatus to give a credible account of this experience on the other. Reception aesthetics had tried to address this problem by placing the recipient of literature as the ground of literary experience at the center of its approaches, but it soon began to lose this very ground as the recipient in question grew more abstract and progressively took on the form of one more layer of mediation between actual recipients and the experience of literature so that we learned, very valuably to be sure, what conditioned and framed the experience of recipients rather than what the actual experience of historically specific readers had been. This state of affairs led some, notably Gumbrecht's University of Siegen colleague Siegfried J. Schmidt, to try to develop ever more empirical ways of ascertaining what the readerly experience had actually been, but this approach increasingly began to take on the appearance of positivistic sociology with all of its attendant theoretical and methodological problems. Gumbrecht adopted a different path, one that came to focus on the very notions of experience and of history.

It may be useful at this juncture to invoke a recent controversy that illustrates very well the difficulties that are precipitated by any attempt to make sense of a historical experience while preserving the nature of this experience. As the events that we can term the collapse of the Soviet empire began to unfold in 1987 and 1988, Francis Fukuyama, the deputy director of the U.S. State Department's policy planning staff, published an essay in the summer of 1988 issue of *The National Interest* entitled "The End of History?", in which he sought to interpret the events in Eastern Europe by means of Hegel's notion that history has an end and that what we were witnessing was indeed such an end. It is universally acknowledged that Fukuyama's interpretation of Hegel is rudimentary and does not go beyond a *Reader's Digest* version of Alexandre Kojève's standard reformulation of the problem. Nonetheless, somewhat surprisingly in the context of the U.S. State Department, Fukuyama had appealed to a theory of history to account for the experience of lived history. In the discussions that ensued what stands out, besides the fact that many of those involved had no idea of what Hegel had said or what a theory of history is, is the disbelief voiced over and over again that anyone could describe by the terms "End of History" a period that seemd on the contrary to be replete with history. Fukuyama's detractors appealed to the experience of their readers and insisted that we were living through a period that was particularly historically eventful and that history seemed to be taking place on all sides of us. According to them it is only through some intellectual perversion, such as philosophy, that one could account for this experience by invoking the end of something that was flourishing with such vigor.

This is not the place to discuss the merits of Fukuyama's underlying thesis. For our purposes here it is more important to point out that the views of Fukuyama and those of his detractors, though apparently irreconcilable, form a notional complex that is precipitated as soon as one tries to give a theoretically motivated account of historical experience. What Fukuyama's opponents were saying was that, at best, his account was counterintuitive. What they failed to consider is that it may very well be in the nature of historical explanation to be such or, to put it more bluntly, that lived historical experience is likely to stand in opposition to any theoretical account of itself. This may very well have been the shoal upon which reception aesthetics has foundered. It is also the channel Gumbrecht has been trying to dredge. Few literary scholars have had the training and the courage to explore the history of historiography with an eye to the understanding of the way in which our own experience is affected by history but also constitutive of it. Gumbrecht has the training, and he certainly has shown the required fortitude.

Contrary to commonly received opinion, History, which I capitalize to designate the discipline, is a relatively recent endeavor. In fact, it begins to emerge at the time when the general principles and tenets of Newtonian mechanics gain wide currency, that is, during the epoch we persist in calling the Enlightenment. This does not mean that there had not existed an interest in the past before, nor that this interest was often referred to by the term *history*, but the nature of this interest was substantially different from what we currently call History. To be sure, one can always find instances of prior usage that resemble ours, but they are isolated and stand at the margins of the periods during which they were formulated. Let us review briefly some of these past conceptions of history, starting with the Middle Ages, the epoch Gumbrecht has studied the most.

Chroniclers and annalists of various sorts consigned elements of dynastic and church history from the earliest Middle Ages, but their activity was limited to the recording of events and happenstances and is usually devoid of any reflection upon the meaning or the significance of the events they record, though, obviously, their selection of data to record confers significance to these data or, at least, attests to the fact that significance had been ascribed to them. Things begin to change in the twelfth century when the Neoplatonists of the School of Chartres, eager to provide a fuller account of the world around them, decide that they can find ways of reconciling those parts of the heritage of antiquity they have received with the then-hegemonic account provided by Christian doctrine. They introduce modes of reading texts that permit them to claim that Plato's account of the origins of the universe in the *Timeus* is not at odds with that of Genesis. This step is extremely important, for it suggests that consistency of account is the primary criterion by which to judge any new data—a mode of reasoning modern science will certainly adopt as its own, so that today the exciting research in superstring theory is judged exclusively on this basis since no one can yet imagine any experimental way of testing its findings. It has the further advantage of suggesting that texts, or even phenomena, that appear to be at considerable odds with received knowledge, or revelation, are not thereby automatically dismissed; rather, they impose upon us the obligation to find the proper way of reconciling them with received knowledge. They are a challenge to our ability to maintain the consistency of revelation. Initially, and certainly among the Chartrians, one would never tamper with the received knowledge; one would read, or interpret, the other text or the new data in such a way that it would fit the tenets of revelation. But the authority of revelation did not prove everlasting.

There is one area in which it proved to be quite complicated to invoke: morals. The sacred texts do enjoin certain forms of behavior and prohibit others, but Christianity differed from Judaism in eschewing a legalization of behavior, preferring on the whole broad injunctions to specific regulations. Inevitably, there arose a need to identify models of proper, and improper, behavior to compensate for the excessive laconism of the New Testament on this topic. Lives of saints were written and accounts of the lives of famous pagans were scrutinized to extract from them the models that would guarantee the moral uplifting of righteous Christians. We know these models under the name of *exempla*, narratives of others' lives, or of events in others' lives, admitting of a moral lesson. The mechanism of *exemplum* is simple: a singular happenstance is related so that it can serve as an instance of a universal principle, which can now be imposed as a moral imperative on the recipient of the story. The universal principle may have been explicitly stated in revelation, but, more often than not, it is enough that it be derived from the *exemplum* in such a way that it is consistent with the rest of revelation. There occurred thus a subtle shift in authority from revelation itself, though it remains unchallenged, to experience, the past experience of the exemplar. Moreover, since the signifying economy of the *exemplum* follows the rule of logical abduction, in which a law is derived from a singular instance to then be generalized to all instances, past experience, which corresponds to the status of the singular instance invoked at the beginning of the abductive process, governs current, and indeed future, experience, as the law that is derived from it is given the status of universal or general law (the distinction between universal and general is not material in this case).

Such an approach is certainly sufficient to provide normativity with the contents it requires, but it has no criteria of normalcy. Nor does it need them: the norms it seeks to impose are absolute and ultimately are vouched for by the absoluteness of revelation. Nonetheless the absence of any criteria of normalcy makes itself felt by skewing the search for exemplars toward ever more extreme instances. In fact, this absence made the inclusion of marvelous, and miraculous, instances possible as well. It fostered a form of curiosity that hankered after the exceptional. It is not difficult to see that both the reliance upon an abductive logic and the valorization of the exception rest upon the fundamental fact of a supernatural transcendence, located in the divine, that guarantees a happy outcome to the abductive process and offers the exceptional as a challenge to the limited capabilities of our finite cognition. The search for norms of behavior was a search for conformity with the divine design, the prior existence of which served as a de jure guarantee that phenomena were not senseless, though not necessarily wholly accessible to human beings. But as soon as Aquinas argued that the divine design conformed to reason and Alain de Lille claimed that the world of existents was governed by natural law, then a human knowledge of the universe began to be conceivable. And when the voyages of discoveries returned their huge profits to those who had wagered on them, calculation, in the form of a search for normalcy, could take the place of the search for normativity.

To be sure the world of nature would, more than ever, be subject to norms, now described as physical laws, but the nature of these laws resided not in their conformity to a divine design but to the normalcy of observable phenomena. Newton's view of the universe gained currency not because Newton had peeked at God's plans but because it predicted phenomenal behavior that was easy to verify. It established what was the normal behavior of things in the universe.

It is a little different in the world of human beings. There is no incentive to search for normalcy initially. Whereas previously the valorization of behavior was a function of the behavior's conformity to an ascertainable divine design, presently behavior became valued inasmuch as it fostered more immediate gains and profits—indeed, when it ensured that returns on investments were maximized. Whereas previously valorized behavior was termed pleasing to God, now it was termed conducive to the progress of humankind. We are now quite familiar with this secularized version of salvational history, but we need to remark upon the fact that the modern conception of history effected a break between the world of nature subject to the permanence of physical laws and the world of human beings engaged in a march of progress. This break posited in effect two distinct experiential realms and perhaps even two distinct rationalities. For the thinkers of the Enlightenment the problem is far from insuperable. Kant, for instance, believes that nature is governed by a general purposiveness and that human activity enacts this purposiveness on behalf of nature.

Kant may have believed that he was thus restoring a monism that threatened to disappear, but even he had to acknowledge the diversity of humankind and, concomitantly the plurality of histories. Where, in the late seventeenth century, a Bossuet could still seriously entertain the project of universal history, one that would of course be written as the unfolding of a divine plan, Kant and his successors had to face the fact that different human beings seemed to be animated by differing forces and to pursue different projects. What is one to make, for example, of the French Revolution? Does it usher in a new stage in the history of humankind and is Napoleon therefore justified in carrying its message by the force of arms across the entire Continent? Or is it the attempt by one nation to impose its values upon others? This question is far from banal, and the need for consistency produced some interesting contortions in the answers it received. There were those who argued that it was in the name of the very principles for which the Revolution had stood that one had to resist the imposition of its order, arguing in effect that they were the defenders of the purity of the Revolution against its perversion. Even simpleminded reactionaries who rejected all of the Revolution had to account to themselves for its occurrence in the first place. Theories of national character flourished and formed the bases for claims to statehood that had to be legitimated by adducing the evidence of determinate national temper in the past. The study of literature was thus mobilized, dressed in the uniform of national literary history, and made to march on behalf of the state's political autonomy. Existing states marshal it to ensure their continuity; nascent and aspiring states, to proclaim their right to existence.

While it is true that the European nineteenth century unfolds under the aegis of History, this History has but little in common with the Universal History that preceded it. In fact, it could be described as a History caught in the precarious tension between the centrifugal forces of positivistic research into the history of nations, states, eventually institutions, and even families, and the centripetal forces of philosophical or speculative History that seek to recover on its behalf a theory of agency that would ensure that the senselessness ultimately lurking at the core of the positivistic approach is held at bay by a comprehensive understanding of an unfolding historical process taking place through the individual and collective actions of historical players. The most famous of these efforts is indeed that of Hegel, who sought to provide a single developmental narrative of the conquest of matter by spirit, and to identify the State with the spirit triumphant. What is remarkable about Hegel's solution is that it deals with the two sources of fragmentation that we have just observed: by positing that spirit conquers matter, it turns the separation of the natural sphere from the human one into an episode in the unfolding of the spirit, and, by its theory of stages or episodes, it turns the individual histories of smaller groups, and even nations, into the building blocks of universal history. His is the last attempt to return to the monism Kant thought he had protected. The more recent attempts of Toynbee, Spengler, and even Voegelin are more restricted and confine themselves to the sphere of human actions, leaving out the world of nature, and this in spite of the fact that the description of this world was increasingly carried out in historical terms, first in geology, then in the theory of evolution, and eventually in astronomical cosmology. Dilthey recognized the limits of the effort to reunify knowledge by attempting to provide all the disciplines dealing with the sphere of human behavior with a body of methodological procedures as complete as, but distinct from, that of the natural sciences.

It is this surrender to the separation of the two types of knowledge that C. P. Snow deplored, more so than the separation between the two research communities of scientists and humanists, to use today's shorthand terms. For what this surrender amounts to is the paradoxical instauration of a historical happenstance into a permanent fact: we know that it is in the Enlightenment that the paths of scientific truth and historical truth diverged, yet we now seem to find ourselves in a position to enforce this divorce and perhaps even to justify it. The consequences are quite momentous: either we maintain the unity of reason and declare that one of these truths is not of a rational nature — this has been the path of German historicism (which vested in the State a higher interest, called significantly the Reason of State) — or we admit to a plurality of rationalities, whose competing claims and encroachments will have to be arbitrated by a superior instance, once again the State, but a State of Power functioning ideally as the manager of an empire in which these diverse rationalities have their own territories. These territories can consist of geosocial entities not unlike the millets of the Ottoman Empire or of intellectual fields or disciplines, for, from this perspective, all that matters is that a different system of laws operates within a field, without regard for the entities to which these laws apply.

There is every indication that currently it is the second option that is being favored. On the one hand, the fragmentation process we had observed earlier is still going on, and it is being legitimated in some quarters by a substantialization of differences in which difference is recovered on behalf of identity. On the other, there is more attention than ever to the play of power and to its economy. These two processes have come to animate the methodological movement known as the New Historicism, which acknowledges the existence of multiple claims to rationality only to dwell upon the way in which these claims are adjudicated by the instance that holds the most power in any given situation. In effect the New Historicism differs from the old in that the old one vested this adjudicatory power in a State that it saw as enforcing its superior interests, whereas the New Historicism hypostatizes power and sees no superior interests as its motivating force except in the form of a manipulatory justification.

The New Historicism rests upon an idiosyncratic interpretation of the two thinkers it sees as its precursors: from Raymond Williams it has taken a nostalgia for a monism that Williams saw as no longer recoverable under conditions of class society; from Michel Foucault it has fashioned the politics of power into a substitute monistic explanation. What Foucault had sought to address in his archaeology was somewhat different and much closer to the concerns we were examining above: how do we deal with the competing claims of scientific truth and of historical truth? The issue was not power but rather how the politics of power have been a way of dealing with the fact that scientific progress takes place in history while relying upon an inner logic that seems to be independent of history. Unlike the positivistic historians of science, for whom he had nothing but scorn, Foucault did not accept as sufficient the idea that advances in the sciences could be accounted for by changing sociocultural conditions. They have a role to play – indeed, a necessary one as he acknowledged on more than one occasion – but it is not sufficient to determine the advances. Neither, however, could Foucault accept the idea that scientific progress was the result of an inner process where an advance dictated the advent of another, for how would one account then for the long periods of waiting between the realization of some advance? In other words, Foucault was attempting to resolve the dilemma that we started out with: why is it that a coherent and elegant account of the progress of scientific thought, one that makes visible all the links between past accomplishments and failures and the new discoveries, appears to be so removed from the historical experience of these discoveries? His solution was archaeology: a mode of inquiry directed by the preservation of this dilemma and a language in which the dilemma would not be occulted. To return to the Hegelian terms: Foucault did not see spirit conquering matter, nor as some easy reversals of Hegel had sought to put it, matter resisting, and eventually conquering, spirit, but described rather the inextricability of matter and spirit. It is for this reason that Foucault did not have a theory of historical agency, or, more precisely, a theory of historical agents. The New Historicism departs sharply from Foucault in this respect, for it does have a theory of historical agents and patients, but in doing so, it marks a regress vis-à-vis Foucault.

Gumbrecht may believe that his work shares some affinity with that of the New Historicists, but this belief is not sustained by a reading of his essays, except perhaps on the most superficial level of a concern with archival and anecdotal historical material. From the historiographer Reinhart Koselleck, Gumbrecht has gathered a sophisticated view of the problems of history and the handling of agency in relation to time in modernity. But even more important, he has drawn abundantly upon the sociological system theory of Niklas Luhmann, a thinker of great importance to postwar Germany who in effect permitted a return to historical thinking without retaining the old categories of such thinking. These issues came to the fore in a memorable debate that opposed Luhmann to Habermas. The latter, as the heir to the tradition of the Frankfurt School, has sought to restore the continuity of German history by taking fully into account the Nazi period and its sequelae against the long-official amnesia that prevailed in Germany after the war. It is well known, and therefore does not need to be rehearsed here, that Habermas takes contemporary society to be suffering from a certain number of dysfunctions that have to do with the substitution of monological expert languages for what had been in the Enlightenment a sphere of public discourse, and he sees himself as the therapist of these dysfunctions.

Luhmann's point of departure is actually the Hegelian notion of an end of history, but with one major modification: whereas in Hegel this end of history culminates with the advent of the almighty state, Luhmann takes the state as the figure that drives history toward its end and that withers away once this end is achieved. Thus, not unlike the French thinkers who have come under the sway of Kojève, such as Blanchot and through him Derrida, Luhmann asks himself how a posthistorical society functions, but whereas the French thinkers do so by examining the dysfunctions and problems of such a posthistorical order, Luhmann has focused on the actual processes by which such a society regulates itself and indeed invents itself. Gumbrecht was quick to see that Luhmann's approach allowed one to remain within the Foucauldian avoidance of a theory of agents while having a theory of agency, and that, moreover, the processes analyzed and described by Luhmann were akin to the reflections of cognitive biologists such as Humberto Maturana and Francisco Varela, who saw organisms as engaged in a process of autopoiesis, a process of self-creation that does not enact some prewritten script but rather represents a most powerful engagement with the contingency of living. Unlike the New Historicists who retained Williams's nostalgic call for interdisciplinariness, Gumbrecht actually summoned Luhmann and Varela to his Dubrovnik colloquia and interrogated them in front of philosophers, historians, and literary theorists, as well as practitioners of other sciences.

The result, as the reader will rapidly see, is not a return to monism, but neither is it a resigned acceptance of dispersion. It is a major displacement of the terms with which we have been working. The reconfiguration Gumbrecht slowly finds himself enacting (for one cannot speak of a process that he either intends or wills here) revolves around the centrality of contingency. Contingency is a paradoxical temporal formation in that it is so unstable it appears to have escaped time altogether, to have no temporal dimension, so that it is only after the fact that one can locate it in some temporal process, on some temporal vector. Because it appears to have no more extension than a point does, it seems to have no structure, and thus to defy analysis. To pursue the analogy, we could say that it is as resistant to study as the latter is, which is fated, in Euclidean geometry, to remain indescribable as long as it not part of a line. But as happened with the non-Euclidean geometries required for the description of the world of subatomic particles (in which points, far from being barely two-dimensional, are extremely tiny and compact structures within which are folded some additional six to ten dimensions), contingencies are shown by Gumbrecht to possess a structure of incredible complexity. In a text devoted to the problems of experience, I may be forgiven for relating my sense of exhilaration at the reading of his essays: what I saw Gumbrecht doing was revealing the folded-in dimensions of contingency, which included those of experience and of its description, very much in the noncausal and nonlinear way in which the autopoiesis of systems takes place in the descriptions currently given of them. What I was seeing was the creation of a new descriptive language or theory that one could term the microphysics of history.

Physicists working on the elementary structure of matter, and currently en-

Part I
Inverted Perspective

Introduction
How Much Sense Does Sense Making Make? Californian Retrospective to a German Question

When I first saw Wlad Godzich's proposal for the selection of articles presented in this volume, it gave me a sense of estrangement. This feeling, of course, was my reaction to a concrete example of the trivial experience that outside observers have the privilege of seeing shapes and profiles that must remain hidden to inside participants. Wlad, from his North American perspective, had been able to discern a specifically German trajectory in my work from the years between 1975 and 1987, which I myself had somehow carefully tried to avoid—and of which I have only become increasingly aware since I came to the United States in September 1989.

The point of departure for that trajectory, thanks to a position as *Wissenschaftlicher Assistent* at the University of Constance that I held from 1971 through 1974, was the boundless optimism that the "school" of reception aesthetics then inspired in West Germany (with a strong echo in the German Democratic Republic): it was hailed—and probably overrated—as a "paradigm change" in literary studies. But while I assume that my distance from the Constance school has meanwhile grown sufficiently to allow for a sensible retrospective, it turns out to be a difficult—if not impossible—task precisely for a lack of such distance to apprehend the position into which my academic beginnings have been transformed over the past fifteen years. Not only must I admit that it is sheer rhetorical constraint that makes me talk of the *continuity* of a "transformation" or the *homogeneity* of

---

Thanks to John Bender, Wlad Godzich, and Margaret Tompkins for helping me to contextualize this text linguistically, intellectually, and "politically."

a "position"; even more intricate is a now doubly precarious situation that motivates me to try and inscribe such a German position into the American humanities agenda, without being able to judge whether I am close enough and/or distant enough on either side.

My uncertainties could be centered on the problem of locating the practices of *sense making*, which one used to see as occupying both the places of the "subject" and of the "object" in our scholarly endeavor. The perspective from which we analyze the phenomena of sense making and the ways in which we think that our own research and teaching "make sense" are now profoundly changed. If it should therefore be at all worthwhile for American readers to witness my highly German trajectory, I think it would be as a result of a frequent shifting of the very figure of "sense making" that the articles translated in this volume trace over the map of our professional field.

Looking back to my point of departure in the early 1970s, it is no longer self-evident today why the project called "reception aesthetics" turned out to be so appealing to the intellectual generation of the (not only European) "student revolution." This problem may arise because the name reception aesthetics, which placed so much emphasis on the reader, can now be seen as somehow misleading. Indeed, none of the many "literary histories of the reader," which were then announced and expected, was ever finished, and despite their titles, Wolfgang Iser's books *The Implied Reader* and *The Act of Reading* were dedicated to the development of a phenomenological theory of the literary text rather than to the extratextual role(s) of its addressees. The truly important change that reception aesthetics stimulated, however, lay in a consequence of the reader-thematization: it was the plurality of meanings attributed to each text in the name of different readers — despite the efforts of some of the movement's founders at least to limit the range of "legitimate" readings — that profoundly transformed the status of the text within our field of research and analysis. The literary text traditionally had appeared as containing *one* meaning (and only one) to be disclosed and administered by the academic critic (the German word *Gehalt* vaguely alluded to the equally vague conviction that the formal aspects of the literary "work" were inseparable from its semantics in a specific, but rather mysterious, way). Now the text — and at first, only implicitly — was explored as a *center of reference for multiple acts of sense "constitution,"* among which the author's "creative act" did not necessarily preserve a position of priority. The function of the critic no longer appeared to be the mediation of a sense found in the text (which had always left open the question of why such mediation was at all necessary). Rather, the task was now the analysis of different modes of sense production and different configurations of sense for which the text was a necessary framework, though not a container or boundary.

Reception theory probably preferred phenomenological concepts of "action" to the then popular Anglo-American "speech act theory" in the grounding of its research because of a historically obvious closeness to the Weberian and to the more strongly phenomenological post-Weberian style of sense-oriented sociology (much of which, through the work of Alfred Schütz, had exerted a certain influence on American interactionism) and because of the presence of Schütz's former student Thomas Luckmann at the University of Constance. From today's perspective one can therefore say that the more important achievement of reception aesthetics for literary studies (and not only for *literary* studies) was its contributions to a theory of text-centered sense constitution—and to a history of its socially institutionalized forms in Western culture. The first manifestos of the Constance school, however, had presented a program that looked considerably different from what, over the years, would become its specific agenda. At that time, some of its representatives were highly concerned, for example, with the "sense" that their reconstructions of acts of sense constitution might make in a wider societal context—in other words, with the (more or less) "political" functions of their scholarly discourse. This was a second, self-reflexive level on which "sense making" became a key topic and in tribute to which hermeneutics now sometimes began to claim the title of being politically *kritisch*. For example, it was one of Hans Robert Jauss's central interests to give evidence to his conviction of how historically indispensable and politically progressive the functions of "literary experience" are, and the new attention given to the readers' sense constitutions contributed to the expectation that it was possible to demonstrate in detail how literary reception had indeed influenced crucial moments and developments in Western history. While this motivation ended up generating an apologetic discourse for the academic profession of the literary critic (it was not by coincidence that one of Jauss's publications in the 1970s went under the title *Kleine Apologie der ästhetischen Erfahrung*), the hopes of the younger generation concentrated on what they saw as the promise of reception aesthetics for more "democratic" ways in the pedagogy and history of literature. There were dreams of a new proletarian appropriation of the classics and, at the same time, Walter Benjamin's idea of a historiography to be written from the perspective "of the defeated" was read as a revelation of the true function of literary history. By that time it was a project of some especially well intentioned literary theorists to demonstrate that literature had always served to keep alive those needs and desires that had been repressed through the official discourses of the public sphere.

In my essay "Consequences of an Aesthetics of Reception" (chapter 1 in this volume), I attempted to tone down some of these high-flying projects. Typically enough, their inviability had to be shown through an argument borrowed from Max Weber. "Literary experience" can never be more than just one of many previously acquired elements of experience that are assembled into "motivations" for subsequent actions, and it is therefore not possible to weigh its importance in relation to other motivations. This dilemma reduced the hope ever to evaluate empirically the function of literature.

My second intervention referred both to a heritage from the Hegelian (and/or Marxist) "philosophy of history" and to a traditional assumption within the discipline of literary history. Before this double background and without further argument, any kind of historically oriented research on literary texts and genres had been considered to be relevant for their aesthetic appreciation in the critic's present. My proposal was to separate the historical from the aesthetic perspective in the analysis of literary texts—even if only for the benefit of gaining time in order to rethink their possible—but highly unclear—connection(s).

In any event, the tendency toward such a distinction was to become a central, although not a particularly original, tendency within West German *Literaturwissenschaft*. On the side of philosophical aesthetics, its representatives remained, to say the least, astonishingly conservative until some of them discovered, very late, the work of such figures as Derrida, Lyotard, and de Man. On the historians' side, however, the new distance from the problems of philosophical aesthetics accounted for a style of research that, seen from today's angle, displayed striking similarities to American new historicism and also to at least part of the French (and Italian) *nouvelle histoire*. Their main difference lies, perhaps, in the contrast between intellectual environments: the new German literary historicism could never be interpreted as a movement "against" deconstruction (as has been the case with new historicism in the United States) for the simple reason that deconstruction, so far, has remained in a quantitatively marginal and institutionally marginalized position at German universities. But historicism in Germany coincides with American new historicism in their shared interest in noncanonized (and often nonliterary) texts; in their focus on an investigation of the historically dynamic connections between "literature" and other fields of social practice (in Germany often referred to as the "historization of the concept of literature"); in their theoretical and methodological sophistication (which on both sides may incidentally include a certain philosophical skepticism concerning the distribution of the truth claims between historical "realities" and fictional texts); and, finally, in the generally, yet not always, maintained conviction that their historiographical practice should be attributable to certain political goals.

Insofar as such historical work in Germany remains linked with reception aesthetics, it might be anecdotally surprising for an American public that the outstanding importance of Michel Foucault's work still seems to be an object of debate for some of its representatives. First of all, this may be a reaction against the subtle strategies by which Foucault's historical studies resist any appropriation from the totalizing side of a Hegelian "philosophy of history"; but in some cases, it also stems from the suspicion that the explicit theoretical basis Foucault gave to his historical investigations through the elaboration of the concept of "discourse" was less differentiated than the framework for which the German tradition of the "sociology of knowledge" (*Wissenssoziologie*) would allow.

In my own case, it was the challenge of developing something like a meta-historical model of historiography as a background for the identification of some historically specific features in medieval historiography (on which topic I was editing a collective volume as part of the handbook *Grundriss der romanischen Literaturen des Mittelalters*) that first drew my attention to the sociological notions of "everyday world" and "life world." The task seemed all the more rewarding because working toward a metahistorical model of historiography implied the possibility of rethinking some of the presuppositions of our own academic tradition of historiography. While the concept of "everyday worlds" (as synonymous with "stocks of knowledge" in different societies) was easily absorbed in the description of historically specific phenomena, the sociological version of Husserl's philosophy of *Lebenswelt* that Schütz and Luckmann had developed seemed to offer a metahistorical basis for the reconstruction of historically specific cases of sense constitution. The fact that the adoption of this theory implied the adoption of Husserl's construction of the transcendental subject as a necessary consequence did not seem at all problematic in the West German intellectual context of the late 1970s and early 1980s.

What Schütz and Luckmann, continuing and specifying Husserl's use of this concept, call *Lebenswelt* can be regarded as the ensemble of those basic structures that underlie any sense-constitutive acts performed by human beings. As such, the "life world" is seen as the general and necessary basis for any action and interaction in society. In a series of articles focusing on historiography and narration (three of which are published in this volume), it was my idea, first, to connect the formal side of texts and genres (through the mediating level of sense-constitutive actions) with such structures of the life world and, second, to associate certain thematic "fascinations" with the desire to cross the boundaries of the life-world in different directions. Therefore, in the case of historiography, the unstructured accumulation of the continuous sequence of experiences that constitutes the stream of consciousness was discussed as a possible metahistorical ground for its narrative character; whereas on its thematic side, historiography was seen as motivated by the desire to establish a relation of presence with events that had taken place before one's birth. What followed from this perspective was, among other things, the impossibility of associating the metahistorical concept of historiography (or equivalent concepts for other genres) with any specific functions. If we define the "function" of a text as its impact on the knowledge of a recipient existing prior to its reception, it can only be located on the level of historical and situational specificity. Therefore, certain *general* claims about the moral or political functions of the (literary) historian's own sense making had to be given up. Historiographical texts may sometimes well fulfill functions of "emancipation" or "justice," but this would depend on their authors' skill in combination with specific dispositions on the readers' side, and an analogous reasoning would apply, for example, to the functions of literary or critical texts. Paradoxically, therefore, the preoccupation with providing a metahistorical frame for the reconstruction of sense-constitutive acts entered into conflict with the project of a *generally* valid "defense and illustration" of literary experience and the critic's work.

But if this recourse to the German tradition of phenomenology turned out to be rather disenchanting with regard to the theorists' political ambitions, it did provide new possibilities for addressing some classical problems in the fields of literary theory and history. Analogous to the proposal to discuss the metahistorical foundations of certain genres within the conceptual framework of *Lebenswelt* philosophy, the problem of a metahistorical definition of literature could now be negotiated in terms of a specific form of experience or of a specific situation of communication. In this context, Erving Goffman's exercises in *Frame Analysis* were received as a general source of inspiration in West Germany, and, at the same time, it was Mikhail Bakhtin's theorization of "carnival" that oriented the development of situational models of literature and fiction toward features like the "absence of intentions," "rules and patterns of behavior," and "situational insularity." In recalling one of the aforementioned parallels between German *Literaturwissenschaft* in the 1970s and 1980s and contemporary American new historicism, it becomes understandable that such theorizing was increasingly concerned with topics and issues that could no longer be regarded as strictly literary: hence the participation of a great number of literary historians in some of the typically German enterprises of *Begriffsgeschichte* (the historization of key concepts in Western culture) whose publication in monumental encyclopedias transformed historical semantics into a serious alternative to more empirical versions of "social history" (my essays "A History of the Concept 'Modern' " and "Who Were the *'Philosophes'*?" [included in this volume] were part of such collections). Finally, I assume that the still equally popular and vague project of *"historische Anthropologie"* can be seen as at least indirectly related to the philosophy of *Lebenswelt*: it implies an understanding of the results of highly specialized historical research as case studies contributing to a metahistorical picture of humankind much like pieces of a mosaic framed by the conceptual boundaries of the life world.

Such was the theoretical horizon for the historically oriented investigations presented in this book. In retrospect, however, their main interest may lie rather in the possibility of reading them as a progressive erosion of the metahistorical status conceded to the transcendental subject that had been taken as the central element of their theoretical grounding. The history of the concept "modern," for example, not only made evident the historical limitations of *historisches Bewusstsein* (historical consciousness) but, by describing a replacement of temporal sequentiality through the spatial paradigm "in/out," implicitly questioned even the linkage between time and sequentiality/narration. From this perspective, the reconstruction of the process whereby the concept of *Klassik* came to convey a specific character to the literary "canon" in Germany after 1800 can also be seen as a symptom for the impossibility of radically maintaining the imperative of historization even in the golden age of historicism: by calling a text *klassisch*, one exempts it from the laws and consequences of historicity, paradoxically underlining at the same time their general validity (because there could be no exemption from a rule without a rule).

Complementarily, my studies on laughter and seriousness in the period of transition between the Middle Ages and early modern Europe, on the *philosophe* as the central social role in the French Enlightenment, and on the literary history of the French Revolution, sum up by outlining a history of the Western subject *in minor*. By calling those essays "a history *in minor*," I try to avoid a more programmatic characterization that they do not deserve, because when I wrote them it was not at all my intention to problematize the Western subject. Rather against the grain of my research, I thematized the price that had been paid for the historical step from oral performance to the subject-centered seriousness of printed "literature"; I became aware of the hypocrisy in the self-staging of the Enlightenment philosopher (to borrow a metaphor from the historian Reinhart Koselleck) and of its problematic transposition to the institutions of parliamentary representation.

In the long run, such historical perspectives made me increasingly suspicious of the enterprise of "rescuing the project of Enlightenment" about which so many intellectuals of my generation were (and still are) gathering around the paternal figure of Jürgen Habermas in Germany. The circumstance, however, that such distance had been growing *from within* a primarily subject-centered position and without an intention to problematize the subject, left me not only without any of those "profound convictions" that German intellectuals are quite naturally expected to proclaim, but also without the possibility of seeing more than just a different set of "profound convictions" in the basic philosophical assumptions of deconstruction. For deconstruction, if it allows for skepticism at all, does so only with regard to other positions.

Entering the contemporary epistemological moment from such an angle, the "postmodern condition" looks like a situation in which our current analytical tools fall well short of conceptualizing some of the most current everyday phenomena. Sports and the media, with which the essay "It's Just a Game" deals, are telling examples. In the impossibility of understanding the increasingly widespread desire to recover the human body as an object of experience ("an object *of pleasure*" would be saying much) and in the ways through which film and television have supplied possibilities of satisfying such desire by offering body simulcra on the screen, philosophy and cultural studies tend to replace analytical work with precipitate value judgments: whence the popularity of Heideggerian gestures of *Kulturkritik* in the field of media research. The same applies to the gloomy comments with which literary critics normally react to the experience that it becomes more and more difficult to motivate the general public—even the public of their graduate students—to read sophisticated books. Such comments are the unmentioned point of reference for the essay "Pathologies in the System of Literature." The hypothesis I put forth in "Pathologies" highlights the predominant and tradition-laden conceptions of "literature" as a paralyzing heritage that makes it difficult to look for phenomena of aesthetic experience without thinking of books, museums, and concert halls. It might be this very difficulty that contributes to a new fascination with the possibility of defining aesthetic experience in terms of *Erhabenheit*—in terms of that which is precisely "out of the frames."

In the context of this retrospective, however, what is more important and more symptomatic than the outcome of that particular essay is its reliance on Niklas Luhmann's version of a theory of social systems. For it is no exaggeration to say that the availability of Luhmann's theory has been a highly important feature on the West German intellectual scene, ever since Luhmann first appeared as a serious challenger of the Frankfurt school in a controversy with Jürgen Habermas published in 1971. What most of its readers found so authentically shocking in this debate were not so much Habermas's and Luhmann's divergent philosophical views on the sociological concept of "sense," which their respective articles tried to develop, as Luhmann's underlying refusal to accept as naturally given the association between the legitimacy of the academic discipline of sociology and a political position on the left. Although it now seems fair to say that, under the influence of Talcott Parsons and perhaps even in the tradition of Max Weber, Luhmann simply tried to keep apart sociological analysis and the political consequences to be drawn from it, his surprising success, in the context of a rather simplistic binary logic, was criticized in the beginning as the symptom of a reaction from the political right more than it was attributed to the strength of his argumentation. It took the West German public more than a decade to accept that what was at stake was the defensibility of basic philosophical assumptions inherited from the European Enlightenment rather than an allegory of everyday politics.

In the absence, and later on with only the reluctant acceptance, of deconstruction, *Systemtheorie* has become something like "the German alternative" to the type of rationality that, going back to its historical origins in the seventeenth and eighteenth centuries, had been canonized as the general norm of human thinking. Since the place of an alternative to classical rationality has been occupied—at least in France and in North America— by deconstruction, it might be an interesting perspective to compare deconstruction and systems theory as functional equivalents, even though they could not be more different in their styles of self-presentation. If systems theory and deconstruction overlap in some of their multiple strategies of decentering the subject and in their radical criticism of traditional theories about representation and reference, there is an affective passion about deconstruction and a correspondingly affective coolness about systems theory that perhaps account for the dramatically different ways in which they both became intellectually influential. By reiterating as key experience the illusionary character of the Western concepts of truth, representation, language, and writing, deconstruction produces an effect—at least among many of its followers—that one might call a *melancholy of reference.* Sometimes such melancholy makes Western culture appear as an overpowering conspiracy to be denounced or, like lost illusions, to be mourned. Compared to such passionate voices, the discourse of systems theory may look to some observers like the cynicism of postmodern sociotechnology; for rather than mourning what is forever lost, it puts itself in a position of *theoretical astonishment* about the improbable fact that such phenomena as "sense," "meaning," and "reference" could ever have come into being. This attitude brings theorists around Luhmann to the (advertently "paradoxical") *project of "seeing from outside" the concepts of sense, meaning, and reference in order to define them.* Sense would be an effect specific to the operations through which social systems and psychic systems proceed with their "autopoiesis," consisting of their capability to perform each of their operations before a horizon of alternative operations that they might have selected instead—without actually selecting them. Meaning and reference, then, appear as consequences of the social and psychic systems' autopoiesis, relying on a difference between "self-reference" and "external reference" ("system/environment") that they produce within themselves. The reason that systems theory converges with deconstruction in a critical attitude toward the traditional evaluations of such effects lies in the premise that autopoietic systems, as "closed" systems, can "see" neither their environment nor, of course, themselves; observed "from outside," their self-reference and their external reference appear to be nonmimetic. Now, the impression of coolness to which I alluded comes from Luhmann's somehow ironic refusal (very unlike deconstruction) to see "any problem" in the implications of such a *Gesellschafts-Anschauung.* The utmost systemic wisdom (displaying a certain Socratic flavor for which Luhmann is definitely not looking) seems to lie in the willingness to admit that, despite their lack of reference, the systems' complexity takes better care of their survival than the best-intentioned theorist could ever hope for; and that, if the survival of the systems should sometimes be to the detriment of humanity, it would be an illusion to believe that one could know.

What matters here for academic disciplines like literary history and literary theory is the innovative perspective from which systemic thinking allows us to view the phenomena of sense making. First of all, the fact that it provides a definition for the notion of sense indicates that we can leave behind us, if we wish, a research situation in which the existence of "sense" has always been presupposed as a given. This perspective does not imply, however, that systems theory would encourage us to believe in the possibility of withholding or even stopping the production of sense. Sense, in relation to social systems and psychic systems, is thought of as *differenzlos*: in other words, those systems cannot help making sense as long as they exist as social or psychic systems. But the proposal to analyze sense making as an intrasystemic operation depending on each system's specific environment (without "picturing" it) generates the new question of whether we have to count, according to the high variation in the frame conditions of sense making, on a multiplicity of different modalities in sense and meaning. So far, I would not take for granted any answer to this question; but its very pursuit seems to be important in an epistemological situation in which we have been aware for quite a long time of the fact that our concepts for the description and the analysis of sense making turn out to be insufficient whenever we apply them to contemporary culture.

In a recent article Wlad Godzich raises similar questions ("Vom Paradox der Sprache zur Dissonanz des Bildes," in *Paradoxien, Dissonanzen, Zusammenbrüche*, ed. H. U. Gumbrecht and K. L. Pfeiffer [Frankfurt, 1991], pp. 747–58). He highlights the contrast between, on the one hand, a world in which written language used to be considered the most important medium by which sense was produced and communicated (with all its specific implications about signification, truth, reference, etc.), and, on the other hand, a present/future in which we will be increasingly confronted with an ultrafast *flow of images* without any semantic depth and without any reference to a world beyond itself. This new surface (which of course we will see as a "surface" only as long as we still remember different ways of signification implying a dimension of "depth"), to say the least, emerges as one of the reasons why our inherited epistemology looks so insufficient and inefficient. As I have tried to argue here, however, it would be an intellectual short circuit, a dangerous confusion between an extremely difficult analytical task and a reaction of moral indignation, to see this change as something like a catastrophe. It certainly announces the near end of a certain conception of "humanity," which, for some while, we had erroneously taken to have a metahistorical status even though it is an almost traditional Nietzschean argument to insist that human life is not synonymous with the ideology of "humanism."

What is at stake, then, is the invention of a new epistemology capable of theorizing and analyzing ways of sense making that perhaps no longer include effects of "meaning" and "reference." The first step in this direction would be to recognize that, at least so far, we simply *do not know* what interfaces such as those between TV and psychic systems, or between computers and social systems, look like. As soon as we are able to develop some understanding of such interfaces, the question will arise of how we can and should use our "insight" in this respect. Systematically speaking, "sense making" will continue to be our field of reference, but perhaps the same will no longer be the case with meaning, representation, and reference. In any event, the phenomena with which we are going to deal will probably look very different from those that we used to associate with the whole horizon of "sense making" — so different that it is now far too early to think about what the relationships between such phenomena (our future "objects" of research) and our discourses might look like; too early also to say how our dealing with new modes of sense making will make sense. Such questions are definitely not—not yet—the topic of the essays presented in this volume. But I assume that the specific perspectives from which they analyze and reconstruct different literary and nonliterary modalities of sense making in Western history prove themselves to be an appropriate *point of departure* for such an agenda.

But if "point of departure" as a metaphor implies an idea of the goals to reach and the ways leading to these goals, it might even be too much to say that we are now *at a point of departure*. What we experience these days is rather the bare inviability of certain concepts and assumptions on which our profession used to be grounded. Our notion of "meaning" still works quite well with texts—but textuality is no longer the predominant form in which knowledge circulates. If we want to maintain the traditional equivalence between "history" and "historiography," we have to admit that history depends as much on an author's subjective intuitions as any other narrative—and it can then hardly serve as a stable ground for any political claims. Finally, what the *New York Times* used to call "the upheaval in Eastern Europe" should make us think whether the division between the private sphere and the public sphere, as well as rationality as a normative orientation of decision making, is still available as a basis for our pathetic concept of "politics." Anyone who raises such issues, at least in Germany, is likely to be labeled a "neo-conservative." But it might turn out that the only obvious reference of the adjective "conservative" is *not* to raise them, that the most dangerous of all fictions is to behave *as if* we could still rely on such traditions as meaning, history, and politics.

Chapter 1
The Consequences of an Aesthetics of Reception: A Deferred Overture

The Way to a Paradigm Change

At the beginning of his essay "Der Leser als Instanz einer neuen Geschichte der Literatur," Hans Robert Jauss points out that only in the future will we be able to provide an answer to the question whether literary criticism's present discussion about the problem of the "reader" is going to be evaluated as a paradigm change.[1] This is a helpful remark, yet it neither suspends the possibility nor does it free us of the obligation to analyze the contemporary debate over theories and methods as well as the epistemological interest of literary criticism. For it is only on a self-reflexive basis that the hope of getting beyond no longer productive, hand-me-down paradigms can be rendered concrete in order to redetermine the field and the tasks literary criticism projects on the cultural horizon. It follows that we must first of all ask what were the phases of the model of "scientific revolutions" in which Thomas S. Kuhn introduced the concept of "paradigmatic change," and, moreover, which of these phases the literary debate about the problem of the reader has reached or already passed beyond.[2]

According to Kuhn, the provocation and the starting point for paradigm changes are, first, new questions, "which a circle of professionals has recognized as highly important." Second, scientific works are considered paradigmatic when they not only provide some convincing answers to those questions at an early stage but also open up new fields and possibilities for managing them in more detail and more precisely. Third, and finally, the phases between two paradigm changes are filled out with so-called normal science, which tries to cash in on the paradigm's promises by extending the knowledge of the published facts which the paradigm considers especially important and by improving the interaction between these facts and the paradigm's predictions.

In this essay, I would like to argue two points. (1) There are two areas of neglect that are behind the insufficiency continually pointed out by both originators and opponents of "reception aesthetics" as a paradigm change:[3] the insufficient specification of the new questions provoked by the paradigm change along with a lack of exemplary answers to these questions. (2) Feedback from the first of these two perspectives requires, as a consequence of reception aesthetics, the integration of this new form of literary criticism into the sociology of communication, which itself is in the process of being constituted.

Those debates about "correct" interpretations of literary texts that dominated the era of immanent interpretation make it abundantly clear that the formula "the discovery of the reader" by no means adequately characterizes the theoretical direction initiated by reception aesthetics. Immanent interpretation could have easily positioned the readers of each text along with their interpretations on an ahistorical scale ranging between "total inadequacy" and "interpretive richness." This is why the change in criticism's ongoing interest is often misunderstood as the dissolution of the text or of the author caused by the reader's ascension to the apex of a hierarchy of concerns. The point is, however, that critical discussion can no longer be primarily considered as a process motivated by an idea of perfectibility, in which the ideal reader is supposed to converge with the correct meaning, but rather as a reconstructive effort whose purpose is to understand the conditions under which various meanings of a given text are generated by readers whose receptive dispositions have different historical and social mediations. The fact that methodologically reflected suggestions for solving this task through concrete "functional histories" or "literary histories of the reader" have often been proclaimed but seldom executed can be taken as a symptom of stagnation in a quantitatively bottomless theoretical debate.

Now, if the question of the correct meaning or the ideal reader corresponded to a precognition of the text as a form constituting and preserving a single content, then reception aesthetics' studies of the conditions for different meanings by different readers is also going to bring it up against the problem of developing a concept of the text adequate to these inquiries. As reception aesthetics is indeed mainly concerned with the relationship between the conditions of textual meanings and these meanings themselves (and not with the evaluation of the meanings as more or less "correct"), its concept of the text only has to fulfill one function: it must be available as a constant background against which we can try to compare different meanings as the results of the text's convergences with different receptive dispositions. A text constituted in this way has the status of a heuristic construct whose value is measured exclusively by its usefulness in understanding the differences between meanings occurring in history.

Wolfgang Iser's suggestion that we replace the traditional concept of the text with the "implicit reader" as the "character of the act of reading inscribed in the text" suffers, to my mind, from its effacement of the difference between a normative and a descriptive history of reception.[4] A normative history would have to constitute and establish its own "correct" reading of the text, which would be its basis for revealing the conditions of adequate and inadequate interpretations, whereas a descriptive history of reception would have to be satisfied with the comprehension of the relationship between each reading and its specific conditions. Iser's concept of the text is supposed to make a broad spectrum of receptive figures comprehensible as the result of stopping up "indeterminate places" in the text. This refilling is dependent on the different receptive dispositions and can thus function within a descriptive history of reception, yet can also be normative to the extent it excludes a large number of historically conceivable meanings because, according to Iser, they were not built into the text. It belongs to the basic premises of post-Gadamerian hermeneutics (to which Iser adheres just as much as Jauss) that normative readings require a legitimizing criterion—which the "implicit reader" lacks.[5] Hence the apparent advantage of Marxist literary historiography is that, as a result of its global perspective on history, it has been outfitted with such a criterion. Karlheinz Stierle, for his part, has shown that a model of fictional texts that might be practicable for a normative history of reception could only be developed on the basis of a particular concept of their reading. He has shown that a particular interpretation of the English novel is taken for granted and functions as the buried premise of Iser's metahistorically intended "implicit reader."[6] That text models, which are supposed to allow us to distinguish between true and false readings or to elicit the minimal constants for every conceivable textual meaning, inevitably need a normative concept of reception and that they cannot be derived from the pure immanence of textual analysis[7] can be proved by the following simple argument: any attempt to establish systematic constants for all of the meanings of a given text through linguistic methods would have to take into account the entire range of this text and, faced with perfectly common everyday phenomena like "skimming" or simply shutting the book, would have to include, as the minimal requirement for a normative model of reception, the postulate of a reception that is constantly attentive to the text as an entirety.

In summary, the distinction between a "normative" and a "descriptive history of reception"—the first of which can be connected with literary pedagogy and the second with the social history of literature—must be supplemented with a differentiation of the criteria for establishing textual concepts adequate for each of them. Whereas a normative history of reception is forced to derive its concept of the text from the development of a normative model of reading, the concept of the text for a descriptive history of reception (with regard to its heuristic function of providing a steady focus for the analysis of different textual meanings) only needs to fulfill a single requirement: it has to be readily adaptable to all sorts of cases for all kinds of literary critics. Within the framework of a descriptive history of reception I would like to recommend using the meaning intended by the author as the background against which other meanings can be understood and compared. From my comments on the value of this reconstruction within a descriptive history, it ought to be clear that I am not pushing for a renaissance of biographical literary historiography, nor do I threaten anew to reduce to "authorial intention" the plurality of historical readings or potential criteria for normative readings.

There are at least five reasons for supporting the suggestion to focus on the author's intention rather than some random reader's as the background for comparing historical meanings. (1) In most cases (biographical criticism not the least) the meaning intended by the author can be easily reconstructed quite independent of literary critics' various presuppositions. (2) The reconstruction of the context of production is also relevant for those kinds of criticism that, in contrast to reception aesthetics, are tied to the interests of ideological textual analysis or to textual interpretation as the reconstruction of social needs. (3) Since an author can develop a meaning for a text only by taking historical types of readers into account, his or her intended meaning hooks the field of historical production up with contemporary literary reception. (4) On the other hand, this investment of the concept of the text in a descriptive history of reception corresponds to the fact that recipients, in order to be able to constitute a text as a significant unity in the first place, must be able to understand it as the result of an author's action. (5) Since the reader's understanding can also be described as action (which still needs to be discussed in more detail), the sociological conception of action could be a way of overcoming a split in the field of literary criticism that has come about because of the lack of clarity concerning its key questions.

The descriptive history of reception, whose tasks and methods must now be described, thus has good reason to begin with the action of the author and the action of the reader as conditions for the historical formation of meanings. One of its key tasks will be to set narrower limits for the special area of aesthetic communication, after which it must take an exact look at the "causal and functional relationships between social structure, social action, and communicative acts" with respect to textual production as well as textual understanding.[8] The constitution of literary criticism as a subdiscipline of the sociology of communication by no means implies its hierarchical subjugation to a "sociological metadiscipline" but is rather a way of giving ourselves a chance to contribute to the development of a theoretical framework for the sociology of communication, which so far we have only projected. Before we go on to elaborate prospects for concrete research problems in a literary criticism tied to the sociology of communication, it is necessary to introduce some basic concepts of cognitive sociology that have already appeared in this essay without sufficient introduction.

Basic Concepts

When the connection between the three levels—social structure, social action, and communicative acts—is established as causal-functional, "causal" refers to the relationship of the superior to the subordinated instance whereas with "functional" the relationship is reversed. So "causality" does not signify, in the sense of the natural sciences, the determination of communicative acts through social action and social action through the social structure; rather it assigns the roles played by social structure as a meaningful framework for social action and by social action for communicative acts. The content of the phrase "meaningful framework" becomes more precise when we define "functional" more narrowly: "In 'general European usage' . . . function means the obligatory performance of a part within the framework of a whole."[9] Thus communicative acts are elements of social action, which in turn is a subdivision of a social structure in all of its complexity. Only by integrating them into a higher framework can the functions of communicative acts and social action be determined and have meaning.[10] The sociology of communication must first investigate the role of social structure and social action as the meaningful framework for the subordinated instances and then the functions of communicative acts and social action within their respective frameworks.

In the following discussion, "communicative acts" will be taken to mean both acts of expression and perception. I am not going to begin, however, with an established inventory of expressive and perceptive acts that, through simple combination, would allow us to construct the various expressive and perceptional actions. Rather it is through an analytic perspective that we arrive at the morphology of communicative acts whose functional interaction makes up communicative action. In borderline cases, the expansion of a communicative act can even coincide with a communicative form of action. In such instances, the communicative act (Akt) will be referred to as "action" (Handeln) when it is understood as purposeful. Thus what fundamentally distinguishes act from action is not expansion (even when it is available in most cases as an extra criterion for differentiation) but rather an accounting for precisely that "design of the action, which is supposed to achieve self-actuality by acting."[11] This last definition contains a further distinction that needs to be more precisely elaborated—that is, between "acting" (handeln) and "action" in the sense of "plot" (Handlung). While the term "acting" designates any procedure that is goal-oriented and that is completed step by step (for instance, in communicative acts), "action" should be understood as that goal that is designed (or in phenomenological terms, "pre-remembered") by the acting subject and that is handed over to "acting" for its realization.[12]

As a subdivision of action, social action, "according to its intended meaning, refers to the behavior of other people."[13] These other people, whose behavior becomes a reference point, do not have to have access to the direct experience of the action: they could also belong to the past and the future.[14] Consequently, all forms of communicative action—hence textual production and understanding, too—represent social action.

At this point we need a fundamental hypothesis for the relationship between text and action. If we accept Schütz's determination of the concept of action as the "predesigned goal of acting," then it seems acceptable to grasp texts as a particular type of action, since at any given time they represent themselves a posteriori as the realization of an author's pre-remembered project. At any rate, this project is keyed to authorial intentions for the text, and the author can plan this effect only on the basis of a hypothesis about the readers' receptive disposition. Therefore an interpreter, whether literary critic or ordinary reader, deals with a text as an action only when he has analyzed it on the basis of a hypothesis about the effects intended by the author. This hypothesis can be considered a "second-degree hypothesis" because the effects intended by the author are themselves grounded in a hypothesis about the audience's receptive disposition. But as soon as texts are read free of every assumption about the context of their production, they are no longer understood as actions.

From this it can be concluded that, in the following conceptual clarification (which deals with knowledge as perceptual action), we must distinguish between two types of cognitive actions. For every type of cognition, which Schütz calls the understanding of objective meaning,[15] the observer arranges "what has been perceived within his own experiential schemata without bringing the acting subject into view at all."[16] Only from the perspective of subjective meaning does the text appear as action in the complete sense, for the problem then is to reconstruct the project of an acting subject on the basis of this text (as completed action).[17] The understanding of objective as well as subjective sense can itself be defined as action because it is subordinated to the realization of projects that the person who understands tries to pursue. Moreover, both types of cognitive actions—text production and understanding—must be considered social actions, since also the constitution of objective meaning is made possible only by a given sequence of words accepted as text, which in turn necessarily refers to an acting alter ego.

The understanding of both objective and subjective meaning can refer to texts as forms of social action. However, if literary theory is going to conceive itself as a theory of the conditions of meaning generation, and if it regards the production of texts by authors and the understanding of texts by readers as these conditions, then it also must get involved with the reader's cognitve actions. More exactly, it must study the purposes to which reading as a cognitive action was subjected (reconstruction of the reader's "in-order-to motivation") and explain the generation of these projects out of the reader's historical and social situation (reconstruction of the reader's "because motivation").[18] Where it takes on its most ambitious goal, namely, the investigation of the "function of literature in the constitution of the social sphere,"[19] a question is posed that brings us to the problem of how experiences derived from readings can become motivations for the readers' action in everyday life.

The Theoretical Status of a Literary Criticism
Based on the Sociology of Communication

To require that understanding of texts also be made into an object of literary studies implies the problem of literary criticism's self-reflection, for surely the critic's understanding is not categorically different from that of the normal reader. Because the effort to understand is primarily aimed at grasping the projections of actions and the sociohistorical framework that constitutes and conditions them (in-order-to and because motivation), a necessary relationship can be demonstrated between the ongoing redefinition of the tasks of criticism and the intensification of the discussion about its historical presuppositions. Hence the usual reproach that shifts in the orientation of criticism are merely "trendy" can be resisted by systematic argument. At the same time, it should be pointed out that the amount of agreement about cognitive interests (as "projects" of critical actions) limits the possibility of cooperation between the representatives of different critical schools. If Jauss believes that he has already "cleaned up" the "false front" between Marxist and bourgeois criticisms by calling attention to the common involvement of both camps in the project of studies on the "function of art in society" and the history of its reception,[20] then he seems to have overlooked the fact that, in the framework of Marxist criticism, this cognitive interest is seen only as a step toward the superimposed project of every science "as a human activity, which (at least indirectly) is aimed at changing the status quo."[21] The guidelines for the literary critic's contribution to this change, which are supposed to pressure the critic into the role of "historian and educator" and simultaneously provide him or her with the criteria for selecting areas of research and evaluating their results, are the "developed socialist system" and the "Third World's ceaseless struggle for freedom."[22] If the debate between Marxist and bourgeois criticisms is going to do more than just concern itself with methods of reconstructing the historical function of texts, then we are going to have to reach some kind of consensus on the preeminent projects of critical action.

Along with criticism's duty to think through its own epistemological aims, it has, due to its embeddedness in the sociology of communication, a growing need to redetermine the predicate "aesthetic." Of course, it is no longer simply a matter of applying the term to texts with given formal qualities but must also tie into the author's expressive action (which can be reconstructed from the text conceived as action) and the reader's perceptive action (whose first purpose is presupposed by a certain anticipation of a given text as an author's "aesthetic act" and which can be performed or modified during the reading process). Hooking onto those suggestions from aesthetic theory, which attempts to locate the particular value of artworks in their contribution to the formation of internalized norms and the questioning of these norms, "aesthetic" could be related to the function (or even its absence) that the reader's experience can have as a motivation for later action, a function which the reader has achieved and which the author's expressive action made possible in the first place.[23] If it is ever going to be possible from this perspective to reach a more narrow consensus about the meaning of "aesthetic" (which, as we have seen, seems more than problematic, given the different criteria for evaluating such functions), then the large-scale revision of the canon of "aesthetic" texts, which would have to proceed by reconstructing their possible functions for the audience's action, could only devolve on a criticism keyed to the sociology of communication. As must still be shown, however, these kinds of investigations run into methodological difficulties.

To begin with, it can be said that such difficulties are a result of the circumstance that, for most studies, the subjects of those actions of expression and understanding that concern the interests of the new literary criticism are accessible only in a contemporary (*mitweltliche*) or a historical (*vorweltliche*) social context. By putting himself in the roles of those acting subjects and asking, say, which project he would induce into a given text as expressive action if he were in the author's historical and social position, the critical observer can posit hypotheses about the motivation for an author's expressive actions, a reader's action of understanding, and the significance of reading experiences as part of the reader's motivation for subsequent action. Hypotheses about motives acquired in this way, however, can never have an assured status, because, in Schütz's words, "a verification of my interpretations of unfamiliar experience [remains] unfulfilled without the observer's self-interpretation."[24]

Embedding criticism in the sociology of communication by no means guarantees certainty in the sense of the empirical sciences, as once was promised by the "linguistification" of literary criticism and which is still retained today by the hardware vocabulary of those varieties of the sociology of communication influenced by information theory. Rather, communication-sociological criticism should share with hermeneutics plausibility and consensus as criteria for evidence. As a doctrine of textual understanding it is different from hermeneutics only through (1) making understanding an object of its interest and (2) grounding this comprehension of textual understanding in a general theory of cognitive action.

Fields of Research

In the course of our attempt to block out the basic concepts of communication sociology, it has been indicated that each assumption of "textual unity" presupposes its inclusion in an authorial "project." To this assumption it could be objected that diaries, for instance, also belong to the traditional subjects of literary criticism — including posthumously published diaries, which are published without the author's express consent and are therefore not addressed to an alter ego. Can an analysis be carried out in such cases on the assumption that social actions are present? To provide a well-founded answer to this question we would have to approach the diary genre by rephrasing the problem considerably. For the moment, we can only note that the authors of diaries, as is shown by the frequent use of an imaginary addressees, must also have recourse to a reader — but that his or her position is occupied by the reflective ego to whom an experiencing ego is reporting. If it is true that the reporting ego and the reflecting ego are unified in the role of the diary writer and that the text of the diary is their "dialogue," then the interpreter's understanding in this case must address itself to the informative actions of the reporting ego and the cognitive actions of the reflecting ego.

In every attempt to reconstruct the motivation that guides textual production — that is, to comprehend the subjective meaning of texts as actions — the critic will arrange the text in segments by means of a functional-structural procedure that starts with a preliminary hypothesis about the author's purpose. This preliminary hypothesis concerning the function ascribed to the text by the author depends in part on the interpreter's hypothesis about the author's assumptions regarding his audience's disposition (which, of course, does not always match their actual disposition). Those segments in which the text is arranged by the interpreter according to his hypothesis about the author's project are understood as the outcome of individual expressive acts whose functional interaction constitutes the text as action. What is interesting about this kind of textual reconstruction is that it opens up the possibility of revising and sharpening the precision of the initial hypothesis about the subjective meaning of the text (the purpose of the author's action), which might seem incomplete or barely plausible against the background of a more exact analysis.

If the question about the in-order-to motivation of textual production has directed our attention to communicative acts subordinated to social action, then the investigation of their because motivation takes us to the level of historical social structures. In order to know why, for instance, Ronsard could have wanted to write sonnets at all, it is no longer enough to search for a satisfactory answer within the reconstructed framework of his subjective intention. Rather it is necessary to develop hypotheses about the function of literary production in general (which the author is usually not even aware of) and about the sonnet within sixteenth-century French society in particular. At this level of a communication-sociology, a new Marxist theory of literary production has recognized its genuine field, sharply delimiting it from the interests of the mimesis (*Widerspiegelung*) debate.[25]

One of the first important tasks of literary criticism would be the reconstruction of the purposes to which historical readers have applied their actions of under-standing objective and subjective textual meanings — in other words, the study of the history of their literary interest. Such an investigation of the in-order-to moti-vation must again be extended into the question of the because motivation, which can be answered only through recourse to social history, that is, by extending them into the social functions of literary reception. A phenomenology of reading would also have to explicate the connection between the level of understanding as social action and the (perceptual) communicative acts that constitute it.[26] In contrast to critical efforts aimed at correlating expressive communicative acts and textual production, this phenomenological work is made more difficult by the lack of objectifications that can be analyzed, such as the text on the author's side.

The understanding of literary texts does not always aim at authorial intention. Objective understanding (where the reader "arranges perception within his or her own experiential schemata" and at best presupposes the text-producing subject as a guarantee for the text's unity) should be accepted at least as an equally valid type of cognitive action. Valéry's Eupalinos dialogue can be read as a philosophical discussion of the necessity of an objective understanding but also of a suitable mode of reception for the modern work of art. Yet it shows at the same time that recipients are forced into this mode of reception by the works only to the extent that the works refuse to answer the apparently self-evident question concerning the producing subject which is the usual point of departure for cognitive actions. In the following words, Socrates depicts for Phaidros the reflections that provided the incentive for the discovery of the "objet ambigu":

> J'ai trouvé une de ces choses rejetées par la mer; une chose blanche, et de la plus pure blancheur; polie, et dure, et douce, et légère: Elle bril-lait au soleil, sur le sable lèche, qui est sombre, et semé d'étincelles. Je la pris; je soufflai sur elle; je la frottai sur mon manteau, et sa forme singulière arrêta toutes mes autres pensées. Qui t'a faite? pensai-je. Tu ne ressembles à rien, et pourtant tu n'est pas informe.[27]

For the reception of most literary texts from the past and for trivial contemporary texts, at least, the question "Qui t'a faite?" (which the modern work of art no longer presumes to answer) can lead to an assumption about the meaning intended by producers and can be expanded into a hypothesis about an authorial role the reader takes on and through which the reader is supposed to feed herself the answers to her own questions about the text. This asymmetrical form of subjective understanding, in which the reader occupies the author's role as the indispensable prerequisite for meaning, is always suitable in those cases where the meaning intended by the author is not immediately apparent to the reader because the latter does not belong to the same social milieu. In the case of reception aesthetics, the hypothesis of the authorial role can get by without being corrected by historical materials, for it performs its function as long as it serves the reader as a presupposition for consistent sense formations. The case is different when a reconstruction of the author's intended meaning is required that is as adequate as possible. There is no systematic relationship, however, between a subjective understanding dependent on heuristic motivation and historical accuracy, and the fact that, for the reception of aesthetic texts, the special form of asymmetrical subjective understanding seems to prevail.

That this kind of asymmetrical subjective understanding has been the normal way of comprehending literary texts for a long time can be demonstrated by two tendencies among the reading public for which there are countless historical examples:[28] its alacrity (which it shares with biographical criticism) in identifying the fictional first person of the text with the ego of its creator (Arcipreste de Hita, Villon, Proust) and the invention of "suitable" authors for anonymous texts (Homer, Aesop, Vitae of Trobadors).[29] Relevant to the history of reception and not just proof of the lack of a "truly" intentional meaning, it is precisely from such changes in public projections that inferences can be developed about the shifting basis for the textual understanding of audiences from different eras and different social groups.

The problems of actions of understanding discussed in this section are less likely to be solved than are studies aimed at the reconstruction of textually productive acts, because only in exceptional cases do we have evidence for the acts of reception. Along with the projections of authorial images already mentioned, there are the traditional documents of the "high cultural dialogue" between great authors (and not just literary ones), for example, "Voltaire's criticism of Rousseau" or "Engels's canonization of Balzac." This kind of material presents us with two difficulties: it provides only indirect conclusions about actions of understanding, for the acquired experiences appear as something already mediated by an inherent goal of textual production (Engels in his letter to Miss Harkness wants first of all to criticize her novel, *City Girl*, by comparing it to the works of Balzac); and in most cases, it goes into only a few aspects of the work, thus allowing only for partial (and indirect) insights into actions of reading.

Since medieval studies is in an especially precarious situation for this sort of demonstration, it has tried to make a virtue out of necessity by focusing on the various reworkings of a given original text as documents of reception.[30] Of course in this respect the question is even more urgent than with the "high cultural

dialogue" just mentioned — whether, for instance, Hartmann von Aue's version of
Iwein may be evaluated as a reflex of his textual understanding or is not rather
a reworking of Chrétien's *Yvain* that serves a new purpose and is for the most part
independent of the specific structure of a previous textual understanding. To express it more pointedly: does the analysis of forms of "creative reception" really
permit any kind of inference at all about the cognitive actions of the "creative
reader"?

Considering these difficulties, literary criticism ought to intensify its efforts to
discover extratextual evidence of cognitive actions in the past. But even when every potential option has been checked out, there will still be two aporias left: for
past eras we will always have to concentrate on the cognition of a privileged audience, namely, those who were in a position to leave evidence of their understanding behind; and moreover, there will always be something problematic
about assembling the results of individual studies in a more general "reception-
history" because such individual studies do not normally provide historical continuity. One way to avoid this second dilemma would be to simulate meanings
for the readings of those eras where we have no receptive materials through sociohistorical reconstructions on the basis of a given social knowledge. Irrespective
of the fact that the necessary socio-historical groundwork for developing this kind
of hypothesis is rarely performed, we must still ask whether it even belongs to
the possible tasks of literary criticism. If we are serious about the plethora of
problems involved in founding a new paradigm, then this sort of hypothetical
sense production is legitimate only in cases where earlier readings belong to the
conditions accessible to later interpreters: thus an interpretation of the preface to
the second part of *Don Quixote* cannot avoid establishing some sort of hypothesis
about the public reaction to the first part. In this instance to be sure, the simulation
of historical acts of understanding is perfectly justified as far as research interests
are concerned — yet remains methodologically problematic.

In contrast to historical levels of reception, contemporary literary reception
gives us a chance to investigate "experimentally," as it were, the cognitive acts
of underprivileged readers, an opportunity that should not be thrown away because of a general distaste for empiricism. There are two sets of circumstances
here that could elicit potential objections to this approach. First, even an op-
timally planned test for reception will distort the conditions of an authentic receptive situation, for instance, because the motivation to participate in the experiment could smother literary interest, because as a guinea pig the reader feels
particularly obliged to read with more intensity than usual and to come up with
an especially original meaning, and also perhaps because he is incapable of
describing his own cognitive actions and receptive experiences. Second, previous
attempts to do empirical research on reception have not been particularly satisfying. Neither of these are acceptable as primary objections because, in our desire
to make our work as rational as possible (in particular, establishing a canon for

literary didactics and generating teaching methods for literature courses), we should not be led astray by epistemological problems. Putting together a test that would satisfy the theoretical claims of a sociology of communication seems to me to be one of the most urgent tasks of literary didactics, which even as a normative didactics can realize its aims only when it is cognitively well founded in the characteristic textual understanding of its various target groups.

Jauss demanded that, in planning this kind of experiment, just as with every critical effort to grasp actions of understanding historically, we should proceed from the "hermeneutic priority of the implied reader." Referring back to the concept of the "implied reader,"[31] we can recommend the following differentiation of his postulate: whenever literary criticism is ultimately concerned with the distinction between "correct" and "inadequate" reading (as is always the case with literary didactics), it is necessary to set up a framework for correct readings based on a normative model. But where its interests are focused on understanding the connection between historical readings (including those that look like encapsulations or misinterpretations) and their conditions, it is advisable to return to the reading intended by the author as a backdrop against which the various historical meanings can be compared.

Reading Experience and Motivation for Actions

If we strictly maintained the limitation of the field of a criticism based on communication sociology that was mentioned at the beginning, then the program of developing problems and solutions coming out of the research on textual production and cognition as forms of social action would already be solved. But since we are concerned here not only with the anticipation of critical problems but primarily with the reconstruction of a fundamental relationship among all of the different styles of research gathered under the title of "reception aesthetics," and hence with suggesting a way of systematizing current discussion as well as putting a damper on a certain euphoria about the odds for the success of these styles, we still have to face up to the greatest ambition of reception aesthetics – reconstruction of literature's influence on history.[32] This project deserves particular attention, because its success would provide strong arguments and apologetics for every sort of interpretation, and thus for literary criticism in general.

What exactly is meant by the assertion that literature has an influence on history? Apparently that literary reception would be a factor in the stabilization, questioning, and evolution – in any case, in the qualitative change – of existing social structures. Such changes can only be effected indirectly, which suggests that the meanings fulfilled by readings of literary texts modify the field of the audience's social knowledge that is the basis of their everyday action. Schütz called this stock of experiences "that system of factors relevant for motivation" (*das Sys-*

tem der Motivationsrelevanzen).[33] Thus literature has an impact on history whenever its reception modifies the knowledge relevant for motivation, which in turn alters the social action of a sufficient number of readers so that this change becomes an incentive for a shift in social structures.

What sounds quite plausible within the framework of a general model cannot be reconstructed in historical detail, however, even when we have access to the readers' actions of understanding. This is mainly because of the often mentioned, but seldom precisely analyzed, fact (the "autonomy" of art) that these actions of understanding literary texts are rarely performed with the purpose of providing an orientation for practical action.[34] If after reading a photography primer I no longer exclusively choose themes like "Aunt Lucille in front of Grant's Tomb" (at best underexposed) but suddenly use a tripod and trap bedewed spider webs in the morning sun on grainy, high-sensitivity film, then I do not need a literary critic versed in the sociology of communication to establish a plausible relationship between my textual reception and the change in my leisure behavior. For precisely such a change was the project of my reading in the first place. Much more problematic would be the development of a similar correlation for a situation where, say, in the course of reading Eric Segal's *Love Story* just for fun, I become aware of my growing interest in female Italian music students and catch myself setting up accidental encounters in the cafeteria or library.[35] While the reader whose reception of a text has the purpose of altering his action makes an effort to replace or extend the action of previous experiences with new ones, he will for the most part not even feel particularly disposed and by no means obliged to read literary texts from a similar perspective.

Yet it is to be assumed that even these kinds of textual offers, after having modified the reader's previous knowledge, can alter his action. Of course we know very little about how such influence works, unless it has originated in a specific project of gathering knowledge. Since hardly any recipient would read *Love Story* in order to choose the nationality and vocation of his future wife, and because the system of values provided by the text will therefore at best interact with the recipient's previously internalized system of values in a manner that has barely been studied and will by no means simply replace or extend that system, it is inadmissible to identify the experience provided by the text of *Love Story* as the because motivation of behavioral changes observed during and after the readings. The aporia in studying the influence of textual reception on the reader's behavior, to put it precisely, lies in the impossibility of isolating, in the context of knowledge relevant for motivating action, that kind of experience that goes back to literary reception and then to evaluate its significance for changes in action.[36] It remains to be pointed out that this aporia is also not canceled in those cases where we are able to question readers about their subjective impressions regarding the significance of literary reception for their actions: in the first place, because estimating the relative weight of different prior experiences for the constitution of an action is of course impossible for the acting individual; and second, because in praxis, conscious action that is partially aware of its motives always comes mixed with unconscious, purely reactive behavior, so that such self-interpretation would probably overestimate the relative weight of conscious motivation (for example, such experience derived from literary reception).

If we cannot expect to succeed in arriving at the connection between experiences that individuals or groups acquire by the reception of literary texts on the one hand, and changes in their acts on the other, then we lack an indispensable initial stage for the positive reconstruction of literature's "influence on history." Moreover, those changes in historical social structures that can be retrospectively determined at all are presented to us as a complex interaction of so many diverse factors that the chances of evaluating one factor, "literary reception," as significant enough to legitimize literature and literary criticism would seem to be slight — even if we had access to a more precise method for investigating the effect on the readers' action.[37] Faced with this series of aporias that arise as we try to describe those phases of concrete analysis that would have to be achieved as a prerequisite for a successful study of the impact of literary texts, we have a tendency to consider statements about the emancipatory or stabilizing role of the works of individual authors as nothing but expressions of "sympathy" or "antipathy" for these authors, clothed in the pathos of critical jargon.[38]

The Promise of the New Paradigm for Criticism

If we adhere strictly to Kuhn's determination of the term "paradigm," then we cannot talk about a new "critical paradigm" because we still lack studies that would provide an exemplary answer to the changed problems of criticism. But at any rate, from the current discussion about reception aesthetics we can derive a more precise determination of this new research field as an interest in the reconstruction of the conditions of meaning production and futhermore as the differentiation of a normative from a descriptive history of reception. My recommendation to limit the field of a communication-sociological criticism to textual production and textual understanding as forms of social action is self-reflectively analogous to the investigations Kuhn mentioned as exemplary of his "paradigms" to the extent that it also makes possible the prognostication of future research.

Within limits, we can see a preliminary confirmation (ex negativo) of the constitution of a new field of descriptive criticism in the fact that it no longer includes the problematic question about the general function of literature, within which only highly hypothetical or trivial propositions could be produced — and these by no means through controlled methods. There is less and less chance that we will quote literary history some day to justify literary communication or literary criticism.

On the other hand as a résumé of this essay, as it were, there is a spectrum of research problems whose mastery should be achieved in the future. Among them is the determination of the particular characteristics of the expressive and receptive actions of literary communication, a historical sketch of the interest in literary reception as the history of the socially given motivations for any actions related to literary texts, the development of a phenomenology of literary reading as a theory of the constitution of cognitive actions out of the perceptual acts subordinated to them, the gradual improvement and testing of theoretically reflected procedures for empirical research on reception, and finally the systematic differentiation of different types of evidence for the reconstruction of historical processes of reception according to their relevance and methods of evaluation. Critical work could profit in all of these fields by embedding itself in a sociology of communication, which is to be conceived as a theory of communicative action.

Part II
Historical Representation and Life World

Chapter 2
Metahistorical Historiography?

Everyday Language and Life World

When literary criticism took off in the 1960s with the lofty purpose of becoming more rigorously scientific, its flaming epistemological enthusiasm made it seem "progressive" for a while to recommend new and exceedingly formal and complex definitions for critical concepts and sometimes, albeit inadvertently, for literary history as well. "The more innovative, the better" was the secret rule of this definitional euphoria. But before this boosterism really got going, its own logic threw a wet blanket on it; for, by generating countless "private terminologies" in the face of a general enthusiasm for "scientific rigor," literary criticism proved to be its own barrier to communication. By itself this *epistemological*—and for many of the people involved, *autobiographical*—experience would suggest the wisdom of accepting the advice to establish the definitions of key terms in literary criticism simply by making more precise certain rules of everyday usage.

This advice corresponds to our intention to introduce a metahistorical concept of "historiography." For it is not a question here of packing the most recent research into a (complex) concept or pointing out promising perspectives for future research. The problem is rather to make us conscious of the problems implied in using terms as metahistorical—and to set up controls for limiting the thematic field of "historiography" through a projection of the current everyday conception of "historical writing." Now if we want to make the definition of the everyday concept of historiography more precise, then we have to avail ourselves of a theoretical foundation that, in the broadest sense, is anthropological; for only an an-

33

thropologically organized theory will be able to adopt the implicit assumption of everyday language that certain genres or genre-like configurations have a meta-historical character. In the context of these problems, we would like to take recourse to Husserl's *Philosophie der Lebenswelt*, because the philosophy of the life world has become the foundation of the sociology of knowledge, which, in its turn, has proved to be a very useful tool in recent medieval studies.[1]

Our reference to the philosophy of the life world as the starting point for the development of a metahistorical concept of historiography has two consequences. First, the path to this development, as we would like to demonstrate, must be strictly deductive. It is clear, however, that the steps leading to this concept were constantly fed back into experiences of dealing with historical texts and the conditions for using the everyday predicate of historiography. Second, by grounding a metahistorical concept of historiography in the concept of the life world we grant it, epistemologically speaking, a specific status. We are not concerned here to defend or criticize its phenomenological implications. For our presentation of medieval historiography, all that is relevant is the opportunity the life-world concept opens up for us to clarify the metahistorical move that is implemented by projecting the everyday concept of historiography into the Middle Ages.

Life World and World-Gone-By

Research oriented toward the sociology of knowledge reconstructs past or present "everyday worlds." This concept designates the specific inventories of the collective knowledge that orients action and the collective attitudes that guide the behavior of societies or social groups—*with regard to their differences*. It is precisely this regard that induces us to use the term everyday worlds solely in the plural. Seen functionally—and this is the central anthropological premise of Weberian sociology—everyday worlds and the social formations they make possible are interpreted as substitutes for the insufficiently developed human instinctual apparatus. More exactly, it follows from this anthropological premise that everyday worlds (stocks of collective knowledge and attitudes) provide human beings with programs: for sense production on various levels—that is to say, instructions for selection from a perceived environmental complexity; with programs for selecting *themes* out of over complex perception ("experience," *Erleben*); for selecting *elements of knowledge* out of a complex inventory of knowledge that can be correlated with the themes selected for the purpose of interpreting them ("practical experience," *Erfahren)*; and for choosing from a plethora of *possibilities for assembling motivations* as configurations of practical individual experiences ("formation of motivations," *Bilden von Handlungsmotiven*). The series "experience-practical experience-the formation of motivations" (*Erleben, Er-*

fahren, Bilden von Handlungsmotiven) is systematic and is not intended to delineate a temporal sequence of phases for sense production.[2]

The term life world assumes that each historical everyday world is grounded in a certain basic stock of sense-constitutive rules of selection, and it represents this metahistorical layer of sense production. The structures of the life world exclude certain forms of experience, practical experience, and action as possible objects of human self-experience; for precisely this reason (i.e., because of its limits) we are able to experience the structures of the life world both theoretically and in praxis. It is not unusual that all those (im)possibilities of experience, practical experience, and action with their respective historical and social forms—possibilities which human beings can imagine but which they *cannot* expect to realize, either for themselves or for their ancestors and posterity—are condensed into transcendental images of gods, "heroes," "supermen." And such collective images enable us to illustrate what the "life world" and its limits mean. For instance, the Christian God is "omnipresent" and "eternal" (whereas the life world implicates human consciousness in a *hic et nunc*); "He gazes into the soul of Everyman" (whereas human experience of other humans, even in the ecstasy of a love relationship, remains exterior); and we could go on for a long time showing that the predicates of God, Hero, or Superman are located beyond the "limits of the life world."

That the contents of consciousness can be articulated at all in "heroes and supermen," idols and stereotypes that are in principle imaginable but are excluded from the actual human experience, shows that the limits of the life world really are experienced as limits and that the contents of consciousness that are located beyond these limits must be assigned the status of "wish objects that are contingent on the life world." If, however, we can say that the desire to transgress the limits of the life world back into the past and forward into the future is an anthropological constant, then we can legitimately assume that all those individual texts whose generation and effects are invested with desires to trespass the limits of the life world share a common ground. In another study, we use Hugo Kuhn's description of such text groups as "fascination types," because they direct our attention to an ostensibly prereflexive fascination with the contents of consciousness outside the limits of the life world.[3] "Historiography" as a fascination type would then be related to two structures of the life world: in the context of the *nunc* of present consciousness and the *irreversibility of time*. By transgressing the temporal and situational bonds of consciousness, we can set up those genres that anticipate the contents of future consciousness together with the historiographical genres: prophecies, utopias, historicophilosophical tracts, prognoses, estimates. With regard to past and future manifestations, both text groups have similar structural limits. There is a past domain, of which I was contemporary; a domain before that, with some of whose contemporaries I was acquainted in my own lifetime; and finally, another borderline domain, which does not even directly overlap with my own lifetime. In the same way, there is a future that I can hope to experience as contemporary; a somewhat more distant future for my younger contemporaries; and a future that none of my contemporaries will experience.

Thus *a broad concept of historiography* could be attached to all those texts that, by transmitting knowledge of the past through the generations, achieve a transgression of the life world's limitation of the *nunc. A narrow concept of historiography* (just as metahistorical but preferable because of its greater allowance for differentiation) also takes into consideration the constituting role of the second limit of the life world, namely, the irreversibility of time. If we want to tentatively understand the possibility of transgressing this limit in texts, then it is necessary to have a more detailed look at the relationship between text forms and the activities of consciousness they stimulate.

Knowledge of the Preworld and Present Experience

When we say—articulating our experience of the irreversibility of time—that "you can't step into the same river twice" or "you can't turn back the wheel of time," then we certainly do not mean that it is impossible to transmit *past experiences*. Rather, such adages point to the fact that it lies beyond the limits of the life world to reexperience in succession, *as if in the present,* those processes through which the "experiences of the past" are or have been formed. Texts, which are supposed to meet the desire to transcend the limitation on the life world by the irreversibility of time, must give their readers the illusion—at least for the time of their reception—that they are contemporaries of the thematized past themselves, that they *relive* it precisely in the phenomenological sense of *erleben*. Now what conditions have to be met so that recipients, for the time of their reading, will have the illusion "of reliving the past," "of existing in a present relationship to it," as if historiography would let them "reverse time"? One of the first of these preconditions surely cannot be met by historiography—namely, being able to put the material objects of perception from a (past) world at the disposal of the recipient, literally within reach. Nevertheless, we can discern a recurrent procedure, even if it is usually overlooked in critical analyses, which is suitable for stimulating their imagination in this direction: it is by no means rare in historiography to find descriptions or even illustrations of the place of the past action, or to be informed that individual objects from the past, frequently quite laden symbolically, can still be seen "today" (whether the ruins of Machu Picchu, the coronation robe of Henry II, or Napoleon's camp bed). In the second place, "experiencing a past world" means interpreting its objects through historical stores of knowledge. The implementation of the second condition for the representation (*Vergegenwärtigung*)[4] of the past has been worked on intensively by historians only for the last couple of decades, beginning at that point in the history of historiography when so-called structural history began to reconstruct collective mentalities. Third, it belongs to the illusion of experiencing a past world through historiography that recipients, on the basis of their knowledge of the past, develop future expectations or prognoses, which are so open and undefined that it looks like they were wholly unaware of the consequences of the thematized past for their own past or present.

Now this last condition (the open temporal horizon that becomes the future of the thematized past) implies that "historiography in the narrow sense" articulates historical knowledge in a manner that allows the recipients to recapitulate the process through which it was acquired. "Historiography in the narrow sense" translates a historical knowledge embedded in *monothetic* structures into the *polythetic* structural process of their acquisition. It is through this specific performance of sense constitution that we become aware of the plausibility of favoring the narrow concept. For if we were to take the broad one, then the difference between historiographical and nonhistoriographical texts would be based solely on the semantic fields evoked by the respective textual groups and their associated referential objects; on the other hand, the translation of monothetic into polythetic sense structures implied in the narrow concept has to be implemented by special *textual procedures*.

At this point we can draw attention to a specific functional possibility for historiography in the narrow sense. The openness of the future horizon coordinated with the thematicized past is, as we have already seen, an illusion in the consciousness of the recipients. Hence authors of historiographical texts can try to recall their audience's monothetic stores of historical knowledge, liquefying them so that they can flow into polythetic sense structures, yet at the same time they try to steer the reacquisition of historical knowledge made possible by these polythetic structures of re-presentation so that new (and again monothetic) structures of historical knowledge can deviate from the originally evoked structures of knowledge. The readers' willingness to accept such a "retelling" will increase to the extent that they are actually brought to try and implement a process of formulating experience themselves. The goal, the renewal of the structures of historical knowledge on which this—only seemingly self-reliant—process of the authorial acquisition of experience is focused, depends on authorial interests whose legitimation in turn should be measured not by their agreement with or divergence from "historical reality" but by social and ethical criteria.

To summarize: If we devise a narrow metahistorical concept of historiography by investing it with two limitations of the life world (namely, the *nunc* of present consciousness and *the irreversibility of time*), then we can say that historiography—prior to every reflection, or even any historically specific intention and anticipation—gives its recipients the illusion of being able to stretch their own lifetimes back into the past at their pleasure. At any rate then, "an ideal historiography" related to this performance would do more than simply constitute the three partial illusions: the illusion of being able to dispose of the perceptual objects of past worlds as if they were physically within reach; the illusion of being able to draw on the specific stores of knowledge of the same past worlds to interpret those objects; and the illusion of the openness of that temporal horizon that, with respect to the thematized past, is the future. An ideal historiography would also have to claim *authenticity* for itself—whatever that might mean in concrete historical terms (for "fictional past worlds" could not be accepted as extensions of the recipients' own lifetimes into the past, since fictional sense structures belong to a style of experience different from biographical self-experience). Moreover, an ideal historiography in the narrow sense will have to put into perspective past action as the prehistory of the recipients (for "natural history" or the "history of a foreign tribe" cannot be attached to the recipients' own lifetimes in a, so to speak, "semantically unilinear" manner).

It is obvious that not every text labeled *historiographical* will be able to produce all five determinate elements of this concept. Besides, we should keep in mind that, by developing these determinate elements, we are *not* concerned with a program for the writing of history so much as with running through and exhausting the possibilities provided by the philosophy of the life world of making the everyday concept of historiography more precise. Finally, it must be noted that the critical comprehension of at least two of these historical characteristics—namely, the illusions that the historical stores of knowledge are available and that the future horizon is open—was first made possible by a complex of modern cognitive prerequisites we are accustomed to call "historical thought." Of course, the fact that the prerequisites for the comprehension of phenomena were not given from time immemorial does not imply (as the application of the philosophy of the life world demonstrates continually) that the existence of these phenomena is also historically limited.

Narrating and Experiencing Antiquity

Our concept of "historiography" connotes the concept of "narration," and this connotation must be made more precise. The attempt has been made semantically to define "narration" as that "text type" that represents processes. The insufficiency of this definition can be demonstrated textually—for instance, theological tracts about the "story of Christ" or reflections on the historical and philosophical significance of the French Revolution, both of which admittedly "represent" certain processes but neither of which anyone would call "narrative." We could say more exactly that narrative texts manifest processes of experience formation—or differently, that, for the duration of the reception, they give the reader the illusion of implementing past processes of experience formation in present time. In our context, this means that those texts whose fascination is their transgression of the life world's limitation on the "irreversibility of time" must be narrative.

It could now be asked whether the metahistorical claim, which belongs to the everyday concept of "story telling" and literary criticism's notion of "narration," could not just as well be grounded in the philosophy of the life world.[5] In such a context an attempt would have to be made to distinguish basic anthropological modes for acquiring or realizing experience (for example, "polythetic" and "monothetic" modes). This in turn would require an answer to the question whether given modes of consciousness (for instance, various levels of "attention span") might be concomitant with given modes for acquiring manifest experience. Finally, metahistorically intended concepts of text typology (like "narration") would have to be defined as sets of texts that evoke specific configurations for the activities of consciousness (styles of experience). At this theoretical level, the narrow metahistorical concept of historiography could become the convergence point for two anthropological dispositions: the fascination of transgressing the limits of the life world in a certain direction and a basic style of experience.

The Foundation of the Life World and the Function of Communication Forms in the Everyday World

Up until now we have avoided talking about *functions* or even *the* function of historiography. Because we were concerned with developing a useful metahistorical concept of historiography and since we had chosen the philosophy of the life world as the theoretical basis of this attempt, *anthropological dispositions* have been our referential field heretofore. Just as we correlated the concepts of "life world" with *anthropological dispositions*, we will now coordinate the *concept of function* with *everyday worlds* at the phenomenal level.

Communicative motivations — or, to use a different formulation, the functional intentions of authors and recipients — constitute themselves out of the intepretations of historically specific objects and situations by specific historical stores of knowledge. In the same way, the effects of textual reception depend on interpretations of texts that point to the historically specific contexts of their generation and that are made by their audience's specifically configurated knowledge. However, the particular historical and social intentions, needs, and structuring performances of authors and recipients are always grounded in common anthropological dispositions (fascinations and styles of experience). Only around them do intentions and needs become historically and socially concrete. They guarantee a rock-bottom minimum of communication and intersubjective interaction.

These sorts of anthropological dispositions are never "purely" articulated, but rather (when they objectify themselves in texts) are always indirectly communicated in historically particular textual contents and structures. Precisely because of the boundless possibilities of form and content, the extrapolation of anthropological dispositions and their possible configurations, which we have attempted in order to delimit the concept of historiography, can make a contribution to the identification of the particularities of the contents and structures of texts bound to their respective everyday worlds.

Chapter 3
The Role of Narration
in Narrative Genres

The topic "Narrative Theory and the History of Genre" implies a reference that is not contained in the concepts "narration" and "genre" themselves. It is possible to formulate a concept of narration that can be generalized and is potentially applicable for metahistorical analysis, whereas we become aware of genres through the perspective of their particular historical occurrence.

What I am getting at is the relationship between "typical basic forms" and genres,[1] between those communicative components that are not exclusively limited to a single genre and genres as "certain historical figures of compatibility between textual components."[2] During the last few years, there have been two kinds of consensus on this problem among literary critics: (1) genres are understood as part of language norms that can be placed historically and socially;[3] and (2) their constitutive components/basic forms are seen partly as anthropological constants, partly as subordinated elements of speech norms,[4] without "belonging to a single realm of reality or a single level of abstraction."[5] This solution to the problem of the relationship between genres and universals is just as unacceptable as it would be to propose that "the morphemes of the modern High German language norm are partly universals and partly belong to the modern High German language norm." Of course it is precisely the assemblage of phenomena with the same status or concepts with the same degree of abstraction that is supposed to aid us in setting up hierarchies for phenomenal fields or levels of abstraction — for instance, the triad "parole/norm/langue." Lining up universals and elements of the language norm on the same phenomenal level renders the distinction of phenomenal levels in itself senseless. Hence the question about the relationship between language universals and genres needs to be approached in a new way. In this essay, I will attempt to discuss this question paradigmatically with regard to the place of a metahistorical concept of "narration" in a genre theory that is conceived as a foundation for historical genre studies. The discussion is divided into four parts. To begin, a historical theory of genre will be developed as a framework within which a metahistorical concept of narration can be located. This sketch must necessarily be followed up with a suggestion for deducing such a metahistorical concept of narration. Only then will we have generated the necessary presuppositions for answering our main question about the relationship between the concepts of narration and genre. We will conclude with a discussion of the relation between narrative and typical communication situations – that is, of the pragmatics of narration.

Genres as "Institutions"[6]

The sociological theory of action and institutions enjoys, at least in West Germany, increasing popularity as the basis for a genre theory keyed to literary history. Describing textual genres as institutions is not a "more adequate representation of reality" than their characterization through "rules of textual generation" or assemblages of "building blocks." Rather, the boom of the institutional concept in literary criticism's theory of genre indicates a clear-cut sociohistorical interest in the literature of the past (we could reconstruct the specific epistemological origins of this interest here if it were not so certain that it would soon make way for other dominant interests). For the conceptualization of genres as institutions means to make them into a part of social history, or more precisely, into the knowledge relevant to action and orientation in past societies.

Reading through those studies that try to establish or already assume the definition of genres as institutions, it is in any case difficult to avoid the impression that literary historians are fairly unaware of the consequences of this conceptual loan from sociology. Which is precisely why I would like to cite a comparatively broad sociological definition of institutions – in order to derive some preliminary criteria for a systematically reflected coordination of the concept of genre and narration by listing the consequences that have grown out of its appropriation by literary criticism. "Institutionalization takes place," according to Peter Berger and Thomas Luckmann, "as soon as habitualized actions are reciprocally typified by types of actors. Every typification undertaken in this manner is an institution."[7] For genre theory, this has five implications. First, the genre concept has its reference at the level of social knowledge, or more specifically, at the level of knowledge about typical actions (which, as I mentioned earlier, is exactly what makes the concept of institution attractive for a social history of literature). Second, genres as knowledge about typical actions become effective as anticipations of actions whereby what is expected from others (for example, from readers) and what is expected from a self (say, what the author expects from the readers' anticipations) are indivisibly entwined. (For this reason, someone who conceives of genres as institutions cannot afford to screen textual production or reception out of his or her reconstructions.) Third, if genres are seen as reciprocal anticipations of typified action, then those "components" that literary historians would like to regard as genre-constituting elements must be so defined that they are categorically compatible with the concept of action. (As I have already pointed out, universals cannot be brought in as components of an institution.) Fourth, a conception of genre based on the theory of institutions implies the assumption that the genesis, stabilization, modification, and dissolution of genres are mainly (not exclusively, to be sure, but all the same) dependent on their functions. Fifth, the conceptual extension of genres described as institutions is fundamentally limited. (It would be sociological and sociohistorical nonsense to regard "the fable from Aesop to Thurber" as an institution).

Narration as a Style of Experience

Terminological chaos may turn out to be the flip side of complex interdisciplinary discussions, such as the debate on narratology. With regard to this chaos, any new attempt to increase its complexity (as this one here surely does) should at least make it clear from the outset which of the main paths used to define narrative it intends to pursue. We would like to distinguish three paths. First, the semiotics of the Paris school locate the concept of narration in the semantic deep structures of the text and dissolve the limits of the concept "narrative":

> La narrativité genéralisée — libérée de son sens restrictif qui la liait aux formes figuratives des récits — est considérée comme le principe organisateur de tout discours. Toute sémiotique pouvant être traitée soit comme système, soit comme procès, les structures narratives peuvent etre définies comme constitutives du niveau profond du procès sémiotique. [8]

As a justification for our exclusion of this definition, we suspect that from a perspective of textual pragmatics, there is scarcely any way to render plausible the semiotic premise that would ground every discourse in narrative (i.e., in basic semantic oppositions). Second, under the influence of the Parisian semiotic theory of basic semantic oppositions, but without its generalization, an explication of the colloquial concept of narration has entered into the language of criticism. According to this second definition of narration, narratives are texts that provide significant articulations of events through conceptual oppositions. The latent subordination of this narrative concept to textual reference is evident in the following formulation: "Only when something relevant has changed is it worth narrating it."[9] It is clear that this narrative concept, among other things, would have to exclude the concept of "narration without a subject," which would be quite compatible with the Parisian semiotic concept of narration. Third, in contrast to the two definitions, one too broadly semiotic and the other too narrowly referential, a perspective on the phenomenal field of "narration" that was conceived by Eberhard Lämmert over twenty-five years ago would seem to be acceptable as a pragmatically grounded theory. Drawing on studies by Herder and Jean Paul, Lämmert describes narration as a type of sense constitution: "The poet, if he intends to make them narratable, is given the task of converting or at least embedding his ideas and opinions, his conceptions of space and character in temporal procedures or events."[10] Narration as a mode of constituting sense can be reconciled with the concept of genres as institutions because, for all of the differences between individual variants of interactive sociology, institutions as the reciprocal anticipation of types of acts and action are always described as complex frames of sense constitution.

Admittedly by using this third approach to unfold a narrative concept with the status of an anthropological constant, we will not be able, as Lämmert recommended, to proceed inductively. For, as Gérard Genette has rightly pointed out, "the longevity" of phenomena "is not a sure indication of their transhistorical character."[11] Here at the beginning of the necessarily deductive path at the end of which we hope to arrive at a valid metahistorical concept of narration, we already sense the phenomenological reconstruction of the life world (*Lebenswelt*). This sort of application of the findings of descriptive phenomenology would correspond exactly to the representation of its heuristic function recommended by Thomas Luckmann—namely, "to produce a general matrix, tailored to the level of human action, for propositions about human behavior."[12]

On the basis of the suggestion to use descriptions of the life world's structures heuristically, it does not follow, of course, that these structures should be regarded merely as heuristic constructs. Rather we would like to begin our deduction by describing the value of the structures of the life world for social anthropology. Social anthropology is grounded in the hypothesis that societies compensate for the specifically human lack of instinctual orientation by constructing and distributing different (but always intersubjective) meanings—or to put it differently, "socially constructed realities." To designate this kind of socially constructed reality, phenomenological sociology uses the term "everyday world" for the most part. Notwithstanding the broad spectrum of everyday worlds whose contents our imaginative capacities can hardly fathom, and whose synchronic and diachronic developments are reconstructed by ethnography and history, they nonetheless all have a common basis in the strategies of sense constitution. This constant anthropological framework of meaningful orientation, which is filled out with given specific contents in the process of which everyday worlds are generated, is called the life world.

The process of sense formation, which can be described as a sequence of three operations, belongs to the basic structures of the life world. By implementing these operations humankind succeeds in orienting itself within an over complex supply of environmental perceptions and, regardless of how we might define the contents of these constant anthropological structures for a particular everyday world, in constituting intersubjectivity within this orientation. The three operations of the life world's process of sense formation are *thematization, interpretation,* and *motivation.* Thematization designates the selection made in each conscious moment of a central object of attention out of a multitude of simultaneous perceptions. Interpretation is that operation in which certain qualities are ascribed to the thematically constituted object of attention by comparing them with concepts drawn from given stores of everyday knowledge. By motivation we mean the development of the notion of a future situation (of a motive) that will serve as an orientation for action.

Language is undoubtedly the most important medium for ensuring intersubjectivity in sense formation; this does not so much unconditionally imply the stabilization of everyday sense structures as the ensuring of intersubjectivity through the variation of sense structures in the everyday world. Seen in this manner, it becomes plausible, from the concept of the life world and its socioanthropological postulates, to distinguish between three constant anthropological forms of discourse that can be functionally coordinated with the constitution of intersubjectivity on the three levels of the process of sense formation. Through narration, the thematizing sequences performed by subjective procedures of consciousness become intersubjective; through descriptions, the results of the interpretation of thematized objects of perception; and through argumentation, subjectively constituted motivations are prepared to take on intersubjectivity. To put it differently, narration is aimed at the intersubjectivity of experience (*Erleben*); description, at the intersubjectivity of completed practical experience (*Erfahrung*); argumentation, at the intersubjectivity of acting (*Handeln*).

It is not immediately plausible, of course, that the narrative concept that is to be formulated within this threefold organization is correlated with the concept of experience (of thematization). The first and most important associative bridge for this correlation is the concept of time. According to Husserl, time is "the form of experience"[13] and narration transforms meanings, as in Lämmert's formulation, "into temporal processes, into events." Defining time as "forms of experience," Husserl conceives the introspectively acquired insight that every actual experience (every actual choice of a perceptual object) is strung out between a remembered "reverberation" of previous, already interpreted perceptual objects (retention) and anticipations of future experiences (empty protentions) derived from retention but not yet confirmed by it. Consummated practical experiences (results of the interpretation of perceptual objects) can be remembered—or more generally, realized—in various ways. Narrative discourse transposes them back into experiential structures, into the temporal structures of their acquisition.

If we take this suggestion for defining narration as a type of discourse that is metahistorically constant and enables intersubjectivity at the symbolic level of experience, and fill it out with the contrastive observation that narration makes experience accessible in the context of its polythetic constitution, whereas description makes possible a monothetic comprehension of experience as results of processes of experiential formation, then two presuppositions for our argumentation must be pointed out. The first presupposition is concerned with the instance of the speaker/author: we normally assume that the use of language articulates previously acquired experience, which means that the narrative discourse makes it possible to return consummated practical experience to the processual structure of its acquisition. The second concerns the listener/reader: each reception of spoken or written texts as well as any text that is coordinated with descriptive or argumentative discourses has a polythetic character. But while the polythetically performed sense constitution of the recipient of a descriptive discourse leads to a meaning complex that can be understood quite monothetically, the immediate result of reading a narrative text is the recapitulation of an experiential sequence, culminating in an image that has practically no contours.[14]

The complicated circumstances of the varying quality of sense structures resulting from the reception of narrative or descriptive texts can be more concisely grasped when we no longer conceive of narration, description, and argumentation as metahistorical types of discourse but as experiential styles provided by the life world.[15] In trying to work out this recommendation, which can only be quickly sketched here, we would also have a way of characterizing nonverbal media like paintings, films, or shows as narrative or descriptive—without having to call them texts any longer as a way of assuaging our conscience. Experiential styles are complex attitudes of sense formation like "absolute attention," "daydreams," "everyday life," or "scientific work," which constitute qualitatively quite different meaning complexes and which in turn are incompatible with one another.

Experiential styles can be distinguished according to at least five categories: the specific level of attention, the dominant form of spontaneity, the particular *epoché*, the specific form of sociality, and the specific form of self-experience.

According to these criteria, we would first of all like to try to characterize narration as an experiential style, and then go on to compare narration, description, and argumentation as types of experiential style from certain specific points of view.

1. It is intuitively plausible that the level of attention during narration is comparatively low (and increases as we go from description to argumentation), and this impression can be illustrated by innumerable reception-guiding signs from familiar literary and nonliterary texts.

Besides, it has been systematically presented by Harald Weinrich within the framework of his *Tempus* theory.[16]

2. The dominant form of spontaneity during the narration and reception of a narrative is association as a principle of passive synthesis, whereas, during description, argumentation, and their respective reception forms, the ego tends to become active as an "engendering and constituting" force.[17]

3. As a specific *epoché*, in Husserl's sense, narration seems to imply a tendency to bracket out doubts about the adequacy of what is narrated (perhaps as a consequence of its low level of attention).

4/5. The narrator experiences him- or herself and is experienced as the subject of the experience (as the subject of the selection of a sequence of perceptual objects); the recipient of the story experiences him- or herself and is experienced as someone recapitulating a sequence of experiences (it is precisely in this recapitulation that intersubjectivity is constituted), but also as a subject who is largely independent from the narrator and who is the subject of a process of interpretation that the experiential sequence renders possible.

It could be conjectured that, analogous to the recipient of a narrative for whom independent interpretation has become possible through the recapitulation of an experiential sequence, the recipient of a description formulates his or her own independent motivation by taking over an experience already constituted by the author, and that the recipient of an argumentation, when he or she adopts the motivation of the speaker or author, subsequently acts independently. For action Schütz and Luckmann presuppose the highest degree of conscious attention, which is exactly why it seems justified to ascribe a higher attention level to the recipient of an argumentation as a potential subject of action than to the recipient of a narration as a potential subject of experiential formation.

We break our speculations off at this point, since they are becoming increasingly schematic and besides, as far as the performance of description and argumentation is concerned, they have already fulfilled their function as a foil to the presentation of narration as experiential style. At any rate, we are encouraged to continue with this sort of investigation by the circumstance that our assessment of the internal and external experiences of communication partners in the experiential styles of "narration," "description," and "argumentation" practically match Karl Bühler's three "semantic functions of the (complex) speech sign." It can be seen as dependent on the sender — narratives allow the recapitulation of the content of the narrator's consciousness; as articulating the coordination of objects and circumstances — the describer constitutes circumstances that are presented to the recipient of the description for his acceptance; and as appealing to the hearer, whose external or internal behavior it steers—the recipient of an argumentation is experienced as a potential actor.[18]

Experiential Styles and Genres, Life World and Institutions

Having introduced the concepts of genre and narrative, we can now go after our central problem, the question of the systematic location of anthropological constants and "narration" with regard to institutions interpreted as genres. To be sure, we have already twice had the opportunity to point out that it is inadmissible to represent this connection as an inclusive relationship. The concept of "experiential style," which is bound to a basic structure of the life world, could be represented as a partial element of the metahistorical concept of the "institution of the speech act." However, the concept of narration as a specific experiential style, which is just as metahistorical, cannot be subordinated in the same way to genres as institutions of particular past societies. Admittedly, an argument for the systematic coordination of the experiential style of "narration" and narrative genres still cannot be derived from the rejection of such an inclusive relationship.

Surely we will gain a presupposition for the solution of our problem by differentiating the still excessively monolithic definition of genres as reciprocal anticipations of typical actions. Which structures could be regarded as the recurrent elements of such anticipations in each historically concrete genre? To answer this, we must return to Wolfgang Iser's model for his phenomenological reconstruction of the act of reading.[19] According to Iser, each text (i.e., each author as the subject of a speech act) offers its audience a textual repertoire and a textual strategy. "Textual repertoire" designates that selection of elements out of the cognitive systems of the textual environment that refers to the lexemes lined up in the text. Likewise, "textual strategies" are the text's instructions or programs for assembling the elements of the repertoire. While knowing something about a genre is going to provide the recipient with certain expectations of the textual repertoire and textual strategies (which are in the mind of the speaker/author as expectations of expectations [*Erwartungserwartungen*]), it is expected from the reader that he is capable of consciously actualizing the elements of knowlege that are marked in the text by lexemes and of transposing the strategic instructions into a construct of the content form:

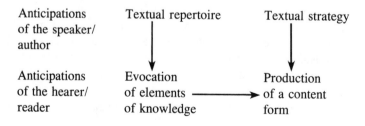

Anticipations of the speaker/ author	Textual repertoire	Textual strategy
Anticipations of the hearer/ reader	Evocation of elements of knowledge	Production of a content form

It is plain that the category of experiential style is to be located in this model as an anthropological foundation for the level of intersubjectivity that will be obtained in communication through the production of textual strategies and their conversion into content forms. For textual strategies and the constitution of content forms based on the experiential style of "narration" it would seem specific that the coordination of the elements of knowledge they evoke are performed in the form of passive syntheses. Outside of the reading, so to speak, the reader of a narrative can of course address herself to the content generated by this kind of passive synthesis and then experience herself as an "engendering, constituting ego" as she attempts to give this content a concise sense independent from the speaker/author. On the other hand, within the framework of the experiential styles of "description" and "argumentation," this kind of "active synthesis" belongs to the reading itself, to the mutual expectations of the communication partners.

What does it mean to postulate a particular experiential style like narration as an anthropological foundation for textual strategies and the activities of recipients directed by these textual strategies, which in turn are themselves elements of specific historical genres and part of the reciprocal expectations of communication partners? To emphasize this for the last time, it mainly means that constant anthropological structures cannot be regarded as constitutive genre elements. This negation problematizes the assumption of countless literary analyses — the premise that there are certain textual strategies, stylistic elements, or rhetorical patterns that can be metahistorically identified as "narrative" (or "descriptive" or "argumentative"). Not even parataxis, usually regarded as the narrative text strategy par excellence, can be seen as a program for inducing intersubjectivity, unless we take into account the interplay of this textual strategy with other text-strategic elements, its role in specific historical and social conventions of communication, and the particular disposition of the communication partners. More as a stimulus for discussion than as a proposition (for the time being), we would like to venture the thesis that a differentiation between narrative, descriptive, and argumentative texts can never be derived from formal analysis but has as its sole basis the recipient's own experience of having heard or read the text.

At this point, it is still undecided what position an anthropological basis (which itself must be deduced in turn from the phenomenology of the life world) would have for the respective text repertoires and the elements of knowledge they evoke. A leitmotiv for this theorizing interest can easily be constructed. Does a constant anthropological horizon for content types also exist parallel to the constant anthropological styles of experience? Now it is self-evident that content types immediately occur to us that we think should be of concern in any everyday world. Nonetheless, a classification of their contents would turn out to be arbitrary and even banal, because the philosophy of the life world does not provide us with a theory from which we can proceed deductively, as was the case with the definition of narration. By consciously waiving systematic completeness and taking recourse to earlier works, we would simply like to provide a few illustrations of what kinds of categories have to be imagined if we are going to develop a second level of anthropological foundation for historical genres.[20]

In the preceding section, we mentioned the socioanthropological premise according to which the structures of the life world compensate for the human lack of instincts. The structures of the life world perform this function by setting limits for each everyday world—in other words, by excluding certain contents of consciousness from all of the everyday worlds. For example, it is not possible to be in several places at the same time; to experience directly what happened before one was born; to know for sure what is going on in the minds of other people; or to get out of one's body. Significantly, only God "is" omnipresent, "has" no beginning and end, "is" omniscient, and "is" pure spirit. To be sure, such divine predication only shows that the contents of consciousness, which the structures of the life world exclude in concrete everyday worlds as objects of human experience (both *Erleben* and *Erfahrung*), can be simulated by language. Language not only enables an intersubjective orientation within the framework of everyday worlds and intersubjectivity in the designs for changing these worlds, as we can see from the course of every enlightenment movement, but also introduces intersubjectivity in simulated transgressions of the life world's limits.

If the limits of the life world are regarded as anthropologically constant, then it can be assumed that their transgression either backward or forward in time is an equally constant anthropological fascination.[21] The fascination of simulating the transgression of the life world's limits in either direction would have to be regarded as part of that anthropological basis for individual genres that we have sought as a parallel to the types of experiential style.

Many genre names seem to refer to this sort of fascination—to concepts that cannot be coordinated with any clearly delimited thematic field, but are nonetheless spontaneously comprehensible, like historiography, bucolics, hagiography, comedy, and tragedy. Historiography, for instance, simulates the transgression of the life world's limits by enabling the reader to reexperience in his consciousness something that happened before he was born. Is it the fascination of a consciousness unencumbered by the body's material existence that is behind all texts identified by literary criticism as "hagiographic"—and many others as well?[22] Doesn't comedy make possible a structuration of the contents of consciousness that is ordinarily excluded from the life world, namely, the simultaneity of incompatible meanings? Naturally in the sense of a metahistorically constant relationship, individual content complexes can no more be coordinated with this sort of fascination than individual stylistic features with experiential styles. Fascination types can be systematically described only by staking out the limits of the life world beyond which they can be found.

At this point it could be asked whether "experiential style" and "fascination"—

hence both of the categories that have been introduced as constant anthropological bases for the two historically variable communicative relationships and out of which every genre generates itself—whether they are not largely compatible with two conceptual modes that have turned up lately in discussions about the theory of genre. The *modes d'enonciation* of Genette are undoubtedly close to our "experiential types of style." On the other hand, Wolf-Dieter Stempel, taking off from Ingarden and Scholes, has spoken about "the sublime, the tragic, the grotesque, the unintelligible" as "modes," which, when recalled by impulses specific to genre, "steer the recipient in one way or another."[23] Certainly it is not a matter here, as Genette seems to believe, of an either/or.[24] When communicative interaction is performed on various levels, then each level, insofar as we are at all interested in getting involved in an anthropological discussion, can be grounded in constant metahistorical dispositions.

In our reflections on the relationship between anthropological constants and historical genres as institutions, we have barely touched on a concept that is usually at the core of theorizing about the pragmatics of genre: the concept of function. We have not avoided its extensive thematization because there is any doubt that the institutionalization of speech acts as genres, their continuity, and their variation are mainly conditioned by their functions. The reason for screening out this theme is rather the recommendation to contain the function concept within the everyday worlds, whether this concept is limited to the conscious subjective motivation of the communication partners or is extended by the historical conditions that make such motivations possible. "The legitimation of a ruling house from a foreign country" is an example of a function in the everyday world that, in all literary and sociohistorical probability, decisively contributed to the origination of the genre of twelfth-century French verse historiography. It can be safely assumed that the elements of the repertoire and the textual strategies typical of (and in any case historically specific to) the texts attributed to this genre are capable of evoking the experiential style of the narration in the recipient and at the same time awakening that fascination that is brought about by the transgression of the temporal boundary toward antiquity. Thus certain constant anthropological dispositions were activated that were suitable for promoting (over other instances of mediation) the recipient's realization of the genre function. Admittedly the activated dispositions have about as little to do with the genre of "twelfth-century verse historiography" as vocal cords do with the institution of a particular language.

The Pragmatics of the Experiential Style of "Narration"

The main question for this final section has already been made concrete through this last example. Is it possible to explain the choice of experiential styles by referring to functions of the "everyday world"? Conversely, can a shift between activated experiential styles contribute to the understanding of functions? Naturally, there is hardly any history of a genre that would not provide interesting results in this respect in one phase of its development or another. At any rate, the agony of having to choose from many examples is considerably lessened by the fact that we can draw on two recent investigations that have shown, quite independent of each other, that two genres of French literature in the second half of the eighteenth century changed their dominant textual strategies so that "narration" was replaced by "description" as an experiential style. They are the beast fable and the utopian novel.[25]

Friederike Hassauer-Roos provides the following summary of her observations about the strategic textual shift in the beast fable:

> In general, three discursive levels . . . can be observed in eighteenth-century fables, all of them related: in the first place, there is a striking expansion of descriptive discourse, together with a marked increase in the length of the text; and second, this is accompanied by a tendency to replace diachronic conceptual transformation with synchronic opposition or with a series of particular narrations. A third characteristic: the protagonists interact less, establishing their positions through dialogue instead; described in spatial relations, this means that they do not change their semantic fields.[26]

Parallel to this shift on the level of text strategies, yet without explicitly referring to them, the authors of fables carry out an extensive discussion in the text about the relationship between the roles of the narrator and the reader. Hassauer-Roos is surely correct to see here a line of development within the framework of the consensus models of the bourgeois Enlightenment, for while at the beginning of this debate the narrator was assigned the role of "midwife" in the formulation of the reader's experience, he ended up in a role that, according to a description by Marmontel, no longer assumed a "didactic abyss" between the roles of the narrator and reader: "Rendre sensible à l'imagination ce qui est évident à la raison."

In an investigation of some twenty utopian novels from the same period, Marion Wedegärtner was able to show that from the middle of the eighteenth century the travel fable, as the dominant structural element of utopian novels, was often reduced to a single page.[27] At the expense of the fictional framework, the description of the ideal society, which was formulated on the basis of abstract concepts with increasing clarity, was extended. Before the utopian novel was finally replaced by sociopolitical programmatic writings during the incubation phase of the Revolution, two further modifications took place: on the one hand, the displacement of the ideal society from the distant island into the future (a first example would be Mercier's novel *L'An deux mille-quatre-cent-quarante* from 1771); on the other, the explicit renunciation by the writers of novels of the genre's previous claim to authenticity:

> Si j'avois voulu suivre la coutume usitée depuis longtemps, j'aurois as-
> sûré avec hardiesse, que cet ouvrage n'est que la traduction d'un
> manuscrit grec, trouvé dans les Ruines d'Herculaneum . . . , mais les
> gens eclaires n'en auroient voulu rien croire. J'avoue donc ingénuement,
> que cette bagatelle est toute entière de moi, et que je suis seul responsa-
> ble de tous les défauts qui la déparent.[28]

If we go back to the category of "experiential style" developed earlier, all of these historical observations can be interpreted as symptoms of a functional shift in literary genres in the late French Enlightenment that was barely perceived by its contemporaries. The transfer from mainly narrative to mainly descriptive textual strategies was accompanied by a change in both the author's and the reader's experiences of their own roles. If the reader previously had to form experiences on the basis of narration, he or she increasingly found him- or herself in a situation that rather suggested the constitution of motivations of action on the basis of an experiential style of description. This means we can understand the tendency toward textual strategies of description in the late French Enlightenment as a sign that perhaps there was a greater need than ever for the traditional genres functionally to mediate between experience and action.

What it functionally means to transpose the dominant textual strategies and the experiential styles they activate—from argumentation and description "back" to narration—is familiar to every teacher at the very least, and, as the pertinent chapters in Quintilian show, to every lawyer as well. It is quite evident that readers are more likely to accept experiences when the author has packaged their acquisition in a polythetic process. Admittedly the choice between strategies that activate a descriptive or narrative style of experience also has something to do with the level of conscious attention that is demanded by descriptions or narrations. This is precisely what seems to be known or instinctively taken into account by the managers of California's amusement parks. For they present shows with dolphins, whales, or carnivores, daring water-skiers, or even the way through the park itself as "narrative." The walk through is supposed to be experienced as a "safari," waterskiing cops defeat evildoers with a little help from Superman, and the killer whales have an opportunity to show what they have learned by saving "unfortunate seamen" from the schemes of Cap'n Hook. If the trained animals were descriptively presented by zoologists, then it would demand a higher attention level from the audience and the same "content" would seem boring. The relaxation that inserts itself into narration—not to be confused with boredom—is also what makes the novel as "bedtime reading" or "the fairytale before going to sleep" the ideal bridge between the daytime and the nighttime level of attention.

Chapter 4
"Narrating the Past Just as if It Were Your Own Time": An Essay on the Anthropology of Historiography

In memory of the historian Wolfgang Nocke
August 21, 1950–December 16, 1980

Historiography: "Fascination Type" Rather Than Genre

In everyday as well as in theoretical language, "the writing of history" is predicated on a concept that is clearly meant to be used in metahistorical and intercultural contexts.[1] It follows theoretically that referential phenomena correlated to this concept are regarded as "anthropological constants." If we lacked such a metahistorical and intercultural concept, we would be unable to respond to works from foreign cultures as "historiographical" and could not assemble texts from completely different eras to study the evolution of "historiography" as a genre; nor could we talk about the affinities, interactions, and conflicts between chronologically simultaneous texts and genres. I must say at the outset that I have nothing against this use of the word. Rather, I am going to be concerned here with rendering the metahistorical and intercultural concept of "historiography" more precise so that its application to the three problem-contexts just mentioned will not remain theoretically precarious.

It is an open question why an effort was not made a long time ago simply to define historiography and then institutionalize such a notion through specialist consensus. One suspects that such a gap in the fundamental categories of history came about because none of the currently dominant textual concepts of genre was suitable enough to serve as a model for a metahistorical and intercultural concept of historiography. Genre theory today has received its best impulses from pragmalinguistics. For instance, it can define genres as "discourses in situations," as "the institutionalized concomitance of contents, structures, and functions," and as

54

"the institutionalized relationship between attitudes and the stock of knowle,
actualized by communication partners for communication." All of these pragmatic suggestions for defining a general concept of genre correlate "genres" and
specific "situations," and all of them provide a clear historical and social limitation
of their field for the determination of individual genres by the components of "institutionalization." It is exactly this historical and social limitation of pragmatic
concepts of genre that cannot be made compatible with history's need for a metahistorical and intercultural concept of historiography.

It is evident that the desired (higher) degree of abstraction of the concept
"historiography" can and must be achieved by crossing out at least one of the three
components—content, structure, function—belonging to any pragmatic concept
of genre. Hence it must be asked whether we want to ground a metahistorical and
intercultural concept of historiography in an assumption about the constancy of
the function, the structure, or the content. For purely practical reasons, the possibility of the assumption of a functional constant is eliminated right away, since
it would presuppose, as "a preliminary condition" so to speak, that there are functional interpretations of all texts that we are accustomed to calling "historiographical" as well as consensus about the interpretive conclusions. Also today,
in an epistemological era that our French colleagues identify as "poststruc-
turalist," we are likely to assess the very possibility of "structural constants" with
a certain amount of skepticism. For if we no longer consider structures to be inherent in the object (that is, as "ontological" factors of data), but concede that the
mental disposition of someone who identifies the structures also participates in
their constitution, then it is clear that we can only arrive at structural constants
when we allow the mental presuppositions of textual interpreters to dominate
those of the author and those of the author's contemporary readers as well. To
formulate it cautiously, the assumption of a constant field of content, therefore,
is left over as the least problematic possibility for establishing a metahistorical
and intercultural concept of historiography.

To designate this kind of content-based conception of text corpora, which has
a higher level of abstraction than pragmatic concepts of genre, the medievalist
and literary theoretician Hugo Kuhn has suggested the term "fascination type."[2]
If we bear in mind the concept Kuhn attaches to this term, then we have a way
of categorically developing metahistorical and intercultural concepts of genre that
could be classified as "anthropologically constant speech acts." Kuhn's key argument is grounded in his observation of thematic affinities among those texts (more
dominant, but not exclusively, during the late Middle Ages) that cannot be approached from the point of view of a function, an intention, or a unifying structure. Instead, he finds symptoms for a constant type of attention, whose continuity
was uninterrupted and which was directed to certain (obviously quite broad)
thematic fields. Because such a constant "type of attention" does not need to think
about itself and its reasons, it is incompatible with categories like "intention" or

"motivation." Kuhn suggests that since certain thematic fields draw into their wake the attention of authors and recipients of every age and class "without them," so to speak, "having had anything to do with it," it is only logical to correlate the relationship between human communication and thematic areas with "fascination," as a concept for a prereflexive state of "being attracted."

On the basis of this short explication of "fascination type," which semantically is a concretion of an "anthropologically constant speech act," it is even possible to expand our theoretical justification of the search for a metahistorically and interculturally applicable concept of historiography. If we have simply focused on the strategic need to coin a working concept for introductory purposes so far, we now have an opportunity to employ the concept "fascination type" in order to establish an anthropologically constant perspective of attention upon which we can build historical consciousness, the interest in history, and thus historiography in all of its varieties. The identification of an anthropologically constant perspective of attention could also be used for a normative pragmatics of historiography (for its "rhetoric"), especially if it could successfully formulate a set of instructions that would demonstrate a way to guarantee the involvement of all historiography in this of attention, thereby assuring its success with a public beyond the narrow circle of specialists of History.

These preliminary theoretical considerations serve mainly to clarify and justify the purpose of our study and to make some prognoses about its future prospects. Our procedure will be strictly inductive when we turn our attention to the development of a concept of historiography that could be used in metahistorical and intercultural ways. In the following section I would like to grasp by introspection those (conscious) anticipations that we automatically bring to all "historiographical" texts and that are therefore part of our everyday knowledge about communication. In conjunction, we will go on to analyze a small body of historiographical texts with quite disparate historical and social origins for recurrent features that will allow us to infer the (preconscious) dispositions hidden in their anticipations. These would have to be assigned to determining elements in the same manner as the conscious anticipations of historiography's anthropologically constant speech acts. And finally, we will use our inductively derived results as the basis for a synthesizing sketch of "the fascination type of historiography" or the anthropologically constant "speech act of historiography."

Anticipations in Everyday Communicative Knowledge Specific to Historiography

To return to communicative competence, we have no difficulty making out two anticipations or expectations that are indirectly related to text and author and are habitually activated in the realm of historiography. We want to designate and descriptively specify them so that they correspond to our interaction with a broad spectrum of historiographical texts. Moreover, there are two anticipations frequently mentioned in recent studies that we would like to dismiss as particular and therefore incapable of being integrated into a model for a metahistorical recurrent speech act.

The First Anticipation

Historiographical texts thematize human action and behavior.
This expectation, which is probably uncontested as far as the author's thematic selection is concerned, should not be understood, say, as a rule for exclusion but as a minimal requirement: historiographical texts can get by without referential objects outside human interaction, but not without human interaction. In individual cases the presentation of situations or natural transformational processes might be thoroughly dominant from a purely quantitative standpoint; nonetheless they must, as Emmanuel Le Roy Ladurie's climatic history has shown, be introduced as a relevant conditional framework for human action.[3]

The extrathematic condition, according to which historiographical texts must have their reference in the past, refers to the relation between the author and his referential material. In other words, "contemporary descriptions" by authors from the distant past might very well constitute a field of sources favored by professional historians, but that does not mean that we have to identify these descriptions with historiography. Actions can be considered as "past" only when their subjects' motivation no longer has an anticipatory status and when their "empty protentions," to put it in phenomenological terms, have been fulfilled in congruence with or in deviation from the motivation.[4]

The Second Anticipation

Historiographical texts refer to reality in every individual part and on every constitutive level.
With the transcription of this second expectation we choose the formulation "refer to reality" instead of "objectivity," the most common predicate in current theoretical discussions about historiography, because for all of this talk about "objectivity" there is also the chance of a "merely subjective" appropriation and reproduction of reality. But within the framework of the history of historiography, the resulting disjunction ought to be considered specifically modern given the traditional conviction that a representation that fits the reference will always be the only one possible and thus is obviously capable of achieving consensus. Now on the other hand, if our description of the second expectation is also going to do justice to modern experiences with historical representation, then it must be presupposed that by "reality" we mean socially institutionalized, more or less

complex, sense structures. From this perspective, Hermann Lübbe's distinction between factual objectivity and consensual objectivity, as practical as it might be for normative purposes, becomes problematical for protomodern as well as for modern historiography.[5]

When we talk about the "reality reference on every constitutive level of the texts," then we intentionally set historiography off from fictional texts. For although authors and their contemporary readers have found pleasure for centuries precisely through the lack of reference in the imaginary worlds evoked by texts, they never hesitated in granting reality to "a deep conceptual level of fictional texts"; the beast fable would be a good example.[6] On the other hand, the referential constraint on historiographical texts must be, as it were, nearly "seamless." For instance, Marxist historiography keeps a tight grip on "the facts of reality" yet is hoping all along that beyond them it is going to uncover a "deep layer of reality" in the form of "historical laws." And a certain "neohistoricism" supports the referential claim of the text surface by taking recourse to the standards of academic historiography (factual objectivity).[7] More comprehensive configurations of meaning can also be considered real but must be located on a "deep narrative level" to satisfy the criteria of "consensual objectivity."

It is well known that the claim of a "seamless" reference to reality can be grounded in quite different ways—by the rules of "academic praxis," by the "correct point of view," by the author's (speaker's) relationship to the represented past ("witness"), by the role, which he or she assumes with respect to the recipients ("priest"). This sort of legitimation, whose context was already theoretically grasped as a pragmatic historiographical problem in antiquity, becomes precarious when what is represented conflicts with the concept of reality ("reality expectation") formulated by the recipients' everyday experience. By slightly differentiating the discourse system, as was done to a certain extent in antiquity through a pragmatic syncretism of myth and historiography, this discrepancy between the recipients' reality expectation and the protagonists' actions simply led to their "redefinition" as demigods. Similar discrepancies are worked out today (according to the communicative context) either through similar categories ("superman," "national hero") or by disqualifying historiographical texts as propaganda literature.

To those anticipations of historiographical texts that are not regarded as metahistorically recurrent belongs the imputation that they have "narrative structure" in the sense that their beginning and end are marked as the basic terms of a binary opposition and that they are mediated by their narrative sequence in such a manner that their theme will always continue to be transformational processes.[8] Neither the elementary form of the chronicle nor the modern "writing of synchronic history" is compatible with such a scheme. Synchronic history is even plainly opposed to this concept of narration, which is so obviously derived from literary criticism, because it requires the assumption that a series of chronologically parallel institutions (even when they are presented in succession) are not going to be subjected to change during a given period.[9] Quite the contrary, the chronicle and structural history could probably be encompassed by Arthur C. Danto's historiographical concept of narration: the "main characteristic feature" of narrative sentences "is the fact that they are related to at least two events temporally separated from one another, although they only describe or make statements about the earlier of the two."[10] By the way, it can be noted in passing that, according to Danto, the particularity of the chronicle in contrast to other historiographical genres is determined by the fact that the series of speech acts constituting it does not feed back into a single moment in the author's present but rather to successive moments of an author's biography or to the lifetimes of various authors, so that under certain circumstances identical actions can be illuminated from different "horizons in the past." For the context of our investigation, however, the only essential point is that Danto's concept of narrative was already implicit in my formulation of the prospects for the thematic selection of historiography—"the presentation of the past" has always meant "connecting two temporally separated events."

"A need for orientation in real contexts of action" is no more a metahistorical, recurrent element of the historiographical speech act than is narrative structure in the sense of literary criticism.[11] It is only in the concluding part of this chapter that we will have a chance to refute this conjecture, which has literally pushed its way into debates about contemporary historical theory. For the moment we can only formulate it as an antithesis, that this "need for orientation" is nothing more, and nothing less, than an articulation of a normative functional determination of historiography dressed up as a pragmalinguistic (descriptive) reconstruction of its speech act.

Induction of Historiographically Specific Dispositions from Historiographical Texts

The terminological opposition between the "expectations," with which I was concerned in the previous section, and the "dispositions," which I now would like to derive from historiographical texts, can be understood with respect to the central distinctions between action/behavior and motivation/attitude in sociology. Conscious motivations can be contrasted with comparatively diffuse (behavioral) attitudes; it is also possible to start with a (gradual) difference between "anticipations," which belong to everyday communicative knowledge and are hence reflexively comprehensible, and precognitive ones, which are for that reason no less relevant as communicative "dispositions." Because they cannot be directly retrieved from everyday knowledge, these kinds of dispositions must be induced from texts, or more exactly, from textual manifestations of historiographers' (most likely precognitive) participation in their audience's disposition.

In a search for metahistorically recurrent speech acts, any attempt to get at the problem by assembling a homogeneous text corpus would be misleading. Rather we use examples whose origins, thematized referential objects, and audience's precognition as imagined by the author are as different as possible.

The Oxford variant of the *Chanson de Roland*, which was presumably set down around the beginning of the twelfth century, is based on events from the eighth century and, with the double claim of offering historical knowledge and entertainment at the same time, was aimed at an "uneducated" audience. The *Crónica general* of Alfonso the Wise was compiled in the thirteenth century, depicts events from the conquest of Spain by the Arabs in the two chapters that interest us here, and although composed in the vernacular language was wholly accommodated to the interests of a highly educated public (by medieval standards). Jules Michelet's *Histoire de la Révolution française* was written at a time far less remote from its thematized events and, as was characteristic of "classical" historiographic texts in the nineteenth century, was just as important for specialized academic debates as for the historical consciousness of the educated bourgeoisie. *Würzburg: Die Jahre nach 1945*, an illustrated volume published in 1974 by the city chronicler of Würzburg, Werner Dettelbacher, presents (mainly through the principles of synchronic history) the *Wiederaufbau* (reconstruction) of the Federal Republic of Germany and surely appealed, if only because of the emphasis on photographic documentation, to groups with very different educational backgrounds. Finally, as an example of modern structural history, there is E. Le Roy Ladurie's masterpiece, *Montaillou, village occitan de 1294 à 1324*, which in the next part will be built into our considerations as a "control" and which, because of countless features in its textual constitution, can in any case be regarded as an example of professional history in the 1970s. It presents life in a village in southwestern France from the thirteenth to the fourteenth century; because it became a best-seller in France as well as a standard academic work it demands inclusion in this essay.[12]

An analysis of these texts suggests that, along with the two anticipations from everyday communicative knowledge already described, we are going to have to ascribe four (precognitive) dispositions to the metahistorical, recurrent speech act of historiography. In the following description we will draw on the pertinent passages from the first four of these texts, with particular emphasis on the interpretive approaches developed by Michelet, especially the chapter about July 14, 1789, in his history of the Revolution.

The First Disposition Specific to Historiography

The thematized world of the past is metonymically present in the world of the recipients through certain objects.[13]

Michelet informed his readers that "still today" the key to the Bastille was stored in an iron cabinet in the archives of the French National Assembly. It is obvious that, within the context of a chapter about July 14, 1789, this object does more than simply realize a metonymic material presence of the past in the present. If the key to the Bastille (the token, as it were, of the arbitrary curtailment of freedom typical of the ancien régime) had been kept ever since in the National Assembly (the most significant organ of the new, bourgeois democratic order), and moreover was locked in an iron cabinet as if it could break out and cause trouble once again, then we have a perfectly clear demonstration of the new political order's determination to prevent any relapse into capricious absolutism.

It is not always the case that those material objects that safeguard the presence of the past in the present have such an intentional interpretive function. Thus Dettelbacher, the author of *Würzburg: Die Jahre nach 1945*, reveals architectural stylistic breaks in the inner city's renovated streets and alleys.[14] His depictions allow an observer educated in art history to recognize that reconstruction in the 1950s was quite often forced to compromise between preserving the historical image and accommodating new economic needs. But for all that, these indirect traces of the bombing of Würzburg on March 16, 1945, are quite incompatible with the book's fundamental intention. By letting the restoration (which is dealt with somewhat critically) seem to be the preservation of "beauty" and the repression of a terrible past at the same time, the breaks in the style of architecture are traces of a destruction obliterated.[15]

In the *Crónica general* there are Arabic toponyms whose meaning and reference could no longer be clear to a thirteenth-century Castilian audience but which nonetheless provided a way etiologically to interject the story of the conquest of Spain by the Arabs. And those relics of Christian saints that Charlemagne's troops had already regarded with astonishment on the Peninsula could still be hunted up by twelfth-century pilgrims in the cloisters along the way to Santiago de Compostela (e.g., *Chanson de Roland*, vv. 3683ff.). Until a few years ago they were still so fascinating for Romance philologists doing research on epics that some colleagues imagined the dominant motive for the genesis of the *Chanson de Roland* was to be the production of a "tourist ad" for these cloisters.

The Second Disposition Specific to Historiography

A given thematized past, at least in its basic concepts, is present in the actualized historical knowledge of the recipients; in any narrative presentation of events this specific store of knowledge embraces at the very least those concepts that correspond to the basic semantic opposition in its deep structure.

This disposition can be inferred from the observation that a series of nouns with definite articles customarily emerges from the introductions to historiographical texts. Thus Michelet begins his history of the Revolution with the theses: "Je définis la Révolution, l'avènement de la Loi, la résurrection du Droit, la réaction de la Justice" (p. i). The first sentences of the chapter on the storming of the Bastille (p. 56) evidently assume that the readers have at their disposal "a concept" of Versailles and Paris at the end of the ancien régime, but, above all, that they can readily contrast them with "concepts" of Versailles and Paris on July 14, 1789. Similarly, the introductory statement of the book on Würzburg not only counts on an image of a *sonntägliche Stadt* (p. 5), a calm Sunday city (before its destruction), but also evokes the readers' knowledge of the night bombing on March 16, 1945, with a temporal adverb—"hatte die Schärfe des Krieges *noch* nicht erlebt." While the reference to the defeat of King Rodrigo ("la batalla . . . uençuda") at the beginning of chapter 560 from the Old Spanish *Crónica* has an intratextual referent in chapter 557, the definite article introducing "the Infant Pelayo" and the determination of his later coronation as a future horizon for subsequent narration can only be explained by assuming that the audience possesses extratextual knowledge about that protagonist's historical role. On the basis of the conceptually quite simple distinction between the use of the definite and indefinite articles, we can already perceive in the first lays of the *Chanson de Roland* exactly what previous historical knowledge the scribe of the Oxford version expected from his public and which elements of his own knowledge he presented in order to expand his audience's precognition. He simply had to remind them of the (ostensibly) successful seven-year Spanish campaign of Charlemagne and of his adversary, King Marsilie, but also of the Franconian emperor's faithful vassals (vv. 104ff.); whereas Blancandrins, Marsilie's adviser, was obviously not sufficiently well known: "Blancandrins fut des plus savies paiens, / De vasselage fut asez chevaler / Prozdon i out pur sun seignur aider / E dist al rei . . . "

The Third Disposition Specific to Historiography

The thematized past is regarded by the recipients as part of "their own" prehistory.

Certainly this third disposition can also be postulated without recourse to texts as soon as we take into account the metonymic material presence of the thematized past in the audience's world and the conceptual knowledge they relate to the thematized past. This reception of a past as the audience's own prehistory is especially striking in medieval texts. Charlemagne, whose realm extended far beyond the settlements of a population speaking protoforms of modern French, for the scribe of the Oxford version of the *Chanson de Roland* and for his public, was "our emperor." From the most variegated skeins of tradition allegedly narrating the past of the occupants of the Iberian Peninsula, long before the beginning of the Reconquista and those integrative movements that generated modern Spain, the Castilian king commissioned the compilation of every available source into the "Spanish chronicle." "This happened," as the prologue says, "so that the origins of the Spaniards would become familiar and so that one would have cognizance of those tribes which had inflicted suffering on Spain" (p. 4).

With respect to the third disposition, it is particularly important that the same representation of the same past can be regarded by different public groups as "their own prehistory." Michelet closes off his reference to the key to the Bastille in the National Assembly's archives with the following sentence: "Ah! puissent, dans l'armoire de fer, venir s'enfermer les clefs de toutes les Bastilles du monde!" Here it becomes clear that, in the first half of the nineteenth century, as is still true today, the French Revolution was already construed as an event both in French national history and in the history of mankind. From the perspective of historiography, it is evident that the general meaning of a text is not unaffected by the differences among the audiences to which it is addressed. Whereas Michelet presents the French with "their Revolution" as a past accomplishment that must be preserved and that places an obligation on the present and the future, for humankind as a whole it can mean the anticipation of a happier future—with the reference to its metonymic material presence in the present shifting to the optative mood.

For "humankind as public," it is self-evident that *any* thematized action and behavior from the past will turn into its "own prehistory," whoever were the subjects of the action and wherever it took place. This seemingly trite statement contains the possibility of introspectively verifying the third disposition. For if we do not perceive the referent of a text as segment of our prehistory as "human beings," then the past aspect of the thematized action is insignificant in comparison with its potentially exotic character. In other words, we can read the same text as historiographical narration or as description, or also—one thinks of Lévi-Strauss—as a contribution to anthropology, or, like eighteenth-century French literature, as a potentially utopian trip into the past.

With these considerations, we have a head start on the question whether biography could be a subgenre of historiography. The eighteenth-century description of the life of the painter Schmitt, who died in 1648, is read by a genealogical researcher named Schmitt as a part of his own family history, so that, as his own prehistory, it becomes a historiographical text; such a reception is possible for a reader of the same text in 1992 named Müller, only if he is also a painter or if, as a German citizen, he is presented with Mr. Schmitt's (violent) death in 1648 as the metonymic realization of a "fateful year in German history."

The Fourth Disposition Specific to Historiography

The historical knowledge actualized by the readers is transposed back into the conditions under which it was first acquired.

We return for the last time to that chapter from Michelet's history of the Revolution, "Prise de la Bastille, 14 juillet 1789," a title connoting a concept that belongs to the audience's stock of historical knowledge. By "concept" we want to stress the fact that the process referred to in that chapter is monothetically rather than polythetically understood by historical knowledge.[16] Naturally an awareness of the processual character of its referential object belongs to this cognitive element ("concept"), but the processual character of a series of events is not realized in the present by the concept "process." Yet it is exactly its realization to which the text of the chapter on the storming of the Bastille leads step by step. We have already pointed out that its very first sentences draw on the readers' knowledge of the concepts "Versailles on the eve of the Revolution" and "Paris on the eve of the Revolution." If we look at these statements more carefully, we notice that with them the transference of the concept "storming of the Bastille" into a realized process in the present has already begun. For Paris and Versailles are both concepts with a double meaning. On the one hand there is the experience of a contemporary on July 13, 1789: "Versailles, avec un gouvernement organisé, un roi, des ministres, un général, une armée . . . / Paris, bouleversé, délaissé de tout autorité légale, dans un désordre apparent." On the other hand, both the knowledge of the event and the historical significance of July 14, 1789, must be assumed, for only taken together can they actually be called "Versailles/Paris on the eve of the revolution": ". . . n'était qu'hésitation, doute, incertitude, dans la plus compléte anarchie morale" / ". . . atteignit, le 14 juillet, ce qui moralement est l'ordre le plus profond, l'unanimité des esprits." In the second sentence of the chapter on the Bastille, the opposition between the two considerations about Paris has already turned into narrative—that is, it is presented as an event—by the *passé simple* ("atteignit"). Thus it becomes clear that the concepts of appearance ("gouvernement organisé" / "désordre apparent") and truth ("anarchie morale" / "unanimité des esprits") are going to function as basic semantic terms in the historiographical narrative of the storming of the Bastille; the concept of the historical process, presupposed by Michelet as part of his audience's knowledge, is dissolved in a conceptual opposition that constitutes narrative.

The three following sentences, all connected with Paris, mark a second step toward transforming the audience's knowledge into the structure of an experience. Anticipations of the immediate future from the evening of July 13, 1789 ("empty protention")—"ne songeait qu' à se défendre" / "il y avait encore des doutes" / "le soir était plein de troubles"—are contrasted with the readers' knowledge about the event of July 14, 1789. This kind of juxtaposition of the protagonists' empty protention of a thematized past with a fulfilled protention known to posterity is characteristic of historiographical discourse, and with this hypothesis we anticipate some of the issues addressed in the next section. Even without having given a precise semantic rendering of "experience" in the phenomenological sense, we can state that an aspect of real experience—hence the experience of the past—is realized precisely by this play with protentions.

The meaning of the formulation, "realization of past experience," is made clear by the further deployment of the author's strategy.[17] After a new contrast between empty and fulfilled protentions (the Bastille was considered invincible / it was taken) and the designation of the subject of the action ("Le peuple, tout le monde," p. 58), which is so crucial for Michelet's political intentions, there is a narrowing of the temporal distance between those points in time (July 13/July 14) in which the basic oppositional concepts had previously been narratively located. In other words, the search for an explanation of the event puts the night between the two days into the thematic center. "Que se passa-t-il dans cette courte nuit, où personne ne dormit, pour qu'au matin tout dissentiment, toute incertitude disparaissant avec l'ombre, ils eussent les mêmes pensées?" To answer this question Michelet simulates the experience of the historical protagonists in a manner that corresponds exactly to the phenomenological concept of experience: the night between the thirteenth and fourteenth of July 1789 is realized as the moment when experiences acquired and accumulated in the past were transformed into future anticipations for the first time and which in turn could motivate collective action for political change:

> L'histoire revînt cette nuit-là, une longue histoire de souffrances, dans l'instinct vengeur du peuple. L'âme des pères, qui, tant de siècles, souffrirent, moururent en silence, revînt dans les fils et parla. Hommes forts, hommes patients, jusque-là si pacifiques, qui deviez frapper en ce jour le grand coup de la Providence, la vue de vos familles, sans ressources autres que vous, n'amollit pas votre coeur. Loin de là, regardant une fois encore vos enfants endormis, ces enfants dont ce jour allait faire la destineé, votre pensée grandie embrassa les libres générations qui sortiraient de leurs berceaux, et sentit dans cette journée tout le combat de l'avenir! . . . L'avenir, le passé faisaient tous deux même réponse: tous deux ils dirent: Va!

This sort of realization of sequences of experience from the past narrows the distance between the later historian (and heir to the French Revolution) and the historical protagonists, of course without raising any suspicion that he wants to abolish it. The pathos of the passage is due to the vocative with which the historian addresses the heroes of July 14, 1789, but in this speech act his own present is strongly articulated. Henceforth a new interpretation of the so-called historical present will be provided by the assumption that its use signals the effort of historiographers to reduce this distance as much as possible and that maybe it can even be abolished entirely for those recipients who are inclined to overidentify. At any rate, for Michelet there is other evidence that, whenever the "historical present" appears, a final stage has been reached in the actualization of the audience's knowledge of past experience. Taking into consideration the passage that presents the penetration of the first "revolutionaries" into the Bastille (pp. 61 ff.), we can make out three phenomena in the text's constitution concomitant with the "historical present." First of all, the paratactic cadencing of short sentences in this kind of situation has often been observed, and it has sometimes been interpreted as an early attempt to distinguish between "the narrated time" and "the narrative's time" (*erzählter Zeit* and *Erzählzeit*). Here it seems more relevant to point out that parataxis is always a renunciation of hypotactical connections, and that to renounce hypotaxis also means renouncing interpretations of the represented objects of experience, which becomes possible only after they have been fulfilled. In the passage we are concerned with here, Michelet shifts back and forth between paragraphs manifesting direct experience ("historical present") and interpretive paragraphs ("imperfect"). Second, there are a striking number of sentences in "direct address." Since they were undoubtedly invented by Michelet, they cannot be tied to a function whose intention is the enhancement of their documentatary value; rather they put the audience in the situation of someone who is experiencing the evoked scene "as if it were in the present" and who must interpret the experience himself, like trying to make sense out of the utterances of people within earshot. Third, along with the "historical present" and the "direct speech dialogues," there are deictic forms, whose use "actually" presupposes that the objects referred to lie within the speaker's and listener's visual field: "Et le voilà en face de l'énorme grille qui fermait la troisième cour."

The other three texts will only supplement the comparatively extensive analysis of the procedural steps by which the audience's historical precognition is transported into the realization of past experience in Michelet's Bastille chapter. They will be able to verify that what we are in fact concerned with is the author's acquiesence in the audience's dispositions. Already in the first two pages of *Würzburg: Die Jahre nach 1945* (the only place where it actually presents the events) we come across all of the textual strategies uncovered in Michelet: the evocation of a concept whose referential object is a process out of the audience's precognition (the year 1945 in the title); its dissolution through the opposition of two partial concepts constituting narrative ("die sonntägliche Stadt" / "die zerstörte Stadt"), which contrasts the empty protention of contemporaries ("who would want to destroy the city now that the war is almost over?") with the fulfilled protention of posterity ("had not yet experienced the war's trenchancy" / "That this harmless city would be destroyed . . . "); and the reduction of the distance between the points in time to which the basic semantic concepts are keyed ("the evening of March 16 was vernal and mild"). There is an unbroken transition between two procedural steps here: the fulfilled protention (namely, the destruction of the city), to which "the evening of March 16" is contrasted, is already articulated by the "historical present." The "historical present" as a maximum level in realizing past direct experiences is kept up beyond the description of the bombing; references to the topography of Würzburg from the bird's-eye perspective of the flight formation ("Marsberg, Dallenberg, Steinberg, Kantstrasse, Greinberg") are functionally equivalent to Michelet's "voilà."

All of these procedures can also be shown in medieval texts, with the exception of the "historical present" in the *Crónica general*, where it could be asked whether the subgenre "chronicle" is not characterized by the absence of certain specific communicative conditions. It is left to the reader's skepticism to check out this assertion textually; for it seems more worthwhile at the moment, before attempting a synthesis of our particular observations, to make a brief digression here and call attention to what is evidently a specific moment in the experiential structure characteristic of medieval societies. "The future," as Niklas Luhmann once maintained, previously "came towards man," while today it "is that open horizon . . . towards which he himself is moving, choosing his direction." Correspondingly, the present, which was previously constituted as duration, has been "reinterpreted as a minimal moment . . . which is itself moving towards the future along a constant scale of dated points in time."[18] If we read the *Chanson de Roland* as a historiographical text, then it is not surprising at first that, on the horizon of those lays thematically focused on the death of the hero, the audience's ("historical") knowledge about his death is evoked. It is not a trivial confirmation of Luhmann's thesis to point out that, in the certain expectation of death (hence with fulfilled protention), Roland kills another heathen, destroys his weapons, remembers "sweet France," but above all experiences "from lay to lay," so to speak, how death is moving toward him: "there Roland senses death's nearness / there Roland senses that death clasped him with firm hand / there Roland senses death grasping him entirely / there Roland senses that he has no more time / dead is Roland" (vv. 2258ff.). It could be asked whether, parallel to a fulfilled future moving itself toward a present constituted by duration, a past that becomes increasingly distant also belongs to the premodern structure of experience. At any rate, that the coordination of past and present in the Middle Ages was different from today's forms of experience is also evident in the fact that in the *Chanson de Roland*, deixis is regularly accompanied by forms of the subjunctive rather than by the "historical present": "ki puis veïst Rollant et Oliver / De lur espeis e ferir et capler!" (vv. 1680f.) / "la veïsez la terre si junchie" (v. 3388).

The Recurrent Speech Act of Historiographical Fascination

In the preceding two sections we were able to constitute anticipations and dispositions but not intentions or needs as elements of historiography's metahistorical, recurrent speech act. This indirectly confirms our suspicion that a pragmatic attempt to develop a metahistorical concept for a genre cannot count on a constant historiographical function, at least if "functions" are taken to mean effects and intentions the communicating subjects can grasp reflexively. Thus, if Michelet's history of the revolution and perhaps the *Crónica general* would seem to support Rüsen's hypothesis that historiographical narration is always a response to "a need for orientation in the present," the post-1945 history of Würzburg and the *Chanson de Roland* require an act of interpretive violence in order to appear as a means of realizing an orienting function. In the same way, the metahistorically intended contention of Maurice Halbwachs — namely, that historical knowledge is written down only when it threatens to fall into oblivion — is not only refuted by the inventories in which selections culled from the epics have been collecting ever since the twelfth century, precisely those articulations of the "mémoire collective" whose special status Halbwachs wanted to emphasize through his hypothesis of the fixation of texts in writing.[19] But also many texts from the "classical" historiography of the nineteenth century, such as Michelet's *Histoire de la Révolution française,* started with available concepts of the "mémoire collective" in order to transpose them back into the framework of experiential structures. Finally, our analyses also give us reason to doubt whether there is a general function valid for any historiographical discourse drawn from that configuration of complex sense structures, from that disordered tangle of heterogeneous individual memories and traditions Hayden White has called the "historical field."[20] Rather it seems indispensable for the historian to feed back into the sense structures already available in the audience's cognition in order to decompose them by the simulation of direct experience. Only when historical knowledge has been "liquefied" in this manner can the historian attempt to influence reader's ex post facto re-creation of an experiential process from the past so that, in the end, newly configured structures of historical knowledge come into existence. But to achieve this restructuration of historical precognition is certainly not, as is shown by examples from remote periods above all, the intention of every historiographer, nor is it the effect of every reception of their texts.

Turning back to our descriptive approaches of the third and fourth dispositions, we can claim for the time being that whereas the reconfiguration of individual elements of the historical field into complex sense structures is normally concerned with a possible function of historiographical texts, only the decomposition of historical precognition has been a recurrent functional purpose in the texts we have been analyzing. This proposal has by no means always been understood by authors and their readers, and yet its realization is a prerequisite for the redemption of all of the complex functions that have been programmatically proclaimed for historiography and for which the orientation of future action is one example. Our claim gives us the opportunity to take up a recommendation by Rüsen and to make it more precise. According to him, historiographical texts mediate not historical knowledge but historical consciousness, which in turn is defined as an "articulation of temporal experience."[21] In fact, a glance at the everyday use of historical knowledge, which (also) monothetically comprehends past processes, makes it clear that merely possessing and using it are not enough to qualify someone as "historically educated." For the settings of historical knowl-edge are so strongly deindividualized and schematic that, just like nonhistorical elements of knowedge, they can serve as tools for the interpretation of everyday perception and experience. The conceptual histories of abstract predicates drawn from the names of historical actors ("Bonapartism," "Caesarism," "Josephinism") prove our proposition every bit as much as the frequent use of the word "revolu-tion" to legitimize morally illegitimate reinvestments of positions of power (the 1964 coup of the Brazilian army was officially called a "revolução").

What the "articulation of temporal experience" as the structural mediation of historical consciousness actually means is the recapitulation of an experiential process in time that allows the recipient to transpose him- or herself back into a situation where those consequences of action that constitute the identity of past processes were still empty protentions. The "historical consciousness" mediated by historical writing is also the awareness that we "could have expected com-pletely different results" and, for many, that it "could have turned out differently." If we take into account that the prerequisite for such a consciousness is a poly-thetic realization of the past, then that "love of [obsession with?] historical detail" in which many professional historians would like to ground their professional ethos seems to unjustifiably hypostatize phenomenal strata as the purpose of historiography. Nevertheless, the writing of history must have recourse to details —if only because the semantic substance of the audience's decomposed mono-thetic precognition of the past is usually insufficient to fill in the individual steps of the past's polythetic rearticulation. In defense of the great East German historian of the French Revolution, Walter Markov, whose "love of detail" appar-ently raised suspicions that he was negligent in his Marxist historiographical duty to formulate concepts, his student, Manfred Kossok, presented precisely the same hypothesis. The image of the historian "bent over his books, buried in documents, making an existential principle out of acribia, is of course a prejudice"; nonethe-less it is "incontestable that detailed knowledge is an irrevocable prerequisite for a historian if he is going to be able to make substantiated judgments, for he is obliged to feed the things which we experience as completed back into the process of their becoming."[22] By stressing the re-creation of past experience and its empty protentions as historiographical performance, it should be obvious that we are not trying to avoid the basic precondition of historiography in the sense of our first anticipation—namely, that this realization of empty protentions is carried out from a lofty citadel, which has at its disposal the knowledge of their fulfillment and which can continually shift this knowledge into a new light within the flow of time.

Up to now we have used the terms central to our argument without explicit and mutual delimitation—"time," "experience" (*Erleben*), "practical experience" (*Erfahrung*), and "knowledge." When Husserl defined time as "a form of ex-perience," he was assuming that experience refers to the successive thematic applications of symbolizing consciousness.[23] These have time as their form (or constitute time), because as given presents they are accompanied by afterimages of what has previously been experienced (retention) and by an anticipation of future experience (protention). Just how wide we should set the boundaries of retention and protention largely depends on the respective field of application for a given phenomenological concept of experience; hence it might be practical for a psychologist to identify "retention" with short-term memory, whereas a historian will match the concept of retention with the experiences a subject actualizes out of his or her stock of knowledge. The elements of experience (first concept of experience, identical with "elements of individual and social knowledge") that can be accessed by retention are instrumentalized for the interpretation of the present contents of consciousness. The results of this interpretation of preexperiential bases are actual experiences (second concept of experience), which either exhaust themselves in the verification of precognition or, when it is a question of "the construction of problems,"[24] can lead to new experiences (i.e., new—for the time being—elements of subjective knowledge). Anticipations about the near future (protentions) are formulated on the basis of the verification, modification, or completion of precognition. When retention and protention are taken into consideration, the temporal structure of practical experience can be defined as an experiential process (the third concept of experience). Only where this third concept is meant does it make any sense to talk about historiography as a mode for mediating (or better, "realizing") historical experience[25] and to distinguish it from texts that transport knowledge of the past without feeding it back into structures of experience (or processes of practical experience). For instance, historical compendia would not be covered by this concept of historiography.

If we have not succeeded in establishing a catchall genre for "historiography," yet have located a series of constant elements (anticipations and dispositions) for the historiographical speech act, then it would seem worthwhile trying to derive a prereflexive "anthropological affinity" that would be acceptable as the basis of a recurrent historiographical speech act from the interaction between these elements. To do this, it is now necessary to return to the first and the third dispositions. Those objects and phenomena to which historiography refers and that metonymically realize the past world in the audience's present world (cf. the first disposition) are coincident on the one side with the audience's lifetime, yet on the other they evoke a temporal dimension stretching beyond this lifetime, which Schütz and Luckman call "world time."[26] The limitation of every individual's lifetime in the face of world time belongs to the basic structures of the life world and can be described in two ways: a human being is irrevocably born into a "situation" that comprises only a segment of world time; and/or, he or she experiences world time as "irreversible." With the concept of irreversibility, this second description stresses above all the impossibility of transgressing lifetime in the direction of the past and, considering the indefinite location of death as a second future-directed boundary of lifetime, it corresponds to the dominant mode of our everyday experience of lifetime's finitude. The historiographical reference to phenomena, whose origin predates the recipients' life-time by far but which is also simultaneously coincident with it, functions as a stimulus at least to take "these phenomena backward" in the imagination and step over the boundaries of the lifetime.

Now all this talk about the "irreversible character of world time" could lead to misunderstandings, for this experiential premise surely does not have a universal function. Hence we have to specify that "world time" is the time of the social world that can only be "experienced as historical on the basis of the subjective experience of the sequence of generations."[27] Seen in this way, it is easy to understand why a genre that invites its audience to transgress lifetime imaginatively in the direction of world time, has to thematize human action but not necessarily transformations in nature (cf. the first anticipation). However, transgressing the boundaries of the lifetime brings us not to arbitrary temporal sequences but simply to that succession from which the experience of the world's irreversibility is derived: to the level of the (familial, national, human) prehistory of the recipients. In this way we have also developed a functional designation for the third historiographic disposition.

Which conditions must we meet now in order to talk in the full sense about the transgression of lifetime toward its own prehistory (*Vorwelt*)? First, we would have to be able to experience and believe in the future of the past as empty protention so that it would be possible for us to influence it—a past that has actually become unalterable because of our own time's limitations on the life world. Second, we would have to be able to experience in a meaningful way material concretions located on the axis of world time before our lifetime. And third, through the process of formulating experience, we would have to be able to feed back into that stock of knowledge that underlies humankind's everyday interpretations of the past. The reference to those objects out of the past that are simultaneous with our own lifetime simulates the satisfaction of the second of these three conditions. The first condition refers to the transposition of monothetic historical knowledge into polythetic experiential structures. Hence the thesis becomes plausible that the fascination of historiography is grounded in a prereflexive anthropological need to transcend the limits of our own lifetime.

A genre whose place in life we would spontaneously locate far away from historiographical genres (namely, the discourse that accompanies magical practices) is characterized by an interrelation between function and textual procedure, which would probably corroborate our thesis if we made a more exact analysis, but here we must limit ourselves to a few examples. With respect to the discourse of magic—for example, the well-known spells in Old High German—there is no need to establish in detail the proposition that it also functioned to transgress the limits of a given lifetime toward world time. To be sure, here it is a matter of attracting a supernatural power, which had manifested itself in the past, into the present. But even if the transgressional direction is diametrically opposed to historiography's, both discourses must simulate the possibility of performing past experience for the audience. This is exactly why magical praxis, like historiography, requires the presence of a material object that was already manifest in the situation when the supernatural force was conjured up. It could be assumed that this object functions not only as a medium, as is regularly emphasized, but also as a sign of the "path" on the axis of world time that the past scene had to traverse on its way toward realization in the *hic et nunc*. Then the material presence of such objects in magic would be, at least in part, functionally equivalent to the typical historiographical reference to phenomena from the world of those recipients who had already existed at the same time as a past that is not yet realized. But if the realization of past experience is undoubtedly a presupposition for the success of magic, then the concomitance between magical praxis and narrative texts can be pointed out as an affirmation of our thesis about the basic anthropological need to which historiography responds. It is a relatively recent insight that, along with the experience of the past through empty protentions and the meaningful perception of its materiality, a third condition (namely, the disposition over a stock of experiences specific to each lifetime) still has to be met if there is ever going to be any possibility of transgressing it in the direction of the prehistoric world (*Vorwelt*). This discovery of the historicity of everyday worlds (or social stocks of knowledge), to use an illustration from literary criticism, took place somewhere between those classical French dramas in which the protagonists of antiquity present themselves as *honnêtes hommes* and the origination of the historical novel. Precisely because the main lines of action constituting the plot of the historical novel have no past reference, it can be "historical" only by realizing the specificity and the "space"—writing itself in the interstices—of past everyday worlds.

Therefore, at least as far as the third condition is concerned, the writing of structural history is a proposal to transgress imaginatively the boundaries of a given lifetime toward the past. But we doubt whether it will also meet both of the other conditions. Somewhat unexpectedly this doubt has been resolved by the text that we have chosen as a paradigm of modern structural history, Le Roy Ladurie's *Montaillou, village occitan de 1294–1324*. In numerous footnotes the author records traces of the elements of knowledge from past societies ("remnants" of past everyday worlds) that are still alive in his and his audience's present: "Dans ce qui reste du folklore de Montaillou (enquête orale 1974), les souvenirs relatifs au rôle magique du curé jouent un rôle important."[28] In the same way, he describes institutionalized future anticipations ("empty protentions") of the past, for instance, the certainty that the arrival of the Antichrist was at hand.[29] We see that structural history has not withdrawn from the need to transgress respective lifetimes and to realize past experience. Rather, by representing the social stocks of knowledge from the past and by adding specific retentions ("spaces of practical experience"), structural history completes the restitution of the empty protentions of past presents performed by other historiographical texts. This amounts to the fact that historical consciousness, which in any case now acquires another dimension, is mediated by structural history just as much as by the representation of events. With respect to the performance of structural history, the static-descriptive character stereotypically ascribed to it is contingent. For the fact that the texts of structural history usually quit once they have reconstructed one experiential framework constituting one everyday world in the past (i.e., the relationship between a social experiential space and its corresponding anticipatory horizon) is due to the complexity of the task and does not mean that it is fundamentally impossible to represent the succession (evolution) of everyday worlds. Only when historical time itself—that is, the question, How is the experience of the past worked out in a concrete situation; how are expectations, hopes, or prognoses of the future formulated?[30]—becomes one of our themes, will we be doing structural history in the full sense.

What is the consequence of our reflections on "a normative pragmatic" for the discipline of historiography? Roughly, the thesis that history cannot fulfill any social task (however well intended, whether from a conservative or an "emancipatory" point of view) as long as its texts do not meet, as the medium of their social effect, our anthropological need to transgress the boundaries of present times. This need is what constitutes the power of historiographical fascination and opens up space for functions that go far beyond its mere gratification. More concretely, a serious sign of just how insufficient our academic historical discourse often is can be found in the fact that, of all texts, it seems to have been the tear-jerking TV series *Holocaust* that first transmitted to a whole generation of Germans a historical consciousness of its own recent past. The countless academic definitions of "fascism" and statistical tables of the monstrous efficiency of the concentration camps only produced a mania untroubled by historical consciousness that discovers "fascistic" phenomena everywhere in the political present, and even worse, makes the pleasingly exonerating offer to compare the performative capacities of Hitler's, Stalin's, and Reagan's annihilation machines. Undoubtedly, disconcertedness about the years 1933 to 1945 has seldom been actively promoted by the discourse of academic history, and, for my part, it is regrettable that the arousal of concern was left to *Holocaust*, because the proposal of the series to recomplete a past experiential process was organized so that in the final reckoning all too much legitimation of the "Western world" remained behind as the new monothetic experience. But Reinhart Koselleck's blow-for-blow attempt to "rerhetoricize" the historical discourse about the recent German past has probably come too late to stimulate a pertinent historiography that could compete narratively with *Holocaust* and would be ethically and normatively superior to it.[31] At any rate, the basic structural element in Koselleck's study provides a useful approach in the contrast of the future expectations ("empty protentions") of concentration camp prisoners reconstructed from dream narratives and precisely those statistics on the extermination enterprise of the Third Reich that are part of our historical knowledge ("fulfilled protentions").

In the event that our pragmatic efforts to develop a supercategory for the genre of "historiography" have yielded some plausible findings, it can be asked whether the underlying anthropological argumentation can also be applied to other histories of text and genre. We justified the hypothesis of a prereflexive anthropological need for historical writing by correlating it with a structural element of the life world ("the lifetime's limits"). This meant understanding the term "life world" as a metahistorical space through whose various investments at any given time historically particular everyday worlds are generated. As we know, the life world is regarded anthropologically as the foundation of the basic function of any everyday world, which compensates for humankind's characteristic lack of instinctual orientation. It is precisely because the structures of the life world and everyday worlds are behavioral orientations mediated by socialization and are not innate that we are able to count on a–particularly human[32]–need to transgress them; and precisely because the situational limitedness of the lifetime and the irreversibility of world time do not make up the only constituted limit for the life world, it is necessary to ask whether other metahistorical recurrent speech acts are not connected to other transgressional needs. At this point we must break off our speculations, but would still like to remind the reader that the life world's limits, for example, are also keyed to the spatial reach of our actions, to our ability to reconstitute the flow of consciousness of other human beings, and to the extension and differentiation of our knowledge.

Epilogue: Historization and Anthropology

Because of the current epistemological trend in Germany, the search for "anthropological constants" is enjoying a boom, and so we hope the same for the specific question that we have approached through certain preliminary considerations. While just a few years ago in academic discussions, the mere mention of "anthropological constants" would have been promptly and summarily regarded as *lapsus linguae*, we are now energetically organizing symposia on them. Even Marxist philosophers no longer regard it as "undialectical" (whatever that might mean) to illuminate a teleologically conceived historical process through recurrences. (As a strategy to cover any potential retreat, they have reserved for themselves the option of redefining "anthropological constants" as "*longue-durée* structures" whose parameters are set so "long" that there is no possibility of returning to any sources whatsoever at a time before their origination.) At the same time in Germany, the search for linguistic universals has once again become acceptable everywhere, and at the world congress of philosophy in 1979 the philosophers anticipated getting information from neurologists, from specialists in the anatomy and physiology of the human brain about the structures that their own thought probably would have shared with the objectivizations of consciousness in the first homines sapientes.

Behind the sequence of a historicizing and anthropologizing tendency that is our shared experience, we could make guesses about a general rhythm of scientific history: phases of historization are necessarily followed by systematizing and abstracting phases, which in turn lead to historical specification a perceptual multiplicity. Seen in this way, the most recent tendency toward anthropology does not require any legitimation. In any case, the foundation of the propensity toward historicization that until quite recently was a dominant disposition has provided a powerful provocation for its justification. As an investigative style, anthropology became discredited to the extent that it was recognized that eighteenth century anthropology had been retained in the cheap ideological outfitting of numerous political and social systems up to our own time and often served to embellish particular interests. Despite this culpability, anthropology is of course not bound in principle to the legitimizing function of the status quo. This is exactly what can also verify the "bourgeois anthropology" of the eighteenth century, if we are willing to explain it through its function of questioning and formulating norms before the "bourgeois revolutions" of the eighteenth and nineteenth centuries. Even today an anthropological reflection with new problems and premises could be attached to similar purposes.

Part III
Failures of Modernity

Chapter 5
A History of the Concept "Modern"

The Present State of Research

There are probably few concepts whose history has been so frequently thematized in the last decades as those marked by the predicates "modern," "modernity," and "die Moderne." Hans Robert Jauss, Fritz Martini, and Jost Schneider have submitted detailed studies that are mainly connected to the field of aesthetic experience and that trace the word's shifts in meaning from the early Middle Ages to the present. Marie Dominique Chenu, Ernst Robert Curtius, Walter Freund, Johannes Spörl, and finally Elizabeth Gössman have described the numerous possibilities for using the topos *antiqui/moderni* in the Middle Ages. Recently, Jochen Schlobach has written a Habilitation that provides us with an apparently exhaustive documentation of the theories about periods and concepts of time between the Renaissance and the early Enlightenment, while Siegrun Bielfeldt's doctoral thesis has enriched the spectrum by considering the theme of modernity from the standpoint of Slavic studies.[1] Thus it was difficult during the preparation of this essay to turn up new evidence — except for the twentieth century, with which Jauss and Martini are but marginally concerned and even then only within the fields of "aesthetics" and "philosophy," both of which, of course, are particularly productive for the history of the concept "modern" because of their semantics. The only way for this essay to do something more than simply summarize already available information would be to disclose material from fields of experience that up until now have barely been associated with the concept of the "modern,"[2] but second and above all to elaborate evidence both new and familiar from the standpoint of particular theoretical premises and a consequently applied method. The following study should therefore also be read as a contribution to the still open-ended discussion about the theory and method of conceptual history[3] – or more precisely, as the application of an approach that has been developed in more detail elsewhere to historical material.[4]

Preliminary Remarks on Theory and Method

Without discussing any of the many individual problems they entail, I would like to introduce here three indispensable assumptions for understanding the structure of this essay and justifying the individual interpretations.

First, the object of conceptual history, when studied within the framework of social history (which is not its only possible epistemological context), is shaped by the "linguistic norm" (that is, by language as a social institution).[5] We use the term here in the sense introduced by Eugenio Coseriu, according to which the aspect of the norm is contrasted on the one hand with the aspect of the system, where language is an "abstract framework of functional oppositions," and on the other hand with the aspect of "speech," which is concerned with "actual language performance."[6] With respect to conceptual history as a method of social history, Coseriu's theory has chiefly two important consequences. Since the language system does not simply comprehend historically concrete language events but, given the phonology, syntax, and semantics of a particular language type, every possible (and in part unrealized) variant as well, the norm can be understood as the result of a collective selection from the possibilities of the language system, a selection depending on the speaker's mutual systems of relevance, shared typifications, and rules of language action.[7] Since individual speakers and authors, in opposition to a given norm, frequently realize innovative features of the language system that do not become social usage because of their failure to match the social dissemination of cognitive elements, inferred meanings can be recognized as socially and historically relevant (that is, as something more than simply evidence for genius or a communication block) only when they have converged with other meanings from the same period and the same social milieu or have proved their membership in the language norm by having been accepted into a lexicon.

Second, the notion of the language norm as a social institution leads to the further assumption that individual words in various fields of experience (in Wittgenstein's sense of *Sprachspiel* or *Lebensform*)[8] are variously applied and understood – that is, assume different meanings. Whenever this context of conceptual history is ignored, there is the danger that the disparate meanings of a word in several instances will be interpreted as diachronic changes, when in reality there is simply a synchronic plurality of uses and meanings in the different fields of experience belonging to a single inclusive language norm. Thus in the following historical presentation, the sections dedicated to individual periods will be further subdivided according to the criteria for these specific fields of experience, without losing track of the semantic interference phenomena between them.

Third, fully aware of the implications of such a heuristic tool, we will now briefly outline the system implicit in the possible meanings of "modern."[9] This will provide us with the groundwork for a systematic description of changes in meaning and will correspond to the theoretical basis of our historical study according to which all of the meanings contained in a given language norm are the result of a socially conditioned selection from its potential senses.

The first possible meaning of "modern" is "present," to which the concept "previous" can be opposed. In this sense, the predicate "modern" is assigned to concepts, objects, or persons that, for any given present, represent an institutional position existing over a long period of time and filled in various ways—for instance, "the modern cut" for the institutional position of fashion that must be reoccupied every year; or *modernus pontifex* for the institutional place of the *successor Petri* that must be refilled when a pope dies.[10]

The second possibility of "modern" is "new"; its opposite is "old." In this sense, the predicate "modern" designates a present experienced as a period set off from previous eras (usually within an evaluative historical and philosophical model of periodic change) by certain qualities that comprehend them as homogeneous in all their complexity.[11] The beginning of this present can be put back as far as desired and its end remains undetermined.

The third possibility of "modern" is "transitory" as opposed to "eternal." This sense of the predicate modern is always possible when a present and its concepts can be understood by contemporaries as "the past of a future present." It assumes its full value when it designates a present that is experienced as passing so rapidly that it is no longer possible—as is the case with the second sense of "modern"—to oppose it with a qualitatively different past but only with eternity as its static pole.[12]

The Use of "Modern" in the Middle Ages

In Gelasius's *Epistolae pontificum* (494/495) we find the earliest known evidence of the adjective *modernus*. The decrees of the Council of Chalcedon (451) that were still in force at the time of the composition of the *epistolae* are set off from the still valid *antiquis regulis* as *admonitiones modernae*.[13] *Modernus* is used here in the sense of the first possible meaning as the designation of a presently valid situation in contrast to the institution it has replaced. In Cassiodorus's "Letter to Symmachus" (507/511), the word is already employed to set the limits of a period; hence in the second meaning, Cassiodorus, who called himself *antiquo-rum diligentissimus imitator*, had the ambition of reestablishing Rome's previous grandeur as a model for the contemporary Gothic empire, thereby earning for himself the title *modernorum nobilissimus institutor*.[14] Here the realization of this goal still implies the work of acting subjects, a task that is not guaranteed by a typological estimation of history, nor is it characterized within a schema implying decadence as unrealizable from the outset. Three and a half centuries later, the period designation *seculum modernum* for Charlemagne's "universal empire" and the initiation of "modern literature" with Boethius still do not suggest any firm values.

Only in the eleventh century, the age of the struggle over investiture, does *modernitas* mean — as we know from Berthold's von der Reichenau report on the Lenten synod of 1075 — that period that had strayed from the precepts of the Fathers and which therefore must be overcome. During the High Middle Ages, above all within the framework of the cultural movement called the "Renaissance of the twelfth century," this kind of negative evaluation of the present gives way to a new confidence that is grounded in a typological historical experience. The past is admired in order to surpass it in the present. In this sense, Bernhard of Chartres designated the *moderni* as dwarves standing on the shoulders of giants, which is precisely why they could see farther.[15] Walter Map, in his *De nugis curialium* (written between 1180 and 1192), was the first to quantify the present as a time span of a hundred years — that is, a period of time that could still be remembered by oral transmission. Like many authors (including those writing in the vernacular),[16] Map defended the high claims of the twelfth century against scoffers: "omnibus seculis sua displicuit modernitas."[17] In formulating his counterargument, he expresses a thought belonging to the prerequisites for using the third meaning ("transitory"), which of course was not available as yet: Map recognized that past eras had also understood themselves as *modernitates*.

After the beginning of the thirteenth century, the paradigm *antiqui/moderni* was employed in conformity with the first meaning to designate the philosophical schools that were in conflict with one another for a while and then simply withdrew. According to this usage, the adjective can sometimes function as a name: thus Aristotelianism was still considered by the Renaissance as "modern" philosophy,[18] and *via moderna* became the current designation of Ockham's nominalism in the fourteenth century. But even in the late Middle Ages, the opposition *antiqui/moderni* served broader differentiations for determining the period's self-image. Medieval theologians set themselves as *moderni* apart from the Church Fathers; with respect to the Christians, Old Testament Jews were considered *antiqui*.

The Present in the Renaissance's Cyclical View of History

Even if "modern" as an adjective for a period oriented to the antique past was apparently only seldom used during the Renaissance as a designation for the present, here we must briefly characterize the notion of history that gave the period its name and, along with other factors, provoked the self-understanding of the Enlightenment. Its rise around the middle of the fourteenth century can be historically located in a text by Petrarch, in which the evaluation of antiquity and the present fixed in medieval typological history's two-phase schema are reversed. In 1341 in his projected work, *De viris illustribus*, Petrarch did not consider it worth his effort to occupy himself with the time that began with the victory of Christianity over the admirable world of ancient Rome: *nolui . . . per tenebras stilum ferre.*[19]

According to this 1341 text, what Petrarch hoped to gain from the classical world (namely, its revival in his own present) was seen by Boccaccio, in a text composed only a little later (*Vita di Dante*, 1357/59), as having already been realized in Dante's poetry: *Per costui la morta poesìa meritamente si può dir suscitata.*[20] And for the end of the fifteenth century, Ficino attests (1492) that the three-stage view of history (classical flowering, Christian decay, Renaissance) that first began to take on shape in Boccaccio's time had become self-evident in the meantime: "Hoc enim seculum tanquam aureum liberales disciplinas, ferme iam extinctas reduxit in lucem."[21] In this view of a present that is separated from an ideal past by a dark age, we find the origin of the period concept called the "Middle Ages." Early Latin instances are *media tempestas* (1469), *media aetas* (1518), and *medium aevum* (1604).[22]

The relationship between the respective present and antiquity will change in the course of those centuries that will later be called the "Renaissance." If at the beginning of the period it was recommendable to imitate the ancients in full awareness of their matchless superiority, *aemulatio* later took the place of the principle *institutio* and with it came the hope of reacquiring, or even improving on, the cultural flowering of Greece and Rome. In his *La deffence et illustration de la langue françoyse*, Joachim du Bellay takes the self-esteem of the politicians and generals of his time as a basis for such self-confidence: if they can bear comparison with their antique predecessors, then why should the arts be condemned to inferiority?[23]

Admittedly, the principle of *aemulatio* is already contextualized by discussions that will ultimately lead to the Enlightenment. It was characteristic of the Renaissance to pattern itself on the classical model, which may be why "modern" was prevented from entering the self-reflection of the time as a predicate for an independent period in the second sense. It seems to have been widely used only as a name for medieval schools of philosophy. As a designation for the present and within the language norm, it does not seem to have had anything to do with the qualitative distinction between periods. Thus in Estienne's French-Latin dictionary (1539), the meaning of *moderne* is defined by the expression *poètes modernes*: modern poets are no longer considered to be Christian authors or those who came after Petrarch, but from the point of view of a purely temporal and quantitative distinction are *poetae recentis memoriae*.[24]

The Enlightenment Consciousness of the Present as the First Step in the Disassociation of Modernity from the Antique Pattern

If evidence from the French language area predominates in the following section, then it does so first of all because it contributes to our understanding of the German Enlightenment (which drew its essential stimulation from France), and also because it facilitates our recognition that the German origin of the European romantic movement was a "response" to a historical and philosophical question left over from the early French Enlightenment – a response in the sense that it was a late reaction to a new consciousness of time that was prepared by the Enlightenment but that still had not entered into the norms of thought and language.[25] It has already been suggested that this new view of history was generated by protests against the fixation of the present on classical antiquity, which had been maintained from the beginning of the Renaissance to the threshold of the eighteenth century.

The polemics aroused by the *Querelle des anciens et des modernes*, which was set off during a meeting of the Académie Française in the 1680s and which went on for over twenty years, were initiated by the *modernes* under the leadership of Charles Perrault in a public declaration of their new sense of superiority over classical antiquity. This was based on their conclusion that the preeminence of the present, if measured on the scale of the perfectibility of science that had been manifest ever since Descartes and Copernicus, would also have to be paralleled by a higher perfection in the arts. Instead of the Renaissance's cyclical view of history, which itself had replaced the typological perspective of the Middle Ages, there was once again a progressive historical model. To be sure, it was no longer motivated by the story of Christ as in the Middle Ages, but was explained in Perrault's main work, *Parallèle des anciens et des modernes* (1688/97) by making the ages of the world parallel to those of humankind.[26] After its youth, antiquity, and with the Renaissance as life's midpoint (the Middle Ages as a "dark" intermediary period is not drawn into the discussion), humankind has now come into its maturity. In Perrault's polemical sentence, "C'est nous qui sommes les Anciens,"[27] the word *anciens* first of all designates the place of the present, that is, of the *modernes* in the periodical sequence of this new historical model. At the same time it stresses its claim that the preeminence previously attributed to the "classical ancients" must now be transferred to the "modern ancients" as representatives of the present, representatives of the end and thus the closure of a historical development. During the discussion of this hypothesis, there had been since the beginning of the Enlightenment a new flourishing of "modern" in the second sense, namely, as the designation of a period accepted as the present in its own right.

The development of the argument in Perrault's book *Parallèle des anciens et des modernes*—which was begun with the purpose of demonstrating the superiority of the *modernes* in all of the arts and sciences through a broad-scale comparison—reflects the course of the discussion for the entire *Querelle*. In attempting to prove the validity of the principle of *perfectibilité* for the arts as well as devaluing antique works of art by submitting them to the criteria of the norms of French neoclassicism, the *modernes* provoked the response from the *anciens* that art can be judged only by the taste of its own time. In turn, the *modernes* were forced to admit that the qualitative distance between antique and contemporary art and the progress in the natural sciences were not necessarily parallel with respect to temporal progression. With these mutual concessions by both parties toward the end of the *Querelle*, the possibility of reevaluating any given present in the course of history was programmed. Admittedly, all of the theoretical consequences were finally exhausted only at the turn of the eighteenth to the nineteenth centuries, and even later the moral of linear progression still belonged to the temporal consciousness of broad social strata. It can be formulated through four insights. (1) If each period's accomplishments are to be judged by their own customs, according to their own tastes, then there can no longer be "dark" and "ideal" ages. Every age deserves the interest of posterity. (2) However, once the principle of individual times is accepted, then the recognition that periods are unrepeatable would forbid historically regressive imitations. (3) Against a self-righteous condemnation of antiquity on the part of the *modernes*, the *ancien* La Bruyère had already used the argument that "nous, qui sommes si modernes, serons anciens dans quelque siècles."[28] When a period succeeds in critically evaluating its own modernity as the past of the future, then the most important presupposition for the use of "modern" in the third sense, the transitoriness of the historical moment, has been satisfied. (4) From Perrault's failure to prove his own present's superiority in the arts through the parallel with the natural sciences, there was the general insight that development in different fields of experience obeyed different laws of periodicity.

If the results of the *Querelle* were not yet converted into a comprehensive new temporal consciousness in the course of the eighteenth century, they nonetheless altered the relationship of many Enlightenment authors to past periods. Already in 1714 Fénelon was demanding that historiography deal with the Middle Ages, which as *antiquité moderne* was recognized by contemporaries in the same way that the *antiquité ancienne* had been previously recognized for antiquity.[29] And around 1750, Bougainville, recapitulating the preliminary results from the study of the Middle Ages as postulated by Fénelon, could claim that the customs of those times that were once scorned as "dark" were in many respects superior.[30] Something that was also largely completed since the end of the *Querelle*, the differentiation between the various realms of experience for judging the status of the present in the course of history, brings us back to the change in the meanings of "modern." Despite his hypothesis that human talent is distributed equally through every age, Voltaire, under the entry "Anciens et Modernes" in his *Dictionnaire philosophique* (1764), grounds his conviction that modern literature is inferior to antique literature in a reference to the history of the French language as "mélange de l'horrible jargon des Celtes et d'un latin corrompu." Yet this verdict on his present language did not stop Voltaire from proudly pointing out hundreds of advancements in the natural sciences "dont les anciens ne soupçonnaient pas même la possibilité." His fundamental attitude toward differentiation behind this sort of praise and blame is formulated in the closing sentence of the text in question. "On conclut enfin qu'heureux est celui qui, dégagé de tous lés préjugés, est sensible au mérite des anciens et des modernes."[31]

This text could have even been the motto for the item "Moderne" in the *Encyclopédie*, where the beginning of the present in various fields is shifted to different times in the past: modern literature started with Boethius (a temporal boundary we have already seen in the Carolingian Renaissance), modern astronomy with Copernicus, and modern physics only with Newton (even though Descartes was already considered to be its founder in the seventeenth century). On the other hand, modern taste could not be determined by a temporal borderline—"non par opposition absolue à ce qui est ancien"—but only through qualitative contrasts with bad taste.[32]

Now, the fact that the *Encyclopédie* had recently adduced antiquity as the criterion of good, hence modern, taste makes it clear that, considering the neoclassicism dominating the eighteenth century, the possibilities opened up by the *Querelle* around the notion that one's own art could be equal to that of all previous periods had not yet been completely realized. This observation helps us to recognize that, within the context of neoclassicism, the adjective "modern" did not serve to displace a self-reliant present from the past but signified a substantive control over the institution of art (drawn from antiquity), thereby attesting to the present's irretrievable inferiority to antiquity. This is made perfectly clear by Montesquieu: "Nos modernes, en cherchant le grand, perdent le simple, ou, en cherchant le simple, perdent le grand."[33]

The rare applications of "modern" to politics and eighteenth-century political theory do not seem to have been influenced by the newly acquired potential of the *Querelle*. In Rousseau's *Contrat social*, the medieval principle of feudal dominion is regarded as "modern" and, within the framework of its decadence schema for human history, verifies the inferiority of the present to antiquity as the period immediately preceding it. "L'idée des Représéntans est moderne: elle nous vient du Gouvernement féodal, de cet inique et absurde Gouvernement dans lequel l'espèce humaine est dégradée. . . . Dans les anciennes Républiques et même dans les monarchies, jamais le Peuple n'eut de réprésentans."[34] In contrast to the classicistic theory of art of the time, Rousseau did not enhance the status of antiquity as a model paradigm. For antique societies were also based on alienation and the division of labor; they too followed the original sin of universal social history.

It may seem surprising at first glance that, during the French Revolution in the speeches to the National Assembly and in the Jacobin Club, "modern" did not become the regular designation for a present in opposition to the "ancien régime." The explanation can be found in the self-image of the revolutionary politicians.[35] They regarded days like July 14, 1789, or August 10, 1792, as clean breaks with an absolutistic past to which there was no way back; yet from the rash sequence of political upheavals they had acquired the new historical insight that their own time was only a preparatory passage to the future and hence that they alone would have to answer for the progressive import of their political actions before the bar of a future humanity. Their consciousness of an absolute duty to progress could then be molded by Saint-Just into an argument for the execution of Louis XVI. If they were to shrink from this deed, then they would expose themselves to posterity's reproach that they were not equal to the republican courage of the classical *tyrannicida*, Brutus: "On s'étonnera un jour qu'au XVIIIe siècle on ait été moins avancé que du temps de César."[36]

If in the course of the eighteenth century such revolutionary experiences were exclusively reserved for the French nation, the conceptual history of "modern" shows that outside France the canon of neoclassical taste as a seventeenth-century inheritance and the achievements of the *Querelle* were received as the primary foundation of the Enlightenment by individual horizons of cultural history. Quite in Voltaire's sense or like the *Encyclopédie*'s distinction between ancients and moderns according to different fields of experience, Jovellanos of the Spanish Enlightenment attributed *más genio* (in the arts) to antiquity and *mas sabiduría* (in science) to the moderns.[37] However, we can read out of Caldaso's *Cartas Maruecas* (1789) that the norms of French taste introduced by the new French royalty conflicted with the self-assurance of the Spanish nation. He reported that an old-fashioned Spaniard reading a satire directed at the modern would lose all of his accumulated *gravedad* for pure joy, but at the slightest praise for the achievements of the present would throw the book into the fireplace and curse the author as a *traídor a su patria*. To this knee-jerk rejection of the modern, resistance to foreign cultural influences, and sense of estrangement from the norms of the *Siglo de Oro*, Cadalso opposes the current attitude of his own generation, which he finds equally senseless: "La generación entera abonima de las generaciones que le han precedido. No lo entiendo."[38]

The German world lacked the focusing power of a national flowering like Spain's *Siglo de Oro* as a motivation for resisting neoclassicist devaluations of the art of the previous century through the norms of antiquity. In his *Versuch einer kritischen Dichtkunst*, which appeared in 1730, Gottsched at first took the side of the *modernes* in the French *Querelle*, but then defended the normative claims of the *anciens* with even greater conviction. Haller took the same position in his 1734 text, *Sermo academicus ostendens quantum antiqui eruditione et industria antecellant modernos*, but in harmony with the position of the French Enlightenment conceded his own period's superiority in natural science. The evidence for the acceptance of this dominant opinion among all of the significant German writers in the eighteenth century has been assembled by Fritz Martini.[39] It is important to note here that none of the dictionaries of the time that were representative of the language norm mentioned the arguments about temporal limitations and the judgment of the modern in comparison to the antique. In *Adelung* (1777), to be sure, *antik* is adduced along with *veraltet* as an antonym of *modern*, but the semantic explanations are attached, according to *Sperander*'s model (1728), solely to our first sense: *neu, von gegenwärtiger Zeit, auf die jetzige Zeit gerichtet.*[40]

This section of the conceptual history of "modern" will remain incomplete as long as we merely confirm that on the one hand the values of French neoclassicism and the results of the *Querelle* were taken over by the German Enlightenment but that, on the other, this reception had no effect on the normal eighteenth-century meaning of "modern." For in the reception of the German Enlightenment, above all in the writings of Winckelmann and Herder, the latent contradiction between neoclassicism and the *Querelle*'s insight into the inner laws and characteristic values of different historical periods is finally recognized and transformed into a question whose answer would later become the key assumption of romanticism's self-image.

Probably developed out of the excerpts he made from early French Enlightenment figures, Winckelmann had the insight that the uniqueness of art in different periods could perhaps be grounded in social history (his new principle of "the history of styles"), yet at the same time and with a certain amount of contradiction he was thoroughly convinced that the imitation of antiquity was "the only way we could achieve greatness, and perhaps even become inimitable."[41] Herder rejected classicistic copying and the imitation of antique art, recommending instead the imaginative return to their time as a way of "constituting genius" and thus rearranging the relationship of historical study and aesthetic praxis for his time.[42] He was probably the first to raise the question about *the historical law behind this change* in the different periods, which according to qualitative assessments no longer seemed to him as being hierarchically organized.[43] He not only drew his conclusions from the recognition of their inner laws but had already adduced the problem of the structure of the sequence of such self-contained periods. It was only at this point, a good half-century after the end of the *Querelle*, that there was enough incentive to transfer its results into a comprehensive redetermination of the relationship of the present to the antique and medieval pasts.

Historicophilosophical Reflection and Its Conversion into the Romantic Determination of "Modern Time"

From the turn of the eighteenth to the nineteenth century on (and different from the period of the Enlightenment), it was Germany whose philosophy and aesthetic theory had been influencing the general discussion in other European countries. My presentation will take this historical shift into account by moving the conceptual history of the German use of "modern" into the center of this discussion. It will demonstrate how the philosophical determination of the characteristic value of "modern time" at the end of the eighteenth century became the prerequisite for a new use of "modern" as a period concept.

In a detailed investigation of two essays by Schiller and Friedrich Schlegel written at the end of 1795, Jauss has tried to answer Herder's question about the "law" behind this periodic change. I would like to summarize his results briefly here.

Both Schlegel and Schiller made an attempt to define the characteristic value of the modern with respect to antiquity. Schlegel concluded that what was *interesting (das Interessante)* was no longer antiquity's *Beauty* but *the ideal of modern poetry*. Schiller introduced the famous distinction between *naive* and *sentimentalische poetry*, or as Schlegel formulated it to characterize the two periods, between *natural* and *artificial education (natürlicher und künstlicher Bildung)*. But whereas Schlegel still devalued "the Interesting" as the principle of modern poetry because of the "lawlessness of the whole" and as an expression of "lacerated feelings" *(zerrissenen Gemüts)* about Beauty, Schiller of course granted that sentimental poetry is characterized precisely by the consciousness of having irretrievably lost the natural perfection of antique poetry, but he no longer inferred an inferiority of the modern period from his understanding of the relationship between the two times. According to his historical and philosophical model, which was supposed to answer the question still open since the *Querelle* about the relationship between independent periods, the antique poet had achieved a perfection through his natural education that cannot be recapitulated by the modern poet, who is separated from nature by an artificial education. Only through the Ideal can one strive for the lost unity. But since the Ideal is infinite, and hence unachievable, the cultivated person can never be complete in the same way as the natural person was. If it seems that because of this, modern art, which is subordinated to a principle of perfectibility, is once again subjected to antiquity, then Schiller turns the traditional values around in his assessment of the goals pursued by sentimental and naive art. "The purpose, toward which mankind strives through culture, [would be] infinitely preferable to the one that it [could] achieve through nature."[44] Wilhelm von Humboldt, whom Schiller felt was the greatest "representative of modern poetry," had explained why the goal pursued by sentimental poetry would have to be given an incomparably higher evaluation than that of naive poetry: "They [the antique peoples] were merely what they were. We still know what we are, and look beyond. Through reflection, we've made ourselves into a double person."[45]

By determining antiquity's and modernity's respective values and their transmission within a historical and philosophical model of progression, Schlegel and Schiller had created the decisive presuppositions for finally freeing contemporary consciousness from the obligatory paradigm of antiquity. In 1808, August Wilhelm Schlegel could ascertain that "the name 'romantic' [had been] invented for the particular spirit of modern art in contrast to the antique or neo-classical."[46] By designating their own time as "romantic" with a specific history stretching back to the literary genre of chivalric romances,[47] the poets of the early nineteenth century instituted the Middle Ages (which was left unmentioned in Perrault's synchronization of world-historical eras with the phases of human life) as the beginning and high point of a Christian period that was completely different from antiquity and at the end of which the romantics found themselves. The French reception of this new historical view by Madame de Staël shows first of all that "classical" as a predicate for the arts of antiquity had lost its normative connotation through the romantics' dismissal of the classical criteria of taste, and second that the distinction between "classical" and "romantic" that had grown out of the discussions about the periodization of art was also more comprehensively applied to the periods of world history:

> Je m'en sers ici [sc. du mot "classique"] dans une autre acception, en considérant la poésie classique comme celle des anciens, et la poésie romantique comme celle qui tient de quelque manière aux traditions chevaleresques. Cette division se rapporte également aux deux ères du monde: celle qui a précedeé l'établissement du christianisme, et celle qui l'a suivi.[48]

In contrast to "modern" in the sense current in the Enlightenment, the new understanding of the present marked by the predicates romantic and modern also found its way into German lexica of the early nineteenth century. If our theoretical preconsiderations on the method of conceptual history are valid, then this evidence for the inclusion of "modern" in the language norm demonstrates that the philosophical discussion about the delimiting of the past and the present, which had been carried on all through the eighteenth century, converges for the first time with the shift in the normal social experience of time. From Schiller's distinction between naive and sentimental art, *Brockhaus' Konversations-Lexikon* in 1817 takes over the world-historical division into antiquity and a Christian modern era. In its narrower determination of the latter, it seems to be interested in legitimizing some of the essential tendencies of the Restoration—*monotheism*, the *monarchist constitution*, *monogamy*—three principles that in turn were supposed to have a common denominator in the so-called Germanic character that had allegedly been dominant since the beginning of the Middle Ages.[49] In the same sense, this designation also appeared in the *Konversations-Lexikon* of Macklot (1818)[50] and in the new *Brockhaus* editions up to and beyond the turn of the period in 1830, whereas the *Teutsche Synonymik of Eberhard/Maass* (1827) and *Heinsius' Enzyklopädisches Hand-Wörterbuch* (1828) only continued to include the first meaning of "modern."[51] In England, *Rees's Cyclopaedia* continued to repeat the differentiated determinations of modern for various fields of experience that had been provided by the French Enlightenment, but, in a deviation from the *Encyclopédie*, conceded that modern architecture could also integrate features of the Gothic "whence it borrows members and ornaments, without proportion or judgment."[52]

Now admittedly, the importation of the romantic definition of modern into the German discussion about aesthetics was preceded by a renewed separation of "modern" and "romantic," which resulted in the elimination of the romantic in the past and a negative evaluation of the modern as the art of most recent present. In his lecture *Geschichte der alten und neuen Litteratur*, published in 1815, F. Schlegel criticized precisely that tendency of modern literature (for him it was already no longer romantic) that would be turned into a principle of unification fifteen years later by the Young Germany movement, which introduces the use of modern in the third sense. This tendency "erroneously sought to effect life by attaching itself completely to the present and thus narrowed reality."[53] Just a few years later in his *Asthetik*, Hegel attached a dominant literary genre, lyric, epic, and drama respectively, to the preantique, antique, and romantic eras. Like F. Schlegel, he also spoke quite negatively about the arts of his own present, which followed on the period of the romantic regarded as a completed whole. So he mentioned Shakespearean figures as being "the opposites of wretched modern characters, for example those of Kotzebue, which seem highly noble, grand, splendid, but which are actually shabby within."[54] According to Hegel, this modern period, which culminated and ended in German classicism, had its origin not in the High Middle Ages but in the "principles of the Reformation."[55]

From the distinction made by F. Schlegel and Hegel between romanticism and the (for the moment negatively assessed) "modern" present, it is an easy transition to the increasingly positive estimation of the *Zeitbewegung* (the dynamics of time) that set in after 1830. But conceptual history as a social-historical method cannot afford to restrict itself to evidence that retrospectively represents the most progressive status of the self-image of any given period from the past. As late as 1820, Goethe still considered a classical education to be the requisite provision for modern art,[56] and in 1821 Achim von Arnim declared the distinction of periods as "antique" or "modern" to be a *brick wall* obstructing any view of the whole.[57] In France in the year of the July Revolution, Hugo propagated exactly this *romantisme* as "libéralisme en littérature," as a principle of art that would be suitable for the time after having overcome the restorative "ancien régime," whose end had been substantiated by Schlegel and Hegel a good decade earlier.[58]

But more indicative of the renewed shift in meaning of modern after 1830 are those documents that, in full awareness of romanticism's difference from the modern present, saw the present as being characterized by the spirit of pragmatism. A paradigm is provided by *Hübner's Zeitungs- und Konversations-Lexikon* (1826) in the entry on "Nordamerikas Freistaaten" where "there is already such a feeling for the modern," meaning that what is "useful" takes precedence.[59] That this lexical item takes up an already common understanding of modern time can be seen in instances like the sentence in Schelling's *Vorlesungen über die Methode des akademischen Studiums*, where he complains about the modern tendency "to overemphasize the pragmatic spirit in history."[60]

The antagonism in these last definitions depicts romanticism as a transitional period in the history of the meanings of modern. During the first decades of the nineteenth century, the detachment of the present from the model of antiquity implicated in the *Querelle* had theoretically been completed and assimilated by the language norm—all of which corresponded to a basic change in the perception of time after 1830.

The Reduction of the Modern to a *Zeitbewegung* in the European Pre-March

"In 1830 a new political generation entered the arena, a generation that hadn't known the old Europe."[61] What Koselleck has confirmed as a prerequisite for political history after the July Revolution is also true for philosophy in the broadest sense, for the arts, and for the natural sciences, and may partly explain why in this period phenomena were experienced as characteristic of the present that would have been merely trends for the Enlightenment and romanticism. Among them was an increased interest in economic questions, in sociology, and in natural science that was generated during these decades; in a complete reversal of general romantic preferences, these were regarded as far more topically relevant than the theory and praxis of aesthetics.[62] However, the "common denominator" of the new generation's changed consciousness of the present was the "experience of acceleration" together with the insight that "every new modernity is destined to surpass itself."[63] We can recapitulate this in the replacement of the common use of modern as a period concept by a present perceived as a point of transition.

When Stendhal in 1832 called the period from the beginning of the Revolution up to his own time the *siècle de la Révolution*, he would seem, like the romantics, to be defining his own period by fixing its beginning (admittedly quite recent). The essentially new moment in his feeling for time becomes evident only through a reflection made during composition, where he imagines a point in the near future when what he has just written could seem to belong to the past and would thence no longer be up-to-date: "Que penserai-je de ce que je me sens disposé à écrire en le relisant vers 1835, si je vis?"[64] But in contrast to La Bruyère, Stendhal, by taking into account the future's judgment of his own time, would henceforth have a new way of evaluating the validity of his action in time: "Ma philosophie est du jour où j'écris."[65]

Nearly three decades later in 1859, Baudelaire, in his *Le peintre de la vie moderne*, had converted this new temporal perception into an aesthetic theory of modernity, which is still applicable to the avant-gardes of the twentieth century and which we would like to outline here in anticipation of the chronology of our conceptual history. Baudelaire is the first to recognize that every past must have experienced itself as a present and its art as modern ("Il y a eu une modernité pour chaque peintre ancien"), and this leads him to the further conclusion that "modern" and "modernity" not only refer to the particularity of the most recent period, as the romantics had still assumed, but rather designate all of the different, but always past, ideas that the people of different periods have made about beauty: "La modernité, c'est le transitoire, le fugitif, le contingent." A concept of modernity, however, that embraces the programs for many different transitory ideals can henceforth no longer be juxtaposed with "antiquity" as the essence of *one* past but only as the "imperishable." Both principles, the modern and the eternal, supplement each other in the "double nature of beauty." It is the task of literature to cull out of the transitory what it contains of the poetic, so that the eternal can constitute itself as the opposite pole of the modern: "Dégager de la mode ce qu'elle peut contenir de poétique dans l'historique, de tirer l'éternel du transitoire."[66]

Baudelaire's theory of modernity does not simply mark a turning point in the self-identification of art. It also allows us to understand how the use of modern in the third sense, as a foil to eternal, results from the "historization of time,"[67] — in Baudelaire's case, from the insight that the periods of the past themselves were once presents. In pre-1848 Europe, the historization of time also became a task for historiography to the degree that the present ceased being a delimitable fixed point from which the past could be judged. Historicism too, in embryo since the fundamental equalization of the periods of world history during the *Querelle*, seems to have been motivated by this new experience. The difficulty with the new temporal experience first became manifest in attempts to understand correctly the history of the present. In 1843 Lorenz von Stein wrote: "The old conditions were overturned, new ones appeared, themselves opposed by the new . . . it is as if historiography were barely able to attend to history."[68] The same insight—namely, that the history of the present no longer existed as a genre of historiography ("Il n'y a plus d'histoire contemporaine")—was more exactly determined by Lamartine in 1849. The sequence of great events shouldering in between actual experience (*oeil*) and remembrance (*mémoire*) was so rapid that those memories from one's own life that previously would have been reckoned to the present now continually seem to be in the distant past—"les jours d'hier semblent déjà enfoncés dans l'ombre du passé."[69] The historization of time moves from a cognitive model to an experience in which the events experienced during a lifetime as being in the present could seem to be in the past.

For members of the Young Germany movement, the point of departure for a similar consciousness was still achieved by explicitly distancing themselves from the immediate past as a period over and done with and qualitatively different from their own present. Heine, one of its spokesmen, had already confirmed in 1828 that "the principle of Goethe's period, the idea of art" had lost its significance, announced "the end of the philosophical revolution" in 1834 after Hegel's death,[70] and as early as 1831 felt that "his old prophecy of the end of the art period that had begun in Goethe's cradle and which will end with his coffin . . . was close to fulfillment."[71] Even Hegel believed that the end of art had been achieved in his time,[72] and Hugo also experienced the period around 1830 as a moment of radical change. Heine is different from Hugo in his struggle to overcome exactly that romantic art whose principles were for him "still rooted in old abandoned regimes, in the past of the Holy Roman Empire," and which Hugo had wanted to posit as revolutionary art, as *libéralisme en littérature*, in place of those classicistic rules (*les règles d'Aubignac*) representing the ancien régime. Like F. Schlegel and Hegel, Heine of course also saw a break between the romantic period and his own time, but he did not share their belief that art was no longer possible in this period or even that it was inferior to that of the antique. On the contrary, it was his opinion that this movement would even be beneficial for it.[73]

This effort to thematize "what could be suitably chosen from the real and existent in suitable contexts" was Heinrich Laube's criterion in an 1835 essay for identifying the "modern manner of writing."[74] In fact, it was the moment of unification for the representatives of a new literature whose "Messiah . . . could only be time itself [i.e., the present], in whose service and working for the ideas of which every individual strength considered itself predestined."[75] Despite this unity with respect to the resolute devotion to the present, modern consciousness did not coincide in all of the Young Germans. On the one side, the new time was organized as a period with specific characteristic tendencies in order to set it off from the past: hence "the struggle of the people's awakening spirit against absolute monarchism" was supposed to be its preeminent political job,[76] the indivisibility of life and writing was the law of modern literature,[77] and prose was the modern way of writing.[78] Where it is used in such a function, "modern" remains a period designation in the second sense, even if the authors of Young Germany transferred the beginning of their present into the immediate past of 1830 – and not several centuries back like their romantic predecessors. On the other side, Karl Ferdinand Gutzkow defined modern as a predicate for "the grace, the aesthetic law" not only of "the new aspirations" but also of *Raffinement* applied to antique, medieval, or romantic arts. Evidently the word signified for him not the substantial peculiarity of a given period but rather a particular relationship of the observer to the phenomena of his own present and past as historical: "Hence the modern would then actually be objectivity in a suspended moment, the fact of time, observed in and for itself, without conflict and contradiction, without relationship." Even for Gutzkow, the experience of his own period as transitory is the result of this sort of temporal historization: "Modern genres are quickly generated, quickly spread, quickly understood and die – often too quick to have experienced criticism."[79]

This use of modern in the third sense still had not come into view at this time within the field of political philosophy. This can be documented by the young Karl Marx's 1843 essay, *Kritik des Hegelschen Staatsrechts*, where he wanted to prove that Hegel's "true idea of the state" was contradicted by existent reality. In section 262 of his *Philosophie des Rechts*, Hegel had established the state as the "real idea, the Spirit, which divides itself as into the two ideal spheres of its concept, the family and bourgeois society as its finitude, in order, out of its ideality, to be for itself endless, real Spirit." Marx criticized the basis of this conception, namely, Hegel's tendency to make what "is" really the subject (here the family and society) into the predicate of what really "is" the predicate (here the state). It would be more accurate to begin with the idea that the state could not exist without the family and society, which in turn makes it transparent that it is alienated from them in political reality. This dualism of state and society already existed in the Middle Ages, but only becomes manifest in modern times, where humankind faces the state objectified in constitutional and bureaucratic forms: "The representative constitution is a great step forward, because it is the open, unfalsified, consequent expression of the modern condition of the State. It is its unconcealed contradiction."[80]

When Marx presupposes the representative constitution as a criterion for the demarcation of the modern from the medieval state, then he is applying a periodization that was current in his time but which differed from that of the eighteenth century. It can be found, for example, in Alexis de Tocqueville, who identified seventeenth-century England as "une nation toute moderne, qui a seulement préservé dans son sein et comme embaumés quelques débris du moyen âge."[81] The essential difference between Marx and Tocqueville is not so much the way they set temporal limits to the "modern" but how they each interpret it. Marx welcomes the accomplishments of the modern state only as a preliminary stage in liquidating the alienation it still contains, whereas Tocqueville celebrates it as an achievement of the past that should be preserved in the present and ultimately realized in every country.

When we analyze the evidence in German lexica from the period before 1848, we see that neither the use of modern to designate a transitory present in aesthetics nor its application as a period term for political philosophy became part of the language norm.[82] Along with the first sense of modern, the *Neueste Konversations-Lexikon für alle Stände* and *Heyse's Allgemeines Fremdwörterbuch* maintain the meaning originating during romanticism.[83] *Pierer's Universal-Lexikon* (1843) is the first to register a narrowing of the "modern" period, even though this does not mean that the third sense has fundamentally replaced the second, since its content was anticipated by Hegel's limitation of the romantic period in his *Ästhetik*: "In the most recent art and literature, the actual modern begins with the period where the older romanticism was modified through the influence of the renewed study of Greek and Roman literature and art."[84] From the precise formulation in *Manz's Allgemeiner Realencyclopädie*, it becomes clear that the new division for defining the historical foundations of idealism is subordinated to German classicism: "The modern that developed in this manner strove henceforth to entwine the antique and the romantic within a higher unity and to validate the domination of the Idea in all of its multiplicity."[85]

But while the period of German classicism was still marked with the predicate romantic by Hegel and F. Schlegel and was set apart from their own "modern time," which they considered decadent in comparison to classical perfection, their three-stage use of modern abolished the distinction between a national classicism and their own present, as for example *Brockhaus* in 1853: "Lately the separation into antique-classical, romantic-medieval, and modern has become quite general."[86] By the middle of the nineteenth century, it became evident that the normative meaning of "modern" was directly juxtaposed to its use by the Young Germany authors, whose work was characterized by a completely new experience of time.

Critique and Development of the New Consciousness of the Present after 1850

"En somme, à l'idole du progrès répondit l'idole de la malédiction du progrès ce qui fit deux lieux communs."[87] With this sentence, Valéry ironically underlines the subject of this and the preceding section—namely, the opposition of two characteristic nineteenth-century experiences of time, the sequence of "stimulus and response," practically in a scientific sense. In order to understand historically the "malediction" of the new consciousness of the present, we must question the motivation behind this response, which doesn't match Valéry's causal scheme. Evidently they are closely connected to the legitimizing function of the socially transmitted consciousness of the present. Institutions with origins that reach back several centuries and with structures and contents still imprinted by the time of these origins require a temporal consciousness in which the present stretches back at least to the time of its origin. Otherwise, as relics of the past in a new present, they could look as if they needed to be changed. In this sense, the romantic concept of the modern, as a Christian time founded in the Middle Ages, could function as a legitimation of the Restoration monarchies. A concept of the present, which might be transmuted but still designated by the word modern and whose beginning approaches and then moves into its own century, or even more, an experience of the present as a transitory moment resulting in an imperative of unremitting change, would necessarily run into criticism by partisans of a social order that needed to be legitimized by the consciousness of widespread historical continuity.

Of course after 1848, Young Germany's characteristic concept of modernity was not only attacked by the representatives of the old guard. A new generation of literary authors called themselves modern, to be sure, but no longer attached any programmatic demand to the use of the word in the first sense. Yet, in a deliberate swerve from their forebears' struggle to be up-to-date, they sought eternally valid guidelines: "We moderns aren't going to fall for any more illusions, for the idioms, literatures, criticisms, and reflections have made us trite and barren, perplexed, confused, and scruffy."[88] Fontane understood realism as precisely the artistic principle that could refill the emptiness due to an exaggerated dependence on the present: "Realism in art is as old as art itself, or even more, it is art. Our modern direction is nothing but a return to the only correct path, the nursing of an invalid back to health."[89] In a similar manner, Stifter wanted to oppose *objectivity*, *naïveté*, and *purity* to the *affectation* and *ornateness* of current taste. But in contrast to Fontane, he reserved "modern" as a designation for those tendencies with which he wanted nothing to do, "the mistakes of modern art and literature."[90]

More characteristic than the self-image of the realists, who wanted to replace what they felt was a worn-out effort to be up-to-date with a new transtemporal principle of art, were the keen polemics in the second half of the nineteenth century against a modernism that was regarded as hostile to traditional rules and values. So for instance, in 1872, the devaluation of the liberal slogan "modern" in the third printing of a collection of "phrases and slogans" edited by A. Reichensperger, the leader of the Catholic faction in the Prussian House of Representatives, turned out to be an attack on cultural-political opponents that did not even need to resort to factual argumentation. Pseudocontradictions were constructed: since "modern" was already used by older writers," it could not actually be modern — as if the value of the signifying concept could be reduced because of its historical derivation. Those "illuminated by the nineteenth century" were infused by a "certain feeling of devotion" whenever the word was mentioned, even though they usually considered themselves above any sort of religious sensation — as if this devotional feeling were reality and not simply effective polemical hyperbole. Modern art, which Reichensperger, as a patron of the restoration of the Cologne Cathedral, obviously hated — is denounced as immoral: its "main strength is nakedness . . . whereby it has nothing in common with the ideal nudity of Ancient Greek art."[91]

The attack on enemy camps allegedly propagating the concept modern concealed in this sort of polemic is even more obvious in a piece entitled "modern" published by Richard Wagner in 1866. Wagner states that the " 'modern' world as our most recent cultural transmitter" should be understood "as a completely new world, no longer having anything to do with previous worlds," and concludes that such a lack of historicity could be blamed on the Jews alone, since "they still had a long way to go to catch up with our cultural efforts of just a half a century earlier." By equating the "modern" and the Young Germany movement that he deprecated as "a malformation in the field of German literature" (and whose most important representatives, Börne and Heine, actually were Jews), Wagner lends his hypothesis a superficial plausibility; it might even camouflage how he twists the Young Germany consciousness of being at the beginning of a new present distinct from German classicism and romanticism into a *war*, a Jewish-national conspiracy against German culture, "well-supported by the forces of finance." And it is from this completely distorted representation that Wagner derives his concluding warning against modern art as "something quite wretched, and especially dangerous for us Germans."[92]

The German studies of the time developed a critical model for the devaluation of the various "modern" directions in art opposed to classicism and romanticism. It argued that German literature achieved so-called flowerings at regular intervals of six hundred years and after its high point around 1800 threatened "to grow out of the ideals . . . that constituted our pride and greatness during Goethe's time."[93] It was the task of German studies to keep the memory of the identifying values of the German "classics" alive during the coming nadir. Although modern time had a completely different position in Nietzsche's theory of the decadence of Western culture than in the texts we have been dealing with so far, in which the criterion was not so much the classical Greek era as the national classicism

immediately prior to their own period, and which propagated its so-called national ideals instead of the defeat of the despised modern by a new human type,
their characteristic efforts even for him were still the object of a critique that was
no less harsh yet incomparably more sagacious. For Nietzsche, "the transition to
mediocrity, to democracy, and *modern ideals*" had been signed and sealed in Germany "with the founding of the Reich in 1871."[94] Already prepared in the eighteenth century (hence the time span of the period labeled "modern"), its realization
originated in the French Revolution[95] and was characterized by the dominance
of three ideals: "sympathy with all suffering, . . . sense of history, . . . and
scientism."[96] Now whereas democracy and science during the nineteenth century
had been frequently mentioned either as human accomplishments or defects,
nothing less than a polemics against the "tireless intricate historicization of all
forms of becoming by modern man" would serve Nietzsche as a way of defining
the new consciousness of the present.[97] His attacks on the historical tendency to
create a distance between the present and the past and his skepticism about what
has become historical were the result of his experience of his own present as transitory and the past as a present that is past. Nietzsche's mockery of the "naive
promoters and eulogizers, the apostles of 'modern ideas' " demonstrates a capability quite unmatched by the other mockers of recognizing the relationship between
diverse and thoroughly "modern" phenomena.[98]

Apparently the sum of the attacks against the concept of the modern that had been
altered by the 1830 generation's consciousness of the present still were not able
to keep it from slowly seeping into the language norm. Even H. Wagener, reactionary member of the Prussian House of Representatives and prominent author
of the *Kreuzzeitung*, in his *Staats- und Gesellschafts-Lexikon* (1863) rejected as
old-fashioned the standard romantic use of modern as a predicate for the whole
Christian Era since the beginning of the Middle Ages. For historiography the concept now encompassed the time "from the origin of the French Revolution . . . up until our own days." "This third period of recent history" was
characterized by the formation of the "modern state." Like Marx and Tocqueville,
Wagener continually acknowledged "class arrangements of various kinds" as a
criterion for distinguishing the modern from the medieval state, but unlike Marx
he expected that the system of representation would bring about "the doctrine of
the balance of powers . . . for the good of the whole."[99] For aesthetics,
Wagener still quoted Hegel's concept of a modern period beginning with the
Reformation, which since 1843 had been an entry in German lexica. Hence for
the first time the varying uses of modern as a period designation were admitted
to political theory and aesthetics as part of the German language norm.

    Meyer's Konversations-Lexikon (1888) shows how the new understanding of
the present continued to put pressure on the norm. For here it was a question of
the "peculiar character of recent artistic creations" as an idiosyncrasy "chiefly of

the nineteenth century."[100] Of course modern remained a period concept, yet in its progressive foreshortening of the present, we approach the third type of meaning.

As a tendency in the second half of the nineteenth century, polemics against the new concept of modernity and its continual effect on the language norm can also be observed outside of Germany. For example, the liberal Spanish writer, Benito Pérez Galdós, in his 1878 novel, *La familia de Léon Roch*, puts a flow of billingsgate into the mouth of his protagonist Onésimo, who is a caricature of the conservatism based on the nobility and the church, a tirade against those *hábitos modernos* that were supposed to have disaccustomed Spanish women of their Christian modesty and beautiful ignorance.[101] The motivation behind such a conservative animosity to every modern claim is mentioned by Galdós a few pages further on, when he talks about the new opportunity to compensate for the advantage of noble birth through service and wealth as being one of the key characteristics of contemporary society.[102]

In France toward the end of the nineteenth century, the lexica, to be sure, took over the conceptual determinations provided by the *Encyclopédie* for various fields, yet two changes kept on turning up that are worth mentioning here. In the edition of *Larousse* published between 1865 and 1878, we see that "modern" was mainly used for phenomena of the current century. At the same time, and like its German counterpart, *moderne* will appear from now on as a historiographical term. Although the beginning of "modern history" was moved way back into the past, to the reign of Francis I, the following postscript to this determination demonstrates that a present with such boundaries was also experienced as the past of its own future and therefore as transitory: "Cette définition deviendra évidemment fausse quand l'époque de François Ier sera devenue une époque ancienne."[103]

In 1864, a year before the first edition of *Larousse* just referred to, the Brothers Goncourt published *Germinie Lacerteux*. Literary history considers it to be an initial work in French naturalism, a doctrine that a quarter of a century later would stimulate a renewed attempt to establish a school of modern literature in Germany. It was the Goncourts' aim to describe modern mankind, whose particular character they saw as having been spread by a general change in the educational experience that had marked an entire generation. According to their preface to *Renée Mauperin* (1875), modern education for men stretched back to the parliamentary beginnings in the epoch-making year of 1830, whereas the decisive tendencies of modern education for women ("l'éducation artistique et garçonnière") only went back about thirty years, that is, to around 1845.[104] This attempt to characterize modern humanity shows that, together with the experience of continual acceleration, even an insight into the plurality of historical sequences hindered a retrospective enclosure of one's own present within a self-contained period. It seems that the theoretical grounding of naturalism formulated by Zola in 1880 got such a wide reception all over Europe precisely because, unlike the Goncourts, he no longer erected it on the actuality of the described object,[105] but rather replaced the determination of traditional models with the demand that literary production implement the positive experimental methods of the natural sciences as a program for the future: "Le point de vue est nouveau, il devient expérimental au lieu d'être philosophique."[106]

The Modern as Program at the Turn of the Century

In an age when the life rhythms for half of humankind are determined by five-year plans and research on the future has become an academic discipline, it is hardly surprising that an artistic or political movement defines its claim to modernity by a still-to-be realized concept, as Zola did for naturalism. Within the historical context of the nineteenth century, however, accordance with the new future-oriented understanding of the present as evidenced in countless manifestos marks that turning point where the "force of tradition" as an orientation for human action is replaced on a broad front by the "forces of selection."[107] In the evidence documented in the foregoing sections of this chapter (as well as in conservative polemics), this adaptation is both a result of the radical change in the experience of time and a point of convergence for its various manifestations. Setting limits to the present as a period by determining its origin in the past seemed impossible from now on because of the accelerated sequence of historical changes and because of the recognition that there was a plurality of heterogeneous historical sequences. Not only was the duration of the present reduced to a point within a temporal flow, but it was also reduced as the past of the future so that it would have a chance to experience the shaping of this future. Thus it was now understood as a space free for the planning of future actions that could be formulated in programs. From the point of view of our retrospective analysis, it seems self-evident that for the designation of such programs "modern" was employed in the third sense. To be sure, in the consciousness of innumerable modern authors at the turn of the century it remained the name of a present period, at whose beginning they believed themselves to be standing and whose end seemed so far off that they felt little pressure to consider their own programs as transitory.

This contradictory self-image was already emphasized in the first manifesto of the *Moderne*, "Thesen zur literarischen Moderne," which was published by Eugen Wolff in 1887 and gave the movement its name.[108] On the one hand, together with representing the "significant powers struggling for significance in present-day life" as one of the tasks of the contemporary writer, there was the duty "to lead the struggle for the future as a prophet and pioneer." On the other, the present had recently been defined as a period with three dominant tendencies: German idealistic philosophy, natural science, and "technical cultural work."[109] In contrast, three years later when Otto Brahm began the newly founded magazine *Freie Bühne für modernes Leben* with a programmatic article "Zum Beginn," he avoided defining his own modernity in the same way—despite his express appeal to naturalism as the momentarily leading theory: "The boundless development of human culture is not bound to any formula, not even the most recent."[110]

When the principles that various representatives of the modern have listed as characteristic are lined up side by side, then we have a broad spectrum of artistic, philosophical, and political theories rather than a unifying doctrine. Michael Georg Conrad hoped for a unification of the "modern" with social democracy;[111] Curt Grottewitz and Leo Berg found the human figure for their own modern time in Nietzsche's Superman who will overcome the Enlightenment-modern idea of compassion.[112] Like Hegel at the beginning of the century, Heinrich Hart celebrated Shakespeare and Goethe as "prophets of the modern."[113] Considering the divergence of these orientations, which soon would elicit criticism from without and dissension within, there was nothing left but the consciousness of being at the beginning of a present that still needed to be formulated: "We're on the razor's edge between two worlds; what we create is only the preparation for a future greatness, which we cannot know but only surmise."[114]

Shortly after its reformulation, the substantive modern was entered in Brockhaus in 1902 as a "designation for the embodiment of the most recent social, literary, and artistic directions."[115] This semantic representation of the language norm is no different from the way it was used by the turn-of-the-century authors we have been quoting. It is somewhere between the second and third sense of "modern," according to whether the most recent directions are seen as a present experienced as just beginning that is nonetheless a complete period or as a present experienced from the outset as transitory.

By conceiving the present as compressed to a transitory point of elapsing time, we seem to have reached a semantic limit of the concept modern, which is transgressed when the present, as it were, anticipates itself as a moment in the shaping of the future. Already in 1895, for the actualism of the naturalist school, one of its main theoreticians, Antoine Albalat, had suggested the predicate "dans-le-mouvement," which however did not pass into the speech norm.[116] More successful was "avant-garde," which came out of the debates about aesthetics around 1900 and originally referred to the representatives of "new revolutionary positions that were clearly opposed to their own cultural and social context and the most recent past."[117]

This brings us to a point in our conceptual history where a new set of contents, which does not include the previous possible meanings of modern prescribed by the language system, is grasped by a predicate, which is already contained in the signifying system of speech and which thus alters its meaning accordingly. Originally a military term, "avant-garde" had already been used occasionally as a metaphoric signifier for the most recent schools of art and future-oriented political groups. However, when the Goncourt brothers in 1879, for instance, called the success of their own novel *Germinie Lacerteux* and Zola's *Assommoir* "des brillants combats d'avant-garde,"[118] the implicit observation that these books were ahead of their time was still slightly negative. Only to the extent that a new understanding of the present as a moment in the shaping of the future might spring up and spread, could "avant-garde" become its signifier in the speech norm and thus undergo an expansion in meaning. Since then, the word modern seems to have been used less and less frequently to designate "the most recent social, literary, and artistic directions."[119] Today its function is largely limited to the first type of meaning.

Our interpretation of the substitution of "avant-garde" for "modern" has confirmed that this present that could be experienced in a new way could no longer allow its periodic limits to be defined by particular qualities in the past. Most representatives of the modern acquired this insight only after their own programs had failed and their opponents' criticisms began to sink in. Already in 1894, Hermann Bahr rebuked the moderns for not having been able, despite their own claims, to arrive at a common "formula" or "program,"[120] and in the same year Cäsar Flaischlen confirmed that "the changes in the individual representatives and in their poetry" had occurred with such "rash precipitation" that none of the original artistic principles of the modern still had any validity.[121] Michael Georg Conrad's protest against the goals of the moderns — "the truly great flame of naturalism will not be choked by any opposing stream" — is simply one more piece of evidence for the accumulating insight into the impossibility of carrying them through as the focus of a new present.[122] In 1908, approximately two decades after its beginning, Josef Kainz was able to condense the historical consequences of this experience to the simple formula: "There are no moderns any more."[123]

This change in aesthetic value — which as our last quotations indicate was the common experience of intellectuals around the turn of the century — became the object of conceptual historical reflection at about the same time. In 1905, Rudolf Borchardt believed the recent devaluation of the concept of modernity was the result of its transfer "from the temporal sphere . . . into the aesthetic, where it had been remodeled into a concept of genre and appreciation."[124] The generality of this interpretation can be contradicted by calling attention, for instance, to romanticism's use of "modern" as an evaluative and a genre concept, but it is nonetheless valid for the years around 1900, insofar as the traditional syncretism of an aesthetic genre concept and a chronological concept of the present with respect to the new experience of time could not be taken any further with the concept of the modern. In his *Wörterbuch der Philosophie* (1910), Friedrich Mauthner formulated the same insight: since the word modern signified "only an undetermined stretch in the flow of the present, literally only the pin-point of the present," the substantive formulation modern could not be used parallel to the period and genre concept of antiquity, which encompassed "a relatively well-defined space of time."[125] In an analogous argument, the *Enciclopedia universal ilustrada* from 1907 said that *modernismo*, Spanish and South American modernism's effort to define itself as an artistic school, was senseless: "Puesto que no siendo el tiempo fijo ni permanente para ninguna cosa de la vida presente, es linaje de temeridad pretender que lo que hoy tiene aspecto de cosa moderna y remozada pueda también tenerlo dentro de unos años."[126]

Official Spain's united front against the modernistic movements in the most differentiated realms of experience was decisively motivated by the Catholic church's war against theological modernism that had been waged ever since the First Vatican Council.[127] Within the field of theology, "modern" has chiefly a general and transhistorical meaning—that is, "progressivism in contrast to conservatism [as a] normal phenomenon in the historical economy of spiritual life."[128] Thus the concept could also be used in the nineteenth century by the Protestant orthodoxy "to characterize the anti-Christian tendencies of the modern world as well as the radicalism of liberal theologians."[129] However, "modernism" was used at the end of the nineteenth and the beginning of the twentieth century in a narrow sense, for the most part as a proper name, in order to signify different efforts at theological renewal within the Catholic churches of France, England, Italy, and to a lesser extent Germany. Pius X introduced the concept in this sense with his encyclicals *Lamentabili* (July 3, 1907) and *Pascendi* (September 8, 1907). Among Protestants and outside the Catholic church, the "modernists" were considered a parliamentary party of Reform Catholicism. But for the Catholic church the word signified only the streams of critical Catholicism and therefore, as usual, "modernism" was marginalized as heretical.

From the standpoint of theological history, "modernism" was simply a continuation of the Catholic reform movements of the seventeenth and eighteenth centuries; seen systematically, it was a construct that brought together various tendencies "in the philosophy of religion, apologetics, Bible studies, the history of dogma, church discipline, and political and social action."[130] Attempts to mediate revelation with reason, Catholicism with cultural, scientific, social, and political reality, were generated within the context of Pius IX's reactions to the increasing secularization of life: the proclamation of the Immaculate Conception (1854); the denouncement of modern science, liberalism, and communism in the *Syllabus* and the encyclical *Quanta cura* (1864); the proclamation of the Pope's all-inclusive episcopalism and the dogma of papal infallibility at the Vatican Council (1869–70); the establishment of Neo-Thomism as the philosophy of the Catholic church; and so forth.

The counterreaction grounded the key moment of its "modernism" in a turn toward subjective mystical piety, withdrawal from the "alienation of religious life,"[131] and the assumption of historical and critical thought in opposition to evolutionism. According to its various fields, a distinction was made between a biblical, a social, and a theological modernism.[132] The Papal Judgment of 1907, followed by excommunications, indexings, and deposals from office, flowed into the so-called oath of anti-modernism (September 1, 1910), which bound the entire Catholic clerisy, with the exception of German university professors, to the encyclicals *Lamentabili* and *Pascendi* and which has remained in effect ever since.

The outbreak of World War I marks the end of the altercations over "modernism," which had been especially determined by the untraconservative reaction to the integralists after 1910. This direction defines "a religious totalitarianism" that "wanted to fundamentally subordinate all questions of private and public life . . . to the *potestas directa* of the Church."[133] Integralism raised the reproach of modernism against Reform Catholicism as a whole. After Pius IX's condemnation of all philosophical and political tendencies toward secularization outside of the Catholic church (e.g., liberalism and communism) in the *Syllabus* and *Quanta cura*, "modernism" was then marginalized as a heretical sediment of "liberalism" within the church.[134] From this time on, "Catholicism" and "antimodernism" made up a united front against modernism, liberalism, and communism. The problems turned loose by modernism, which were repressed rather than worked through, led to a continuation of the discussion between the two world wars. After World War II, there emerged Théologie Nouvelle, Left Catholicism, and Teilhardism, in which the boundaries between modernism and Reform Catholicism were blurred. Along with the Roman Catholic modernism, the concept had a second meaning as a proper name, which designated similar tendencies in the Anglican church. The adversaries of Anglican modernism are fundamentalism and Anglo-Catholicism.

While the Catholic church could protect its traditional self-image from the consequences of a changed consciousness of time with authoritarian decrees from the Curia well into the middle of the twentieth century, after the failure of "modernism" around the turn of the century many artistic movements were faced with the task of redefining their relationship to their own time, to the past, and to the time to come. Anyone (e.g., Erik Ernst Schwabach in 1913) who announced the beginning of a new modern period that was supposed to include "the now and the next two decades at least" simply had not grasped the historical significance of the turn-of-the-century aesthetic discussions—that is, the concrete experience that it was no longer possible to live through any present or plan it as a unified period.[135] Anyone turning away from the disoriented present who looked back to the past, such as innumerable Spanish authors in the early twentieth century, was aware that the literature of the previous century no longer served as a normative model but could stay alive only if an understanding of how it had changed was reached: "Los clásicos . . . deben ser revisados e interpretados bajo una luz moderna.

. . . No viviría el pasado si no estuviera sujeto a oscilaciones . . . la obra de arte está en perpétua evolución."[136]

To be sure, a different relationship of the artist to time is characteristic of the twentieth century. Instead of the idea of diachronically arranged series of styles and aesthetic theories specific to a given period, whose respective last link is the art of the present, we imagine at every present moment that we are able to scoop up subjects and procedures out of a synchronic cornucopia.[137] The present, then, is the moment of selection out of the possibilities available for shaping the future, and it must maintain itself as the past of this future.

The Consciousness of Modernity in the Twentieth Century as an Imperative for Change

The comprehensive entry under "modernité" in the fourth edition of the French *Encyclopaedia universalis* (1973) confirms the definitive acceptance into the speech norm of the third sense of "modern." Here we will no longer try to determine the "modernity" of the final (that is, our own) present by disqualifying the past, but rather will define modernity as a category of movement, as a *morale canonique du changement*. Such an imperative of change results from an awareness of the present as a future-oriented transitory moment that is diametrically opposed to an orientation to tradition as the basis for a type of civilization: "C'est un mode de civilisation caractéristique, qui s'oppose au mode de la tradition."[138] Of course, it is not unusual in the contemporary use of "modern" that the first and the third meanings converge. For example, anyone who talks about the modern university could mean in the first sense the momentarily dominant characteristics shaping a traditional institution, but can also in the third sense simultaneously imply that this shaping is connected to the future and will have to be changed in the future. The acceptance of the third sense of modern by the speech norm and the return of its use in the second sense as a period designation may, of course, be accepted as general complementary tendencies for our conceptual history in the twentieth century, even if they are not equally valid for speech use in every field of experience. It is precisely the growing recognition of the difference of historical, hence semantic, developments in various contexts of life that is one of the achievements of our present-day consciousness of modernity, and it is this that dictates the divisions of the following discussion.

Twentieth-century aesthetic praxis and its accompanying philosophical reflection can be interpreted as the redemption and growing understanding of Baudelaire's concept of modernity from 1859.[139] The transitory character of modern works of art is no longer felt as a fatal destiny, but as a willed negativity, as a form of resistance against an alienated society: "Pour échapper à l'aliénation de la société présente, il n'y a plus que ce moyen: la fuite en avant."[140] Nearly sixty years ago,

Breton had already celebrated Picasso's 1913 collages, their colors having faded in the meantime, as great art because they had actually been created in the consciousness that they were documents of their own transitoriness: "le périssable et l'éphémère, à rebours de tout ce qui fait généralement l'objet de la délectation et de la vanité artistiques, par lui ont même été recherchés pour eux-mêmes."[141]

At best, this kind of negative aesthetics can elude social alienation. In any case, it distances itself from the general public by its self-imposed duty to liquidate the latest artistic movement precisely in the moment that it becomes concrete. Since around 1960, a new generation of artists has tried to confront this dilemma of "Grandpa's modernism" in two ways.[142] By replacing the work of art with its performance, conceptual art announces "the end of the concept of the avant-garde." Instead of the material triangle, "atelier-gallery-museum," we have the temporal triangle, "idea-demonstration-agitation."[143] But if this program can do nothing more than help us adjust to the feeling of acceleration in the turnover of styles that was already the common avant-garde experience at the turn of the century, then the basic principle of pop art (namely, that any object is potentially aesthetic) matches the new recognition that modern artists can permanently choose from and adapt their creative processes to an abundance of synchronic possibilities. The given viewpoint of the observer will then designate the actualized forms respectively as "in" or "out," while the oppositional pair old/modern that corresponds to the diachronic sequential schema no longer plays any role in the conception of pop art.

In responding to the new experience of time, historiography had to develop methods to deal with the present history and fence this problematic field off from the more easily surveyed, self-contained periods of the past. Already in the title of his book *Der Untergang des Abendlandes*, Oswald Spengler was registering one of the first attempts to clear a path through the jungle of traditional patterns of historiography. In the foreword to the 1917 edition, he drew attention to "a phase in world history encompassing many centuries at whose beginning we presently find ourselves." The consciousness of being at such a decisive historical crossroads, together with his growing awareness of unsynchronized historical developments outside of "the small partial world" of Europe, led Spengler to repudiate the traditional segmentation of periods into antiquity, Middle Ages, and the modern "as an unbelievably paltry and senseless schema." It was precisely "the transfer of the beginning of the modern from the Crusades to the Renaissance and then to the beginning of the nineteenth century" made by his immediate predecessors that had proved to Spengler the fruitlessness of trying to articulate a historical development that in his opinion could only have been understood and represented as a whole from the very beginning.[144]

When the basic features of the old schema are retained today, modern usually designates the last period of the past that can generally be regarded as self-contained. At the same time it is set apart from present history, which is still open and hence inaccessible with the same methods. In the 1931 *Larousse, modern history* is defined as the time between the end of the Middle Ages dated at 1453 and *histoire contemporaine* beginning with the French Revolution.[145] Thus "modern" names a time that lies in the past but just touches the present.[146]

Only recently has the temporal conceptual pair progressive/conservative as a way of labeling and distinguishing political groups and their goals been detached from its functional use for social or occupational communities. Luhmann has shown that, given the increasing complexity of social relationships, this substitution was necessary, insofar as membership in the same class or occupation no longer guaranteed a community of political interests.[147] The choice of temporal concepts was evident because, considering the "temporalization of all existence" [*Temporalisierung alles Seienden*] in bourgeois society, they can be applied to practically any given object. Luhmann's hypothesis does not explain, however, just why it is the predicates progressive and conservative that have such an astounding popularity and not, for instance, an opposition like modern/old, or to use a concrete example, why it is quite possible to call a conservative politician like Kurt Georg Kiesinger modern,[148] but scarcely progressive. On the basis of our interpretation of the shift in the experience of the present at the turn of the century, we can suggest an answer to this open question. While designations like modern and old only coordinate the signified objects or persons with the periods understood as present or past, the political code of progressive and conservative in the narrower sense of present political acts and concepts of action distinguishes between two types, each according to whether it is patterned on the past or sets itself the task of shaping the future. Hence it manifests and constitutes an opposition between two forms of temporal experience, which has appeared only in the late phase of bourgeois society.

In sociology, "modernization" has been used specifically since about 1960 to describe the developmental efforts of Third World countries.[149] That this substantive could scarcely be used to describe political, social, and economic change in the industrialized nations indicates that the two kinds of change are not simultaneous. From our perspective at least, modernization in the underdeveloped countries is determined by the desire to catch up with present levels in the industrialized countries, and is thus taking place somewhere between decolonialization and our own present. At the same time, the industrial nations are moving out of this present into an open future, without being able to predict the way to it or what it might conceivably look like.

Only in the natural sciences has the paradigm of a permanent progress building on the accomplishments of the past — and hence, the concept of modernity as well — remained undebatedly valid. The recognition that the natural sciences had their own laws was already one of the consequences of the *Querelle des anciens et des modernes.* Yet at the same time, as Valéry argued in 1931, it is precisely this sort of differentiating historical cognition that makes us skeptical about the global progressive optimism built up around the achievements of the natural sciences. Valéry established "accroissement de netteté et de précision, accroissement de puissance" as the essential accomplishments of modern times, from which he derived his hopes for an improvement in human existence with respect to "conversation, diffusion et relation."[150] But as far as the social politics of the 1970s is concerned, it is exactly this correlation of technical-scientific achievements and "the quality of life" that has become questionable.

The continuation of this correlation in social knowledge is the focus of countless advertising strategies. With modern furniture or cigarettes "for modern people," we also ransom ourselves free of the collective fear of being considered old-fashioned, which is apparently motivated by the experience of a present that is constantly outstripping and disengaging itself from its past. Admittedly, "the wave of nostalgia" has been effectively interpreted by social psychology at the level of popular science as a countermovement to this sort of restlessness, yet it is not to be understood as a new awareness of tradition. For rock and roll and Jugendstil are also "in," which means that they are both valid results of the selection from the ahistorical reservoir and could be set aside tomorrow by a new collective choice and thus be "out." Therefore, the "nostalgia" mode does not go against the grain of the present temporal consciousness but finds its contingency in it.

Historiographic Consequences

The history of the concept "modern" confirms the conjecture that "since the middle of the eighteenth century a thoroughgoing change in the meanings of classical *topoi* has been carried out and . . . old words have acquired new senses that no longer require translation as they approach our present." Right at the end of the eighteenth century, during that debate about aesthetics at the threshold of German classicism and European romanticism, the detachment of the present as a "modern" period from the normative model of antiquity was completed, becoming in turn the point of departure for a philosophical understanding of the new consciousness of the present that would fundamentally alter the concept of modernity. This clear historical localization of the decisive shift in meaning can be performed only within the framework of the theoretical concepts developed at the beginning of this study, where it was argued that, as a method of social history, conceptual history must concentrate above all on changes in the speech norm. For instance, if we were to concentrate exclusively on the sequence of first appearances, that is, on the innovative selections of individual authors out of all the possibilities embedded in the language system, then the *Querelle* — and not the shift from classicism to romanticism—would seem to be the turning point in the development of the concept of modernity. The consequent orientation of action to antique paradigms was maintained up to the end of the Enlightenment, and this lets us assume that the theoretical disclosure of a new understanding of time that was implemented by the *Querelle* did not converge with collective experience for an entire century and was therefore only really used in isolated instances. It was merely because the questions that Friedrich Schlegel and Schiller had left open since the end of the seventeenth century were raised once again, and as a result of the answers they developed for the romantic consciousness of modernity, that the *Querelle* took on a social-historical significance as an event in the humanities.

Now for its part, the origin of the romantic concept of "modern" is simply a first step, observable after 1830, toward the substitution of the third for the second sense of "modern" within the speech norm. It is the feeling of temporal acceleration derived from this substitution that gives this conceptual history a perspective relevant for social history. But therefore its contribution to social history exists only because it can legitimize itself by pointing to an ongoing research project; for Koselleck and Luhmann have already posed the question about the reasons for the change in the consciousness of the present that sets in around 1830 and have arrived at complementary answers. Whereas Koselleck explains the change in the experience of time as an adjustment to the "empirical preconditions of a world that had increasingly technologized itself,"[151] Luhmann sees it as determined by the necessity of projecting into the future a surplus for potential action that has recently entered consciousness and that is not acquired from the paradigm of the past.[152] It can be concluded that ever since then the duty of selection as a way of formulating the future has detached itself from the pressures of tradition. Luhmann introduces the increasing functional differentiation of systems as the main presupposition for the resulting "surplus of possibilities." The technologizing of the world, however, is inseparable from the intensification of system differentiation.

Chapter 6
Laughter and Arbitrariness, Subjectivity and Seriousness: The *Libro de buen amor,* the *Celestina,* and the Style of Sense Production in Early Modern Times

Dedicated to the memory of Wilhelm Kellermann,
serene connoisseur of the Spanish Middle Ages

An Eccentric Perspective

Comparing and contrasting the *Libro de buen amor,* a work that, on the basis of the manuscript transmission, can be safely assumed to fall in the first half of the fourteenth century, with the *Celestina,* which was first printed shortly before the end of the fifteenth century, has been a classical approach in Hispanic literary history for many years. Without wishing to deprecate the often admirable results such studies have contributed to the understanding of a special case in cultural history – namely, the unbroken transition from the late Middle Ages to the golden age in Spanish literature – there can be little doubt that, rather than heuristic considerations, it is first of all the way these texts belong to the canon of an unspecialized reading public in Spanish-speaking countries today that urges the conjunction of the *Libro* and the *Celestina.* In recent years, both texts have been filmed, admittedly with quite different pretensions; many of their passages belong to the repertoire of popular Spanish songwriters; and the central protagonists, Arcipreste de Hita and Celestina, have become part of those stereotypes through which everyday realities are constituted and interpreted in Spanish-speaking countries.

Processes of canonization always provide perspectives for measuring the semantic potential of the texts that they render "classic." Around the middle of the nineteenth century, there was a growing enthusiasm for both these texts in two sharply opposed groups in Spanish society that ended up leading to their present "classicality." Such a shared enthusiasm from two different angles of reception, whose respective motivations and manifestations are almost opposite, makes us suspect that the sense structures of the *Libro* and the *Celestina* contain a specific ambivalence. Since the end of the nineteenth century, Spanish cultural critics have used the expression "the two Spains" to describe an opposition that had already begun in the late Spanish Enlightenment and that still has not completely disappeared today, an opposition, on the one hand, between the conservative effort to preserve Spanish identitity in traditions from the feudal Christian Era, and on the other, the tendency of bourgeois intellectuals to locate, formulate, and propagate a new national identity through two instances—the discovery of an alternative social and cultural history of Spain and the reception of Central European literature and philosophy. Conservative Spain is convinced that, since our two texts appear as historically "avant-garde," they are simply one more proof among many of the timeless truth of the Spanish worldview. In the *Libro*'s and the *Celestina*'s breaking of taboos, in their heterodox tendencies, their willingness to accept elements from Arabic, Jewish, and popular culture, the proponents of a modern Spain have uncovered objectifications of that "other" Spanish history through whose progressive disclosure it has hoped to build its "own" national identity.

These short remarks are meant to show that the *Libro* and the *Celestina* owe their canonization as "two Spanish masterpieces"[1] to particular historical conditions, which readers outside of Spain normally become familiar with only if they receive training as Hispanists. At any rate, the divergence between these two approaches to reading, the centripetal interpretation of the conservatives and the centrifugal one of the liberals, might also suggest that the *Libro* and the *Celestina* could become classical for medievalists in a completely different sense—namely, as paradigms for a shift in the style of sense production at the threshold from the late Middle Ages to the Renaissance whose reconstruction has recently been at the center of attention in medieval studies.[2] The perspective, from which we are therefore going to attempt a comparative interpretation of the *Libro* and the *Celestina* is the heterogeneity of the sense structures constitituted by the texts, a heterogeneity that is both the condition for the possibility and a provocation for the development of new (i.e., modern) types of reception.

But the question about the reciprocity between heterogeneous meanings and their different receptions is not just a heuristically new approach to the threshold between the late Middle Ages and the Renaissance; we find the same structure at the center of some theories about comedy and laughter. Now it is precisely this shared focus that puts the theme of the comic in medieval literature and the question of the threshold between periods into a systematic relationship that may be somewhat surprising.

Theoretical Premises: The Pragmatics of Laughter and the Evolution of Knowledge

Despite all of their divergences, the few (but in the meantime canonical) reflections on this theme from philosophy, anthropology, and psychology tend to agree that, from the perspective of cognitive theory, laughing and crying are symptoms of an insufficiency dependent on certain situations. According to Joachim Ritter and Helmut Plessner, they are involuntary (that is, removed from rational control) physical reactions to the simultaneous experience of sense complexes whose mediation or compatibilization the subject is incapable of performing.[3] Of course, in contrast to crying, laughter is not only a mark of insufficiency but also of the privilege of not having to cope with one or the other of the incompatible figures of meaning. It is a sign of the opportunity to keep these figures at a distance (that in a very broad sense is aesthetic).

The sociology of knowledge developed by Mannheim, Schütz, Berger and Luckmann, and especially Niklas Luhmann's "theory of social systems," recommends comprehending the phenomena of social evolution (equivalent here to the "evolution of social knowledge") through models of the various relationships between complex, collectively internalized (and here not individually experienced) sense structures.[4] One of the anthropological premises of the sociology of knowledge is that knowledge functions to compensate for a lack of instincts (specific to human beings) as a means of orientation within a highly complex environment. The selection of elements out of environment perceptions and the sense formation out of these selected elements are completed in two acts of screening: by screening out the nonselected parts of the inventory and by screening out the possibilities for assembling selected elements. Assuming that those objects of perception and those models for assembling objects of perception that were screened out of the data of consciousness can be turned back into these data at any time, then sense production can be called "negation," whether it is implemented by the subject or experienced as socially prescribed.

Having associated social evolution with the evolution of collective knowledge and having defined sense production as a two-level act of negation, we can now set up the theoretical presuppositions for distinguishing different types of social evolution as based on different types of negation.[5] Normally, in social evolution some (but not all) of the elements and structures of knowledge positivized by a system (A) are screened out by a subsequent system (B), while (B) positivizes some (but not all) of those elements and structures of knowledge that were screened out by system (A). This type of evolution constitutes an *asymmetrical negation*. A second type of negation/evolution—which is a pure theoretical (and sometimes fictional) possibility, but can never historically materialize—might then be called a *symmetrical negation*. Here the second system indeed screens out *all* the elements and stuctures that constitute the first system in order to positivize all of the elements and structures negated by the first system (this would mean a radically new beginning of any human existence and thought). A third type of negation/evolution, which I will call *purely recursive negation*, has, in contrast to symmetrical negation, references in history, but it should be regarded, in contrast to asymmetrical negation, as an exceptional case, presumably as a form of transition typical of many of those phases in history that we call "period thresholds": here system (B) positivizes all of the elements and structures of knowledge screened out by system (A), without excluding any of the elements and structures characteristic for system (A). Historical transitions in the form of purely recursive negations constitute moments of social and cultural chaos.

If we apply this typology to a series of vernacular texts familiar to every medievalist, then we find three conceivable positions. (1) Texts whose sense structures stage themselves as a symmetrical negation to their audience's knowledge can be mainly found in the High Middle Ages; and at the level of a functional history we can presume that these texts served to release their recipients from the pressures of everyday sense structures (dogmatic solemnity, imposed renunciation of drives, etc.), whereby it is exactly the *impossible* character of the symmetrical negation that shields everyday knowledge from being seriously problematized. (2) The chaos into which previously quite stable genres glide in the late medieval period and the heterogeneous meanings of many of its individual texts can be characterized as a recursive negation, resulting from the selective weakness of social systems, and hence as a symptom of crisis. (3) This explosion of meanings and forms in the Late Middle Ages seems to have prepared or made necessary a new style of sense formation: at first simply in the key works of our humanistic tradition, then later in increasingly wide fields of art, of science, but also of everyday life, meaning was no longer experienced – in terms of the medieval cosmology – as something objectively given in a world created by God, but as an achievement of humans in the position of subjecthood.

Thanks to the intensive reception of Mikhail Bakhtin in the last few years, we do not have to justify our shift back to a pragmatics of laughter from a typology of social evolution and our proposal to apply both theories to the threshold between the late Middle Ages and the early modern period.[6] For in his cultural and typological category of the carnival Bakhtin sets out a mediation between evolutionary processes of social history and the pragmatics of laughter. What is laughed at in the carnival is the solemnity of everyday life, whose source and support are vaguely designated by Bakhtin as "official culture." On the basis of our theoretical preconsiderations, we can, on the one hand, now regard official cul-ture as the horizon of meaning that provides an integrating framework for all the particular stores of social knowledge interrelated in an everyday world. On the other side, Bakhtin's rich supply of examples suggests that we define the relation-ship between the world of the carnival and feudal Christian cosmology (the "official culture" of the European Middle Ages) as the ratio of a purely recursive negation.

Now of course, "official culture" and "carnival" were current in medieval studies long before the reception of Bakhtin. But his work on medieval culture has sharpened our focus on those situational conditions that secure a temporary dominance of the carnival's compensatory and releasing function by preventing its chaos from encroaching on everyday life. I am referring here to Bakhtin's con-cept of "the insularity of the carnival," its isolation from everyday life, which in the High Middle Ages was ensured by the position of the carnival in the ecclesiati-cal year: the collective effects of the carnival could be cushioned by the asceticism of subsequent fasting. From this perspective, we are faced with new questions about the transition from the late Middle Ages to the Renaissance as if seen as a change in the style of sense production: should the crisis in the everyday world of the High Middle Ages be described as an increasing penetration of the carnival into everyday life, well beyond the limits of its insularity? Are we to suppose that the Renaissance had discovered new modes for isolating sense, thus replacing the carnival and its position in the ecclesiastical year as modes that questioned official culture?

Especially the second of these two questions intersects precisely with what we called the excentric side of our comparative analysis of the *Libro* and the *Celes-tina*. I begin their reading with an outline of the most important elements of both texts (the text repertoire), not yet taking into consideration those structures through which the repertoire achieves form. The structures that provide form (text strategies)[7] involve a second analytical step, which in turn is concerned with three levels of sense configuration: thematic relevance, interpretive relevance, and motivational relevance (those complexes of meaning through which the pro-tagonists' behavior and action become comprehensible). It is only on the basis of the textual analyses implemented from these points of view that we can ade-quately focus our central question about the shift in sense constitution between the late Middle Ages and the Renaissance. Then, on the basis of a reconstruction of the implicit communication situation inscribed in the texts, we will try to recon-struct and historically understand their respective *Sitz im Leben*.

Text Repertoire

The *Libro* begins with a prayer of lamentation by a prisoner whose (allegorical or real?) prison is not localized and whom the copyist of the most important manuscript identifies in a heading with the first-person protagonist, who in later passages of the text often refers to himself as Juan Ruiz, archpriest of Hita. The ten stanzas of the lamentation, which are in the *cuaderna via*, the standard meter for vulgate clerical poetry during the Spanish Middle Ages, are followed by a prose prologue in which reflections about the book's intention and possible ways of reading it are developed through biblical quotes and contemporary principles of exegetical praxis. Returning to the *cuaderna via*, the first-person narrator (whom literary historians, with few exceptions, have not hesitated to identify with "the author") begs God to help him complete his work, and following this appendix to the prologue, there are two songs on the seven joys of Mary in a meter of popular verse. The topic of the ambiguities of interpretation, which was already theologically prefigured in the prose prologue, is subsequently rearticulated within the context of a burlesque example-story about a fight between a Greek and a Roman.

It is only at this point (after the seventieth stanza) that the first-person narrator also assumes the role of the central protagonist. Up until stanza 949, a series of love affairs is depicted, which the sinful archpriest tries to instigate with the help of the procuress, Trotaconventos (a precursor of the protagonist in the *Celestina*). At the center of the book is not only the theme of clerical sex, but also the perspectives and forms of its textual presentation, which are mostly defined by medieval Latin culture. Hardly a single episode is not interpreted through an exemplum (mostly beast fables), and one episode can even be read as an adaptation, in parts as a translation, of the Middle Latin "Pamphilus" comedy (also a model for the author of the *Celestina*). The protagonist extracts contradictory messages out of the love affairs, on the one hand by taking recourse to astrology and on the other by developing two nocturnal dialogues with Don Amor and Doña Venus, well-known allegorical protagonists from antique literature. After the last meeting with the procuress, the first-person protagonist takes off for a hike through the mountains, which leads him into the arms of four farm ladies; they are called *serranas*, and the last one seems to be a sister of the "monster at the spring" from Arthurian romance. The travel narrative and the inserted metrical songs of the farm women in the mountains vary not so much the theme as its forms of articulation—they are adapted to the tradition of pastoral poetry. On his way home from the mountains, the archpriest stops at a shrine for Mary; there he dedicates to Mary two meditations on Christ's sufferings.

This topic opens up a temporal and semantic bridge to the following sequence. During dinner on the Thursday before Ash Wednesday, the protagonist (his name has now been changed to Don Carnal [Mr. Flesh]) is challenged to a duel by Doña

Quaresma (Mrs. Lent). The deployment of the troops of meat dishes as a kind of metonymic representation of the carnival's sensual lust and their defeat by the Lenten dishes (on Ash Wednesday), the capture of Don Carnal, his escape, and finally the expulsion of Doña Quaresma accord on the whole with the model for a well-known allegorical narrative in French literature.[8] The adaptation of the names and origins of the meat and Lenten dishes to the knowledge of the Spanish recipients certainly belongs to the medieval concept of "translation" just as much as the way Don Carnal's escape route is worked out to take him through regions renowned for their cattle and cities with large Jewish communities—his only chance of surviving Lent.

After Don Amor's triumphal entry on Easter morning (this scene replaces the anticipated return of Don Carnal and is based on forms of the celebration of spring in courtly culture), a fifth part begins. Its unity is provided by common reference to a horizon of folklore culture: the motif of the Mass as a love market (it will turn up again two hundred years later in the picaresque novel) as well as the archpriest's love of a nun and an Arabic woman. These episodes are extended by a catalogue of ideal attributes of beauty, by an inventory of over forty aphrodisiacs, and a tract on the differences between Christian and Arabic musical instruments. With the death of the procuress, to whom the first-person narrator dedicates two epitaphs, the variations on the theme of love are concluded for the time being.

The conclusion of the *Libro* is just as heterogeneous as its introduction. A list of the many qualities that are supposed to predestine small women for love is followed by a catalogue of vices of the loutish servant, who wants to take over the role of the dead procuress—another familiar motif from popular literature. After some more instructions how to read the *Libro*, there are, again with parallels to the introduction, a series of psalms to Mary, some songs of the blind (*cantares de ciegos*), so beloved in the literature of the Spanish Middle Ages, and a few examples of Scholastic poetry. The text ends with twenty stanzas in *cuaderna via*, which many interpreters read as proof of its autobiographical authenticity: "the song of the clerics of Talavera" includes the laments and protests of clerics, who were forbidden to take mistresses by the archbishop of Toledo. And in fact this interdiction was issued in the 1320s at a synod in Toledo.

The name *La Celestina*, which is normally given to a work by Fernando de Rojas that probably first appeared in 1499, is a concretion of a particular perspective of reception, which was most likely not the author's intention. Originally the text was called *Tragicomedia de Calixto y Melibea;* the title *La Celestina* "first shows up in an Italian translation from 1519 in the Alcalá edition of 1569."[9] If the original title is connected to the love story of Calisto and Melibea, thoroughly imprinted by Middle Latin and early humanistic traditions, the usual title today, *La Celestina,* directs our attention to another tradition of subject matter and cultural history that is integrated in the love story: the milieu of magic, crime, and prostitution. Because of the widespread heterodoxy in the Spain of the *Reyes Católicos,* this representation is also interesting for historians.[10] Calisto—a young man "of noble birth, a brilliantly gifted mind . . . advantageous education . . . reasonably rich," as we read at the beginning of the early edition of the *Celestina* —falls in love with Melibea—who is consummate in beauty and virtue, the only daughter and sole heiress of a wealthy family. Since Melibea does not return Calisto's advances, Calisto succumbs to his servants' advice to engage the services of the procuress, Celestina, which he does, promising her an enormous payment should Melibea give in to his desires. Celestina, who makes a deal with Calisto's servants to divide the reward with them, sets them up with two prostitutes living in her house, and supports them. Through various types of black magic, but also through an amazing power of persuasion, Celestina convinces Melibea to receive Calisto for a tryst in the garden.

When Celestina refuses to pay the servants their promised share of the reward, they murder her. But they, too, find death directly after their deed in flight from the reach of justice. The prostitutes, left destitute by Celestina's death and once again "single" since the death of the servants, decide to revenge themselves on Calisto, even though he is totally unaware of the consequences of his act. During an evening of love in Melibea's garden, he hears voices on the other side of the garden wall and, concerned about his and Melibea's reputation, tries to find out who is disturbing their idyllic evening; he slips and falls from the garden wall to his death. Melibea calls for her father, climbs a high tower in her parents' presence and explains to her father, before following Calisto by plunging to her own death, that she knows very well the injustice she does to her loving parents, but that since life without Calisto would be empty, the only choice left to her is to renounce this life in order to be reunited with him in the beyond. It is precisely Melibea's closing monologue that demonstrates how the tragicomedy draws together not only different milieux and their protagonists but also quite diverse forms of heterodoxy: for Celestina's black arts are no closer to orthodox Christianity, the accepted "official culture," than the self-evident manner with which Melibea disposes of her earthly existence and anticipates a happy existence in the beyond following her suicide.

Strategies of Sense Configuration

The plot structures of the *Libro* and the *Celestina* could, from the perspective of a literary historian, easily look like a mere superstructure on which mutually heterogeneous elements are assembled. Yet why do we have the impression that the *Libro*'s plurisignificance is carnivalesque, that it did and can elicit laughter, whereas in the *Celestina* it seems to enable a fictional approximation of the "real world"?

As far as the *Libro* is concerned, it has been said that the text's content is medieval and its (biographical) form modern.[11] On the other hand, it should by no means be forgotten that not all of the thematic inconsistencies are abolished by integrating heterogeneous material into the biographical structure. This is why the text also seems to be close to the *cancioneros*, the collections of lyrical texts characteristic of late medieval Spanish literature. With respect to the inconsistency of the narrative plot, it is remarkable how frequently the name of the narrator and protagonist, Arcipreste de Hita, is replaced by the names of other characters who themselves had been the main protagonists in other texts prior to their integration into the *Libro*. Thus in certain passages from the part that goes back to the Pamphilus comedy, the name Don Melón has been left over. The name Arcipreste comes up just as infrequently during the allegorical narration of the battle between the Lenten dishes and the meat dishes, where his role is taken over by Don Carnal. In turn, in the Easter scene celebrating the return of sensual joy, Don Carnal is represented by Don Amor, a figure who had been Arcipreste's conversational partner in a previous part. Equally inconsistent is the chronology alternating between the mountain journey and the allegorical story of Lent. The protagonist sets off on his trip in March; Ash Wednesday, when Doña Quaresma's reign begins, is located after the return of the first-person protagonist, consequently at the end of March, when according to the church calendar Lent would already have begun. After all the (historically inadequate) expectations of a modern reader, used to biographical narration, are not sufficient to establish a line of development for the series of episodes in which the main protagonist appears. The biographical structure integrating isolated complexes is not (yet) filled out by them in a way that would allow this pattern to become concrete in a specific plot.

On the other hand, the *Celestina*'s plot constellations accomplish exactly this by constantly motivating the transgression of the limits of the refined world of the lovers on the one side and Celestina's on the other. The procuress herself, who has acquired her professional competence outside of social bounds and who, as long as she practices her profession, must lead a life outside of society, becomes a promoter of this sort of social encounter.[12] Hence we can agree that, while the *Libro*'s heterogeneous materials require an integrative structure for their presentation (that is, while here the content predominates over the structure), it is difficult to decide in *La Celestina* whether it is primarily the plurisignificance that needs the complex plot, or the plot that needs its plurisignificant repertoire for its realization. What in everyday language might be called the text's worldview can largely be identified with the knowledge proposed and presumed by the text for interpreting perceptions and experiences – the knowledge relevant to interpretation. If the *Libro* can be characterized as "inconsistent" at the level of plot (that is, the function of its knowledge in constituting themes), we also have to deal with contradictions on the second level of the same text – internal contradictions between the various elements of knowledge relevant to interpretation—and contradictions between many of these elements and official culture. Internal incompatibility and partial incompatibility with official culture suggest that we characterize the relationship between the meaning proposed by the *Libro* and the official culture as "purely recursive." A good illustration is a passage in the second part (stanzas 693ff.) where, unless some sort of adjustment to mutual communication is made, completely different interpretive horizons are brought into play in order to discuss the instances on which the success or failure of the protagonist's love affairs might depend. As a substratum of primitive religiosity, there are the ill-intentioned spirits of fate (*fados*); with God's help and the protagonist's own effort (*trabajo grande*), these spirits can be defeated. Just one stanza further on, the text seems to regard anonymous fate (*ventura*) as an instance above God. Four stanzas more and it is finally Amor, the allegorical god, who helps the lovesick priest succeed. As we see, equivalent elements of knowledge from primitive conceptions of transcendence (*fados*), from Arabic culture (*ventura*), from classical mythology (*amor*), and from the Christian doctrine of good works (*trabajo*) are set in a series without the text giving us any hint whatsoever how this interpretational potential should be hierarchically arranged.

More complex (and thus less evident from the point of view of interpretation) is a contradiction overshadowing the entire episode of the struggle between the meat and Lenten dishes. The temporal course of this narrative is marked off by concepts taken from the structure of the ecclesiastical year. To mention only one example, the struggle begins with Lent on Ash Wednesday and concludes with the end of Lent on Easter Sunday. Now this recourse to the ecclesiastical year has a series of implications. Of course Lent must be regarded by devout Christians as a suspended phase, an enclave whose identity is to be found in the intensification of its demands on everyday ethical solemnity. More pointedly, however, the few carnival days tolerated by the church would also be an enclave embedded between everyday ethical demands and their intensification during Lent. Precisely this relationship between the normality of the ecclesiastical year plus Lent on the one hand and the carnival enclave on the other is reversed in the *Libro*. The protagonist returns from his mountain journey seven days before the beginning of Lent, and these seven days, according to the ecclesiastical year, are given to the carnival enclave. But in the *Libro*, carnival's beginning is by no means emphasized as a kind of caesura; only Ash Wednesday (allegorized by the onset of the attack on Don Carnal and his warriors, the meat dishes) and Easter Sunday (with the return of Don Amor) are experienced as caesurae. According to the *Libro*, Don Carnal, Don Amor, and the Arcipreste, which are surely specific concretions of the carnival king described by Bakhtin, rule for the whole year, except for Lent, which is reinterpreted as the enclave in which Don Carnal is imprisoned and from which he must escape. The grave Doña Quaresma, on the other hand, dominates only during the forty days of fasting, having to spend the rest of the time far away . . . "on a crusade." This temporal structure inscribed in the text, which is carnivalesque in the concrete sense, contradicts the extratextual structure of the ecclesiastical year, which to be sure is still present in the temporal markers used by the text. It lets us intuit a substratum of cyclical, pre-Christian orderings of time, whose rhythm is provided by the continual banishment and return of the carnival king.

Now it can be assumed that the contradictions on the cognitive level relevant to interpretation that have been pointed out so far simply slipped past the author of the *Libro*—that is, they were unintended. Elsewhere certainly, this sort of potential inconsistency (for example, the ambiguity of individual predicates in the text that are left unreduced) was obviously implemented for the plot according to plan. For instance, in stanza 825 it illustrates the procuress's suasive skills: "¿Cómo vienes, amiga?" says the mother to a young lady, when Trotaconventos knocks on her door in order to ask "why" she has come. Trotaconventos sidesteps the disagreeable obligation to answer by not understanding the cómo of the question in the ordinary everyday sense of "why" but literally in the sense of "how." Hence she answers: "How am I doing? I don't know how to put it . . . tense and bitter."

The semantic ambiguity of individual predicates also plays an important role in *La Celestina*'s dialogue. But here the different uses of the words serve to formulate the character or situational frame of mind of the protagonists, and even if it could perhaps be conceived as the author's wordplay, it could by no means be seen, as in the case of Trotaconventos, as a protagonist's wordplay. When at the beginning of the tragicomedy the servant Sempronio suggests to his rejected master, Calisto, that he should look for another lover, Calisto gruffly replies, "How little you understand of steadfastness [*firmeza*]." Sempronio snaps back mockingly: "Perseverance [*perseuerancia*] in a bad situation shouldn't be confused with constancy [*constancia*]; where I come from we tend to call it blockheadedness [*dureza ó pertinacia*]." As we see, Calisto interprets his own behavior quite differently than his servant; their dialogue suggests that we should contrast the subjectivity of the worldview of the protagonists in the *Celestina* with the *Libro*'s internal and external cognitive inconsistencies at the level of interpretive relevance, just as we contrasted the different kinds of plot inconsistency at the level of thematic relevance. Examples of subjective interpretation by the protagonists in the *Celestina* could be multiplied at random. For the moment it is enough to point out that in the dialogue between Celestina and Melibea, the young woman of a noble birth, befitting her upbringing, considers the age of the procuress (seen from the outside) as honorable, while for Celestina herself it can only be experienced as the phase of decrepitude. When E. Leube correctly distinguishes Celestina as an individual from Trotaconventos's role as procuress in the *Libro*, he apparently is not only thinking of the fact that the titular figure, like all of the protagonists in *Celestina*, is an instance of sense production.[13] Rather her estimations and interpretations of the (fictional) world around her, her self-respect, and finally her personal identity were apparently so surprising for the contemporary audience that plausibility could be established only through a faked (individualizing) biographical narrative of Celestina. Her solicitude for Pármeno, Calisto's young servant, which runs against the grain of her principle of consequent material egotism, causes Celestina to talk about those (subjectively!) happier times when, together with Pármeno's mother, she prevailed over the milieu of prostitutes and criminals. Shortly before her death, when Sempronio, with rough words and threats, demands two-thirds of the match-making fee paid by Calisto, Celestina defends the honor that is due to her as well as to any other human beings who have fulfilled God's providence in their lives:

SEMPRONIO: Give us two parts of the money that you received from Calisto—or maybe we'll let it become known just exactly who you are? You can try your gab on someone else, you old hag.

CELESTINA: Who am I then, Sempronio? Have you ever seen me anywhere else but in the prostitution scene? Shut up and stop cursing my gray hair, for I am an old woman as God made me and no worse than anybody else. I live from my profession as every professional lives from his: honestly.

By trying to distinguish the respective modes through which sense structures in the fictional worlds of the *Libro* and the *Celestina* are presented with respect to their interpretive function (the key words were "contradiction" and "subjectivity"), we have moved onto a third level of the field of textual strategies: How is the relationship presented between stocks of experience on the one hand, and the protagonists' types of behavior or actions on the other? How is the motivational relevance of knowledge presented? If we were to apply the standards of contemporary theories of identity, then we would have to conclude (which admittedly would be senseless for a hermeneutically reflected interpretation) that the first-person protagonist of the *Libro* has a divided consciousness.[14] For in many passages, individual experiences (again, without any attempt to mediate them) are bound to contrary plot motivations. When Don Amor introduces the archpriest to the arts of love in the second part of the book, the first-person protagonist tries to turn back the God of Love, cursing him for tempting his holy soul; when Doña Venus provides similar instructions, his gratitude knows no bounds. In two passages from the fifth part of the book, there is a similarly crass opposition that projects an event from the fictional plot, namely the procuress's death, on the horizon of future actions: the motif of the *memento mori* in Trotaconventos's epitaph is a summons to enjoy the pleasures of this life before it is too late—yet it also reminds us of the duty to lead a virtuous life, the only way to avert God's punishment after death. The experiences consummated by the protagonists are indifferent to the actions connected to them; far from ascribing a split consciousness to the first-person protagonist, readers of the *Libro* are more likely for long stretches to lose sight of and stop integrating—not the least because of this indifference—the diverse meaning complexes built into the structure of the narrative.

In the *Celestina*, on the other hand, contrary perspectives on the motivational relevance of identical experiences are constantly presented within the complex role conflicts. That this interpretation is not anachronistic is shown by the prologue to the 1502 Seville edition, which stresses internal and external struggle (*lid*) as the central experience of human existence, as the central theme of the text, and as its main interpretive problem. That a reader of *La Celestina* is immediately willing to relate contrary motives to the respective protagonists in the sense of motivational conflict, while a reader of the *Libro* tends to lose sight of the protagonists as the focus of contrary motives, can be explained by the fact that contrary motives in *Celestina* are always rendered plausible by the contrary roles assigned to the respective protagonists within the framework of the plot. Calisto's servants vacillate between loyalty to their kind master and the greed and sexual drive that Celestina promises to satisfy. Melibea vacillates between the propriety of the daughter of a noble house and the growing love for Calisto in her conversations with the procuress—in the closing monologue, between her wish to end a life that has become meaningless without Calisto and the numerous responsibilities (not the least, economical) that she, as an only daughter, feels toward her solicitous parents. Even greed-driven Celestina is influenced by motherly feelings, as we have already seen in her behavior toward Pármeno. Despite the distance, the "qualitative leap" implied by the structural use of motivational conflict as textual strategy in the *Celestina* when compared with the *Libro*, the narrative plausibility of the motivational conflicts is still a long way from the subtlety that only a hundred years later will characterize the picaresque novel at its zenith as a narrative genre.[15] For there, the whole (fictional) biography of the pícaro, which is presented as unique, functions as a model for understanding his often contradictory actions. In comparison, the autobiographical flashbacks of the *Celestina* are fragmentary.

The Implicit Role of the Reader

We hope that it earlier became clear just how similar the material repertoires of the *Libro* and the *Celestina* are when we confine our attention to their semantic substance without looking at their presentation structures. As far as some parts of the *Libro* are concerned, this similarity is consolidated by distinct parallels, which the study of sources (to be sure, with quite different interests) already uncovered decades ago. Just as evident as the source of the repertoires is the threshold of selection: materials from popular poetry, but above all materials closely connected to the Christian religion, hardly appear in the *Celestina*. Connotatively at any rate, the structures of the Christian cosmos have also gone into the framework of the *tragicomedia:* life outside of society, to which Celestina and the prostitutes are damned, or Melibea's spontaneous resistance to the amiable Calisto and the persuasion of the procuress are, along with many other textual moments, symptoms of a still quite self-evident Christian line of demarcation between sin and virtue. But in the sum of their elements, both texts break through the limits and taboos of the Christian worldview. Since this worldview is transgressed on the one hand yet is denotatively or connotatively evoked by the texts on the other, we can ascertain that both of them are in a relationship of purely recursive negation to the "official culture."

At the same time, the styles of sense production ascribed to the protagonists in both texts have shown themselves to be fundamentally different. Thus Fernando de Rojas seems to start with the practical experience that each conceptual and judgmental act is dependent on the situation of the person doing the understanding and judging. Thus the shift in the relationships of sense production introduces something like a desubstantialization of phenomena into the *Celestina:* the imperturbable love of Calisto, who is rejected at first, is interpreted by himself as faithfulness, but by his servant as blockheadedness; in Melibea's eyes Celestina's age makes her particularly worthy, while for the procuress herself age is mainly decrepitude.

Of course we have not been primarily concerned with the extraction of the affinities and differences between the *Libro* and *La Celestina*. Despite its range, the multilevel textual comparison that has been carried is in the last analysis merely an essential prerequisite if we are to attempt to answer the questions raised at the beginning: How can we explain that recipients of the *Libro* and the *Celestina* have reacted and still react to similar, even largely parallel, textual repertoires, in completely different ways—sometimes with laughter, sometimes in all seriousness, and even with tears? Which structures of the (typical) communication situations of both texts were implicated in the function of preventing their semantic potential for negation from encroaching on the audience's everyday sense production? A few observations on the reader's (text-immanent) role and on the *Sitz im Leben* (which can only be reconstrued from contexts external to the text) will provide us with perspectives to answer our questions about period typologies and styles of communication.

In the *Libro*'s prose prologue, which is interspersed with the cognitive structures of medieval theological exegesis, the recipient is first of all assigned, as could be expected, the role of the sinner who is worried about the state of his soul and who is thus capable of learning from exempla:

And I compiled this new book, setting out some of the treacherous paths, secret ways, and ruses of foolish worldly love, which many employ in order to sin. If men or women who wish to save themselves read this in the right spirit, then they will be able to choose and let themselves be guided by it. And they will be able to say with the Psalmist: The Path of Truth, et cetera. Even those of lesser intellect will not founder, for when obstinate folk read or contemplate evil, which they do make or intend with their evil ruses, and when their multifarious arts of seduction, which they use for sin and the beguilement of women, are made public, then they repent and do not despise their own reputation; for he is without feeling who despises his own reputation—so sayeth the law. And they will love themselves more than sin, for the duty of human love begins with one's self—so is it decreed. And they will reject and abominate the paths and ruses of foolish love, which cause souls to founder and fall into God's wrath, shorten life, make for a bad reputation and dishonor, and which visit the body with many troubles.

Surprisingly, there is after this a complete reversal in the prologue's instructions as to reception:

On the other hand, since sinning is something human, those who would like to abandon themselves to foolish love, which I do not recommend, might find here some way thither. And thus can this my book say to everyone, to every man and every woman, to the reasonable and unreasonable, to him who recognizes the good and chooses deliverance and acts in the Light of God, as well as to him who cultivates the foolish love that he commits: I will give you understanding, et cetera. And I beg everyone and advise him who sees or hears it that in his soul he attend well to three things: first, that he may understand my intention and take into account why I am writing and the inner meaning of the content, and not the ugly sound of the words; for it is always so that the words serve the intention and not the intention the words. And God knows that it was not my intention to give cause to sin nor to speak badly; rather it was my intention to call to mind right action and to proffer examples for good manners and admonishing patterns for deliverance; and so that all would be initiated and could better protect themselves from such secret ways used by many for foolish love.

With respect to our main questions, it is particularly interesting that the narrator-author quite decisively distances himself from the "sinful" manner of reception—whether the archpriest of Hita actually was the author or his real name has remained unknown, whether this disavowal is to be taken seriously or is asserted purely for his own protection. For the final sentences of the prologue just quoted are counting on a recipient for whom it is self-evident that he takes on a role and can use the text in a manner that is bound neither to the author's express intention nor to the Christian commandments. Two stanzas, one from the beginning and one from the end of the *Libro*, concretize our conception of that communication situation, which the text attributes to itself in order to reserve a particular freedom of sense production for its audience:

> I, the book, am related to every instrument: how I talk will depend on whether you play me well or badly; open me up and stop wherever you want so that I'll speak; if you know how to play me, you'll always have me in your mind. (stanza 70)

> Everybody who hears it can, if he knows how to invent good poetry, add and improve, if he wants: it [the book] should pass from hand to hand, to everyone who wants it, like the ball with the ladies: everyone who can, should take it. (stanza 1629)

"The book should be played like a musical instrument": If we assemble the hints about the organization of reception from these stanzas and take the verb "play" seriously, then we can stake out a new position in the debate that has already been waged for over a century about the intended meaning of the *Libro*.[16] For the attitude that the text recalls in the audience meets all of John Huizinga's criteria for characterizing the situation of play.[17] (1) The *Libro* does not provide readers with a binding motivation for their acts of reading, but the author is counting on the fact that the recipients' dispose over a certain competence in games of love and poetry as well as over rules with which they can reciprocally coordinate their receptive actions. In the prose prologue, he even points out that the book itself can be used as material for learning these rules: "And I put this new book together in order to provide instructions and examples of metrical language, of rhymes, and of composition." (2) With the invitation in stanza 1629 to add new poems to the book and to improve on his own pieces, the author is assigning participatory roles to himself and to his readers in a poetry game. (3) Now this poetic game, as countless formulations imply, can be well or poorly mastered: hence the author and the audience are in a situation where they compete with each other – the situation of a (latent) poetry contest.

Nearly forty years ago, Ramón Menéndez Pidal had already located the *Libro* within the milieu of minstrelsy (*arte de juglaría*) on the basis of the passages steering reception.[18] In the Spanish Middle Ages, there was scarcely any demarcation between "minstrel" and "goliardic" poetry, and thus it is thoroughly plausible for Menéndez Pidal to support his hypothesis about the pragmatics of the *Libro* by arguing that minstrel techniques might have been interjected into the situation of the goliardic levity. To this there is very little to add, except perhaps to note, as a contribution to greater precision, that indeed there are forms in the *Libro* that, if taken literally, would presuppose an oral communication situation, but that they no more definitively prove that orality was the primary or even authorially intended form of the poetry game than does Menéndez Pidal's discovery in a fifteenth-century volume of minstrelsy of an announcement for "the archpriest's book." Even in the reception of a single reader, the formulas of minstrelsy connote a particular, originally oral, communication situation and hence might, but not necessarily, evoke receptive attitudes bound to orality. Thus it is quite possible (a possibility we will return to in the next section) that we will have to regard the importation of the *Libro* into a minstrel's repertoire as a "reoralization," *sit venia verbo*. Here we would like to bear in mind that the particular form of the audience's subjectivity was arbitrary sense production, and it was precisely this subjectivity on which the *Libro*'s stock of meanings, its development of a purely recursive negation of official culture, was counting. Such a distance from the supply of meanings, which permits arbitrariness in the first place, belonged to the structural peculiarities of a communication situation removed from everyday life and which staged itself as a game with poetry. That such a situation could also be objectified in special forms of sociability during the course of its institutionalization is shown by phenomena like *gaya ciencia*—the *puys* or *minnesang* in late medieval Catalonian, Provençal, northern French, and German literature. If it is correct that the *Libro* implies a role for the reader that allows the freedom of arbitrary sense production, then we can assume that the structural markers in this text, which we have labeled with "inconsistence," "contradiction," and "indifference," were not experienced by fourteenth- and fifteenth-century audiences as lacking something, as being insufficiently concrete from a semantic point of view. Rather, we should imagine it the other way around, that a closed plot, like that of the *Celestina*, would have run counter to the arbitrariness of the poetry game's sense production. However strongly divergent in details the instructions about reception are with which the tragicomedy's sequence of editions is framed by the prologue and epilogue, they nonetheless agree that the work should be read or heard in a serious mood. But in the context of mutual solemnity, *La Celestina* seems to be able to depend on its audience's subjectivity as an instance of sense production just as the *Libro* depended on general laughter. In the prologue of the Seville edition of 1502 we read:

> So I wouldn't be surprised if the work before you had caused strife and discord among its readers, had sown dissent among them, since every one of them will have tendered his judgment according to his own will. . . . The first age of life smudges and tears these pages, the second is unable to read them, the third, merry youth, doesn't agree with them. Many gnaw the bone of no nourishment (I mean the whole story), hastening through the text like a stretch of road and putting to no good use what was strewn about in this story; others pick out pretty phrases and platitudes, praising them with passion and letting that pass which would have been more useful for themselves. But those who are pleased by the entire work leave the course of the story to the side,

grasping its more profound sense for its own purposes, laughing over witticisms, preserving the aphorisms and sayings of philosophers in their memory in order to induce them into their own actions and designs at a suitable opportunity. Thus if ten people gathered together to watch this comedy, and if, as is usually the case, they were as different among themselves as the above-mentioned ages, then who would deny that strife would grow up around an object that can be understood in so many different manners.

Now how can we more narrowly characterize an implied reader that, confronted with a text repertoire for the most part similar to the *Libro*'s, produces a contrary reaction? The rhymed epilogue of Alonso de Proaza, who saw the Seville edition through its printing (*corrector de la impresión*) points us toward a possible answer. According to Proaza, the work is correctly called a tragicomedy, and not a comedy, because a sympathetic reader would be moved to tears by the fate of Calisto and Melibea. At the same time, Proaza addresses the "sympathetic reader" (*discreto lector*) as someone reciting Calisto's role (we see that the text is supposed to be performed with various roles for recital) and gives him the following recommendation:

> If you, as reciter of Calisto's role, wish to induce greater attentiveness in your listeners, then make sure that you succeed in speaking between your teeth, sometimes with relish, hope, and passion, sometimes angry and quite confused. When reciting, imitate a thousand manners of speaking, use all of them in the questions and answers, laugh and cry by occasion.

The task assigned the reciter here would nowadays belong to the production of illusion; we are quite accustomed to regard identification as a type of reception produced by illusion. The particular form of audience subjectivity supplied by *La Celestina*'s text would not be subjectivity in the sense that set pieces are arbitrarily chosen from the whole repertoire and then assembled into a given configuration, but a subjectivity that realizes itself by choosing a protagonist as a model for identification in order to then manipulate the plot in various ways toward seriousness or even tears. Identification as a subjective attitude of reception is made possible by the astonishing complexity (compared to the *Libro*) of the protagonists, by refracting unilinear roles, by what we have called motivational conflicts.

So we see that the concept of "subjectivity" does not sufficiently characterize the style of sense production in the early modern period. The textual focus for such subjectivity must also be taken into account in order to describe it as a specific style of sense production, all the more so since different forms of subjectivity also maintain specific relationships with the everyday action of the recipients.[19]

Sitz im Leben

Whenever efforts to reconstruct the *Sitz im Leben* are directed toward institution-alized communication situations (and not toward unique or individually specific implementations), they steer, at the phenomenal level of the past world, everyday knowledge, or more exactly, communicative competence. This means that the question of the *Sitz im Leben* cannot be merged into a description of the respective forms for realizing text-immanent readers' roles, but rather that it is a question, as far as readers are concerned, of the prerequisites for realizing these roles, and, for authors, of historically specific, communicative stores of knowledge as the *Weil-Motiv* in the sense of Alfred Schütz ("horizon of feasibility") for generating text-immanent readers' roles.[20]

These quite general comments about the status of the *Sitz im Leben* appear at the beginning of this final section in order to make two points perfectly clear. On the one hand, we definitively have to transgress the sphere of textual immanence. (Hugo Kuhn has shown that, hermeneutically speaking, an indirect text-immanent reconstruction of the *Sitz im Leben* was one of the temptations particu-lar to medieval scholarship.)[21] But on the other hand it must also be clear how little it helps us to know that the *Libro* was written in Alfonso XI's Castile during an age of continual domestic intrigue and constant warfare between the petty kingdoms of the Iberian Peninsula, or that *La Celestina* appeared during the rule of the *Reyes Católicos*, when a modern political and cultural leadership, by in-tegrating the five Iberian kingdoms, first began to consolidate what would later become the Spain of Charles V. If we are serious about reconstructing the *Sitz im Leben*, then we must have recourse to the much more specific — and, some-times, positivistic — reports of expert medieval knowledge.[22]

The impression that the *Libro* includes an expectation of specialized theological understanding, a communicative competence that had to be particularly sensitive to religious texts as media, has been confirmed (as far as medievalists can) by the state of the three oldest manuscripts. They all date from the turn of the fourteenth to the fifteenth century, "and all three clearly indicate that the text circulated in edu-cated milieux, for manuscript T comes from the Cathedrale of Toledo, manuscript S from the College of San Bartolomé in the University of Salamanca, and manu-script I must have a similar origin."[23] In all likelihood from the last third of the fourteenth century, a translation of the text existed from the original Castilian into the medieval ancestor of modern Portuguese, and just a little later there must have been a Latin poetics, which quotes two stanzas out of the *Libro* as vulgate exempli-fications of its poetic rules. On the other hand, the famous fifteenth-century *can-cioneros* do not, at least explicitly, refer to the *Libro*, which can certainly be ex-plained by the absence of a "rhetorical and beautiful eloquence" (*retorica e pulchra eloquençia*), as the *Libro*'s proem formulates it. This sort of evidence, both nega-tive and positive, the manifest localization of this text in a milieu that Jacques Le

Goff has called the "intellectuals of the Middle Ages,"[24] is completely backed up by Menéndez Pidal's meticulously reconstructed biography of Alfonso de Paradinas, whose name, in the signature of the copyist, ends manuscript S.[25] He came from Peñaranda, today a small town in the diocese of Salamanca, and as a student in 1417 lived in the College of San Bartolomé: "It was undoubtedly during those years, when he copied for the College library the codex, which was preserved there until 1807." Paradinas was later a professor of canon law in Salamanca, and during his apparently ninety years of life traveled twice to Rome, where he had a hostel and a church built in honor of Saint James (Santiago); in Spain he rose as far as the archdean of Ledesma (in the diocese of Salamanca), and later even became bishop of the neighboring diocese of Ciudad Rodrigo.

Although we do not owe the text, but only the most important manuscript to Alfonso de Paradinas, his exemplary clerical career is of great relevance for literary history, since it proves that "official culture" can hardly have censured him for his intensive occupation with a (potentially) heterodox book. In contrast to the expectations based on our experience of contemporary religion's institutional reality, it must be understood that being a priest, a professor of theology, and a bishop was first of all a job; and certain "avocational" life forms belonged to this job like the game that did not shrink back from blasphemy and the medium of which was the *Libro*. No one felt obliged to harmonize these avocational life forms with the solemnity of the priestly office.

Our embedding of the text in situations where medieval students and clerics are engaged in intellectual play receives a final confirmation in two observations about the manuscript. The paper used was of an extraordinarily high quality. And on many of the pages the script luxuriates in the drolleries so typical of Gothic manuscripts (but, of each and every subject? of each and every milieu?), none of which derives from Alfonso de Paradinas.[26] These (somewhat careless) drawings of fabulous creatures, grimaces, and hands with pointing forefingers may be functionally interpreted as extratextual reading guides. But seen as forms whose background is the written text corpus, they surely belong to those transgressional borderline malformations in which Bakhtin sees the most certain symptom of the carnivalesque fulfillment of life.[27] Despite the subjective style of sense production demanded by the *Libro*, we suspect that it was precisely the insularity of the carnivalesque poetry game that could prevent the arbitrarily generated figures of sense from encroaching on the everyday world. Of course, insularity does not have to mean here that the communication situation is spatially or temporally distant from the everyday world. It could have very well been made concrete simply by the marked division of roles between the priest's profession and the intellectual games of clerics.

A profusion of unbiased historical factors comes together in the certainty that the *Sitz im Leben* of *La Celestina* was that humanistically educated urban milieu of citizens (admittedly, being "bourgeois" in the Spain of the High Middle Ages mainly meant being neither cleric nor aristocrat) on which the economic and cultural politics of the *Reyes Católicos* relied. Above all there is the recipients' presumable educational level, which, with respect to a classical education and in contrast to the *Libro*, has become more complex by several dimensions, but which no longer presupposes specialized theological knowledge. There is the woodcut in the 1502 edition, which turns up lightly retouched in other Spanish prints whose derivation is unequivocally humanistic, and there are the many humanistic conventions in the final printed version.[28] But most of all, there is the biography of the author of the *Celestina*, Fernando de Rojas, for which literary history has accumulated an abundance of details. "He was born in 1465. His academic title, to which he alludes in the preface to his *El auctor a un su amigo*, was acquired through the study of law. From around 1517 on he lived in Talavera de la Reina, where he became mayor and where he died in 1541. His education can only be guessed at indirectly, and we know nothing about his other literary activity. In the final analysis he found it best to make as little as possible out of his Jewish origins."[29] What this information corroborates and possibly explains is clear: Fernando de Rojas could have acquired the education manifested in *La Celestina* without belonging to either the clerisy or the nobility. Moreover, it suggests that the discrepancy, so obvious to the modern reader, between the plot and the two prologues, both of which can be undoubtedly ascribed to him, should be attributed to the typical situation of a *cristiano nuevo*—that is, the pressure of having to conceal a heterodox worldview behind an appearance of perfect congruence with Christian orthodoxy. For the denouement—which means the death of practically all of the protagonists—is presented in the prologues as an instructive exemplar of the inevitability of divine punishment for sin, although in each case, more or less clearly, the connection between "sin" and the cause of death seems contingent. Quite possibly the interment of Fernando de Rojas behind a Franciscan cowl (his step-father at any rate was interrogated by the Inquisition) is just as clear a symptom for the double life imposed on the *cristianos nuevos* as is the relationship between the author's prologues and *Celestina*'s plot.

All of these unbiased historical factors still do not add up to an explanation why the dominant form of reception of *La Celestina* was subjective identification with individual protagonists. It is not so much that the communicative situation of the closet drama alluded to in the epilogue could not also be demonstrated elsewhere as a typically humanistic form of educated social life. It is a question of the grounds on which we can grasp the connection between this form of reception and the social status of the recipients. We can approach a preliminary hypothesis when we compare the audience's modes for assuming roles in bourgeois social life in (roughly) the eighteenth century with those of the High Middle Ages. The Enlightenment's implicit (or in the beginning, explicit) aesthetics of the novel and the drama presupposed that the audience's core of personal identity or—normatively—its "pure humanity" would prevail as the basis of identification with fictional protagonists. During the Middle Ages, on the other hand (this also speaks for our analysis of the *Libro*), the audience's pleasure in the playful assumption of text-immanent roles seems to have grown, aside from a few exceptions, in direct proportion to the distance of this role from their recipients' identity. Medieval identification, if we want to use the term anachronistically, turned into participation in a masquerade, within the framework of which, quite in contradistinction to the eighteenth century, even individual recipients could continually change masks and roles.

Our considerations have brought us to the final thesis that the "official cultures" in the Middle Ages were protected from negative stocks of knowledge by keeping them at a certain distance from one another, whereas ever since the early modern period the uniqueness of the reader's or spectator's individuality has taken over this distancing function. To put it even more generally, the position held by a communicative game, whose conventions stage role exchanges between performers and audience as well as between authors and readers and whose medium was a text with indefinite contours, was taken over by the triad of the (solitary) author as creator, the text as the author's work and object of the reading, and the (solitary) reader as a sympathetic individual ready to identify with the reading.

Those intellectuals who invest so much verbiage in complaining about the functional insignificance of literature and art did not need to wait until the twentieth century to find out that the solitary role of the reader could be quite effective in protecting "official cultures" from the serious consequences of negation. As early as 1758 in his famous "Lettre à d'Alembert," Rousseau formulated his moral verdict against a species of drama that merely indulges itself in self-love and self-pity:

> Mais n'adoptons point ces spectacles exclusifs qui renferment tristement un petit nombre de gens dans un antre obscur; qui les tiennent craintifs et immobiles dans le silence et l'inaction. . . . Plantez au milieu d'une place un piquet couronné de fleurs, rassemblez-y le peuple et vous aurez une fête. Faites mieux encore: donnez les spectateurs en spectacle; rendez-les acteurs eux-mêmes; faites que chacun se voit et s'aime dans les autres, afin que tous en soient mieux unis.[30]

It was not to confirm Rousseau's argument that I went to the trouble of reconstructing two communication situations at the threshold between the late Middle Ages and the early modern period. Rather I found it important, by working my way through two specific texts, to problematize a belief in the anthropologically constant status of certain communication structures that are all too often taken for granted—but that are simply modern.

Chapter 7
Who Were the *Philosophes*?

Philosophie, the Basic Structure of the Enlightenment

The General Structure of the Historical Course of the Concept

In theoretical discourse, as well as in generally educated conversation, the word Enlightenment can be used both as a designation for a typological concept and as a name. The concept Enlightenment is an abstraction of those historical processes in which old stocks of collective knowledge are replaced or revised by new ones, with the new knowledge presenting itself as a more adequate representation of reality. On the other hand, as a name, Enlightenment refers to a single strand of the various historical strands that went into the concept's formation and that can be specified in four ways: (1) it occurred mainly in eighteenth-century Europe; (2) by shifting the dominant images of society from a theocentric to an anthropocentric basis, it effected not only the contents of collective stocks of knowledge but also and above all their basic principle of constitution; (3) hence it established stocks of knowledge whose basic principles have not undergone revision up until the present and are still considered adequate; and (4) in the eighteenth century the Enlightenment was understood first of all as a historical development but at the same time as an effective orientation or motivation for action.

By reconstructing and presenting the concepts *philosophe* and *philosophie*, it is possible to recapitulate the essential phases of the eighteenth-century Enlightenment. For if *philosophie* outlines the Enlightenment's content and way of think-

133

ing, then the *philosophe* is its subject, or more precisely, the role to which the task of constituting the new collective knowledge and questioning the old is assigned, and also the role whose institutionalization accompanied the new knowledge's step-by-step assumption of socially founding functions. If such elements from collective knowledge, which effect the formulation of other, particular elements of knowledge, can be defined as *basic* concepts,[1] then by conceiving the *philosophe* as a subject of the Enlightenment and *philosophie* as the direction of its thought and line of action, it follows that both of these concepts are indeed basic concepts of the Enlightenment. For the unity of Enlightenment thought is based on the conviction that all of its individual elements were coordinated with the cognitive style of the *philosophe* and at the same time are supposed to ground philosophical action.

As a fundamental Enlightenment concept, the history of the *philosophe* begins by dissociating an interactive role characteristic of seventeenth-century court society from its still "feudal" origins and ends by setting the stage for the incorporation into bourgeois society of a professional role whose institutional foundations in France were created by the empire. It is between these two types of society that the conceptual history of the *philosophe* makes the history of the Enlightenment comprehensible: from his constitution as a subject of the Enlightenment in which reflection and social action converge, it feeds into the polemics between *philosophes* and *antiphilosophes;* from the canonization of the *philosophes* as the elite of the ancien régime up to the normative status of the canon of their writings during the revolutionary years and finally up to its transposition into a powerfully legitimizing horizon of a past detached from the present.

Methodological Problems

Since *philosophe* and *philosophie* and their derivatives are unusually well documented, their high value for social history has been recognized since the second half of the eighteenth century, and they have often been used historiographically,[2] the following presentation is faced with an especially comprehensive body of material. Yet it is neither a question of optimizing the "definition" of *philosophe*[3] and *philosophie* in the eighteenth century, since the effort of arriving at semantically unequivocal definitions is bound to flatten precisely that abundance of meanings and applications to which conceptual history as a method owes its social-historical status in the first place; nor should we conclude anything about the "thing signified" directly from the signifier, since our view of the concept *philosophe* as a symptom shows that our epistemological goal is located "behind" its semantics. And so our hypothesis is focused on the notion that the ancien régime had provided practically ideal conditions for the development of enlightened knowledge, the constitution of its subject, and the institutionalization of its communicative space. In other words, the rise of the *philosophes* in the eighteenth century is closely connected with the declining "public involvement" of established groups in government and society and with the origination of a new "bourgeois" public together with its tendency to exhibit solidarity with the politically persecuted.

The pertinent sources raise two other problems. One concerns the contextual use of the concepts *philosophe* and *philosophie* in France between the late seventeenth and early nineteenth centuries. However striking the recognizable semantic change for this time might be, semantic differences between different positions within given historical phases are rare. To be sure, speech acts, common to the use of the concept by proponents as well as opponents of the Enlightenment, are diametrically opposed as self-apotheosis and condemnation, yet the concepts remain almost identical for both contexts, even down to the finest nuances when regarded semantically. It is much the same for the dictionaries, which more frequently serve as part of a polemic opposing *philosophes* and *antiphilosophes* than as confirmation of the acceptance of different sense variants by the speech norm.

Second, the enormously broad horizon of significance behind *philosophe* and *philosophie*—it seems to have reached its greatest extent between 1680 and 1820—forces us to concentrate our presentation on those semantic structures in which both concepts were effective over and beyond long-term constant stores of sense potential. Hence we will only touch in passing on the fact that the predicate *philosophe* between 1680 and 1820 could also mean "friend of wisdom," someone who "reflected on the natural causes of phenomena and on maxims of behavior," as well as "schools of thinkers in antiquity," a didactic profession in all of its historical forms, but also the "holder of the *pierre philosophale*." Instead we will reconstruct two levels of meaning that make up the particularity of the conceptual history of *philosophe* during the Enlightenment. First of all, there is the relationship of the *philosophe* to society; he can be regarded with respect to his detachment from society, which in turn can be interpreted as superiority or eccentricity. In other contexts, in contrast, the concept thematizes various modes of performing subjective actions and behavior in society, so that the *philosophe* is not far from the social sophistication of the *honnête homme* and can adjust his thought and action to the purposes of "common good" and "equality." The second level of sense, with which the long-range constant spectrum of *philosophe* in the Enlightenment is extended, contains two opposing attitudes toward intellectual style. Beyond all scholarship and intellectual brilliance, the Enlightenment philosophers in their own positive self-image were characterized by the strict foundation of their thought in human reason, the "unprejudiced" observation of their natural environment, and self-reflection as the consequent self-determination of thought and action. The polemic image of the *philosophes* as enemies, which had been worked up by the *antiphilosophes* since the middle of the eighteenth century, was based on the repolarization of the individual elements of this figure of identification: the claim of self-determination becomes *fanatisme*; the principle of reason, *esprit de système*; social dignity, the presumption of authority.

Throwing off the Interactive Role of Social Conventions: The *Philosophe* as Stoic and Misanthrope (ca. 1670–1730)

A nonverbal motivation for the extension of the concept *philosophe*, which conclusively demonstrates that etymology is insufficient to understand its meaning in French,[4] can be found in the aristocratic and above all courtly forms of interaction during the seventeenth century and their function in regulating the aristocracy's affectivity.[5] Appeals to self-respect (*amour-propre*), moralizing the repetitive behavior of the interactive partner (*plaire*), and finally the adjustment of behavior to others' expectations and the expectations of expectations—these were the basic principles of social intercourse that were supposed to secure the regulation of affectivity. They were supplemented by the more specifically interactive maxim of *sincérité*[6] but found themselves in a precarious relationship to it from the very beginning. Simply because honesty cannot always please, symbolic forms must have soon been generated, which on the one hand supported the claim to *sincérité* but on the other turned out to be a mask behind which the courtier could dissimilate knowledge, experiences, and emotions; which was Rémond des Cours's experience at court: "C'est lá où les gens ont le plus d'honnêteté et le moins de sincérité."[7]

Those who were really serious about *sincérité* would have to withdraw from courtly society and get by without its "group narcissism,"[8] within which the fulfillment of the new interactive norms was both confirmed and considered worthwhile. To be a *philosophe* became the role of the upright person who, because of *sincérité,* maintained a certain distance from "good society," and cultivated self-reflection and those feelings of self-esteem that depend on the effect they have on others. The main role in Molière's *Misanthrope* (1666) was already motivated by the experience of the incompatibility of "honesty" and "being pleasing"; its reception earned for it the label *philosophe* ("Ce chagrin philosophe est un peu sauvage"), although a milder "philosophical"—stoic—attitude not so detached from social intercourse was considered preferable.[9] Then in 1678, La Rochefoucauld provided a less ambivalent maxim:

> L'attachement ou l'indifférence que les philosophes avaient pour la vie n'était qu'un goût de leur amour-propre, dont on ne doit non plus disputer que du goût de la langue, ou du choix des couleurs.[10]

Here it is confirmed that the degree of distance to and from society was dependent on the specific formulation of the *amour-propre*. It would be possible to see the move toward self-reflection as a decisive phase on the way to anthropocentricity, as the constitutional principle of enlightened knowledge. The fact that in the beginning social detachment was bound up with it shows, at any rate, why the mental point of departure for the Enlightenment was a "private inner space."[11]

Late seventeenth-century dictionaries indicate that, from a sociological point of view, it was already quite current to designate this excentric role by the predicate *philosophe* during the lifetime of Louis XIV. Moreover, they also take notice of two contrary evaluations of the phenomenon. In *Richelet* (1680), the neutral definition of *philosophe* ("Celui qui s'est détaché des choses du monde par la connoissance qu'il a de leur peu de valeur") is followed simply by an entry that confirms the negative symbolic value of the role ("Ce mot se prend quelquefois en mauvais part, & alors il signifie une espèce d'esprit qui ne se soucie de rien, une manière de fou insensible").[12] The same sense can be found in *Furetière* (1690)[13] and in the *Academy Dictionary* (1695): "Il se dit aussi quelquefois absolument d'un homme qui, par libertinage d'esprit se met au-dessus des devoirs & des obligations ordinaires de la vie civile & chrétienne."[14] To be a *philosophe* outside of society was obviously a new attitude, which on the one hand was experienced as a break with social conventions, as lacking a sense of duty, and even as madness. But on the other hand, the position of the *philosophe* outside of aristocratic society was also seen as the condition and expression of his superiority: "On appelle aussi *philosophe*, un homme sage, qui mène une vie tranquille & retiré, hors de l'embarras des affaires."[15] This already requires *philosophie*— that is, a study of "nature" and "morality" grounded in *raisonnement*, a power unsullied by the ideas of the "common people," which still seemed reconcilable with natural science and Christianity.[16]

Since the distribution of the meanings of *philosophe* among the various upper-class milieux and contexts of use is not sufficiently obvious, the questions of just who the *philosophes* of the late seventeenth century may have been and who admired or condemned their social reserve cannot be unambiguously answered by conceptual history. In the same way, however, that domestic opposition to Bourbon absolutism found an example in the aristocracy repressed by Bourbon power (and not in the bourgeoisie),[17] the members of the old nobility, if anybody, must have regarded the courtly culture of interaction as a provocation, insofar as it enabled the crossing of class lines and reduced the exclusivity of their social rank. So they were happy to avoid the milieu at court; already at the turn of the eighteenth century, they seem to have been accused of *incivilité* because of their lukewarm conformity with the new, heavily moralized norms of conduct—and precisely by those social climbers in the service of absolutism.[18] Saint-Simon, a member of the old nobility, provides a linguistic piece of evidence for his peers' disposition to put a positive value on social excentricity by simply listing the virtues of Marshal Catinat, who had a lower rank in the social hierarchy (withdrawal from society, contempt for wealth, simple life-style).[19] In a similar manner, Marais appraised the royal chancellor d'Aguesseau's marriage, one that was quite inappropriate from the point of view of class: "M. de Faljoran est un philosophe, qui ne se soucioit de rien."[20]

If a parliamentary adviser like Marais could agree with Saint-Simon to reevaluate positively the previously negative secondary sense of philosophe and philosophie over against the préjugés,[21] then this indicates that in the early eighteenth century an originally aristocratic negligence of disciplined social norms began to insinuate itself into the high bourgeoisie and also that a philosophie critical of authority—for all of its protestations of traditional proximity to theology[22]—would necessarily become opposed to religion, much to the sorrow of the Jesuits.[23] And in fact, at the Paris Jesuit Collège Louis-le-Grand in May 1720, *Le philosophe à la mode*, a satirical play by Father J.-A. Du Cerceau, was performed in order to warn students against withdrawing, like the negative protagonist Narcisse, from orderly social intercourse and from the duties of submission as well as against the development of their own, unauthorized theories:

> Le Philosophe donc n'est chargé que de lui
> Et tout autre soin remet sur autrui;
> Redevable à lui seul, et borné dans lui-même,
> Il n'a qu'un seul devoir, il s'aime.[24]

This obviously was meant as a necessary attempt at immunization, for a detailed review of the performance tells us that already in the title Du Cerceau was denouncing an unfortunately widespread and pernicious new attitude: "Il l'appelle philosophe à la mode, parce qu'il paroit, dit-it, que cette philosophie a grand nombre de sectateurs."[25] Hence the semantic development of *philosophie* from a free-thinking aristocratic gesture in preservation of the old class hierarchy to the philosophe as the "subject of bourgeois Enlightenment," as it later appeared, did not take place immediately in a straight line but was transmitted by the high bourgeoisie, with anticourt eccentricity merging into a withdrawal from the more general social norms. At first this individualistic social disassociation excluded socially relevant "political" action, and yet it created exactly its essential preconditions: only through a distance from traditional social norms and on the basis of the self-reflection it made possible was the *philosophe* able to formulate his enlightening function—in order then to embody socially relevant action in a new sense.

Constituting the Enlightenment Subject: The Role of the *Philosophe* as Convergence of Reflection and Social Action (ca. 1730–51)

How this process unfolded in detail cannot be reconstructed from available information. In the 1730s, however, there is an accumulation of evidence that a new sense of *philosophie* that was no longer purely scientific and unpolitical but critical of prejudice and authority had pushed out of the private space of retirement and that the *philosophe* was increasingly allotted the role of social enlightenment. The earliest striking piece of evidence and at the same time a factor in this shift in meaning was Voltaire's *Lettres anglaises ou philosophiques*, which was published anonymously in Amsterdam in 1734 and reprinted at least eleven times by 1793, although the French Parliament had immediately interdicted it and condemned it to be symbolically scourged and burned: "comme scandaleux, contraire à la Religion, aux bonnes moeurs et au respect dû aux Puissances."[26] Voltaire was putting his own role in the new concept of *philosophie* into perspective by taking Bacon as the prototype of the *grand philosophe* who had established *philosophie expérimentale* and who had enlightened not only himself but also his fellow human beings ("s'éclairer soi-même et les autres").[27] At the same time, he praised Locke's sensualism as an example of a philosophy guided by reason, which, to be sure, distinguished itself from belief but which could never cause as much uproar as religious zealots: "Jamais les Philosophes ne feront une Secte de Religion." And finally, Voltaire compared the French practice of aristocratic art patronage with the much greater official recognition and endowment in high offices, as was the case with deserving writers in England.[28]

This model of a scientifically enlightening and yet ideologically neutral *philosophie* played down its own threat, but it obviously already possessed such a great power of attraction and had managed to conceal its antireligious critical potential so well that for several editions (1732–40) the Jesuit *Dictionnaire de Trévoux* made the *philosophe* equal to the stoic. It had nothing but praise for his strict rejection of cringing servility before the "grandees," explained the uniform distribution of the competence of his *philosophie* among logic, ethics, physics, metaphysics, and, in contrast to earlier editions, granted a high moral significance to his self-reflective attitude and detachment from society. It even tried to canonize him in a positive sense:

> PHILOSOPHE, se dit aussi d'un esprit ferme, & élevé au-dessus des autres; qui est guéri de la préocupation, & des erreurs populaires, & désabusé des vanités du monde, qui aime les honnêtes plaisirs; qui préfère la vie privée au fracas du monde; ami fidèle, peu dangereux ennemi; utile, si on le met en oeuvre, content de n'y être pas; atentif au présent, peu inquiet pour l'avenir.[29]

That this affirmation of the superiority of the "true philosophers" to the people is disengaged from a subjective feeling of superiority ("Un vrai philosophe ne s'élève point fièrement au-dessus du Vulgaire, comme s'il avoit seul la raison en partage") lets us sense how two decades later the opponents of the Enlightenment will play the *philosophes'* demand for leadership against their popularity.

However, the decisive turning point in the conceptual history of the *philosophe* during the Enlightenment is marked by the year 1743, when Diderot deliberately inserted the still-developing new sense of the word in his very first publication.[30] In the debate among his contemporaries, whether the honorable title of *philosophe* justly pertained only to the devout Christian[31] or rather — instead of the misanthrope — to the urbane and virtuous citizen and paterfamilias,[32] the decisive event was provided by the "materialist" Dumarsais in his treatise *Le philosophe.* For a while it was circulated in manuscript and was first published in an anonymous collection of pamphlets, *Nouvelles libertés de penser* (Amsterdam, 1743). By 1777 it had been published in a dozen other contexts with changing titles and attributions of authorship (Voltaire, Helvétius, etc.), sometimes with slight changes in the text, and also appeared in the *Encyclopédie.*[33] In this text, which had a sustained effect on the Enlightenment self-understanding of roles, the aspect of self-reflection, previously always dependent on social detachment, converged with that socially relevant action, whose postulation had begun, for instance, with the *Lettres philosophiques.* This convergence became possible because educated society (*le monde*) as a horizon of reference, in front of which the role of the *philosophe* could assume various forms, was no longer occupied by a framework of rigid, highly complicated interactive norms, but by a circle of potential recipients: the public was on its way to political institutionalization. By opening himself up to the public, the *philosophe* found a task that gave him a feeling of self-esteem that could never have been yielded by the normative framework of the honnête homme:

> Notre philosophe ne se croit pas en exil en ce monde; il ne croit point être en pays ennemi, il veut jouir en sage Econome des biens que la nature lui offre . . . c'est un honnête homme qui veut plaire et se rendre utile.[34]

On the one hand, the action of the *philosophe* is grounded in society and for society by free and unprejudiced empirical observation ("une infinité d'observations particulières"), and, on the other, mainly in the gesture of self-reflection, whose convergence with action is manifested by the machine metaphor so dear to the eighteenth century:

> Le Philosophe est une machine humaine comme un autre homme; mais c'est une machine qui par sa constitution méchanique, réfléchit sur ses mouvemens. Les autres hommes sont déterminés à agir sans sentir ni connoître les causes qui les font mouvoir. Le Philosophe au contraire démêle les causes autant qu'il est en lui . . . c'est une horloge qui se monte pour ainsi dire quelquefois elle-même. Le Philosophe dans ses passions même n'agit qu'après réflexion; il marche dans la nuit, mais il est précédé d'un flambeau.[35]

By constituting the *philosophe* as the subject of the Enlightenment at the point where reflection and action converge, those negative aspects of meaning were screened out that up until then had been connected both with self-reflection and with the *philosophe*'s social echo. The fashionable role of the "misanthrope" and self-sufficient "thought systems" were distinguished from truly "philosophical" self-reflection,[36] just as the courtier's libertine critique of religion, his arrogance, and flattery were distinguished from the philosopher's service to society.[37] It was precisely because of such a negation of the vices once imputed to the "courtier," but also because the *honnête homme* had partly "bourgeoized" himself since the end of the seventeenth century, that this concept and the related virtues of *honnêteté* and *probité* could henceforth serve to define the main ethical components of the enlightening role of the *philosophe*.[38] In any case, the new image of his role became acceptable for larger social groups through this link with an institutionalized, by 1743 already faded, ideal social type. But at the same time, in the superficial assimilation with the unpolitical and individualistic *honnête homme*, a blind spot objectivized itself within the Enlightenment's self-image:[39] by establishing the *philosophe*'s social action in reflection and the private sphere, the enlighteners were able to overlook, repress, and deny his politically active status.

Not only do we have the first proof in the 1740s for the convergence of the concept "*philosophe*" with reflection and social action, but also, in a series of typical attitudes, the new structure of meaning seems to have already been institutionalized toward the end of the decade. So a widely read moral treatise from 1748 can present a detailed discussion of the role of the *philosophe* in, of all places, the chapter on piety — surely in order, on the one hand, to defend the *philosophes* from the already current reproach of irreligiosity, but also, on the other, to appease the reservations some had about their allegedly patronizing attitudes and charges of social agitation.[40] Argenson's entries in his diary between 1739 and 1756 confirm the decisive structural shift in the meaning norm of *philosophe* from the image of a stoic to the subject of the Enlightenment. At the same time, they elucidate the anxieties and aggression that the perception of this new social role could evoke in a representative of the aristocracy: in 1739 the Marquis still dreamed of the moderate contemplation (médiocrité) of a life at some distance from society and the sphere of power ("La Philosophie bien approfondie retranche les goûts, mais ne les éteint pas"). Twelve years later he sensed a "vent philosophique de gouvernement libre et antimonarchique" wafting over from England to France with its hostility to religion, its *matérialisme* and *fanatisme,* and that it was slowly settling into the opinions of most educated people. Could this feeling of threat only be countered with anti-Enlightenment measures? Were the new values and needs articulated by the *philosophes* incompatible with royal interests? Argenson felt that the king, weakened by the struggles with the higher courts, could still consolidate his authority if he would just put himself at the head of a *philosophie* on the side of "justice" and "reason."[41] He was forced to realize, however, that the orthodox Catholic circles at court "intolerantly" restricted the

freedom necessary for the work of the *savants philosophiques:* "Le gouvernement, effrayé par les dévots, est devenu plus censeur, plus inquisiteur, plus misér-
able sur les matières philosophiques."[42] Indeed, around this time there was an increase in the number of interdictions of texts by the state board of censorship as
well as the incarceration of literati and publishers in the Bastille.[43] Also the secret
reports compiled by the royal secret service agent, D'Hémery, between 1748 and
1753 on 453 Parisian authors is a demonstration of the state's growing insecurity
over "philosophical" writers and books.[44]

From 1751 on, this sort of defensive reaction was kindled and intensified by
the appearance of the *Encyclopédie* above all. Right at the outset, d'Alembert's
preface to the Enlightenment's most lucrative publication located its project
within the program of a *philosophie* that had been laboriously struggling for "freedom" against the "despotisme théologique" and the "goût des systèmes" but which,
as far as progress and esteem were concerned, had now outstripped its forerunners, science and literature:

> La philosophie, qui forme le goût dominant de notre siècle, semble par
> les progrès qu'elle fait parmi nous, vouloir réparer le temps qu'elle a
> perdu, et se venger de l'espèce de mépris que lui avoient marqué nos
> pères. Ce mépris est aujourd'hui retombé sur l'érudition.[45]

And in a comprehensive diagram, exempting only history and poetry, he subordinated all fields of human thought to *philosophie* — from physics and mathematics
through ethics and logic and over to "Science de Dieu" and the "Métaphysique
générale."[46] Diderot declared the whole *Encyclopédie* the trustee and pace-maker
of the new "philosophical" observational and experimental sciences: "Aujourd'hui
que la Philosophie . . . soûmet à son empire tous les objets de son ressort; que
son ton est le ton dominant, & qu'on commence à secouer le joug de l'autorité &
de l'exemple pour s'en tenir aux lois de la raison."[47] The entry "Philosophe"
repeated then Dumarsais's 1743 text, though with deletions, in particular of the
earlier equivalence with the *honnête homme.*[48] The new understanding of the
philosophe's role had become so completely autonomous and politicized in the
meantime that it had severed itself from the *honnête homme* and in the subsequent
period would no longer be defined along with it. The anonymous *Encyclopédie*
entry *"Philosophie"* (which because of the censor was first published in 1765, although edited earlier) took d'Alembert's concept over, since he, too, opposed
philosophie as an empiricocritical method of epistemology guided by reason to
blind belief in authority, to a dogmatic "esprit systematique," and to préjugés and
"passions."[49] In a discussion, the *Journal encyclopédique* emphasized exactly
these last two articles and noted with satisfaction that meanwhile the real "philosophers," who were quite distinguishable from the prolific and presumptuous "faux
philosophes," had climbed high in public esteem:

C'est un titre sans doute fort respectable que celui de Philosophe,
lorsque c'est d'après ses actions, ses écrits, & la reconnoissance publique qu'on en est décoré. . . . Le vrai Philosophe est modeste.[50]

Now if we ask which social group functioned as this "subject of the Enlightenment," then recent research has made it more than clear that a blanket allusion
to the "bourgeoisie" needs to be overhauled. The conceptual and historical evidence fits rather to the hypothesis that the Enlightenment writers had gradually
moved into a social space left open by the withdrawal of the old nobility from
the absolutistic court at the end of the seventeenth century.[51] And according to
studies on the social structure of the provincial academies, eighteenth-century
journalists, and 144 authors of the *Encyclopédie*, among whom most of our references can be found, the *philosophes* around 1750 belonged overwhelmingly to
a class-crossing, "mixed" educational elite of economically secure and, in their
economic behavior, thoroughly traditional officeholders, rentiers, and "free-
lance" scientists and technicians, whose share of clerical and aristocratic members was, to be sure, quite recessive.[52]

Conquering the Public (ca. 1751–76): The Publicity War between *Philosophes* and *Anti-Philosophes* and the Institutionalization of the New *Philosophie* in the Enlightened Public

If in the course of the 1740s the *philosophe* as a socially secluded misanthrope
and bookworm with no knowledge of life had been reinterpreted as an engaged
enlightener, then it was only in the subsequent two decades that this new understanding of the word and the role permeated the educated to a greater extent —
indeed, even seeming to achieve a distinct influence on governmental praxis. This
was not just a result of the persuasiveness of Enlightenment argumentation and
self-representation, which organized and articulated itself through an increasing
number of magazines, books, and societies for a "bourgeois" public, but was also
favored by a crisis in the system of the ancien régime, as was expressed, among
other things, by Damiens's attempt to assassinate Louis XV, by France's humilia-
tion in the Seven Years' War, in a series of sensational judicial scandals, in the
expulsion of the Jesuits from the kingdom, and in the power struggle between
crown and parliament. As a result of all this, the anxiety of the old conservative
upper classes intensified from vague fears to panic and made them aggressively
defensive. This provided the new *philosophie* with a nationwide resonance, more
than ever evoked a clear group consciousness by the *philosophes*, strengthened
their inner coherence, and paradoxically contributed essentially to their successes.

The decisive journalistic altercations, the fight over the meanings of the key concepts *philosophie* and *philosophe*, occurred in the early 1760s. The climax came with Palissot's comedy *Les philosophes,* which in 1760 led to a regular pamphlet war and a whole series of less spectacular imitations. Thereafter, the frequency of new related texts declined sharply, yet leveled off at a higher point than before 1750. In contrast to before, "antiphilosophical" tracts were now clearly in the majority. Of course they had to argue for the most part and increasingly from a defensive position against a *philosophie* that no longer had to struggle for recognition. Taken altogether, the debates of the 1760s only served to recharge what had been up until then quite abstract concepts. While the *philosophes* induced diffuse fears in their opponents, they turned their argument around so that it looked like a "pursuit of virtue," an affirmation of the claim that their own criticism was morally grounded. What was the argumentative strategy of these innumerable pamphlets of which only a few examples can be presented here, and how were they received by the developing public?

Philosophe *and* Philosophie *in Cross Fire*

The most persistent accusation against the *philosophes* was that they were anti-clerical and hostile to religion. As soon as the *Encyclopédie* began appearing, Argenson noticed an intensification of the Jesuit practice of charging anybody who expressed himself "philosophically" of "irréligion" and "matérialisme" ("ce goût de philosopher du siècle") and to agitate for the interdiction of the *Encyclopédie.*[53] Indeed, the Jesuits' twenty-volume reply to it made an arrogant clique of atheists out of Voltaire and the *"philosophes"*: "Ces hommes audacieux dont la Philosophie consiste à se déchaîner contre une Religion dont la vérité . . . irrite leur orgueil."[54] Extensive treatises pilloried in particular the "anti-Christian character" of the new *philosophie.*[55] And when a conference of the Catholic bishops of France drew up a pastoral letter against "false doctrines," the bishops originally wanted to call it "Instruction Pastorale antiphilosophique" but ultimately chose a more theological title: "Une Instruction où ils [the prelates] renversent cette Philosophie irréligieuse qui voudroit lutter contre l'Eglise et en frapper les fondements."[56] Holbach's radical pamphlet-dictionary caricatured the orthodox Catholic denunciation with deliberate exaggeration:

> *Philosophes:* Ce sont les prétendus amis de la sagesse & du bon sens; d'où l'on voit que ce sont des marauts, des voleurs, des fripons, des pendarts, des impies, des gens détestables pour l'Eglise, à qui la société ne doit que des fagots & des bûchers.[57]

On the other hand, the public well understood that the *philosophes* often gave due cause for such charges—for instance, by systematically ganging up against the clerical members in the Academy of Fine Arts, taking credit for the increasing lack of recruits to the religious orders as a direct effect of their "philosophy,"[58] and ironically dismissing efforts to reconcile Christianity and *philosophie:* "Le but de Maupertuis est de prouver qu'on ne peut être heureux que par religion."[59]

Thus isolated attempts to close the gap between *philosophie* and revealed religion, and thereby to bend *philosophie* back to its traditional meaning, found little echo. Not just in special disputatious Catholic dictionaries[60] but also in conversations on the promenades, the concepts *philosophie* and *philosophe* were so self-evidently connected with the ideas of "atheism" and "materialism"[61] that the *Dictionnaire de Trévoux* recanted its previously hesitant agreement with the "misanthropic philosopher":

> Dans le monde on décore aussi du nom de philosophe ces fendus esprits fort, qui . . . se mettent au-dessus des devoirs et des obligations de la vie civile et chrétienne; et qui, affranchis de tout ce qu'ils appellent préjugés de l'éducation en matière de religion, se mocquent des pauvres humains, assez faibles pour respecter les lois établis, et assez imbéciles pour n'oser secouer le joug d'une très ancienne superstition.[62]

On occasion the spokesmen for the *philosophes* appeasingly replied to all of this that they had no doubts about Christianity whatsoever but were only fighting against its misuse by the clergy.[63] But for the most part they reacted with the recrimination of "religious fanaticism": "L'ennemi né du philosophe est ce fanatique atrabilaire qui défend sa secte avec le poignard & la flamme des bûchers."[64] For even Voltaire put the entry "Philosophe" in his *Dictionnaire philosophique* to a large extent under the label of unjust persecution, to which most of the deserving *philosophes* from Charon to Descartes and Gassendi and on to Bayle and Fontenelle had been subjected: "Nous avons toujours vu les philosophes persécutés par des fanatiques."[65]

On the other hand, the opponents of the Enlightenment unmasked the persecution anxieties of successful *philosophes* who made such a show out of the publicly effective, but artificial, self-stagings of the well-known motif of *vertu persécutée:* "Il est si doux de jouer le mérite persécuté, ou prêt l'être! On se rend si considérable en renonçant à la considération! Ce charlatanisme a quelque chose de si séduisant pour ce même public que l'on méprise."[66] Beyond this, they simply turned the reproach of fanaticism back on the *philosophes.* "Ils demandent la tolérance, ils renversent tout. Ils crient contre le fanatisme, et jamais on ne vit des fanatiques plus furieux" was the criticism of a Catholic pamphleteer in 1765 on the occasion of d'Alembert's paper against the Jesuits, which even Enlightenment circles found too extreme.[67] Linguet used up sixty pages to point out the *philosophes'* arrogance, impatience with other opinions, militant propagation of exaggerated compulsive ideas, the demand for unconditional obedience, and obsessive vying for proselytes.[68] This disconcerted the Enlighteners, but their opponent Fréron recommended reading it:

Le fanatisme religieux se baigne quelquefois dans le sang . . . Mais celui de la Philosophie, moins destructeur en apparence, n'est pas moins dangereux. . . . Le fanatisme philosophiques est à la fois destructeur, lâche & timide. Il opprime, il dégrade les hommes.[69]

No wonder the Catholic counter-Enlightenment sought to institutionalize this criticism lexically in the concept *philosophes:* "Ils prêchent la tolérance comme des séditieux prêchent la soumission; ils veulent qu'on tolere ce qui vient de leur part, et ils sont les plus impatiens de tous les intolérans, vis-à-vis de ceux qui leur remontrent leurs écarts."[70]

Hence the reciprocal reproaches of mutual backscratching and sectarianism were closely related. As a reaction to the radical Enlightenment writings of Helvétius and Holbach, Fréron coined the slogan "Philosophistes" or made references to "M. de Voltaire et toute la Philosophaille."[71] A conservative dictionary characterized the *philosophes'* alleged claim to exclusivity with the words: "Toute la science de la Philosophie étoit renfermé dans leur école; le reste du genre humain n'étoit point éclaireé."[72] Even more neutral observers spoke of a new "Secte de Philosophes audacieux,"[73] and the benevolent Baron Grimm accurately commented on a "parti philosophique" that was forming itself against the dévots within the French Academy.[74] Above all, within the context of this argumentation, *philosophes* became a synonym for the names *Encyclopédistes*[75] and *Physiocrates:*

> Les Economistes sont des Philosophes politiques, écrivant principalement sur les matières agraires & l'administration intérieure. . . . Quoique n'étant, à proprement parler, qu'une foible émanation des *Encyclopédistes*, ils n'ont pas tardé à se révolter. . . . Ces Philosophes commencent à faire corps.[76]

Such a congruence of name and predicate betrays a tendency to stylize the *philosophes* as a collective subject to whom conspiracies against society can be easily ascribed. Of course the Encyclopedists were not a radical conspiratory sect but a loose association of mostly bourgeois intellectuals working together and integrated into the ancien régime, from which Voltaire, Rousseau, d'Alembert, and others soon withdrew. Nor did the Physiocrats make up a solid "party." All in all, as Rousseau bitterly ascertained, most of the "philosophical" writers were more concerned with profit and social climbing than with "truth";[77] moreover, ever since the 1760s tensions between moderates and radicals, *arrivistes* and unemployed *philosophes* had been increasing. Nonetheless, it is evident that ever since the 1750s the enlighteners had developed their tendency toward common basic values and mutual support into a feeling of community and solidarity. Of course this occurred essentially as a reaction to the public offensive of the *antiphilosophes,* as the new slogan went.[78] From now on they expressly admitted a certain partisanship, justifying it as self-defense against "fanatic persecution."

Especially Voltaire's correspondence from this time contains a long series of appeals for unity to his followers (often addressed as "mon cher philosophe"), in which an ostensible persecution mania slipped over into the war cry "Écrasez l'infâme!"

> Par quelle fatalité se peut-il que tant de fanatiques imbéciles aient fondés des sectes de fous, et que tant d'esprits supérieurs puissent à peine venir à bout à fonder une petite école de raison? C'est peut-être parce qu'ils sont sages; . . . ils se contentent de rire des erreurs des hommes, au lieu de les écraser.[79]

> Exhortez sans cesse tous le philosophes à marcher les rangs serres contre l'ennemi. Ils seront les maîtres de la nation s'ils s'entendent.[80]

It is particularly in such appeals that the *Correspondences* reveal themselves as the ideal genre, thanks to which the *philosophes* dominated public opinion and at the same time could convincingly preserve the self-image of a persecuted minority. After all, the letters of famous Enlightenment figures were addressed to a public circle of subscribers and, with its verbal gesture of intimacy, gave every single recipient the impression of belonging to a small group of "initiates."[81]

A fourth facet of the polemics touched on the new *philosophie*'s way of thinking and its ethics. What was condemned by the anti-Enlightenment as a rigid mathematico-analytical system of thought unsuited to questions of feeling and morality[82] was justified by Enlightenment spokesmen as an empirico-critical *esprit philosophique*, which was on the verge of overcoming the dogmatically determined *esprit systématique*:

> . . . par esprit systématique, je n'entends pas celui qui lie les vérités entr'elles, pour former des démonstrations, ce qui n'est autre chose que le véritable esprit philosophique, mais je désigne celui qui bâtit des plans & forme des systêmes de l'univers, auxquels il veut ensuite ajuster, de gré ou de force, les phénomènes.[83]

Therefore they declared their *philosophie* as a pioneer of *vérité, justice, raison,* and *progrès* against the dark forces of *préjugé, fanatisme, ignorance, injustice,* and *barbarie.*[84] While Catholic dictionaries were accusing the *philosophes* of perniciously corrupting manners and morals,[85] they claimed a social educative function for themselves: "Travailler à corriger les défauts qu'on trouve dans le sistéme d'éducation d'un Peuple, vouloir éclairer sa Nation & s'appliquer à contribuer au bonheur géneral, c'est la tâche d'un Philosophe."[86] And an entire text devoted itself to the amplification of the opinion that the "true philosopher" — due to his new humanitarian dedication to society, his *vertus sociales,* and his *urbanité,* in short his ethical duty to the triad *Société-Vérité-Vertu* — had also been nominated for this task before all other citizens.[87]

Nevertheless—or even because of it—the polemics of the opposition culminated in the statement that the *philosophes* were undermining the foundations of society and the state. It was exactly this point that the "antiphilosophical" theatrical writers considered the most important; and therefore they put more antiabsolutistic than antireligious lines into the mouths of the *philosophes* they were criticizing.[88] Spokesmen for the Catholic church carried on the attack:

O siècle dixhuit! . . . que vous êtes frivole, que vous êtes corrompu: grâce aux Philosophes, à ces Savans universel, dont la plûpart comme les gens de qualité, savent tout sans avoir rien appri! Où est l'honneur, la probité? Où sont les moeurs purs, la bonne foi dans les affaires, la fidélité conjugale, la tendresse filiale, l'amour paternel? Toutes ces vertus ne sont-elles pas frappées dans leur fondement par les Ouvrages philosophiques? D'où viennent les troubles de L'Etat, l'autorité compromise, l'obéissance forcée, le vice accrédité, la vertu abbattue? Si non de cette liberté de penser, de cette raison, de cet audacieux égoïsme; principes fondamentaux du moderne philosophisme, sources inépuisables de désordre . . . [89]

The Parisian Parliament joined in and intensified the persecution of pamphlets criticizing church and state that were successfully smuggled in under the collective designation *livres philosophiques* and which made up the main part of forbidden underground literature in the second half of the eighteenth century:[90]

Les philosophes se sont élevés en précepteurs du genre humain. Liberté de penser, voilà leur cri, et ce cri s'ést fait entendre d'une extrémité du monde à l'autre. D'une main, ils ont tenté d'ébranler le trône; de l'autre, ils ont voulu renverser les autels. Leur objet était de faire prendre un autre cours aux esprits sur les Institutions civiles et religieuses. . . . La contagion a pénétré dans les ateliers et jusque dans les chaumières.[91]

To this Enlightenment spokesmen asserted that the *philosophe* did not aspire to governmental power but only to theoretical understanding[92]—but without missing a chance to lay claim to their function as political advisers:

. . . Quel est le philosophe qui ait ensanglanté les trônes & armé les hommes contre les hommes? . . . Faites asseoir le philosophe au pied de trônes, & vous ne verrez point ces grands crimes . . . Le philosophe est le plus pacifique des hommes. Il unit les sujets aux rois, & les rois entr'eux. Il empêche les peuples de s'exterminer pour des sophismes.[93]

This whole multifaceted polemic had already developed in the 1740s but with the appearance of the *Encyclopédie* assumed a novel trenchancy, density, and resonance. Besides, the whole repertoire of meanings for *philosophe* and *philosophie*—and this is an essential point—could be employed just as self-evidently by Enlightenment spokesmen as by their opponents. To be sure, certain given aspects of meaning were thematized, criticized, and thus—at least theoretically—faded out of the language norm by anti-Enlightenment spokesmen, whereas the *philosophes* at any given time were forced to concern themselves with the criticism of such critiques and the negation of (potential) negations. But in the public mind in front of which the antagonists staged their debates, it was necessary to implant *one* concept—not only could the aspects of meaning that were being fought over *not* be postponed but they had absolute priority. Precisely because in several respects the opposition accepted the position of a "symmetrical negation"[94] as the self-image of the *philosophes,* a certain agreement was introduced into its use. And it was precisely because the concept *philosophe* had institutionalized itself through negations of negations that the 1743 tract *Le philosophe* was able to preserve its actuality for so long; for there, too, the concept had been constituted through negations of negations. To be sure, it had been radicalized and politicized in the meantime, had further developed its anticlerical and antiabsolutistic implications, and now entirely linked the conceptual role of self-reflection with an ethics of engaged social action, against what the *philosophes* defined as "fanaticism" and "despotism" and for Enlightenment, "justice," and "freedom."

The Practical Political and Social Effects of **Philosophie's** Success with the Public

The Theater Scandal of 1760. That Enlightenment spokesmen were ultimately the victors in the disputes about the fundamental positions of their *philosophie* was to a decisive degree a result of the scandal around Palissot's play *Les philosophes.*[95] In this comedy, which is modeled on Molière's *Ecole des femmes* and takes over a scene from Moreau's *Cacouacs,*[96] a clan of cynical and hypocritical *philosophes* profit from a rich widow's blind enthusiasm for the "philosophie du jour." By putting Diderot, Helvétius, Rousseau, and Duclos—with fictitious but readily decodable names—on the publicly effective and particularly sensitive forum of the stage and giving them low qualities of character and ridiculous poses, Palissot and other opponents of the Enlightenment, including the foreign minister Choiseul, the patron of the play, hoped to annihilate the reputation of all of the *philosophes* by attacking the honor of some of the leading Encyclopedists. But precisely the radicalism of this novel attack both on the fundamental "protection of the individual" of the time as well as on the traditions of French drama, which had not previously experienced personal defamation as the main theme of a whole play, made it possible for Enlightenment spokesmen to identify Palissot and his "backers" as *persécuteurs* and thus to turn what looked at first sight like a dangerous attack into an affirmation of their own public role. Hence the outraged reaction of the *Correspondance littéraire:*

Toute la finesse et tout le sel de la Comédie des *Philosophes* consistent
à dire que philosophe et fripon sont synonymes; à attaquer les moeurs
de M. Diderot, de M. Helvétius et d'autres personnes, à les traduire sur
la scene comme des scélérats et de mauvais Citoyens, et à faire
marcher Jean Jacques Rousseau sur quatre pattes. . . . que cette farce
ait été jouée sur le théâtre des Corneilles, sous l'autorité du gouvernement; que la police, qui poursuit en ce pays-ci avec tant de sévérité
tous les ouvrages satyriques, se soit écartée de ses principes, et ait
permis que plusieurs Citoyens fussent insultés publiquement par une sa-
tyre atroce, voilà ce qui n'est point indifférent et ce qui marque . . . la
faveur et la protection que les lettres et la philosophie ont à attendre
désormais de la part du gouvernement.[97]

If it could have been expected that Enlightenment commentators would unite
themselves behind the banner of "persecuted virtue" to counter Palissot's attack,[98]
then it proves all the more the comedy's exaggeration that even neutral observers
objected to its malignity[99] and that even Fréron had to admit dejectedly that the
feelings of much of the audience were offended.[100] Hence the unusually large audience at the beginning, which had been additionally inflated by free tickets, fell
from 1,439 at the first performance to 462 by the fourteenth (May 2–31, 1760),
and after two more badly attended performances the play was removed from the
Comédie Française's program.[101] For the *philosophes* had immediately used their
opponents' weakness for a merciless publicity war of extermination against Palissot: "Nous avons des loix contre les *Libelles diffamatoires*. La diffamation sur le
théâtre est la plus publique, le plus grande & la plus criminelle de toutes."[102]
When the pamphlet war began to slacken after a few months, they triumphantly
ascertained that Palissot had become a ridiculous figure, his play forgotten, and
that the whole scandal had only served to increase their popularity.[103]

The "Anti-Philosophes" on the Defensive. "The exhibition game" deciding the fate
of Palissot's *Philosophes* was the spectacular culmination and turning point of the
years-long trench warfare between the Enlightenment and the anti-Enlightment
for the favor of the public; its outcome could not be foreseen. With the publication
of the first volumes of the *Encyclopédie,* the adherents of the new criticoration-
alistic *philosophie* had so visibly increased that Fréron abandoned his use of the
concept, which as late as 1751 had still been positive: "L'étude de la Philosophie
commence parmi nous à prévaloir sur la belle Littérature; le plus mince écrivain
veut passer pour philosophe: c'est la maladie ou, pour mieux dire, la folie du
jour."[104] Innumerable attacks of this sort put the *philosophes* on the defensive for
a while. When the Académie Française offered a prize for the question "En quoi
consiste l'esprit philosophique?" it was won by a Jesuit pastor who denigrated the
new "freethinking" as a pernicious fad and rejected it, adding, "On se pique aujourd'hui de Philosophie: voilà le goût dominant, et j'oserai dire, la passion générale de notre siècle."[105]

By 1760, however, Enlightenment spokesmen retrieved the initiative and drove critics increasingly on the defensive. One, Fréron, had fair reason to complain that "les Philosophes, M. de Voltaire à leur tête, crient sans cesse à la persécution, & ce sont eux-mêmes qui m'ont persécuté de toute leur fureur & de toute leur adresse."[106] Voltaire's crowing reports of success to "initiates" frankly show this:

> Il me semble que tous ceux qui ont écrit contre les philosophes sont punis dans ce monde. Les jésuites ont été chassés; Abraham Chaumeix s'est enfui à Moscou; Berthier est mort d'un poison froid; Fréron a été honni sur tous les théâtres, et Vernet sera pilori infailliblement.[107]

> On crie contre les philosophes. On a raison, car si l'opinion est la Reine du monde, les philosophes gouvernent cette reine. Vous ne sauriez combien leur empire s'étend.[108]

And actually there is a whole series of indications that, in the course of the 1760s, the *philosophes* had succeeded more and more in establishing themselves as the leaders of public opinion. For one thing, they could now afford to take an ironic distance to their own fashionable fellow-travelers. If the *Correspondance littéraire* had presupposed in 1757 that soon all of the "fainénants de nos cafés" would pretend to the title of *philosophe,* within ten years it had to substantiate that "tout est aujourd'hui philosophe, philosophique et philosophie en France."[109] This mode was given a striking literary figuration in the self-made *philosophe* who meets Rameau's nephew in Diderot's novel; he stages his role primarily by ostentatiously feigning a great distance from the café milieu, which he frequents nonetheless, forcing him to put up with the ironic greeting, "Ah! ah! vous voilà, monsieur le philosophe." This kind of seemingly playful expression is symptomatic of the fact that ever since the early 1770s more and more young writers had been flowing into Paris in order to make a name for themselves like Voltaire.[110]

At the same time, the opposition began to realize that the new *philosophie* was not simply limited to a little "sect" but had acquired broader social influence:

> C'est elle [la philosophie] qui donne le ton. Elle s'insinue de cent manieres différentes. Son poison de trouve répandu & apprété dans le Livres de morale, dans les ouvrages de physique, dan les Histoires générales & particulieres, dans les Dictionnaires & les Enciclopédies, dans les Traités de politique, dans les projets concernant l'Agriculture, le commerce & les Arts; dans les relations de voyages, dans les piéces dramatiques, dans les brochures périodiques.[111]

Truly, even the apologists of Catholic dogma found it so difficult to escape the attraction of the Enlightenment model of knowledge that an antiphilosophical dictionary was called *Dictionnaire philosophique* notwithstanding, and, despite vigorous resistance to the "false doctrines" of the Enlightenment, its essential purpose was conceived as the demonstration of the convergence of religion and "philosophie":

> . . . nous adoptons avec plaisir un Esprit véritablement philosophique; et nous le regardons, cet Esprit, comme la chose la plus digne de notre estime. . . . Mais en quoi consiste-t-il? . . . le véritable Esprit philosophique en un mot, c'est une manière de penser qui adopte toujours comme deux flambeaux également nécessaires, la raison et la révélation.[112]

Moreover, spokesmen for the Enlightenment, as Fréron resignedly recognized, gradually took over the Académie Française and other institutions formulating public opinion.[113] Already at the beginning of the 1770s the identity of the *philosophe* had become unequivocally preponderant among the members of academies and educated circles in the capital, as well as in the provinces, and the conviction grew that this development was the concrete demonstration of a law of historical necessity.[114] The highly moral self-image of the *philosophes* was no longer merely the role of "persecuted virtue" but was also grounded in a historical and philosophical argument. Texts like Suard's inaugural address in the Académie Française in August 1774 show that the social improvement of their own role was experienced by Enlightenment spokesmen as confirmation of their historical and philosophical speculations:

> Se déchaîner donc contre le siècle, parce qu'il est le siècle de la philosophie, c'est se déchaîner contre les arrêts de la nécessité, c'est se révolter contre la loi qui régla de toute éternité la conduite humaine. Nous sommes plus philosophes que nos pères, parce que nous sommes venus après eux; nous le sommes, parce que nous ne pouvons pas être autre chose.[115]

Here we can see how indispensable it was for the status of *philosophie* as an eighteenth-century emblem of identity not to assimilate into their public self-image the fact that they had long since been completely integrated into the historically antiquated ancien régime.

Besides, Enlightenment figures were now practically presentable at court. Already since the 1750s, the *Correspondance littéraire,* in which Grimm resolutely advocated the *philosophes'* new understanding of their role, owed its duration and the profit it rendered to the editorial staff to the concealed interest of numerous European royal adherents of *philosophie.*[116] When the young Danish king Christian VII undertook an educational journey to Paris in 1768, he expressly insisted on meeting the *philosophes,* gathering eighteen of them for a roundtable discussion—among them, d'Alembert, Condillac, Diderot, Grimm, Helvétius, Holbach, and Marmontel: "Le roi fit d'abord le tour du cercle . . . Après ce premier tour, le roi en fit un second, et causa avec les principaux de ces philosophes."[117] This event seems symptomatic of a significant shift in the center of gravity of social worth in educated society. Marked as an outsider in the early eighteenth century because of his withdrawal from courtly conventions, the *philosophe* now saw himself courted by princes. Fully conscious of this acquired prestige, it was no longer necessary for the *philosophes* merely to offer their "useful" services to society, as had been the case thirty years earlier as their role was being formulated. Now they could ascribe their dedication to society as merit and demand princely rewards in the name of humanity, as can be seen in d'Alembert's speech to the Académie des Sciences at the reception for Christian VII:

> Messieurs, la philosophie, toute portée qu'elle est à fuir l'éclat de l'appareil, a cependant quelque droit à l'estime des hommes, puisqu'elle travaille à les éclairer. . . . Peu imposante et peu active, elle a besoin, pour se produire avec confiance, de protecteurs puissants et respectés. Il est réservé aux rois de rendre ce service à la philosophie, ou plutôt aux hommes.[118]

Finally, the emanation of the new *philosophie* was not limited to high society and the capital, but even affected provincial cities like Montpellier:

> La lecture des livres philosophiques a tellement saisi l'esprit de la plupart du monde, surtout des jeunes gens, qu'on n'avait jamais vu tant de déistes comme il y en a aujourd'hui.[119]

Already in 1755 an anonymous brochure out of the circle of the *Bibliothèque bleue* reported on the "philosophical" pretensions of the folkloristic robber and smuggler captain Mandrin:

> Les Livres qu'il lisoit par préférence, étoient des ouvrages clandestins, faits contre le Roi, le Gouvernement, la Magistrature & la Religion. . . . Mandrin se regardoit comme un Philosophe: il croyoit avoir avec Auteurs qu'on lisoit, le privilége exclusif de sçavoir penser. Le peuple végète, disoit-il, & nous pensons.[120]

The Philosophes as Reformers. The *philosophes* even achieved a certain influence on sociopolitical decisions and French administrative praxis. For instance, when Voltaire added a paragraph to the entry "Philosophie" in the 1771 edition of his *Dictionnaire philosophique* in which he attributed, among other things, the establishment of religious peace in the ancien régime and the extinguishing of the Inquisition's *auto-da-fé* in Spain to *philosophie* (p. 605), he was projecting the solid "philosophical" successes of his own time into the past. These were mainly in three fields.

As their first great victory—which was more than mere publicity—the *philosophes* celebrated the dissolution of the Jesuit order in France and their exile from the kingdom in 1762–64. Actually this had been fought for by the Jansenists and the parliaments in a temporary expedient alliance; but since Enlightenment spokesmen had quickly occupied the public vacuum left by the interdiction of the order and the simultaneous silence of the Jansenists, they were able to present themselves convincingly as the real conquerors of institutionalized "fanaticism":

> La philosophie, à laquelle les jansénistes avaient déclaré la guerre presque aussi vive que la compagnie de Jésus, avait fait, malgré eux et par bonheur pour eux des progrès sensibles. . . . C'est proprement la philosophie qui, par la bouche des magistrats, a porté l'arrêt contre les Jésuites; le jansénisme n'en a été que le solliciteur. La nation et les philosophes à sa tête, voulaient l'anéantissement de ces pères, parce qu'ils sont intolérans, persécuteurs, turbulens et redoutables.[121]

Even more effective than publicity was the *philosophes'* engagement in a series of judicial scandals, which seemed to confirm their persecution hypothesis and at the same time provide them with the possibility of appearing as pioneers of *humanité*. Probably the most widespread and protracted reaction was to the case of the Protestant businessman Jean Calas in Toulouse. His condemnation and execution for an alleged religiously motivated heretical murder in 1762 unleashed—not the least because of Voltaire's manifestos—a nationwide wave of indignation that lasted until the victim's official exoneration in 1765:

> On doit dire, à la louange de notre siècle et à celle de la philosophie, que les Calas n'ont reçu les secours qui ont réparé leur malheur que des personnes instruites et sages qui foulent le fanatisme à leurs pieds.[122]

Finally, Enlightenment figures came fairly close to their demand for administrative power when the young Louis XVI nominated Turgot as general comptroller and let himself be convinced to undertake some serious reforms. For it was precisely his desire to break up the encrusted structure of the guilds, tear down internal barriers to trade, and get rid of "feudal" villenage that proved Turgot to be—as his fellow worker and later biographer emphasized—a true *philosophe*.[123] But Turgot's failure due to the resistance of the privileged and their anxieties about their prerogatives makes it perfectly clear that, despite everything, the political influence of the *philosophes* had quite real limits and that in the France of the time they were not able to carry through an Enlightenment absolutism. A resigned Voltaire wrote to Frederick the Great on May 21, 1776:

> Nous avons grand besoin que votre majesté philosophique règne longtemps; nous avions chez les Velches [that is, in France] deux ministres philosophes [Turgot and Malesherbes], les voilà tous deux à la fois exclus du ministère; et qui sait si les scènes des la Barre et des d'Etallonde [two other "victims of misjustice"] ne se renouvelleront pas dans notre malheureux pays?[124]

The *philosophes'* overestimation of their influence was followed by disenchantment. Nonetheless the engaged participation of many Enlightenment figures in the struggles over church, law, and political reform had a catalytic effect that went far beyond individual successes to the extent that it directed the *philosophes'* understanding of their own role to a greater degree toward political and social praxis.

The Century's Self-Apotheosis and Prerevolutionary Radicalization (1776–88): *Philosophie* as a Fashionable Life-Style and Its Dispersion

The Confirmation of the Self-Image of "Persecuted Virtue"

If Turgot's failure disappointed his supporters' hopes for a "political takeover," it nevertheless served to confirm the image of the *philosophe* as someone unappreciated in his own country, the persecuted embodiment of "virtue," and thus retained for the *philosophes* the strategic advantage of being able to conceal the publicly achieved power they had garnered behind their conflicts with the traditional ecclesiastical and state authorities, even while they continued to improve their image and legitimize themselves through these conflicts. It is striking how little the *philosophes* had connected the reforms introduced during Turgot's ministry with *philosophie*, just as Turgot himself obviously avoided using the irritating word in his preambles to his reforms. But now his fellow traveler Condorcet, who as standing secretary of the Académie des Sciences drew a royal pension and had not been prosecuted for his forbidden pamphlets, began to complain about the increased danger of persecution and ominously conjured up the custody of Diderot, Morellet, and Mirabeau in Vincennes and the Bastille, as well as the court's public burnings of texts by Boncerf and Raynal.[125] And the church denied Voltaire, certainly the most successful *philosophe*, a regular funeral in Paris, thus making his "lifelong martyrdom" the main theme of the memorial address.[126] Although Diderot had been interned not in the tower but in the Palace of Vincennes for a few days and had freely received visitors like Rousseau, his texts appeared as the just revenge for his "jail sufferings":

> Diderot, rugissant au donjon de Vincenne,
> Y jura sur ses fers, alimens de la haine,
> De chercher des vengeurs, et d'éteindre à la fois.
> Les foudres du pontife et la race des rois.[127]

The Antiphilosophical Polemics Begin to Slacken

In other respects, appearances also justified the *philosophes'* moral arguments; during the last two decades of the ancien régime the number of publications attacking them exceeded by far the number of express apologetics:

> Les pamphlets de toute espèce contre la philosophie et les philosophes
> se multiplient tous les jours, et le but de tous ces écrits est d'accuser la

secte des Encyclopédistes de tous nos désordres et de tous les malheurs, de la dépravation générale, des excès du libertinage, de la décadence du goût, des progrès du luxe, de l'avilissement de tous les ordres de l'Etat, des mauvais récoltes, de la cherté des vivres, etc.[128]

Among the continued attacks on the basic positions of the *philosophes*, three stand out for their particular vehemence. An alleged "roman philosophique" exploited the popularity of the novel in order to deride their communicative "infrastructure" with deadly aim—the meetings of the *philosophes* on the promenades, in cafés, in salons led by women ("bureaux d'esprit"), and at "dîners philosophiques."[129] It accused them of "saturnalian convocations," where they were supposed to have set up regular lists of proscriptions for the annihilation of their critics.[130] Another anonymously published novel traced the fading piety and moral collapse of a young woman to the pernicious influence of *philosophie* so drastically that even the conservative press was critical.[131] And a "livre de théologie et même de controverse" by Madame de Genlis completely gave up whatever meaning was left over from the concept of *philosophe* still clung to by the conservatives; for her, it stood for nothing but "a sect hostile to religion," thus renewing the old reproach of fanaticism by denouncing certain texts by Turgot, Holbach, Raynal, and Condorcet:[132]

Il n'y avoit plus de fanatisme en France avant que la secte des Philosophes modernes fut formée. . . . Ainsi, voilà donc des Philosophes, et les philosophes les plus renommés, qui exhortent les peuples de toutes les Nations de détruire les temples et le culte, à massacrer les Rois, les Souverains, et à ne souffrir aucune autorité, excepté celle des *Philosophes!* Je demande à toute personne impartiale, si ce fanatisme horrible n'est pas mille fois plus dangereux que le fanatisme inspiré par la Religion?[133]

Yet aside from these cases, the "antiphilosophical" writers gave up their polemics of the 1760s and had no illusions about their general retreat. In the theater, the positions of the *philosophes* were directly attacked for the last time in 1775 (Duval, *La nouvelle philosophie à vau l'eau*), and in 1777 living *philosophes* were personally caricatured for the last time (Madame Geoffrin and her salon in Rudlidge's *Le bureau d'esprit*). Henceforth, "antiphilosophical" comedies would limit themselves to the presentation of the *philosophe soi-disant* (the title of several plays) as an immoral, eccentric, misanthropic muddleheaded thinker.[134] Even the author of the antienlightenment novel *Faustin ou le siècle philosophique* was satisfied to make fun of blind enthusiasm for *philosophie* rather than setting forth the conservative position: "Nous avons la philosophie de la nature, la philosophie de l'histoire, philosophie de la vie commune, philosophie de tous états, philosophie de la quenouille, et même une philosophe de la canaille."[135] An increasing number of theological writings now considered parts of the new *philosophie* as valid or even made an effort to reconcile it with religion – for example, the Canon Yvon in Coutances: "Philosophe à la fois & théologien."[136] Other clerics harmlessly preached charity where engaged Catholics expected hard words against the *philosophes*.[137] Whenever the church officially condemned this, it involuntarily confirmed their widespread effectivity: "Les leçons de la nouvelle philosophie retentissent jusque dans les ateliers des artisans et sous l'humble toit du cultivateur."[138] And for all of his individual criticisms of the "arrogance" and "fashionable affectations" of many *philosophes*, a steadfast conservative journalist like Mallet Du Pan spontaneously adopted their ethics of social action: "Je suis pénétré de respect pour la Philosophie qui consiste dans la pratique des vertus sociales et dans l'étude des vérités utiles."[139]

The Victory of Philosophie and Its Various Contextualizations

The Self-Apotheosis of Enlightenment Figures. The retreat of the *antiphilosophes* was in direct proportion to the growing public recognition of the *philosophes*. If they still fell into miscredit occasionally, it was because of radical statements from their own ranks.[140] The fact that even provincial newspapers had taken up *philosophie*, thus publicly institutionalizing it in urban centers outside of Paris, shows the extent to which the role of the "subject of the Enlightenment," which at first was only postulated by the *philosophe*, had since become social reality: "Cet esprit de philosophie, qui lui [notre siècle] imprime un caractère si sublime, est en partie le fruit de la propagation presque instantanée des lumières en tout genre qui s'opère d'un bout du monde l'autre par à la voie des journaux."[141]

Conscious of their worth, the parvenu inheritors of prominent Enlightenment figures ten years before the French Revolution already regarded the struggle for *philosophie* as the glorious past, whereby the constitutive significance of the antiphilosophical polemic for the social success of the role of the *philosophe* was already correctly evaluated.[142] In particular we see the first outlines of a canonization of certain representative Enlightenment schemata. We could begin with Montesquieu's *Lettres persanes* and Voltaire's *Lettres philosophiques* and let them develop for three generations, through the *Encyclopédistes*, the *Economistes*, and the *Patriotes*.[143] But we could also choose the *empire de l'opinion publique* as a historiographical criterion and then set the beginning of the Enlightenment at the appearance of the first volumes of the *Encyclopédie*.[144]

The Image of the Prominent Philosophe. Already regarded as "historical" after their public victory, the surviving *philosophes* and their *philosophie* had become an emblem of identity in the 1780s in a double respect: for foreign intellectuals they were representatives of France's head-start into the Enlightenment, and for the educated French, they embodied the essential achievements of the eighteenth century. The public, which by now was institutionalized, experienced the *philosophes* as a group of writers who were marked by an intellectual style grounded in *raison*, who had proved themselves through humanitarian engagement as well as the accomplishment of the century, the *Encyclopédie*, and whose high moral legitimacy and consequence in thought and action should be honored because of their "persecuted virtue." The emblematic character and symbolic value of the "philosophical" life form was not only positively manifested as, for instance, in this draft for an inscription on Rousseau's monument:

> Philosophe / persécuté par les soi-disants tels. /Ami / de la vérité. / Apôtre / de la vertu. / . . . Politique / lumineux & profond. / Implacable ennemi / de l'oppression & de la tyrannie. / Républicain / comme CATON. Citoyen / comme ARISTIDE . . .[145]

But too, a particularly vehement damnation of Voltaire, in its scornful twisting of his many virtues and accomplishments into just as many vices and misdeeds, testifies to the model effect emanating from the *philosophe*'s life form:

> Parmi nous, qu'est-ce qu'un Philosophe? . . . Prenons, par exemple, l'idole de la nation Française, le fondateur, le patriarche de la moderne philosophie, le grand homme, le Philosophe par excellence, le divin & jamais assez loué *Voltaire* . . . [146]

The case of the Abbé Raynal, which was topical in the 1780s, shows how socially real and historically effective the image of this role could be, despite its somewhat questionable factual basis: Raynal's self-stylization as the pattern of "virtue," the spokesman of the repressed "folk," the uncorruptible pioneer of "liberty," the cosmopolitan interpreter of the future—which he developed in his *Histoire philosophique et politique des . . . deux Indes*. The enormous success of this work put increasing pressure on him actually to live this role, until the French Revolution burst the bubble of this illusion.[147]

To be sure, the figure of the successful *philosophe* presented in these examples began to lose its social basis to the same extent that, between 1778 and 1785 with Voltaire, Rousseau, Diderot, Condillac, d'Alembert, and Mably, the most prominent *philosophes* had died;[148] to be sure, the third Enlightenment generation of Suard and La Harpe had inherited their lucrative and highly prestigious sinecures, but, with a few exceptions like Raynal and Condorcet, they withdrew to politically harmless *belles lettres* and by no means sought lasting fame as *philosophes*.

The Image of the Marginalized Intellectual. The gradual fading away of the "great" *philosophes* and their weary heirs was only the sociohistorical side of the late Enlightenment. On the other, there were more and more young intellectuals (although this concept appeared only a century later, it is justified insofar as the phenomenon that it comprehends seems to have been generated in the late eighteenth century)[149] streaming into Paris fascinated by the myth of the *philosophe* and determined to imitate the life-style of the prominent *philosophe*. Once there, they made the bitter discovery that the elite of the *philosophes* had already made its arrangements with the aristocracy and the state and occupied the sinecures of science and literature, whereas they were forced to struggle at the margins of society as police informers, book smugglers, and, above all, as occasional writers. Yet they did not abandon the dream of the *philosophe* as a life form. Despised in established circles as *libellistes*, they presented their mostly sensational writings as *philosophie*, despite their pornographic, antireligious, or antimonarchistic contents,[150] thus gilding the most trivial sort of entertainment, for themselves as well as for the reader, with the appearance of moral action. Seen semantically, this new minting of the role of the *philosophe* was based on a generalization of those components that had put his "persecuted virtue" in perspective: the "philosopher" wasn't simply someone who could brag about having been persecuted by the old church and state, but was already every author and reader who (potentially) exposed himself to persecution by transgressing the taboos of official significance. Therefore the polemics between Enlightenment spokesmen and theologians from the middle years of the eighteenth century found a curious continuation: it was a game because the persecution of *philosophie* as a determining structure had largely been forgotten; but at the same time it was serious because the young socially *declassés* writers could not count on the same level of tolerance as the successful heirs of the *philosophes*, but above all, because it turned out to have significant consequences for political history. For many of these "back-alley Rousseaus," as Restif de la Bretonne once called them, would become powerful politicians in the Revolution, for whose acts their prerevolutionary experience provided invaluable training.

Now from the point of view of conceptual history, it is important that these marginalized *philosophes* in the late Enlightenment positivized the reality of their life form in a new figure of identity, as described by Mercier in the *Tableau de Paris*. Having been a struggling writer himself, his "vrai Philosophe" sounds like a precursor of the intellectual *bohémien*. His milieu is the big city, where he can "fade" into the crowd and enjoy a new freedom—the freedom of social borderlines, yet also a class-crossing freedom that leveled differences in rank, and which no longer needed to be taken up into the social elite in order to reach a broader public, as had been the case at midcentury:

> C'est dans les grandes villes que le philosophe lui-même se plaît, tout en les condamnant; parce qu'il y cache mieux qu'ailleurs sa médiocre fortune; parce qu'il n'a pas du moins à en rougir; parce qu'il y vit plus libre, noyé dans la foule; parce qu'il y trouve plus d'égalité dans la confusion des rangs.[151]

Mercier's "vrais Philosophes" are the forerunners of the artists and intellectuals of the nineteenth century. Like the *bohémiens* a good half century later, they felt that they embodied the French capital's fame and identity. Also from this perspective, they are successors and forerunners at the same time:

Voilà ce qui fait chérir Paris, voilà ce qui compense la foule de ses in-
commodités. Vous y trouvez des philosophes dont la conversation est
un charme toujours renaissant. Tout ce que les arts & les sciences ont
de plus délicat & de plus sublime, vous est révélé par ces hommes qui,
sans être séparés des affaires, ne s'y abandonnent point, & pour qui
l'Europe entière est un spectacle mouvant & curieux dont ils jugent les
acteurs divers. . . . Il ne faut pas les confondre avec ces ridicules
connoisseurs désoeuvrés & stériles.[152]

And it was precisely the representatives of this life-style like Brissot and Carra
(see below) who helped politicize the concept of *philosophie* in the 1780s.[153]

Prerevolutionary Politicization of Philosophie

After Turgot's failure, the *philosophes* still had practically no direct influence
on the administration, yet their exemplary role remained undisputed in any effective sense. Thus during the final decade of the ancient régime, they made an even
greater claim, on the basis of their *philosophie*, to functions in every field of administrative and social action. They were the authoritative shapers and communi-
cators of meaning:

Le Magistrat rend la justice, le Philosophe apprend au Magistrat ce que
c'est le juste & l'injuste. Le Militaire défend la patrie; le Philosophe apprend au Militaire ce que c'est une patrie. Le Prêtre recommande au
peuple l'amour & le respect pour les Dieux; le Philosophe apprend aux
Prêtres ce que c'est que les Dieux. Le Souverain commande à tous; le
Philosophe apprend au Souverain quelle est l'origine & la limite de son
autorité. Chaque homme a des devoirs à remplir dans sa famille & dans
la société; le Philosophe apprend à chacun quels sont ces devoirs.
L'homme est exposé à l'infortune & à la douleur; le Philosophe apprend
à l'homme à souffrir.[154]

What the older Diderot theoretically concluded here from the example of the
philosophe Seneca had been updated in extensions that for the most part he made
himself and in the countless reeditions of Raynal's *Histoire philosophique et politique*; it was intensified into an activist summons to all *philosophes* to denounce
worldwide political repression and slavery as a glaring offense against the in-
alienable right to freedom.[155] Admittedly, the self-confident belief in an impend-
ing and rapid government takeover by *philosophie*[156]—not to mention its advan-
tages for the monarchs themselves[157]—was relativized by the recognition that
Louis XVI had supported the American War of Independence not in the name of
philosophie—that is, the principle of the "just government" and the "right to
resistance"—but purely out of the usual considerations of power politics.[158]

The politicized image of the *philosophe* as spokesman and pioneer of the
"folk," of human rights, and of the life interests of the lower classes and the un-

privileged was more intensely represented by socially marginalized intellectuals than by Diderot and Raynal. So not only did Brissot bind the *philosophe* once again to the obligation of "truth," active "humanity," and "usefulness,"[159] but he went on to legitimize him through his urban background, his miserable economic situation, and the consequent dependency;[160] with renewed clarity, he distinguished between him and both the parvenu "pseudophilosophes" and the "grands philosophes" who looked down with contempt on the common man: "Il n'existe plus de lien d'union entre lui [le philosophe] et le grand homme qu'il juge."[161] Combining the same marginal social status with moral integrity, Carra, as an anonymous "prophéte philosophe," made himself into the radical plaintiff of the "prétendus maîtres de la Terre": "Prêtres, fuyez! le masque tombe. Rois, tremblez sur le trône, vos flatteurs sont anéantis!"[162]

Once again evidence for a politicized *philosophie* in actual practice can be found in the field of law especially. When several provincial academies in the early 1780s published competitions on the questions of current criminal law, the overwhelming majority of the answers sent in were like those of Bernardi, himself a lawyer who demanded the humanization of antiquated "barbaric" paragraphs in the name of *philosophie*:

> Le charme est rompu, la révolution s'approche, les philosophes et les orateurs l'ont préparé par des éscrits que la reconnoissance a déjâ consacrés à l'immortalité; leur noble enthousiasme a passé dans le coeurs.[163]

The "banner of philosophy" also served as an appellant means in the new legal scandals,[164] indeed as a precedent for a concrete example of annulment in a case where in 1713 the highest court of Bordeaux had granted the compulsory service of the serfs to a lord of the manor despite the lack of any documentary authentication:

> L'humanité regagne peu à ses droits, & la philosophie répand sensiblement sa lumière. Quand je dis philosophie, je ne parle pas de celle qui n'est remarquable que par la hardiesse de ses paradoxes, mais de cette philosophie bienfaisante qui éclaire les hommes & les porte au soulagement des malheureux. Le plus grand soulagement qu'elle puisse leur procurer, est la diminution des redevances tyranniques, triste suite du gouvernement féodal.[165]

Furthermore, even the moderate press attributed plans for reform and actual advances in the most varied social and political fields to Enlightenment influences and the versatility of *philosophie*, whether it was a new slaughterhouse,[166] a movement for the abolishment of slavery,[167] or the novel freedom in questions of rank and etiquette shown by the notables meeting in 1787.[168] The common semantic denominator of such efficacy was the "philosophical" feature of beneficence and public usefulness as a continuation of Christian *charité*:

La philosophie . . . cherche à se distinguer aujourd'hui par de bonnes oeuvres, par des éstablissements charitables et des fondations pieuses. Tant de zèle portera sur des objets utiles à la société, quel que puisse en être le motif secret, il méritera toujours la reconnaissance et l'estime des âmes honnêtes et sensibles. Il est à craindre seulement que le zèle philosophique ne dégénère un jour, comme tant d'autres, en une vaine ostentation.[169]

The Devaluation of Philosophie into a Fashionable Life-Style

It was this last concern that actually came true. Scarcely debated any more as a pattern of behavior, aspired to by more and more writers, employed as never before in so many various fields of social and administrative life—the concepts *philosophie* and *philosophe* were already showing clear signs of decay at the height of their significance and semantic expansion toward the end of the ancien régime. The most trustworthy and up-to-date dictionary before the Revolution mentions a whole series of neologisms that attached pejorative suffixes to *philosophie* (*philosophâille, philosopherie, philosophesque, philosophiser, philosophisme, philosophiste*),[170] formulations, which in publications before 1779 could only be found in isolation but which now began to pop up with greater frequency.[171] From the point of view of the clerical lexicographer Féraud, these pejoratives were "language's revenge" on the enlighteners for their "antireligious" worldview:

Mots nouveaux, et qui commencent à s'acréditer. L'indignation, qu'ont excitée dans les bons esprits les horribles écarts de certains faux Philosophes modernes, a fait inventer ces mots assez singulières. Ils ne sont bons que dans le st[yle] critiq[ue] et mocqueur, ou polémique et mordant.[172]

However, since the arguments between *philosophes* and *antiphilosophes* had been much more vigorous around 1760, the discrediting of philosophie that set in during the 1780s can only be explained by bringing in other causes. First of all, these pejoratives seem to have been functionally motivated within language; according to a fundamental law in the economy of the language norm, the performative signification of the predicates *philosophe* and *philosophie* lost in precision in direct proportion to the growth in the number of fields in which they were employed:

On a tellement prodigué dans ces dernières années, le nom de Philosophie & de Philosophe, & on en a fait des applications si sin-

gulières, que c'est aujourd'hui un problème que de déterminer précisé-
ment ce que c'est qu'un Philosophe.[173]

Another presupposition for this decline was that *philosophie* had become
fashionable and was thus exposed, beyond the circle of the educated, to a trivializ-
ing and superficial imitation with all inflationary and exploitive consequences, as
Mercier summarized it in 1788 in his chapter "Ce qu'on appelle Philosophe":

> Les folliculaires & les partisans du despotisme ont tant crié contre la
> philosophie & contre les philosophes, que ce dernier terme roule au-
> jourd'hui parmi le peuple, qui l'a défiguré à sa manière, & en le mettant
> à toutes sauces. Or, dans chaque maison il y a toujours quelqu'un qu'on
> appelle *philosophe*. Si un garçon marchand, un clerc de procureur, font
> quelques commentaires qui sortent du cercle ordinaire des idées, c'est
> un philosophe. . . . Ce terme est une injure mitigée dans la bouche
> des délateurs, de vos ennemis secrets, de ceux enfin qui veulent vous
> nuire. On appelle encore *philosophes* beaucoup de gens qui ne le sont
> guère. . . . Le terme est donc tombé, mais la chose ne l'est pas.[174]

In fact, this "matter," this Enlightenment knowledge implemented in programs
whose formation and proliferation were co-ordinated with the *philosophe* as their
subject, was now faced with its practical application to politics, which in turn also
profited from the term *philosophe*. The evidence from our conceptual history,
however, that the downfall of the concept and the role of the *philosophe* had already set in before the Revolution, contradicts the myth of Enlightenment
philosophie as the direct precursor of the French Revolution.

Exorcising and Adjuring the Past (1788–99): The Revolutionary Self-Image of *Philosophie* and *Philosophes*

The reactualization of *philosophie* during the French Revolution had the double
function of bestowing an aura of dignity on the acts of revolutionary politicians
that were not anchored in an unbroken tradition and of filling out the future horizon that was always uncertain because of the radicalization of the Revolution. To
the extent that philosophically based action became public political action with
real consequences, the previous nonbinding prognoses acquired a programmatic
status. Instead of criticizing the ancien régime and its institutions, *philosophie*
was now called upon to legitimize the decisions of a new state and demonstrate
its capacity for praxis.

"Cette incroyable révolution, préparée par la philosophie."[175]

That the French Revolution would be the daughter, heiress, and practical continuation of Enlightenment *philosophie* was the spontaneous—and soon enough

the conventional—conviction of many revolutionaries, thereby contributing essentially to the stylization of the historical dialectics of Enlightenment and Revolution as the myth of a direct causal relationship. Immediately after the storming of the Bastille, the populist preacher and politician Fauchet brought this self-legitimation into a salvational scheme of Enlightenment promise and revolutionary fulfillment:

> La Liberté française n'existe que depuis un mois. . . . La Philosophie elle-même a été l'instrument dont la Providence s'est servie pour ce prodige. C'est elle qui a jetté les idées de liberté dans les âmes, échauffé les coeurs & animé les courrages.[176]

Revolutionary journalists conceived of themselves as the successors of the *philosophes* who had actually carried their *philosophie* to victory: "C'est aux lumières de la philosophie que nous devons la révolution, c'est aux lumières des écrivains patriotiques que nous devrons son triomphe."[177]

During the first years of the Revolution, it was above all the supreme symbolic figure of Voltaire who personified the Enlightenment's pioneering struggle:

> Notre glorieuse Révolution est le fruit de ses ouvrages: s'il n'eût pas fait des philosophes, le fanatisme serait encore debout au sein de la capitale. Ce sont les philosophes, qui ont fait les décrets; ce sont des philosophes qui les propagent et les défendent.[178]

As a figure of identification become historical, Voltaire was the occasion for the foundation and festive consecration of the Panthéon as the national monument to the great sons of France. To be sure, there were some reservations about Voltaire—that his elitism was no longer up-to-date and that he was being favored before, for instance, the dead revolutionary Mirabeau;[179] yet the public was dominated by the social need and political will to glorify him as the twice-interned prisoner in the Bastille, as someone "persecuted" into his grave, the passionate advocate of the victims of justice, the spiritual liberator, in short, as the *philosophe*.[180] Hence his sarcophagus, which was the centerpiece of the festive procession that went from the ruins of the Bastille to the new Panthéon on July 11, 1791, bore an inscription that was widely distributed by the press and in broadsheet graphics: "Il vengea Calas, Labarre, Sirven & Montbailly. / Poëte, philosophe, historien; il a fait prendre un grand essor à l'esprit humain, et nous a préparés à devenir libres."[181]

Only Rousseau—"ce philosophe vertueux . . . , ce vengeur indomptable des droits de l'homme asservi"[182]—received the same governmental "canonization" as an Enlightenment forerunner of the Revolution and then only in the festivities of October 12, 1793, after many decrees and the long controversies that flared up because of his "more democratic" character when compared to Voltaire.[183] For beneath this official level and increasingly with the radicalization of the Revolution, even the least-known of the dead *philosophes* were conjured up as political emblems and father figures, whether in the form of busts in reactionary clubs[184] or in bourgeois political catechisms:

D[emande:] Quels sont les hommes qui par leurs écrits ont préparé la révolution? – R[éponse:] Helvetius, Mably, J. J. Rousseau, Voltaire, Franklin. – D. Comment nommes-tu ces grands hommes? – R. Philosophes. – D. Que veut dire ce mot? – R. Sage, ami de l'humanité.[185]

Philosophie: *The Positive Principle of the French Revolution*

The adjuration of the Enlightenment by revolutionary politicians and writers not only functioned to build a framework of meaning around the causes and the outbreak of the French Revolution; it also served to confirm the character and course of this Revolution itself, whose domestic and foreign policy were interpreted as the victorious struggle of the proponents of *philosophie* against the backward defenders of fanaticism and despotism: "Les uns armés de la philosophie voulaient détruire tous les abus, les autres, cuirassés par les préjugés, voulaient tout défendre."[186] On the basis of its multifaceted applicability, the revolutionaries made demands on *philosophie* for every sort of political question. As the schoolmaster of "equality," it supported demands for the abolition of tax privileges and the repeal of class divisions at the Etats Généraux;[187] as the essence of "freedom," it justified the deposing of Louis XVI[188] and the planting of *arbres de liberté* in the areas conquered by the revolutionary troops;[189] as the signpost of a fundamental and propitious political order, it created the constitution of 1795;[190] as the principle of a progressive patriotic disposition, it even glorified extreme measures during the Terror like the mass executions in the Loire:

La Révolution marche à pas de géant; préjugés et fanatisme, tout croule aujourd'hui devant la force irrésistible de la raison; le flambeau de la philosophie éclaire tout, brûle ses ennemis.[191]

If, for all of their pathos, these uses of the concept were relatively isolated, that aspect of Enlightenment philosophy that was hostile to religion and the church underwent a coherent reactualization. In 1789, a revolutionary enthusiast like the Abbé Fauchet could still hope for the reconciliation of *philosophie* and religion under the sign of the Revolution: "La Philosophie & la Religion s'embrassent."[192] But with the de-Christianization movement in the year II, the Revolution seemed to radical reporters to have become more and more a "lutte philosophique à l'église entre les prêtres et les hommes de bon sens."[193] Whether ministers officially abjured their priestly offices in the church of the little town of Rochefort (the building had been renamed the "Temple of Truth"),[194] whether a Catholic priest got married in the Breton harbor village of Saint-Malo,[195] or whether communities in the Département Seine-et-Marne replaced their Catholic priest with a republican teacher and the mass with education in citizenship[196] – it was all a sansculottes celebration of the victory of *philosophie* over religious "fanaticism":

> Le hideux fanatisme est enfin désarmé et la raison triomphe. De toutes parts dans la République Française, les idoles tombent en poudre sous les coups de la philosophie, les temples de l'imposture et du crime s'écroulent.[197]

But this militant anti-Catholicism in the name of *philosophie* was concentrated in the period from autumn 1793 to spring 1794 and was limited to a single group of political activists. Robespierre avoided this sort of language and charged the de-Christianization movement with pernicious *philosophisme*.[198] Then after Thermidor – with decreasing respect for the republican calendar and with church attendance increasing – it became possible to be ironical about the attempt to introduce *philosophie tricolore* as a national revolutionary religion.[199] In any case, isolated attempts to defuse the rivalry between religion and *philosophie* by declaring them complementary[200] or to interpret the concordat between Bonaparte and the pope in 1801 as the final reconciliation between the Catholic church and "true philosophy"[201] found little response: the Enlightenment and the revolutionary de-Catholization movement had bound *philosophie* far too strongly and inflexibly to anticlericalism and atheism.[202]

As the comments just quoted intimate, the adjuration of the "philosophical" character of the French Revolution was fragile, and the more the Revolution's own dynamics took charge, the more questionable it became even for supporters of the Revolution. The regret of moderate journalists that the Revolution had deviated from its well-defined path of *philosophie* with the persecution of priests and the petit-bourgeois club movement,[203] and Marat's repeated statements that *philosophie* had admittedly prepared the way for the Revolution but, as a nonviolent energy guided by reason, simply was not suitable for the revolutionary struggle of the "people" against "despotism" and "privilege,"[204] were based on the common experience that the philosophy of the Enlightenment could hardly be expected to furnish concrete instructions for revolutionary praxis. The leaders of the Jacobin revolutionary government practically never referred to *philosophie*.[205] On the other hand, the post-Thermidorian reaction could then be interpreted as the return of the Revolution to the commonsense middle way of *philosophie*,[206] and C. F. E. Dupin, the administrative commissioner and later prefect of the Département Seine, even claimed retrospectively that during the entire course of the Revolution he could recognize the divine omniscience of *philosophie* generating freedom, a republican yet moderate power:

> C'est cette puissance de la philosophie, qui avait préparé la Révolution, qui avait renversé la Bastille, qui avait armé toute la France pour la défense de sa liberté, cette même puissance de la philosophie qui a dé-

trôné Robespierre, qui a fait le 18 fructidor, qui a accepté la Constitution de l'an III et qui la soutiendra.[207]

But by bracketing the phase of the Jacobin dictatorship as a "blunder," such harmonizing efforts went rather to confirm the tension between *philosophie* and the French Revolution.

The Philosophe *as Revolutionary?*

Just how fragile the claim actually was for a "philosophical" continuity between the Enlightenment and the Revolution is shown even more clearly by the *philosophe*'s image of his own role; for neither could the Enlightenment spokesmen maintain themselves as revolutionaries nor could revolutionaries continue to play the roles of *philosophes*.

Next to the heirs of the great figures of the Enlightenment, who squeezed through the revolutionary period as inconspicuously as possible,[208] Raynal and Condorcet exemplify the two extremes of the prominent *philosophe* in the Revolution. The former condemned the nationalization of church property, the formation of parties, the club movement, and antimonarchist tendencies as violations of property, individual freedom, central political authority, and public order, taking care all along to maintain a safe distance from the Revolution in the names of the *philosophes:*

> Mais non, jamais les conceptions hardies de la philosophie n'ont été présentées par nous comme la mesure rigoureuse des actes de législation. Vous ne pouvez vous attribuer, sans erreur, ce qui n'a pu résulter que d'une fausse interprétation de nos principes. . . . Alors aucun motif ne m'appellait à en faire l'application .[209]

Condorcet, on the other hand, so strongly engaged himself in the Revolution—for the introduction of the republic, for a democratic constitution, and a new educational system—that his political friends could quite believably recommend him as a revolutionary *philosophe*.[210] Raynal lost his credibility during an excited public debate: "Philosophe, tu as renié la philosophie."[211] Precisely because of his beliefs, Condorcet tried to transfer the enlightened philosophical search for truth to the Jacobin politics of persecution; he ended up a suicide.[212] Thus, both demonstrated the *philosophes*' ineffectiveness for programming and mastering political revolution. Not as political shapers but only as precursors who had retreated into the past were the *philosophes* able to preserve their glory and functional legitimation in the Revolution. We have already seen this in the pantheonizing of Voltaire and Rousseau, in the bourgeois catechisms, and in official holidays. What they all have in common is a gesture of causality, but also the qualitative distinction between Enlightenment and Revolution:

> Grâces vous soient rendues, génies immortels qui avez posé les pre-
> mières bases de l'édifice de la liberté du monde! . . . Voltaire, Mon-
> tesquieu, Raynal, Diderot, Mably, et toi, illustre citoyen de Genève,
> divin Rousseau, c'est de vos écrits qu'est jailli ce torrent de lumières
> qui, entraînant dans sa course toutes les vieilles institutions et tous les
> étais de la royauté, a aplani le terrain et préparé l'établissement de la
> République.[213]

On the other hand, marginalized late Enlightenment intellectuals, who had
made more out of their political career than their prominent forerunners, seldom
understood themselves as *philosophes*. Of course Brissot defended his "fellow
party member" Condorcet with this concept, and Carra was outraged at the
representative A. Dillin, whose disqualification of the National Assembly as a
"société de soi-disant philosophes" was supposed to have calumniated the Bearers
of the Revolution.[214] Neither of them, however, claimed the role for himself, nor
did others ascribe it to them.

At any rate, the concept *philosophe* was certainly used for the members of the
National Assembly — sometimes as support or praise,[215] sometimes even polemi-
cally[216] — and generally signified the patriots and followers of the Revolution according to the given context;[217] yet this did not completely account for the role
of the active revolutionary. On the contrary, after the experience of the Terror
the "true" *philosophes* were differentiated from revolutionary politicians with a
new clarity:

> Si les ennemis de toute philosophie persistent à les confondre, il suffira
> de prendre les ouvrages de Montesquieu ou de Voltaire d'une main, &
> celui de Saint-Just de l'autre . . . la distance qui sépare Saint-Just &
> nos philosophes, est toute celle qui sépare l'ignorance la plus abjecte du
> savoir, la folie & la férocité, de la raison la plus élevée & la plus
> éclairée.[218]

Consequently, if the enlightener as *philosophe* failed in the Revolution and the
revolutionary conjured up the philosophical role out of the heroic past without
taking it over for his own time, then this can be explained by the fact that the
French Revolution had largely abolished the favorable political and social conditions in which the role of the *philosophe* had been developed. By ripping down
the old partition between rulers and ruled and opening up chances for political
influence and decision making for intellectuals, the Revolution first of all
devalued the game of criticizing authority even more radically yet even less surely
insofar as that game was further from actual use and correspondingly more incon-
sequent; the sense of criticizing authority as constitutive of the role of the
philosophe was still confirmed by Raynal's *Adresse*. And second, when the Revolution broke up the old power positions of church and state and refilled them with
its own supporters, the aura of innocence and moral integrity was detached from

the role of the politically persecuted. For despite internal struggles over the revolutionary line,[219] persecution no longer befell the critics but the defenders of the ancien régime. Nor could the new phantom of the "aristocratic conspiracy"[220] take over the strategic function of the myth of "persecuted innocence," because the conspirator was not (as yet) the proprietor of political power. Third, the revolutionary displacement of sovereignty from the monarch to the "people" weakened the *philosophe*'s claim to be the "teacher of the people." For this elitist role was not only superfluous to the extent that the sansculottes understood themselves as "une immense famille de philosophes,"[221] that anyone was capable of becoming a *philosophe*,[222] that even the petite bourgeoisie sensed an Enlightenment mandate,[223] and that *philosophie* was certified for the people from the cradle to the battlefield.[224] Yet it could also become a burden for a revolutionary politician to the extent that he drew his legitimation not from the work of the Enlightenment but from a plausible interpretation of the "people's will,"[225] not from instruction but from his representation of the people:

> Ne donnons pas le titre de philosophes à tous ces misérables pédants que le peuple a jusqu'ici trop réverés. La véritable philosophie ne consiste pas seulement à régler les opinions, mais elle consiste aussi à bien connaître l'opinion publique. Il ne suffit pas qu'une opinion soit bonne pour l'adopter, il est nécessaire qu'elle soit génerale.[226]

Since the role of the *philosophe* lost the position it had acquired during the ancien régime through the revolutionary change to a new political system, it could be institutionalized in the developing "bourgeois" society only at the price of a renewed detachment from society.[227] The *philosophe* could remain a hero only within that myth of the "Enlightenment as the preparation for the new society" with which it has legitimized itself ever since; he had become a hero of the past.

That the accelerated development of the meaning of the concept *philosophe* that had been traversed in less than a lifetime could already be recognized at the turn of the century can be seen in a newspaper article and an entry in the Almanac in which La Harpe biographically clothed his answer to the question "Qu'est-ce donc qu'un philosophe?" in a series of personal experiences. They fairly well match the conceptual history whose phases we have been reconstructing. (1) The starting point for the Enlightenment role of the *philosophe* is the attitude of a conscious withdrawal from society: "Lorsque j'étois au collège, un écolier qui fuyoit ses camarades, qui avoit un air sauvage et sombre, on l'appeloit un *philosophe*." (2) Their own public, that reading public that was so proud to attribute *philosophie* to themselves, had been constituted by the *philosophes* through their criticism of religious dogmas and institutions and in debates with their representatives: "Quand j'entrai dans le monde, on appeloit *philosophe* un homme qui se moquoit de la religion, qui ne croyoit ni à l'existence de la divinité, ni à la moralité des hommes. . . . J'avois grande envie d'être philosophe." Thus here, too, the trivialization of *philosophie* to a fashionable role is interpreted as a symptom of the collapse of the ancien régime. (3) If the *philosophes* in the late Enlightenment still employ a relatively mild irony, then the Jacobin claim to have founded their political action in *philosophie* valorizes the most aggressive polemics; and with this abrupt shift in tone, their text confirms our hypothesis about the chronological limit of canon formation at the end of the eighteenth century:

> Alors les philosophes étoient ridicules, mais ils sont devenus atroces depuis que la philosophie a fait naître parmi nous les jacobins, cette nouvelle race d'hommes qui n'a presque rien de commun avec l'espèce humaine et pour lesquels on devroit ouvrir un nouveau chapitre dans non dictionnaires d'histoire naturelle.

(4) Nonetheless, even the time of such threats by the *philosophes* is put in the past. The gain in experience from just a few years of social and political change had made "society" cautious: "Ah! messieurs les philosophes . . . aujourd'hui le monde a les yeux ouverts; vous devez vous estimer fort heureux, si vous n'êtes attendus qu'aux Petites-Maisons."[228]

However partisan this whole retrospective might be, at any rate it clarifies one important insight: with the end of the ancien régime, those specific framing conditions were suspended, the only ones under which the *philosophes* could have presented themselves to their public and allowed themselves to be celebrated as the "subject of the Enlightenment." In bourgeois society, however, this role was not only glorified as part of a legitimizing past but, with respect to its own present and future, was simultaneously pushed into a comparatively marginal position.

Neutralization and Inclusion in Bourgeois Society: *Philosophe* and *Philosophie* (1795–1820)

Reactualizing the Philosophie *Debate and the Historicization of the* Philosophes

The removal of *philosophie* into the past did not simply occur during the peaceful institutionalization of a historical mythos and the canonization of "great authors" in its revolutionary self-image; at the same time, it also took place within the revival of the publicistic clashes between critics and defenders of the *philosophes*.

In 1789, the conservatives merely had to fire up the old reproaches of *philosophie*'s atheistic, morally corrupt, and politically subversive influence, in order to throw all blame on the Revolution and to interpret it as a confirmation of their previous warnings.[229] And many who at first had held tight to the fashionable life-style of the *philosophe,* now began, in the face of the increasingly fierce ideological struggles, to keep a safe distance from it; for instance, the author of the following pamphlet:

PHILOSOPHES. Souffleurs dans la tragi-atroci-absurdo-comédie-parade, appellée la révolution. . . . Ces philosophes, je leur croyois au moins le coeur bon. Les mots de bienfaissance, d'humanité, de tolérance m'avoient séduit. Quelle étoit ma simplicité! Je ne voyois pas que leur métaphysique digne du onzième siècle, leur ardeur pour le proselytisme, jointe à leur indifférence sur le choix des moyens, devoient en faire des êtres essentiellement malfaisans. J'abjure mon erreur.[230]

Nonetheless, it was the experience of the Jacobin terror and persecution — hence, those processes precisely that had been largely bypassed during the revolutionary co-optation of *philosophie* — that nourished an "antiphilosophical" polemics of renewed intensity and aggression; it exploded after Thermidor with the result that the role of the *philosophe* was depleted of its specific Enlightenment features. The political dictionaries were dominated by the pejorative labels *philosophisme* and *philosophiste*,[231] whereas the revolutionary lexica avoided the concept *philosophe*.[232] The polemics were mainly ignited by La Harpe's pamphlet *Du fanatisme dans la langue révolutionnaire, ou De la persécution suscitée par les barbares du dix-huitième siècle, contre la religion et ses ministres* (Winter 1796–97). The pamphlet was printed at least nineteen times within a brief period, and its vigorous, partially brilliant formulations reactivated the conventional reproaches of persecution (which had been completely repolarized once again), religious intolerance, and an arrogant attitude to the general public, yet it also made possible another, positive use of *philosophe* by stating that it had been misused in the past by the Enlightenment:

Vous n'oserez pas nier que ce soit votre *philosophie,* qui ait fait la révolution: vous vous en êtes si souvent glorifiés, avant qu'elle vous eût écrasés vous-mêmes. . . . Pauvre *philosophie* du dix-huitième siècle! à quel point tes disciples t'ont compromise! Ils ne t'ont pas même associée au butin pour te payer tes leçons, et ils ont même égorgé nombre de leurs maîtres et docteurs.[233]

Rivarol — who, in contrast to Voltaire's erstwhile disciple La Harpe, had already advocated the official positions of the ancien régime before 1789 and who had not returned to France from self-exile after Thermidor — showed more analytic acuteness. He devoted an entire piece to demonstrating that, as soon as their involvement in political action became really possible, the *philosophes* would necessarily become entangled in contradictions with their own role due to their work on the Enlightenment and their proliferation of the postulate of equality. By underlining the fact that the political public was *philosophie*'s field of action,[234] Rivarol made it obvious that the *philosophes* ought to be watched over by church and state.

The most comprehensive rebukes, well studded with numerous quotes from the writings of the *philosophes,* were made by Abbé Barruel. He attempted to unmask Jacobinism, this "barbarie des modernes Vandales,"[235] as the final stage of a long-range Satanic conspiracy of three generations of *philosophes,* who supposedly first deposed God and religion in the late Enlightenment (the generation of "Sophistes de l'impiété"), then overthrew the monarchy in 1792 ("Sophistes de la rébellion"), and finally established anarchy ("Sophistes de l'anarchie").[236] As the key means during the first phase of the conspiracy, the Abbé denounced the *Encyclopédie,* the interdiction of the Jesuits, the Enlightenment formation of groups and publicity, the infiltration of the academies by *philosophes,* and Turgot's ministry[237] – precisely the factors that our conceptual history has shown as decisive for the public success of *philosophie* between 1750 and 1775 and which had contributed considerably to the legitimation of the *philosophe:*

> En se donnant le titre d'incrédules et d'ennemis du Christianisme, Voltaire et d'Alembert auraient révolté les esprits. Ils se donnèrent le nom de *philosophes,* et l'on crut qu'ils l'ètaient. La vénération attachée à ce titre passa à leur école; aujourd'hui encore, malgré tous les forfaits et tous les désastres de la révolution qui a suivi, qui devait naturellement suivre leur conjuration, est appelé le siècle de la philosophie; et tout homme qui pense comme eux en fait de religion, s'appelle Philosophe.[238]

The critique of the *esprit philosophique,* which was composed by the lawyer and representative Portalis around the same time (that is, between 1797 and 1800), took an intermediate, historically objective position. On the one hand, he pertinently rejected the conspiracy theory,[239] as well as the reduction of the *philosophes* to scapegoats;[240] he explained their influence as the result of their apparent harmlessness and defenselessness, the model character of their lifestyle, and the social and governmental power vacuum that had simultaneously occurred.[241] On the other hand, he acknowledged the new method of thought based on observation, experiment, analysis, and reason, its practical use for domestic reform under Louis XVI.[242] But he condemned the "materialistic" and atheistic excrescences of this *esprit philosophique,* its tendency toward intolerance and fanaticism, its improper application to areas he considered inaccessible like emotion, morality, and religion.[243]

In many respects, this intermediate position was not very far from that of the advocates of *philosophie.* Morellet, who had directed one of the most vigorous pamphlets against Palissot in 1760, once again engaged himself on behalf of the *philosophes:* Had not the proliferation of their writings been too small and too slow to cause broad-scale alterations in basic mentalities? Was it their fault if the politicians, whose diagnosis was theoretically pertinent, had chosen an overdose of the wrong drug in the power of the people? Not they, but the failure of public power and the seductive force of words, should be blamed for the Revolution. And Morellet supported this apology by a long table juxtaposing the "theoretical programs of *philosophie*" with the "contrary praxis of the French Revolution."[244]

To La Harpe's arguments, it could have been replied that not a single prominent *philosophe* could be found among the leading politicians of the French Revolution, that men like Condorcet belonged rather to the victims of the Terror, and that the meaning of the concept *philosophe* was not negatively defined.[245] In any case, the played-down contrary definition is tantamount to a suppression of the Enlightenment:

> La *Philosophie* est la recherche de la vérité, en descendant des causes aux effets, ou en remontant des effets aux causes. . . . cette définition, la seule juste, la seule vraie de la *Philosophie,* exclut pour ses partisans toute espèce de fanatisme.[246]

Even Barruel's charges provoked an extensive reply, composed by Mounier, a leading prerevolutionary politician of the early National Assembly. Mounier's stress on *philosophie*'s practical and humanitarian, albeit limited, effects on a whole series of reforms in the late ancien régime[247] corresponds to our historical reconstruction of the concept as well as to his hypothesis of the prerevolutionary decadence of *philosophie*[248] and his denial that there was any direct responsibility for the French Revolution on the part of the *philosophes:*

> Ils ont contribué à repandre dans toutes les classes la haine du pouvoir arbitraire: mais la philosophie n'a aucun rapport avec les circonstances qui ont produit la révolution. Les crimes et les malheurs ont été principalement les effets de la composition des ordres, des imprudences de la cour, de l'ignorance des principes politiques et de la corruption des moeurs.[249]

Compared to the debates in the 1780s, the balance of power between the antagonistic groups had been completely reversed. Now it was the proponents of *philosophie* who were on the defensive, who had to bear the brunt of the more aggressive pamphlets after 1800,[250] who complained about the interdiction of Enlightenment writings,[251] and who, once again and even more concretely than around 1760, got themselves into a situation of latent persecution, as a supportive newspaper, *Citoyen français,* was forced to admit:

> Il s'est depuis quelque temps formé, comme on sait, une conjuration de pygmés anti-philosophes, qui osent contester aux grands écrivains du XVIIIᵉ siècle jusqu'au bon sens et á la probité. Il est, parmi nos nouveaux tartufes, de bon ton d'insulter à la mémoire des morts et à l'honneur des vivants.[252]

To be sure, in their vehement delaying actions, the retreating defenders of *philosophie* were still able to unmask many a new *antiphilosophe* as a turncoat,[253] to ironize the argumentative contortions of their critics,[254] and to declare the staying power, the long-range effective inheritance of the writings of the much-despised *coterie philosophique*:[255] as the incarnation of the reactionary press, a colored etching from 1819 shows four "fanatic" priests attempting in vain to extinguish the breath of life of Fénelon, Condorcet, Franklin, and Buffon.[256] But on the whole after 1800, the defenders found the public echo largely hostile and in the long run increasingly less interested. The old polemics flared up once more in 1815 in the pamphlet-dictionaries dominated by the restoration,[257] only subsequently to ebb into incidental skirmishes.[258]

The fading of the Enlightenment concept of philosophy and the splintering of its sustaining groups into little isolated *cénacles* are related to the circumstances, among others, that even in government the role of the *philosophe* had lost its power of suggestion by differentiating its previously combined functions into the scientist, the administrator, and the publicly engaged intellectual, and that the increasingly consolidated state after Brumaire systematically controlled the public and the press, without having to declare its own stance in the conflict of opinions. The regular police reports of the consulate and the empire show how little the security agencies cared about the publicistic encirclement and slow extermination of the dispersed heirs of the *philosophes*,[259] and how they refused—as long as their influence remained limited to café society—to take their tirades against the institutions of the new state seriously:

> Les philosophes se plaignent amèrement de ce qu'on cherche à leur attribuer tous les malheurs de la Révolution et la destruction des anciens établissements. . . . A la suite de ces plaintes, ils se permettent le plus souvent des propos contre le gouvernement. On entend aussi dans les cafés des malveillants. . . . On repousse ordinairement ces discours avec indignation, et ils n'affaiblissent en rien la confiance générale dans le gouvernement.[260]

It can scarcely have been "tolerance" that motivated this observation by the Napoleonic police but rather the insight—won from the experience of the Enlightenment period—that the precipitate repression of polemics hostile to the state was often just a touch more dangerous than the polemics itself.

In this sort of context, the Enlightenment conceptions of *philosophie* and the role of *philosophe* were doomed to a slow demise. Now whether *philosophie* was celebrated by the revolutionaries as the glorious pathfinder of the Revolution, or was condemned by the opponents of the Revolution as a "philosophistic" perversion of "true philosophy" and as the generator of the Reign of Terror, or whether it was defended by later adherents as the humanitarian reform movement of the eighteenth century—all of these positions amounted to the historicization of the Enlightenment concept of philosophy and hence set it off from the action-oriented social knowledge of the early nineteenth century.

Philosophie *as Academic Discipline and the* Philosophe *as Professional Scholar (1793–1835)*

With the *philosophie du dix-huitième siècle* safely deposited in the past, the semantically depoliticized predicates *philosophe* and *philosophie* could now be reinstitutionalized within the developing "bourgeois" society as a neutral, scientifically oriented conceptual pair.

Junius Frey, the Austrian emigrant Jacobin, can be taken as a forerunner of this process. As early as 1793, he had already devoted an anonymous tract to his Parisian club with the title *Philosophie sociale*, which (analogous to the somewhat simultaneous conception of an *art social*)[261] argued for an objective politicological science that would have to be something more than simply *la science des gouvernans pour tromper les gouvernés:*

> Eloigné de tout esprit de parti, je cherche la vérité, je ne m'attache qu'à elle, et au peu de voyageurs que je rencontre sur cette route pénible. La philosophie sociale est la science la moins avancée et la plus incertaine de toutes. Elle est encore dans son berceau.[262]

But for the most part the new academic concept of philosophy was propagated by the *Idéologues*, an elite group of late Enlightenment figures who had gathered themselves around the writings of Condillac in the last decades of the ancien régime, had been supported during the Directory by the foundation of the "Institute," and exercised a certain fascination on many politicians. If out of the complex semantics of the concept of philosophy the *philosophes* had mainly hypothesized their dedication to society, then the unbiased observation of nature was the intellectual style of the *Idéologues*.[263] Their primary interest was to constitute a science of human thought;[264] and the fact that *Science de l'homme* as a paradigm for thought and research in France goes back to this project—which has held good up until now—demonstrates their affinity with the institutional complex of science in bourgeois society. Hence it is symptomatic that—precisely in those years when it was fashionable to legitimize radical-republican politics by grounding it in *philosophie*—the *Idéologues* were engaged in the development of a *philosophie* in the sense of an academic discipline. In the prospectus of their magazine *Décade philosophique*, the predicate *philosophie* (the most frequent concept in the magazine) is applied to one of three groups of science, the others being *Sciences mathématiques* and *Sciences politiques:*

> La section philosophique renfermera non-seulement la Métaphysique, la Logique et la Morale; c'est-à dire, l'art de conduire sa raison dans l'étude des sciences, et de se conduire soi-même dans la carrière de la vie, mais aussi l'Economie publique, ou l'art social, avec toutes ses subdivisions.[265]

Admittedly, it seems as if their reservations about everyday politics have qualified *Idéologie* as the forerunner of modern science in France less than their argumentative and methodological rigor. Characteristically, it was precisely in their magazine that Roederer, the managing editor of the *Journal de Paris,* made a statement in a review of Rivalrol's "antiphilosophical" pamphlet, in which he described *philosophie* as an objective, empirical observational science that could provide a way out of the debates between the *philosophes* and *antiphilosophes:*

> Pour moi, voici à-peu-près ce que j'entends par la Philosophie moderne. D'abord elle a de commun avec l'ancienne, d'être l'amour de la sagesse et la recherche de la vérité. Ensuite, ce qui me semble la distinguer de celle ci, c'est la sûreté de ses méthodes pour la direction de cette recherche, c'est aussi l'étendue de ses découvertes. Une connaissance plus approfondie de l'entendement et de l'origine des idées, a fait remonter aux vrais moyens d'en acquérir et de les vérifier. Ainsi l'expérience et l'observation ont remplacé dans toutes les sciences l'arbitraire des hypothèses et la manie des systèmes.[266]

If it was bound to happen that an *Idéologie* that sought scientific neutrality without being politically complaisant would quickly collide with Napoleonic absolutism and thus lose its official support, it nonetheless established a permanent role, in which the production of knowledge was set apart from political action and in which the reciprocal relationship between the performance of the knowledge produced and a nonspecialist public was relaxed. The bourgeois states soon built up their universities as places for the production of such knowledge, thus taking over the function of the religious knowledge of revelation, which in the ancien régime had been the ultimate valid instance for an "adequate" grasp of reality. Here the role of the scientist folded into a bourgeois role, and it is their role as the precursors of scientists that distinguishes the *Idéologues* from the Enlightenment *philosophes.*

In the following period, their social institutionalization can be seen in the Academie dictionary of 1835 in its grouping of definitions for *philosophie*[267] and *philosophe:* "Celui qui s'applique à l'étude des sciences, et qui cherche à connaître les effets par leurs causes et par leurs principes."[268] The only traces of the dramatic conceptual development of the Enlightenment and the Revolution are the (historical) example of *La philosophie du dix-huitième siècle* and the special expressions that had grown out of the polemics — *philosophaille, philosophailler, philosophastre, philosopherie, philosophesque, philosophesse,* and *philosophiste,* which were relegated to the supplement.[269] Still, the eighteenth-century concept of *philosophie* as a political and ethical legacy and as a latent critical potential remained subliminally in the collective memory. Whenever scientists and artists in bourgeois society succeeded in influencing public opinion and thus acquiring a certain political role — whether in the memorial celebrations of the early Third Republic,[270] in the Dreyfus affair, or in the protest movements of the late 1960s—this latent memory becomes presence. Wherever there are dreams of a convergence of social reflection and action keyed to social needs, of a reconciliation between theory and praxis, then the French Enlightenment is reactualized as the pattern of the past. Even the West German student movement had its Club Voltaire.[271]

Chapter 8
Outline of a Literary History of the French Revolution

Why Write a Literary History of the French Revolution?

In the periodization favored by the standard presentations of French literature, there is scarcely any space for those texts that were written and received between 1789 and 1799. A chapter devoted to the Enlightenment, which usually skips the last decade of the eighteenth century, is followed by French romanticism, whose chronological limits commonly correspond—aside from a few "precursors" (for instance, Chateaubriand) always mentioned without fail—to the Restoration beginning in 1815. The resulting space in between, twenty-five years after all, appears only indirectly—that is, as a precondition for romanticism, which can be interpreted as a contrary movement to the literature of the Revolution. This interpretation is supported by the self-understanding of early romanticism; a pertinent example is found in Victor Hugo's preface to his *Odes et Ballades* from February 1824:

> Contemporary literature is perhaps partly the result of the revolution, but certainly not its expression. The society generated by the revolution had its literature, as ugly and inaccessible as itself. This literature and this society died together and are not going to come back to life. Order was restored in every field of life; the arts were also renewed. Religion sanctions freedom; we have citizens. Belief purifies imagination; we have poets. Truth returns everywhere, to the customs, to the laws, to the arts.

Nonetheless, if literary histories screened out the period of the Revolution, their unquestionable interest in the Enlightenment presupposes this Revolution as its historical and philosophical focus – indeed, as its result.[1] For contemporaries, the causal relationship between Enlightenment and Revolution was evident. After all, they were concerned with the legitimation of the Revolution as a historical break in continuity, even though the Enlightenment efforts prior to 1789 had been more concentrated on reform.[2] As Count Mirabeau put it in a speech to the French National Assembly on September 10, 1791: "The present Revolution is the work of literature and philosophy. . . . Let us beware of the belief that the arts are mere external ornamentation on political considerations."[3]

How can it be explained that, whereas the retrospective devotion to the French Enlightenment was grounded in its being interpreted as the pioneer of the Revolution, there has never been a literary history of the Revolution? Three observations are particularly important here. First of all, the humanistic period called "Enlightenment" (siècle des lumières) has no sociohistorical equivalent (the signification "ancien régime" encompasses the seventeenth as well as the eighteenth century) in which we could find evidence for a preponderant humanistic interest in the time between 1680 and 1789. Second, the lack of something corresponding in the history of the humanities to the politicohistorical label "Revolution" for the years between 1789 and 1799 proves once again that literary and philosophical history has skipped these years. And finally, it can be noted that the political and social historiography of the Revolution has clearly focused on the years from 1789 to 1794, which is why the time from the overthrow of Robespierre (July 1794) until Napoleon's coup d'état (November 1799) has quite rightly been characterized as the "stepchild of the history of the Revolution." Until today, the return to the philosophical and literary history of the Enlightenment has actualized the theories and utopias with which every kind of government in the nineteenth and twentieth centuries has been accustomed to justify its actions. The Revolution is regarded as that political and sociohistorical transformation that was the condition for realizing the promises of the Enlightenment. Seen so, it is understandable that the humanistic history of the French Revolution has barely been thematized: these years can hardly be said to have produced new political theories or novel literary forms that would become powerfully effective in the following period. The French literary historian Albert Thibaudet was of the opinion that "an extraordinary talent of invention and creativity in the field of action had been paid for in the literary field with the disappearance of taste, the poverty of forms, the sterility of the theater and the book."[4]

It is mainly this third observation that is important as a justification for dealing with the literature of this period.[5] It is of course correct that it was exactly between 1795 and 1799 that the Revolution led to those complex changes in the interests of the upper middle class through which it has passed into the writing of history – that is, after the "years of terror" (1793 and 1794), which had been characterized by governmental concessions to the petite bourgeoisie and the forerunners of today's proletariat. But hitherto, it has scarcely been considered that the Revolution was only able to flow into bourgeois channels because the enthusiastic efforts after 1789 to politically implement the promises of the Enlightenment were increasingly abandoned after 1794. If this thesis is accurate, the Enlightenment no longer seems to be a program that has been widely realized but is rather a legitimizing potential that can easily block vision of our own present. A literary history of the French Revolution could move the Enlightenment into a historical distance that will continue to strike us as somewhat strange as long as secondary schools go on presenting Kant's categorical imperative as a still valid maxim for individual action and both socialists and conservatives go on regarding Rousseau's *Contrat social* as the very pattern for (divergent) concepts of political systems of action. Such an "estrangement" of the Enlightenment does not seem to have been attempted up until now because the question of the realization of Enlightenment programs by the Revolution has not been asked seriously enough. The representation of the French Revolution in political and social history did not thematize the Enlightenment but rather the ancien régime as its prehistory. Moreover, the social renewals envisaged by the Enlightenment were supposed to be founded in a change in its communication structures.[6] It is precisely the miscarriage of this hoped-for renewal that can be best demonstrated within the framework of an extensive concept of literary history.

We take 1799 as the "end of the Revolution," because with Napoleon's coup d'état the onset of the institutionalization of those interests can be seen whose realization the upper middle class had been demanding since the middle of the eighteenth century. The ten years constituting the revolutionary period are divided by the decapitation of Robespierre and the liquidation of the Montagne movement (both in July 1794). The historical significance of this date (called Thermidor according to the revolutionary calendar instituted by the National Assembly in September 1792) is the political disintegration of a regime that had attempted to mediate between petit bourgeois and proletarian interests on the one hand and those of the upper middle class on the other. For us, it is significant that the revolutionary administrations had long since lost sight of the Enlightenment goal of a general welfare in which every citizen would share.

Both of the large phases of the Revolution before and after Thermidor can be subdivided once again: first, by the deposition of Louis XVI on August 10, 1792, which was followed by the declaration of the Republic barely a month later (for its first years, there was the characteristic insight—as a first miscarriage of the Enlightenment—that general social welfare could no longer be realized through the free consensus of the citizens but only through political negotiations); second, by Vendémiaire (October) 1795, when an attempted putsch by right-wing forces was beaten down. At that time, newly aroused hopes simply withered away, the hopes that once again "the free play of opinion" could flow into unforced consensus and thus provide models for political action.[7]

Reception of the Enlightenment during the French Revolution

In this sketch of a literary history during the age the French Revolution, we assume that—like other intellectual movements—the sociohistorical role of the Enlightenment could only be to manifest an initially latent situation of needs for contemporaries and later to provide them with models for the restructuring of society. Within this explanatory framework, we must now correct three clichés. First, none of the canonized Enlightenment spokesmen in France had predicted or even expected the political movement of the Revolution and its social consequences; rather, a constitutional monarchy along the lines of England seems to have been the dominant projection of a political system that would supposedly assure the future happiness of humankind. Furthermore, it can hardly be assumed that consciousness of their own needs and hence resistance to the ancien régime had continuously grown among the protagonists of Enlightenment until finally the absolutistic state could no longer contain the increasing pressure. The ancien régime seems to have survived its most difficult crisis in the 1770s. Rather, the calling up of the Etats Généraux by the king in August 1788 was the result of a chain of political mistakes, and it was only through a series of further tactical bunglings that Louis XVI provoked his own dethroning in August 1792. Finally, the hypothesis of the French Revolution as a bourgeois revolution can only be considered valid—if at all—as its result but not as its genesis: in the French provincial academies and discussion groups of the late eighteenth century, aristocrats and bourgeois were almost equally represented, and the share of bourgeois members only slowly increased.[8] That the Enlightenment had become a real mode, even in aristocratic circles, is already reported in 1799 by Mallet Du Pan, a publicist who immigrated from Geneva:

> Since it had already become indispensable thirty years ago, along with the claims derived from birth and property, to lay claim to being an enlightened person, one flatters the distributers of this title in order to get one. Out of fear of being considered uneducated, one clothed oneself in the gown of "liberté" and disbelief. A courtier, a captain, a minister, or an actress considered themselves immortal, once they had been honored with the noble patent of "Philosophie" in a personal letter of d'Alembert and Voltaire or in a Parisian journal.[9]

This seemingly paradoxical enthusiasm on the part of the old nobility and those families who had bought titles in the course of the seventeenth and eighteenth centuries for an Enlightenment promising freedom from and hostility to the nobility can, by the way, also be explained economically. For at the end of the eighteenth century the ancien régime and its characteristic centralized economic management had suffered a serious crisis in growth. Thus the Revolution is a consequence of a comprehensive structural crisis in the absolutistic state that was potentialized by repeated governmental misjudgments. To be more precise, it can only be considered "bourgeois" insofar as it was the representatives of this class that perhaps best understood how to profit from the precipitation of events and their consequences, the growing invalidation of traditional institutions.

It is well known that the French Revolution's ideologies manifested the need for change above all in an anthropology based on the concept of nature that enabled criticism of the existent state and society and that was the presupposition for the development of models of the future. Now if we ask more concretely about its contribution to the historically unique course of the French Revolution (and not just about its role in the preparation of political and social change that was never concretely planned), then it must be stressed that this anthropology always claimed to speak in the name of all humankind and not just a specific class. This is exactly why its ideologies facilitated coalitions between social groups with conflicting interests: the demand for freedom was abstract enough to unify, in the last years of the ancien régime and the first years of the Revolution, the claims of the nobility and the bourgeoisie for more freedom of action with respect to the state, however divergent their individual interests might have been. After the king's overthrow, the interests of the upper middle class and the petite bourgeoisie could be reconciled under the slogan of "equality" as long as a distinction was not made between an equality before the law that had already been conceded and an economic equality that was unacceptable for property holders.

From a different perspective, the Enlightenment almost seems to be a product of the Revolution—especially when we ask about the unity of the movement. Only in recent years has social history been able to demonstrate in a series of case studies[10] that there was a much larger gap at the end of the ancien régime between successful Enlightenment spokesmen like Voltaire or Holbach and marginal literary figures like Restif de la Bretonne or Sylvain Maréchal than in the opposition between representatives of the political status quo and its critics to which the image of bourgeois Enlightenment and Revolution has directed our attention. The "back-alley literati" were—like the Parisian petite bourgeoisie, the later sansculottes—among the actual victims of the economic stagnation. Lured to Paris by the myth of equality in a "republic of intellectuals," they experienced the disdain of the exclusive salons, had to satisfy themselves with literary, mainly journalistic, piecework, and sought their audience among readers for whom indignation about the obscenities at court was a justification for their consumption of pornographic writings. Within this pornographic literature, the *Gazette noire*, published in London by Charles Théveneau de Morande during the 1780s, became especially renowned.

It was the "Grub Street literati," far more than those writers regarded as the legitimate successors of the canonized Enlightenment figures, who made their influence felt in all sorts of political positions during the revolutionary years— mostly through their proliferation and popularization of the ideology of the Enlightenment. Mallet Du Pan spoke of "pen pushers, legal secretaries, provincial lawyers, runaway monks, businessmen, parish employees, novelizers, newspaper compilers." The situation of these intellectuals in the last years before the Revolution explains, first of all, their veneration for Rousseau, whom they called "Jean-Jacques" and not, as later, the "author of the *Contrat social*." In his defensive autobiographical writings, they found a figure they could identify with, at least as far as the now successfully mastered past of the ancien régime was concerned. And second, it explains their retrospective effort to give the Enlightenment an aura of having anticipated social equality, through which they could also lay claim to the prestige of its most famous protagonists. Precisely in this sense, the Revolution also created the myth of the Enlightenment.

In the following analysis, I would like—with respect to the Revolution's reception of Enlightenment ideologies—to concentrate above all on two global models of communication and interaction that furnished the framework for the further development of traditional as well as for the generation of new genres. First of all, there was the idea of an enlightened public as the basis of democratic politics; or to put it more concretely, the idea that the admission of every individual to an uncensored play of opinion must necessarily flow into a consensus geared for action. Second, there was the idea of the festivals of the citizens, whose participants, by always being the performers of themselves and audience at the same time, supposedly made possible a sensual experience of an already achieved freedom and equality.[11]

Public interaction and festival are communication situations whose institutionalization was implicated from the very beginning in the programs of the revolutionary politicians. Their history gives us an opportunity to test the hypothesis of the miscarriage of the Enlightenment promise. But we are also going to have to deal with the theater from 1789 to 1799 and with those texts that, so to speak, by slipping past the disposition to collective communication, directed themselves at the reader as an individual. As we will see, the history of revolutionary theater was, to be sure, impregnated with cultural-political models, yet at the same time responded considerably to the public's unpolitical needs, like lyric and the novel. Significantly, the last two genres barely show up in the scant attempts to present the literature of the Revolution, for it is difficult to trace the influences of the various governments in their development. But it is exactly here that we have an opportunity to delineate the symptoms of literature's global functional change (and hence, indirectly, also the structural change in society at the end of the eighteenth century), because, in those areas neglected by the politicians, hardly any author was committed to the program of fulfilling the promises of the Enlightenment.

We want to include all of those genres in our tableau that claimed to address a public not limited by class or previous knowledge. That the horizon of what could be called "literary" would be extended by the attempt to institutionalize an enlightened public was already anticipated, at any rate, by Joachim Heinrich Campe in his *Briefe aus Paris, während der Französischen Revolution geschrieben* (1789):

> All of this—especially the present elevation of the French spirit by the new feeling of freedom, by the happily achieved rights of thought, speech, and writing, by the continuing inflamed and exhausting struggle against despotism and tyranny of every kind, and by the presently achieved opening to so many glittering stages on which talents in every area have been able to develop, perform, and win applause—gradually promises the language, the literature, the arts, and sciences of this people such a generally provident melting pot, that the others, for whom these advantages have not arrived, will probably have a great deal of difficulty in the future keeping up with them.[12]

Furthermore, we will only take into consideration those publications that first appeared after the summoning of the Etats Généraux and before Napoleon's coup d'état. This limitation cannot be solely derived from our primary interest in a history of four communication situations, for if that were the case, the continued or newly instituted reception of works of earlier decades would be just as illuminating. Yet this would require years of investigation. Finally, we would like to leave aside all of those texts that admittedly appeared during the revolutionary period but not in France. For their thematization would return us, apart from a few exceptions, to a history of emigrant literature—as literary history has happily practiced from time immemorial in its presentations of the 1790s as early French romanticism.

The Political Public

The term "political public" contradicts the self-image of the enlightened public. For, along with the general freedom of being able to participate in discussions, the right to an uncensored expression of opinion, and the expectation of a spontaneously occurring consensus, there was a fourth feature to the "enlightened public": the participants in public discussions were not supposed to speak as representatives of a class or profession, but as "private persons." Formulated in the language of the time, they were only supposed to obey the voice of reason and the feelings of pure humanity. Hence the texts I will deal with here always explicitly address themselves to a public of "private persons," even if today—quite in contrast to the understanding of their authors and readers—we tend to interpret them as means in the argumentative interactions between group interests about questions relevant to the whole society, ultimately even in the struggle for "state power."

The diverse measures by the revolutionary governments—above all in the first years after 1789—document the effort to institutionalize an ideal model of the public. Already on August 26, 1789, all limitations on the right to publish and all instances of censorship were suspended. This formally solved the demand for free access to public discussion and unlimited freedom of expression. Moreover, by financing the printing of parlimentary speeches and decrees, the National Assembly itself actively contributed to the animation of those discussions whose institutional frameworks it had created. The various attempts at literacy and a number of projects on school reform must also be evaluated as further measures for the realization of the ideal Enlightenment model, although recent sociohistorical research leads one to suspect that these efforts at educational politics were scarcely blessed with success: the proportion of adult French who could read and write at the end of the ancien régime—a third of the whole population, approximately 75 percent in the cities—does not seem to have risen until the end of the eighteenth century.[13]

In presenting the various genres that served as media in the context of the communication situation of the political public, we come up against a specific problem. These genres largely overlap (for example, "broadsheets," "flysheets," and "pamphlets"), are formed according to quite heterogeneous criteria (for example, "brochures" and "catechisms"), and not uncommonly project inadequate conceptions of our own present into the late eighteenth century (for instance, "journals"). For several years, a desideratum of French writings on social history has been the elaboration of precise genre distinctions grounded in the historical understanding of their situations. However, there has not been any essential progress so far. In what follows, I would primarily like to produce three functions to which a number of genres in the space of the political public can be attributed—the communication of knowledge (e.g., catechisms, animal fables, almanacs, journals), the polemical problematizing of knowledge (pamphlets), and the engineering of consensus (discourses, parliamentary speeches, the party press).[14]

The procedure of communicating knowledge in prescribed questions and answers that is characteristic of catechism is associated today with theological pedagogics; throughout the eighteenth century, however, it was also a significant medium for spreading the new knowledge of the Enlightenment, which revolutionary cultural politics appropriated for the teaching of citizenship. The communication situation of the public and the genre of the catechism show two clear affinities: on the one hand, the pathos of an instruction that is not aesthetically veiled, and on the other, the basic conviction of the neutrality of knowledge. Nobody in the eighteenth century seems to have criticized the fact that the interests of the pupil are inperceptibly steered by the typical catechismal questions, as the introduction to the *Catéchisme du genre humain* (1792) demonstrates:

Question: Who brought you here?
Answer: My mother.
Question: For what reason?
Answer: To learn how to work for the happiness of my fellow man.

The first of these two questions is supposed to make the pupil aware that—as we would say today—secondary socialization by the school is a continuation of the primary socialization by the family; the second question—quite in the sense of the Enlightenment—ties education above all to a practical interest, which, to be sure, as the second answer shows, goes far beyond the preparation for a job. Now in the following pages of the *Catéchisme du genre humain*, the traditional relationship between questioner and answerer in this genre is reversed. The questions have to be ascribed to the pupil and the answers to the teacher. If we look at them more closely, we clearly recognize the catechism's didactic procedure. It prompts questions that could hardly be expected from a child just beginning school: "Question: In your opinion, what does the happiness of your fellow man consist of? / Answer: In his body's health, strength, and dexterity, in the peace and satisfaction of his soul, and the possesion of the essential goods for an extremely simple life." There seems to be a constant characteristic shift between such relatively complex and other, much more limited questions, which are aimed at the gradual differentiation and extraction of central meanings out of overlapping answers: for example, "Why do you say 'for the most simple life'?" In many places in this book, it can be seen—and this, too, is typical of the genre—that the didactic skill of its author is not sufficient to do more than simply transpose theoretical governmental ideogemes (above all Rousseau's) into another textual schema: "Question: Does education really have an essential function in the recognition and implementation of all of these means?"

Despite the publication of a series of collections of fables during the years of the French Revolution, the political change, above all in the efforts to institutionalize the enlightened public, does not seem to have advanced this genre that was so popular in the Enlightenment. That Sylvain Maréchal could choose as the motto of his *Apologues modernes, à l'usage du Dauphin, première leçon du fils aîné d'un roi* (To women and kings one must speak in instructive fables; published in Brussels in 1788), is a clear indication that it would be an insult to use fables as a way of instructing a republican fully conscious of his new role. Besides, the imagery of a genre so close to the idyll could hardly be compatible with the revolutionaries' favorite symbols from Roman antiquity. Hence it is not surprising that Florian, the best-known author of fables during the revolutionary period, was still defending a constitutional monarchy in his collection published in 1792; or that Vitalis in 1796 used the genre primarily as a way of eluding censorship. At the end of his fable "The Republic of Animals," he asked, "Does one really have to spill so much blood to achieve this result?"[15]

But a genre that the culture-political decrees would hardly have considered worthy of mention reached a far larger public in the eighteenth century. The almanacs used the structure of the calendar for the communication of practical everyday hints, prophecies, tales with the most varied contents, satires, songs—in short, every sort of reading material that could be fitted to the taste of less-educated readers. Almanac titles like *Le fléau des aristocrats (The scourge of aristocrats)* and *Nostradamus moderne* indicate that already before 1789 this genre was as little interested in avoiding untimely connotations as it was in anticipating political events. Such polyvalence in the communicative function predestined the almanac to become the medium for the debates of different political groups. In this manner, the former comedian, Collot d'Herbois, who had advanced himself to the writing of dramas and who was a member of the Jacobin Club, published an *Almanach du Père Gérard* in 1791, a title that alluded to a member of the National Assembly, a Breton farmer named Michel Gérard, who was admired because of his naïveté but also fondly laughed at. Symbolic nominations of this kind during the revolutionary years were a regular procedure. They structured the content of public expectation and, at the same time, appealed to a specific group—that is, those readers who could sympathize with "Père Gérard" on the basis of their social status and their rudimentary education. It says something about the success of this procedure that exactly in the same year the royalist opposition published a satiric reply to Collot d'Herbois's almanac, *Entretiens de la mère Gérard.*

With respect to the history of almanacs, it is remarkable that, in the years 1793 to 1794, they quite commonly took on the function of a republican songbook or evangelium, whereas the administrations after Thermidor 1794 increasingly abandoned the genre to the royalist reaction. By its very nature, it was the perfect medium after 1792 for the propagation of the revolutionary calendar. In 1788, Sylvain Maréchal had already taken advantage of this opportunity in his *Almanach de honnêtes gens;* he dated it from the "first year of the dominion of reason," let the year begin—logically—with the spring month of March, and marked the months with roman numerals. For the saints' days, he put a phalanx of historically great figures, which throws an interesting light on the historical knowledge of those underprivileged groups of late Enlightenment literati to which Maréchal undoubtedly belonged: Moses stands next to Hobbes, Mohammed next to Voltaire, Pascal next to Socrates. Maréchal's biography could be considered as the classic illustration of the role of the "Grub Street literati." Born in 1750 the son of a vintner in les Halles of Paris, Maréchal studied law after graduating from the Collège, could not find work at first (which he later—quite in the style of Rousseau's following—knew how to use as a legitimation of his resistance to the ancien régime), and finally became an employee in the library of the Collège Mazarin in 1781. During these years, he published, among other things, erotic poems under the pseudonym "the Shepherd Sylvain." He lost his position at the

Collège Mazarin when a parody of the Bible appeared that was clearly from his pen: *Le livre échappé au déluge* (1784). In the early years of the Revolution, he advanced to become editor of the successful anticlerical magazine *Le tonneau de Diogène*. Forever striving to belong to the extreme left, Maréchal achieved one of the greatest public successes of the revolutionary theater with his play *Le jugement dernier des rois* in the fall of 1793. This work, which successfully achieved the rare synthesis of political ideologizing and popular entertainment, offered a justification of the execution of Marie Antoinette, which had taken place two days before its first performance.

If there is any atypical characteristic in Maréchal's biography, it would be his fidelity to the sansculotte ideology. It manifested itself after Thermidor 1794 through his membership in the "conspiracy of equals," which planned a coup d'état under the leadership of Babeuf and was subsequently liquidated by the Directory in May 1797. Maréchal escaped the death penalty, although it is considered certain that he was the author of the *Manifeste des Egaux* (1796). Finally, it speaks for his own lack of opportunism, a charge he applied to Marie-Joseph Chénier (who was indeed able to adapt to every revolutionary administration without exception), that Maréchal, in his brochure *Culte et lois d'une société d'hommes sans dieu* (1798), was competing with the efforts of the Directory to establish a deistic state religion; in 1800, he finally published his *Dictionnaire des athées anciens et modernes*.

The meager sum of *Journaux*, periodicals appearing daily, in the eighteenth century can mainly be explained by not inconsiderable technical difficulties. They were printed on the same presses as books, which allowed the production of barely more than 150 copies per hour and which in turn lets us draw some conclusions about the (for us) astonishingly low circulation. Moreover, after the alterations in the political institutions brought about by the Revolution, the editors and the public only considered information about daily events as knowledge and as worthy of being circulated in a printed form. For the postulate of unlimited publicity could be realized only when the debates in the National Assembly and other commissions were at least potentially accessible to every citizen. Thus the *Journal de Paris*, which was founded a few years before the beginning of the revolutionary period, the *Moniteur universel*, which was edited by Panckoucke, one of the most influential publishers of the late Enlightenment, and, as its title already betrays, the *Journal des débats* devoted themselves primarily to parliamentary journalism. Even before the development of stenography, a "Société logographique" was set up to work out a system of abbreviations that would make possible the complete notation of the discussions in the new political boards. This company sold—as the forerunner of today's news agencies—its documentations to various daily newspapers. When *Le Logographe, Journal national* appeared between 1793 and 1794, its publisher, for a considerable price, even received from the Société certain exclusive rights with respect to its information.

Wall newspapers, like the ones we have become familiar with from various "cultural revolutionary" movements in our own time, were quite common at that time. In this manner, the Paris Commune published daily *affiches* in 1793 and 1794 with the protocols of their sessions.[16] It is interesting that these *affiches* were generally called "journaux" in the preamble to the first edition (which shows how distant the concept of journal was from its present-day meaning). This form of informational exchange, as Campe's *Briefe* show us once again, had already become current in the first months of the Revolution:

> These bills or announcements can be seen in every street, especially on the walls of corner houses and all along the walls of official buildings, on the quais and other open spaces—such a huge lot of them that a hale and hearty pedestrian and practiced rapid reader could run around and read all day, from morning to evening without ever finishing all that is plastered up anew every day. In front of every house plastered over with the same bills, which are printed up in large sheets with big type, one sees an infinitely motley, mixed public of laborers and fine gentlemen, fishwives and noble ladies, soldiers and priests, gathered together in thick but always peaceful throngs, all of them with their heads raised up, all of them scarfing up the contents with greedy eyes, sometimes quietly, sometimes reading aloud, judging and debating.[17]

It was above all the journals completely limited to the communication of political information that were able to maintain themselves in the years after 1794. At the same time, those learned weekly and monthly magazines, which perhaps had been the most important medium of the Enlightenment, also experienced a new boom, especially the "Décade philosophique, littéraire, et politique" (since April 1794). That neither they nor the political journals were actually ever really "neutral" has been established beyond question by contemporary research; but it was exactly this claim and the eighteenth century's trust in objective reporting that saved them from the turbulent fate of those periodicals that frankly represented a particular political position.

The flysheets—short publications, mostly stapled together (whence the name "brochure")—whose authors took a polemic position on the questions of the day, were a genre oppositional forces had been using in their struggles against established governments ever since the invention of printing. Now with the assembly of the Etats Généraux, they took on a modified function: between 1788 and 1790 there was a vast flood of thin notebooks whose authors for the most part explicitly addressed themselves to the representatives of the Etats généraux—but implicitly, as the publication in the form of a brochure proves, were directed at the enlightened public. *Requête d'une société rustique à toutes les Assemblées Générales provinciales du royaume par un curé de campagne,* published by a country priest (1788), *Voeux sur la Dernière Classe du peuple à l'assemblées des notables* (n.d.), *La vie et les doléances d'un pauvre-diable, pour servir de ce qu'on voudra aux prochains Etats-Généraux* (1789), *Protestation d'un serf du Mont-Jura, contre l'Assemblées des Notables, le Mémoire des Princes du Sang, le Clergé, la Noblesse et le Tiers Etat, au Roi* (1789), *Le plus fort des Pamphletes—l'ordre des paysans aux Etats-Généraux* (1789), *Plaintes et représentations d'un citoyen décrété passif, aux citoyens dé crété actifs* (1790)—these are some of the characteristic titles showing that at the beginning of the Revolution it was hoped that the effects of the procedure for recruiting representatives for the Etats Généraux, which was still in no sense democratic, could be compensated for if attention were drawn to the needs of the part of the French population not represented there. Since these sorts of flysheets were basically taken from asides in the *Cahiers de doléances* and their assemblage had been commissioned by the government in every province, they are not formulated in as polemical a tone as their titles would lead us to expect (*protestation, pamphlet, plaintes*). It is more characteristic when the author of "The Most Powerful Pamphlet of All" addresses "his noble, just, and honorable fellow citizens," when he renders thanks to Louis XVI for letting him speak henceforth as a "man" rather than as a "vassal." As long as it was believed that the model of an enlightened public was realizable, pamphlets had no polemical accents. Texts designated as "pamphlets" were conceived by authors and readers as a medium for communicating knowledge that was supposed to be the basis for the formulation of political consensus. With respect to our guiding question, it can be noted that the number of such texts after 1790 rapidly sank for a while, but they were soon replaced by authentic pamphlets, usually without official permission.

According to the current meaning of the word, pamphlet, usually subordinated within the genre of broadsheets, has the function of questioning institutionalized knowledge, that is, social cognition internalized by all of its members. Characteristic for it is its indirect mode, in quite various forms, of articulating needs. This is why the genre of pamphlet and the idea of an enlightened public sphere are mutually exclusive, and why it is not rare for pamphlet authors to take recourse in traditional textual schemata for communicating knowledge, which can be ascribed to the attempt, on the one side, to elude inattentive censors and, on the other, to make evident to the readers the difference between institutionalized knowledge and that knowledge propagated by the author. So for instance, a pamphlet by the long-suffering Sylvain Maréchal from the time of the ancien régime bore the seemingly harmless (for the uninitiated) title *Catéchisme du curé Meslier* (1790), behind which was concealed a polemic against Christianity and which for sheer aggressiveness could hardly have been surpassed. But anyone who considered himself a *philosophe* would know what the choice of just this particular fictitious name signified. The allusion to that early eighteenth-century country priest, whose final testament expressed an atheism that even Voltaire found frighteningly consequent, was regarded as one of the most important documents of Enlightenment religious criticism and was supposed to arouse the expected response in its recipients. The following two answers and questions from this "catechism" clearly show how suitable its text schema was to recall continually the reader's religious education. For the most part, blasphemous answers are opposed to the questions:

On Incarnation
Question: What does it mean that God has become a man?
Answer: It means that a man tries to pass himself off as God.
Question: Is he really God and man and both in one?
Answer: Stupid question, stupid answer.

For our hypothesis about the situational framework of the pamphlet genre, it is interesting that Maréchal begins the preface to this 1790 catechism with the sentence: "This book is not a pamphlet." Now it is possible to publish, says the author, what "the friends of order and truth" have long been whispering in each others' ears.

The pamphlets opposing the revolutionary administrations after 1792 have barely been investigated. At least one genre feature—this much seems certain—also remained constant in the Republic, that is, the recourse to religious and bureaucratic textual schemes: what was catechism or litany for the old pamphleteers of the ancien régime had become decrees and constitutions by the late years of the Revolution.

If the previously described texts can be considered as forms preparatory for public discussions, then in three other genres we have the debates themselves. The texts belonging to them show two common characteristics. They are subordinated to the answering of still-open questions, since the beginning of the Revolution there had been a tendency to regard questions that were previously purely academic (one thinks of the prizewinning questions of the academies so typical of the eighteenth century) as being practically relevant now and hence political in a broader sense. Furthermore, the authors make it clear that they wish to present their own point of view—thus an opinion and not "neutral" knowledge (which is why most of the brochures we will now discuss bear the names of their authors).

Under the genre *discourse,* we will include texts related to the tradition of learned speech in Enlightenment academies, but which now are directed to the nation. Their prefaces address themselves to "the people," "to all Frenchmen who want to be free," indeed "mankind whatever his class and in whatever country he might be." Primarily, they deal with problems of political and social organization and for this reason not infrequently sound like abstracts of the utopian novels of the eighteenth century. So for instance François Joseph L'Ange attached to his brochure published in 1793, *Remède à tout, constitution invulnérable de la félicité publique,* "the recommendation of a Heavenly Weapon for the welfare of all peoples"—concretely, a plan to employ the discovery of the hot-air balloons by the Montgolfier brothers in organizing military air forces.[18] But even such scientific discourses seem to have been withdrawn again from the enlightened public in the late years of the Revolution. On October 25, 1795, the Institut Français was founded, the national academy of sciences that has maintained its authority in France to this very day and is divided into three sections, physics and mathematics, literature and *beaux arts,* ethics and politics. Instead of setting aside the texts of the Enlightenment and the early Revolution as "popular science," it should be stressed, on the contrary, that with the founding of the institute scientific knowledge officially became specialist knowledge, which, separated from social needs, was allowed to follow the "immanent logic" of its questions and on which the government could draw in case of need. It is significant that Bonaparte had several members of the Institut Français accompany his expedition to Egypt.

Far more than the scientific prose of the positivistic nineteenth century, whose history in France is irrevocably tied up with the institute's, the discourses of the early revolutionary years have the argumentative structure of a group of participants contributing to a given discussion. The authors regularly lay claim to the prestige of heroic models from Roman antiquity, but also to the popularity of Enlightenment figures quoted in support of their own standpoint; they deflate possible counterarguments, much as if they had been interrupted during a lecture and were obliged to reply; and they conclude with summaries of the argument and consensus-begging suggestions for practical action. Not infrequently these features recall an actual oral communication situation—for instance, in the publication of parliamentary speeches financed by the administration. In this genre, addressing the representatives present was always accompanied by the image of an ideal public—which in fact could only be reached when the speeches were published as brochures.

The evaluation of the enormous corpus of speeches that were given in the various parliaments of the French Revolution is still controversial. On the one side, it has been pointed out, quite correctly, that the argumentative schemes and fields of imagery that are keyed to Roman models have a conventional character. There is scarcely a significant revolutionary politician who was not celebrated as "Brutus" or "Cato," nor castigated as "Catiline" or "Tarquinius." In the face of such allusions, not particularly surprising against the background of eighteenth-century classicism, it has been forgotten that the imagery of the gothic novel also went into parliamentary speeches. This connection is clear, for instance, in the portrait Vergniaud (who, along with Mirabeau, was perhaps the most talented revolutionary speaker) sketched of France after the execution of Louis XVI (which he wished to avert): "It is to be feared that France—despite her triumphs—will one day be like those famous monuments that have outlasted time in Egypt. The traveler admires their size; but what does he find when he penetrates their interiors? The ashes of the dead and the silence of the grave" (speech from December 31, 1792). Against the efforts, for the most part by literary history, to analyze, as it were, the parliamentary rhetoric of the French Revolution by coordinating it with contemporary conventions of text production, there is the unlimited admiration of historians from Michelet to Soboul. As an appreciation of public debates that were really the presuppositions for political decisions, this attitude has a nostalgic touch. Admittedly, if we trace the history of the parliamentary rhetoric of the French Revolution through the texts, we see that the representatives' claim to have manifested the model of an enlightened public never completely corresponded to communicative reality and quickly became an illusion. Mirabeau, the hero of the first revolutionary parliament, was superior to his colleagues and the court because he was the first to recognize the new implications for speech acts that had been acquired by traditional schemes after July 14, 1789. For instance, when he convinced his colleagues on July 16, 1789, to thank the king—in the face of all contrary evidence—for having proved himself a true father of the people, he did this mainly in order to force Louis XVI to accept the political line of Parliament. For after the storming of the Bastille, Louis XVI and his advisers could readily imagine what the immediate consequences would have been if he had rejected this homage as beneath his dignity. The trial against the king during the winter of 1792–93 that was held in Parliament acquires historical significance less because of its result, the beheading of Louis XVI, than because of the conclusive development of parliamentary factions, which made the continual evocation of the representative as a reasoning private person look more and more like a fiction. During the autocracy of the Montagne faction organized by Robespierre, which began with the exclusion of the Girondistes at the end of May 1793, we can no longer speak of "debates." Up until Thermidor 1794, Parliament merely delivered official interpretations of the political events of the day and derived from them prognoses about the future of the Revolution that mollified collective anxieties and whose coercive force was assured by indirect allusions to the guillotine. This successive estrangement from political decision making ultimately reached its zenith in the work of both of the chambers of the Directory. They were mainly occupied in developing representations of the revolutionary events pleasing to the administrations—which had entered history ever since the decision had been made to work toward ending the Revolution and no longer toward fulfilling it, as had been the case up until 1794.

Clear parallels to the history of parliamentary rhetoric in the French Revolution can be seen in the simultaneous development of the newspapers bound to a particular party line. At the outset of the Revolution, they could barely be distinguished from those brochures that served to articulate the needs of social groups not represented in the Etats Généraux. For all that, the complete title of the *Cahiers du quatrième ordre,* which appeared from April 1789 on, indicates that they were not only concerned with the information of the parliamentarians and the public they represented but were meant to further the self-confidence of a particular group: "Brochures of the Fourth Class, that of poor day laborers, the weak, the needy, etc., the holy class of the underprivileged; or philanthropic correspondence between underprivileged, sensitive people and the Etats Généraux: as a compensation for every French person's right, which this class does not enjoy, to send their own representatives to the Etats Généraux." The contributions the aristocratic editor of the *Cahiers,* Dufourny de Villiers, requested from the susceptible public prove that the belief in the suasive power of information had not yet been brought into question; he wanted to publish thoughtful pieces like "The Reasons for Poverty in Various Districts," "The Living Conditions of the Poor," and "The Inequality of the Tax Burden."

The history of those Jacobin party tabloids, whose names have become part of general knowledge—Marat's *Ami du peuple,* Desmoulin's *Vieux cordelier,* and finally Hébert's *Père Duchesne*—permits the assumption that periodicals developed simultaneously with the increasingly more open formation of parliamentary factions, which undercut a basic postulate of the concept of an enlightened public by addressing themselves exclusively to the constituents—and in Paris to the political shock troops—of precisely those political factions. As could only be expected, the party tabloids also fell into line after the elimination of all parliamentary opposition. If we say that Hébert, whose biography is quite parallel to Maréchal's, was the author and not the editor of *Père Duchesne,* then it becomes clear that behind the individual titles of the party press the more or less periodic and consistently formatted flysheets that appeared concealed identical authors. Insofar as they addressed themselves to the public, we can observe the same procedure in *Père Duchesne* as in the *Almanach du Père Gérard.* At any rate, there probably never was a historical Père Duchesne; the name signifies rather a symbolic figure of identification for the Parisian petite bourgeoisie, a suburban ovenmaker to whom political fearlessness was ascribed and who showed a healthy liking for salty oaths. Whoever it was who published his "newspaper" under this name, he provided educated readers with amusement at the expense of the sympathetic underprivileged (a variant of the "noble savage"), yet at the same time, he activated that public that could identify with Père Duchesne and his political positions. Hence, it is not surprising that numerous authors and publishers fought over the rights to this symbolic figure, and this is exactly why the front page of every edition of Hébert's newspaper ran the header: "Fuck 'em all, I'm the real Père Duchesne."[19]

Hébert's tabloid appeared three times a week; a monthly subscription cost about two days' pay for his sansculotte readers. By taking a look at a given edition, we can get a more concrete idea of his paper. I have selected issue number 299 (*Père Duchesne* was undated), which appeared immediately after the beheading of Marie Antoinette on October 16, 1793. Like most periodicals, it usually began with a short summary of its contents, which helped newspaper and book salesmen (the "colporteurs") to hawk their wares. Hébert always began this section with the formula "Père Duchesne's great annoyance/pleasure," making it perfectly clear that his purpose was less to report daily events than to comment on them. To put it more concretely: he tried to bring into unison his readers' "lived meaning" of these events with the "desired meaning" of the community of which he was a prominent member,[20] whereby *Père Duchesne* probably assumes a politically important role mainly because it was regularly read aloud during the meetings of the various sansculotte sections in Paris.

Now the historians tell us – and this is important to understand number 299 of *Père Duchesne* – that the reaction of the sansculottes to the beheading of the deposed queen did not at all match the expectations of the politicians. During the trial, the once-hated Marie Antoinette, now called "Widow Capet," won the public's admiration. On the scaffold, she stumbled and stepped on the executioner's foot, and is supposed to have said to him, "I beg your pardon, Monsieur," audible to everyone standing nearby. When the executioner finally raised and exposed the queen's head to the crowd, it was reported by witnesses that there was complete silence on the place de la Republique. As with the decapitation of the king in January of the same year, the revolutionaries seemed to have been frightened by their own courage. It is this sort of "lived meaning" that the concluding passage of number 299 of *Père Duchesne* tries to negate:

All of you who were reduced to servitude under our old tyranny; you who shed tears for a father, a son, a husband who died for the republic; be comforted, for you have been revenged. I saw the head of the feminine veto[21] drop in the sack. May I be fucked if I don't wish that I could depict for you, with enough power, how great was the satisfaction of the sansculottes when the arch-tigress was driven in the cart of the judged through Paris. Not by her beautiful white horses with ornamental harness was she drawn – no, a couple of nags were hitched up and they seemed so satisfied in being able to contribute to the freeing of the republic that it looked as if they wanted to gallop in order to get to the fatal place sooner. The bitch was impertinent and fresh. In any case, she got weak in the knees as if she needed to lie down, probably because she was afraid of receiving an even more frightening judgment after death than the one to which she was now doomed. Her goddamned head was finally separated from her stork's neck and may I be fucked once again if heaven didn't resound with the cries of "Vive la Republique!"

It is characteristic for Hébert's *Père Duchesne* – and in general for public notices during the Terror – that the text does not explicitly negate the reader's unwanted reaction to the queen's execution. Rather the report is presented as a message of joy. Since the execution here becomes the fulfillment of revenge, the text reawakens its recipients' memories of the popular image of the hated queen of the ancien règime, which was in danger of evaporating during the days of her trial. The queen's execution did not compromise the people in whose name it was carried out, but was a just punishment for previous humiliations. That the "Widow Capet" tripped is interpreted as the expression of her fear of the judge in the next world—hence he and nature (the "satisfied" hacks harnessed to the wagon of the judged) implicitly justify the decision of the revolutionary tribunal. Finally the queen's comment to the executioner, which had unwillingly aroused admiration, is not mentioned, but seems to be the cause of the cheekiness attributed to her. Amidst such an accumulation of manipulatory processes, it scarcely weighs in the balance that the spectators' cries of joy—certainly hoped for by the government but apparently absent in reality—were added by the author to his tableau of revolutionary unanimity.

When we turn to the style of the text, we are above all struck by the mixture of the author's unrepressed educated imagery (the anaphora at the beginning of the quotation, formulations like "the fatal place"), and those breaks in the context of printed language as they must have been put in the mouth of the fictional author "Père Duchesne" and have been familiar to Hébert's readers: the frequently repeated "foutre" in *Père Duchesne,* calling the queen a "bitch" and talking about her "stork's neck."

Père Duchesne is considered to be the most aggressive product of the sansculotte party press; but we can assume that the process of manipulation of which we have just had an example can also be found in those party newspapers that took great pains to achieve an impeccable style. In any case, *Père Duchesne* is already one of the late samples of the genre; by the time of Hébert's greatest political influence in the late summer and fall of 1793, all of those newspapers that did not serve to propagate and legitimize Robespierre's politics had been forbidden. Following Thermidor 1794, there was a short flowering of royalistic tabloids, but after Vendémiaire 1795, the efforts of the bureau of censorship clearly tended toward the suppression of the party press in general—whatever their provenance. The *Tribun du peuple ou défenseur des droits de l'homme* of Gracchus Babeuf (who had taken the side of the new government after the political shift following Thermidor, but soon pursued the rehabilitation of Robespierre and a radical-democratic course) had to be secretly printed and circulated as early as 1795, which led to a situation where the individual issues appeared at ever longer intervals and thus were also more comprehensive. Babeuf, like Rousseau before him, thus interpreted the police measures and censorship imposed on him as symptoms of administrative insanity. The government had apparently recognized that the most effective way of justifying its own politics was to disguise journalistic praise as "objective information." It had already been a long time since one could talk about the realization of the Enlightenment postulate of the unlimited expression of opinion and the clash of opinion as the basis of political consensus.

Revolutionary Festivals

"The most original creation of the Revolution was undoubtedly the art of national festivals."[22] Such a judgment may provoke contradiction, but in any case it allows us to recognize that a literary history of the French Revolution must be willing to include communication situations that usually are only mentioned in passing by social historians. In this study, which is focused on the attempts to institutionalize the ideal communication models of the Enlightenment, the revolutionary festivals take on a special significance, because it was there—at least in the first years after 1789—that theoretical principles and social needs converged. It is easier to place them within the literary system of the period if we keep in mind that Rousseau developed the ideal image of a republican festival and its legitimation precisely in his *Lettre à d'Alembert sur les spectacles* (1758), which has gone down as probably the most sagacious polemic against the theater in the history of literature. Jean Starobinski has analyzed the function Rousseau—together with his adepts, the cultural politicians of the revolutionary period—ascribed to festivals: their participants are actors and spectators at the same time. Just what they present and experience in this double role has been made clear by Starobinski through a reference to a conceptual parallel between the *Lettre à d'Alembert* and the *Contrat social*. The double role of the participant in a festival corresponds to that of the citizen, who is governed as a member of society and who within that society takes over the role of the ruler, thus becoming part of the government himself. Therefore, the festive participant experiences the respective other as "sovereign" but at the same time he also imagines himself in precisely this role. This experience, according to Rousseau, is blocked in the collective receptive situation of the theater because it draws the attention of all of the spectators to the events on stage and puts its fictional situation as an "obstacle" between the spectators' gaze, which, in the festival, "becomes transparent" to one another.[23] Although Rousseau, as we see, achieved a possibility for describing the political function of republican festivals in his argument against theater, it cannot be interpreted as a substitute for plays. Rather the revolutionary festivals appear as the successors to the utopias of the Enlightenment, since in them, apparently, the situation has been actually reached that the utopian texts had imagined.

Admittedly, this does not allow us simply to make this intended function of the revolutionary festivals equal to their actual psychosocial effect. If, at least in the years up until 1794, the oath of allegiance to the new state formed its ceremonial center, then it becomes clear that it offered a way of providing sanctions for a future that the abolition of traditional institutions had made unpredictable. Connected with the political oath of allegiance, which every festival participant had to swear, was the generally soothing experience that the citizens were also ready to continue the Revolution and to guarantee its accomplishments. A second possibility of making predictable with one blow the frighteningly open future that had existed ever since July 1789 was offered by the commemorations of great days like July 14 or August 10. By integrating them into a festival calendar and thus prescribing a commemoration that always had to be repeated, these events gradually lost their "revolutionary" aftertaste, which had contributed to the insecurity of future expectations. In this manner, the history of the Revolution as "lived meaning" conformed to the "desired meaning" of the administrations. Of course it must be taken into account that these festivities had a tendency to deviate from Rousseau's conception of the republican festival. For commemorative festivals need an allegorical or mimetic representation of the past that inevitably diminishes the transparence of the reciprocal experiences of the participants.

If the sociological interpretation of the phenomenon "festival" has up until today continued to be influenced by the *Lettre à d'Alembert* and its reception by the cultural politicians of the French Revolution, then it was Sigmund Freud who set up alongside it a diametrically opposed model of understanding. In festivals he saw enclaves in the course of a society's lifetime that permitted the transgression of its characteristic social norms and thus contributed to social stability by enabling the discharge of aggressions directed against these norms and the repressions they erect. To be sure, it is difficult to find such transgressional signs in the festivals of the French Revolution; they only allowed for excess when aimed at institutions that had already lost their validity through the political events following on July 14, 1789.

Social historians agree that the "Fête de la Fédération" on July 14, 1790, came closest to the model of Rousseau. On the first anniversary of the storming of the Bastille, the king, the highest-ranking government officials, and representatives of the individual classes and provinces made a solemn oath of allegiance to the new political order on the Champs de Mars: "I swear eternal fealty to the Nation, the Law, and the King; I swear to observe the constitution concluded by the National Assembly and ratified by the King; by law to protect security, property, the free circulation of grain and other foodstuffs inside the kingdom and all forms of public taxation. I swear to be unified with all Frenchmen through the insoluble bond of brotherhood." On the basis of the foregoing theoretical considerations about the revolutionary festival, it is possible to list several reasons for the success of the Fête de la Fédération. Just a year after the beginning of the political shift, there must have already been a widespread need indeed for the French reciprocally to experience themselves in their new capacity as citizens. At the same time, and with respect to fresh memories of the ancien régime, the socially integrative character of this festival (for example, in comparison to the court festivals at Versailles) could still be experienced as the breaking of a taboo. Moreover, the festivals of the Revolution did not take on any aggressive features as long as the king was still considered the "Father of the People," as long as the already achieved partial victories on the way to equality before the law and the hope for its complete realization squelched any serious reflection on economic inequality and hence class tensions.

Since 1790, songs had been the medium of communal experience in the Fêtes de la Fédération. It is reported that their texts were published and handed out to participants during the festivities. If "Ça ira" was the most popular in 1790–91, the success story of the "Marseillaise," France's present national anthem, had its first high point during the national festival of 1792. To be sure, Rouget de Lisle, an otherwise completely insignificant author and composer, did not write it for this occasion but first sang it on the evening of April 26, 1792, in the mayor of Strasbourg's house as the "song of the Army of the Rhine." Now how can we explain the overwhelming success of the marching song of the representatives of Marseille (hence the name of the French national anthem), which a scant three months later became the song of the national festival? The text presumably goes back to a recruiting poster from April 25, 1792, asking volunteers to join the Army of the Rhine. When we compare the text of this poster, which was composed wholly in the style of that sort of military appeal, with the text of the "Marseillaise," then we have a way of understanding its unparalled success:

> To arms, citizens! The banner of war is unfurled, the signal is given. To arms! To fight, victory or death, is the commandment of the hour. . . . So let them tremble, the crowned despots! The shine of freedom will light up for all mankind! . . . Let us march! Let us be free to the last breath, our wishes should always be in the constant service of the happiness of the nation and the happiness of the whole human race." (text of the Strasbourg poster of April 25, 1792)[24]

> Allons enfants de la Patrie
> Le jour de gloire est arrivé.
> contre nous de la tyrannie
> l'Etandard sanglant est levé.
> Entendez-vous dans les campagnes
> mugir ces féroces soldats?
> Ils viennent jusque dans vos bras
> égorger vos fils, vos compagnes.
> Aux armes, Citoyens!
> Formez vos bataillons!
> Marchez, marchez
> qu'un sang impur
> abreuve nos sillons!

Let's go, children of the nation!
The day of fame has arrived.
The bloody flag of tyranny has been raised against us.
Do you hear the war cry

of these horrible soldiers on the fields?
They come up into your arms,
to strangle your sons, your friends.
To arms, citizens!
Form your batallions!
March, march,
so that an impure blood fills our furrows!

("Marseillaise")

Two characteristic features of revolutionary songs—and texts read at revolutionary festivals—are common to both the poster and the "Marseillaise." First, the ideal of the unity of the citizens is thematized before a background of threat by an external enemy; second, a future in freedom and victory in battle are already prophesied to the citizens going into battle, but their courage will be needed to achieve this promised goal. The essential modifications that the "Marseillaise" makes with the Strasbourg poster are text-syntactic. Even before there is any talk about the enemy threat, the sentence "the day of fame has arrived" implies the promise of victory. At the same time, in more detail and more frighteningly than in the military appeal, there is a description of the enemy, who threatens not only the nation but also the lives of the children and friends of French citizens. The cry "Aux armes" in the second-to-last sentence is thus simultaneously the precondition for turning the collective misfortune aside as well as for cashing in on the promise of victory in battle with which the "Marseillaise" begins and ends. Moreover, it is worth noting that in the "Marseillaise" the alternative "victory or death" is replaced by more positive prophecies and that the unity of the citizens, who are called up to protect the lives of their children, is not merely political and theoretical, nor simply enforced by a momentary threat, but has an emotional content as well: they themselves appear as the "children of the nation."

As the example of the "Marseillaise" shows, the pervasive feature of all of the texts established for communal singing and mass recitation at revolutionary festivals is the juxtaposition of the promise of a fortuitous future, which provides revolutionary action with self-confidence, and of appeals to the citizens, whose content depends on the situation and whose implementation will create the presuppositions for the fulfillment of that promise. The linguistic outcome of this interaction can be found in an ambivalent use of the future morpheme specific to revolutionary texts. Where it is said, for instance, at the beginning of the poem "Commandements de la Patrie" (1789), "From now on you will defend your freedom with enthusiasm," this sentence can be understood both as challenge and as prognosis. It is noteworthy that the emphasis—despite the essential retention of the semantic double meaning—in the sequence of these fifteen "national commandments" is increasingly put on prognosis. The last commandment states: "And you who were once a slave will certainly become happy and free." The same motif of a future that is promised and at the same time shaped by his own action also dominates Marie-Joseph Chénier's "Chant du départ" from 1794. Its structure is like that of an oratorium: one after another, a representative, a mother, two old men, a child, a wife, and a young girl assure the soldiers to whom the poem is addressed that their hopes for a happy future depend only on them, the defenders of the nation. The alternative evoked in the refrain "victory or death" loses its force when it is announced that whoever tries to avoid it is not worthy of living in freedom.

If we arrange the "Commandements de la Patrie" (1789), the "Marseillaise" (1792), and the "Chant du départ" (1794) as a historical series, then it becomes evident that external threat is gradually replacing spontaneous readiness for fraternity as the condition of the unity of the citizens. This is why the Fête de la Fédération seems to have been unique, and also why it later became necessary to meticulously stage the intentional communal experience through which there was a change in the function of the texts recited or sung at the festivals that previously had served as the fulfillment of that communal experience. Hence the strange genre of the "festival program," whose actual task was to stand in for the dwindling spontaneity of the festival's participants and whose texts were largely taken over for newspaper reportage on the national festivals—much to the concern of the Revolution's historians. The descriptions of the festivals also show that it had now become increasingly necessary (against Rousseau's verdict) to reintroduce visuality as a dimension of the festival. The festival in honor of the new republican constitution on August 10, 1793, was organized by the painter David as a procession at whose various stations allegorical scenes graphically presented abstract formulations of revolutionary discourses: out of the breasts of a sphinx standing on the rubble of the Bastille streamed water that the president of the National Assembly caught in a chalice and passed on to the representatives of the various social groups; at what is now the place de la Concorde a pyramid was set up as a symbol of tyranny—it was solemnly put to the torch; and finally, on the Champs de Mars, the goal of the parade, an artificial mountain symbolized the political faction called the Montagne in whose hands the fate of France had lain since the end of May 1793. The allegorical character of the Jacobin revolutionary festivals not only corresponds to the taste of the time, but also seems to manifest the effort to find a compromise between organizational needs and the Rousseauian model of a "transparent festival" free of content. To be sure, the numerous allegories were barely comprehensible to most of the participants, which explains why their meaning had to be made clear through inscriptions. Out of the burning pyramid (the ancien régime) flew doves around whose necks were silk banners saying "We are free, follow our example!"

That such efforts were unable to hinder the decline from the ideal of the republican festival is shown by the increasing repetition of particularly successful allegorical scenes together with their musical accompaniment on the opera stages of

Paris. Evidence for this is provided by the genre of *Scènes religieuses* in musical theater that was totally bound to the historical context of the Revolution. The "Marseillaise," for instance, was presented in the form of an oratorio with the title "Offrande à la liberté." The name of the genre points to the affinity between revolutionary festival and revolutionary religion. In the "Fête de l'Etre Suprême" (June 8, 1794) initiated by Robespierre, the godhead focused the attention of the participants in a manner that was supposed to engender community. By the way, parliamentary debates about the religion of the Revolution barely veil political hopes of compensating for dwindling enthusiasm with the communal belief in a "supreme being." After Thermidor 1794, there were scarcely any more misgivings about allowing the festivals of the Revolution to deteriorate into open-air plays. With increasing technical perfection, the storming of the Bastille and the victories of the French armies were presented on the Champs de Mars; the actors were soldiers or cadets of the military academy. Nonetheless, as could be expected, the history of the Revolution's festivals did not end on the stages of the Parisian playhouses. On the contrary, the high point of the "Festival of the Founding of the Republic" on September 22, 1796, was a chariot race; and the commentary in the *Journal de Paris* makes us suspect that—also with respect to social function—a preliminary staging of the huge athletic events of our own time had been achieved, which quite obviously served to release collective aggressions:

> It seems as if the chariot races had made a big impression on the audience, but they aroused more pity than pleasure. Could anyone have watched without pain how one of the contestants continually beat his horses as hard as he could with a riding cane? These poor animals got as many blows as the paces they ran. One asks: "Does the fastest yoke or the most insensitive torturer of animals win?" We dare to say that the spectacle of this executioner's tour is of small moral worth.

The Revolution had ceased to be the content of public festivals. Of course, Parliament and the various governmental committees were often still concerned with institutionalizing the *culte de la raison,* but this initiative of Robespierre, who had been damned as a tyrant and guillotined, was only halfheartedly maintained. This is also demonstrated by the tolerance toward private religious circles like the Theophilanthropists and an atheism driven by a veritable religious zeal as represented by Sylvain Maréchal in his aforementioned brochure *Culte et loix d'une société d'hommes sans dieu.* The following excerpt from the philanthropic morning prayer is symptomatic in two respects. It shows that the new ethics were related solely to the actions of the individual and that hope for a happy future depended anew on trust in a supreme being. The connection between action in the new society and the promise of common prosperity was dissolved:

> In no way will I direct wishes to you that do not behoove me: You know the creatures who have left your hands; neither their needs nor

their most secret thoughts escape your glance. I only beg you to cancel the mistakes of others and my own mistakes; for almost everything that distresses mankind is the result of its mistakes. With complete trust in your justice, your goodness, I become a part of all that happens; my only wish is that your will be done.[25]

Theater

"From Rousseau himself you can learn that the pity aroused by a play is a sterile pity, which delights in a few tears but which has never brought forth the least act of humanity. If one has a wife, children, a nation, then the theater—at least—is superfluous. Frenchmen of today, don't you believe that Jean-Jacques addressed these words to us precisely today?" These sentences from the representative Michel-Edme Petit's panegyric to Rousseau (January 1793) show how seriously revolutionary cultural politicians took the verdict against the theater in the *Lettre à d'Alembert.* On the other hand, it is obvious that they had to take advantage of the possibilities for political propaganda proffered by theater. Moreover, there was the prescribed duty of Enlightenment philosophy to try and realize a piece of the postulate of social equality by publicly rehabilitating the class of actors, who had been so despised by the feudal state. Hence, the National Assembly had to deal several times in the spring of 1791 with the refusal of a clergyman to administer to the actor Talma the sacrament of marriage.[26]

This is why, despite Rousseau, the number of political measures to furthering theater is not surprising—from state financing of productions of "patriotic pieces" with free tickets in 1793–94 to the decision that brochures with the texts of ideologically conformist dramas should be included in the backpack of every revolutionary soldier. In the face of such measures, it is astonishing that the postulates of the ideal model of the enlightened public had found their way into the theater only relatively late, namely, on January 13, 1791—the day when a short period began that was wholly free from government censorship. Anyone who wanted, provided he had the financial means, could establish a theater. Even if a number of entrepreneurs attempted to grasp this opportunity—admittedly without much lasting success for the most part—it is possible to presuppose a relatively simple distinction between audience and repertoire in the Parisian theatrical world. The company of the Comédie Française, in its new house that had been inaugurated a few years before the Revolution on the left bank of the Seine (the finest neighborhood in Paris at that time), continued to cultivate classical French drama and, as far as contemporary production is concerned, mainly presented tragedies. The many playhouses in the environs of the Palais Royal, where the Comédie Française is situated today, promoted sentimental drama that was so typical of the Enlightenment era and, among other things, adjusted themselves to the taste of a primarily high-bourgeois public by staging *comédies lyriques* (a protoform of the operetta) and comedies whose theme was contemporary society. Ultimately the boulevard du Temple on the northeastern periphery of Paris continued to be the center of popular (i.e., mainly petit bourgeois) entertainment. Long before the Revolution, the theaters located here had latched onto the tradition of the "Théâtre de la Foire" (the theater of the annual fair).

With respect to its themes and the form of their presentation, theater in the early years of the Revolution is barely distinguishable from the dramatic production of the late Enlightenment. To be sure, it was possible after July 14, 1789, to bring material on the stage that, going back to actual encroachments of the absolutistic state, had inflamed the outrage of Enlightenment spokesmen and their audiences and which had become a myth in the meantime—for instance, the fate of Jean Calas, a Huguenot who had been the victim of a miscarriage of justice. But such plays, for which the genre name *Tragédie nationale* was quickly invented in the enthusiasm of the general new beginning, merely reproduced a constellation of protagonists that had been fascinating theater audiences for centuries. The hero was fitted out with all of the positive traits of bourgeois ethics (Jean Calas, for instance, appeared as *vertu persécutée*); his tormentors were almost always members of the aristocracy or their opportunistic henchmen; the end of the drama regularly saw the distribution of retribution, to each his or her just punishment or reward. If the effect of these pieces on the audience was supposed to have matched the intentions of the authors as they had been worked out in numerous poetological tracts, then the relief of the happy end would have paid the empathetic spectator for the "pleasure" of the tears that he had wept for the hero during his persecution. That is to say, he would have become aware of his empathy, which according to Enlightenment anthropology was the basic trait of human character.

Nonetheless, one of the dramas built on this model, *Charles IX ou l'école des rois* by Marie-Joseph Chénier, became a part of theater history. Written in 1788, it thematized one of the favorite objects of enlightened outrage, the Saint Bartholomew's Eve massacre, and was at first subjected to censorship. For it showed how the Huguenots, whose representatives in this piece spoke the language of the deputies to the Etats Généraux, were persecuted by the Queen Mother of the Medici family, how the young King Charles IX, torn between the two parties, took the side of evil in the end and ultimately admitted his own despair (a modification of the usual happy end): "I have betrayed my country and honor and the law / by punishing me, heaven sets an example for kings." This could be read as a warning aimed at Louis XVI to represent the Etats Généraux—and not the court. It is not without reason that Chénier addresses him in the preface as a "king filled with justice and goodness."

Texts that were meant to put pressure on the king in a soft way were the regular thing after July 14, 1789. Nonetheless, the actors of the Comédie Française refused to stage Chénier's piece even after the storming of the Bastille. This was the starting point for the "Bataille de Charles IX," a heated struggle over the public's right to insist upon the production of a given piece, which lasted into 1791. There was, in fact, a relatively early and much acclaimed first performance as early as November 4, 1789, but the actors of the Comédie Française, the majority of whom were conservative and who probably took July 14 and the abolition of feudal rights as nothing more than an insignificant crisis, continued to polemicize against the staging of Chénier's attacks on the monarchy by a state-supported theater. Far more than its (modest) qualities, it was the consequences of the "Bataille de Charles IX" that had made the piece into what was probably the most-quoted theater text in the revolutionary period. For one thing, the public debate quite clearly influenced the cultural legislation of the National Assembly; and also, the "Bataille" ended up by splitting the company of the Comédie Française—François-Joseph Talma, who had played the role of the young king with a pathos that would probably be unbearable today, established the Théâtre de la République in the Palais Royal, the location of the Comédie Française today, along with several other actors who were just as decidedly on the side of the Revolution as he was. His conservative colleagues continued the classical tradition for the time being in their own building of the Comédie Française on the left bank of the Seine.

Like Chénier's Saint Bartholomew's drama, Gabriel-Marie-Jean-Baptiste Legouvé's tragedy *La mort d'Abel* (1792) picked up one of the favorite themes of the Enlightenment—the question of human inequality, to which Rousseau had provided a much more acute answer in his "second discourse," *Discours sur l'origine de l'inégalité parmi les hommes* (1754). Indeed, Legouvé made an effort, in imitation of a text by the Swiss Enlightenment figure, Gessner, to motivate Cain's crime as the result of the unjustly withheld love of his father and the god of creation; and of course, the audience's pity is aroused when Cain predicts in a dream the fate of his successors, the underprivileged, who as serfs will be forced to provide for the welfare of Abel's children. But Legouvé's answer to the implicit question remains a little ambivalent, for, with the reference to the Old Testament myth, "inequality among men" must necessarily seem like a punishment for a crime, even if it is also motivated against the biblical model. Perhaps it is precisely this ambivalence that is the reason for the popularity of *La mort d'Abel* in the later years of the Revolution.

Even if we were able to assume that the receptive disposition for such materials was changed the moment the Revolution broke out (the Revolution could be interpreted from a historical and philosophical point of view as a late revenge for all the injustice that was ever inflicted on the just), even if it now became possible to stage plays that were previously forbidden by the censor—a real break in the history of French theater in the eighteenth century is first marked in the summer of 1792 in the course of which the king was deposed and which ended with the declaration of the Republic. In these months, the failure of the final piece in Beaumarchais's *Almaviva* trilogy, *La mère coupable*, proved how clearly the disposition of the theater audience had shifted — which in any case had never regarded Beaumarchais before 1789 as a "prerevolutionary author" to anywhere near the extent acknowledged by literary history. The metamorphosis of the aristocratic Spanish family into a bourgeois community sympathetic to the Revolution that it depicts seemed like a political affront for which not even its vigorous polemic against the clergy could compensate. The audience's spontaneous rejection might have encouraged the cultural politicians of the group of Jacobins who had become the most powerful faction in the winter of 1792–93 to return to the practice of theater censorship, albeit in an altered form. The staging of a piece aimed at Robespierre by Laya, *L'ami des lois*, in the Comédie Française was broken up in January 1793 by gangs from the sansculottes' communes. In August of the same year, it had gone so far that the production of a dramatic adaptation of the most popular novel material in the European Enlightenment, *Paméla ou la vertu recompensée,* by François de Neufchateau, resulted in the arrest of the actors and the closing of the stage until Thermidor 1794. At any rate, it is also astounding that this thoroughly opportunistic author (he later became a member of the Directory) went back to an adaptation of Richardson's novel by Goldoni, in which, unlike the English model, it is discovered in the course of the happy ending that Pamela, the heroine, was born noble.

The criteria formulated by theater criticism from 1792 to 1794 for the production of contemporary dramatic texts reflect these protests against traditionally contrived pieces: "No more kings in our theaters, unless they are presented as cruel, bloodthirsty, barbaric, or hypocritical — in a word, as they really are," demanded the *Journal des spectacles* on September 11, 1793. If the conversion of evil persons was forbidden in historical pieces, whereas dramas about the revolutionary present — this was the complementary postulate — could only depict the triumph of virtue, then the thematic tradition of *vertu persécutée* had definitely come to an end. These regulations, however, seem motivated above all by the cultural politicians' fears that kings of the past, who were converted to good, or kings of the present, who had triumphed over their subjects, might reawaken the anxiety of a new theater public that did not possess the self-reflective culture presupposed by traditional bourgeois drama. Of course as long as the evil hero had no chance to be converted and their virtuous antagonists were condemned to triumph, it was difficult to sustain the audience's attention. "Too much declamation, too little action" was the pithy commentary of the *Journal des spectacles* on September 8, 1793, on a piece in honor of the friend of the people, Marat, who had been murdered two months before.

Only a few authors from 1792 to 1794 succeeded in finding new dramatic forms for the taste of a new public rather than persevere in the space of the varieties of traditional theater circumscribed by political censorship. This merit goes to Sylvain Maréchal and his *prophétie* of the *Jugement dernier des rois* (1794).

The piece was first performed in the Théâtre de la République on October 18, 1793, two days before the beheading of the queen, and its success would be hard to grasp without knowing this political context. Maréchal picked up a utopian tale from his 1788 *Apologues modernes:* all peoples—so goes this late Enlightenment wish fulfillment—arrest their kings and deport them to a desert island where a life according to the laws of nature awaited them. With the rapid eruption of strife and horrifying slaughter among the despots, it is certain that Maréchal only wanted to point out their incorrigibly depraved character; but in October 1793, this denouement amounted to a justification of the execution of the royal family by rendering the judgment of the revolutionary tribunal in such a way that it looked like the fulfillment of natural laws.

The *Jugement dernier des rois* is larded with the favorite motifs of the late Enlightenment: on a distant island "noble savages" live in idyllic harmony; it goes without saying that they recognize their brothers in the sansculottes of all countries, who have now taken over the deportation of the kings; they are accustomed to address as "mon papa" an old man who has already been living on the island for quite a while after having avenged himself on the aristocratic seducers of his daughter; and finally the eruption of a volcano at the end of the play not only gave the Théâtre de la République the opportunity to throw in the "special effects" that were so popular with the public, but also made it palpable that nature itself demanded the king's death. It was certainly an important prerequisite of Maréchal's success that he reactualized the traditions of popular theater, or more precisely, the "farce," in his piece. The sanctimonious pope, the king of Prussia hacking around with his scepter, and Catherine of Russia, whose repulsive ugliness blocks the satisfaction of her sexual desires—all are the targets of aggressive laughter. Finally, in anticipation of our discussion of the novel during the revolutionary period, it can be noted that Maréchal, by extending the dramatic personae to the European kings and the European sansculottes, once again opened up space for a utopian theme at a point in time when every utopia connected with France would have had to be considered an affront to the pretensions of the Jacobin administration. Precisely this new future horizon of a European revolution makes it understandable why six thousand copies of the *Jugement dernier* were distributed to soldiers in the revolutionary armies, why the piece was seen by no fewer than 100,000 spectators during the months of its performance, and why "Père Duchesne" (issue number 310) took his wife to the Théâtre de la République in order to see how "all of the tyrants of Europe would have to gobble each other up and be swallowed by a volcano at the end of the play. That's really a spectacle for republican eyes!"

The population of Paris reacted to the political events of Thermidor with a number of balls and previously unheard of enthusiasm for the theater. The *Décade philosophique, littéraire et politique* reports on these days:

All of the playhouses in Paris draw unusually large crowds now; people push through the gates of the various theaters; they press into the orchestra after having driven the musicians away; and often a large number of eager spectators have to return home without having gotten a ticket. What is the explanation for these extraordinary crowds?

Nowadays an answer to this question could be easily formulated in the slogan "collective discharge," and in fact, such a wholesale explanation is confirmed by the plays from the second half of 1794. As in the summer of 1789, actors were in a hurry to get all those dramas on stage that had fallen to the censor during the Terror; and of course authors made an effort to respecify and refocus the context of their originally quite generalized tirades against tyranny. The flexible Marie-Joseph Chénier prefaced his *Timoléon,* a tragedy with an antique touch, with by an ode aimed at Robespierre and his accomplices, which he claimed to have written before Robespierre's overthrow; today this seems all the more improbable considering that, despite his friendship with influential Jacobins, Chénier made no attempt to save his brother André, who was decapitated only two days before Robespierre. Already after a few weeks it was possible to proffer texts that present Robespierre's political overthrow on stage. *Chute du dernier tyran ou la journée du 9 Thermidor* was performed as early as September 4, 1794.

But even this kind of management of the past was just a passing fashion. Up until the fall of 1794, two types of drama in particular dominated the Parisian stage: on the one hand, comedies, whose action was located in the time after Thermidor and which allowed their audiences to laugh to their hearts' content at the powerful Jacobins who are now forced to conceal themselves from their former victims but who are nonetheless unmasked without fail; on the other, pieces in the tradition of late Enlightenment bourgeois drama, whose virtuous protagonists had been repeatedly persecuted, to be sure, by evil despots, without these persecutions and the sudden wheeling around to a happy end having anything directly to do with the events of Thermidor, as was customary in the summer of 1794. But how can it be explained that this action is often set in the Scottish Highlands or in Goa, the Portuguese province in India? Probably such displacements were the result of a political compromise between the revolutionary administration and the royalistic *jeunesse dorée* who set the tone after Thermidor on the boulevards, in the cafés, and in the theaters of Paris. For if the pieces would only lightly allude to the political reversal of the immediate past, then they best suited the new government's wish to let the political past be forgotten (after all, they had been party comrades of Robespierre's for a long time, and yet they did not completely exclude the possibility that the theater performances might turn into veritably political orgies of revenge) — above all for the audience of the playhouses around the Palais Royal, which was as reactionary as it was wealthy. Hence, the popular game of tossing notes with anti-Jacobin and sometimes anti-Republican occasional poems on them to those actors who had once sympathized with the sans-culottes in order to force them to read them aloud. A final observation about the time between Thermidor 1794 and Vendémiaire 1795 has a particular significance. Indeed, dramas with the motif of *vertu persécutée* and a happy ending pick up for the most part conventions of the late Enlightenment, but it is striking that increasingly and obviously the protagonists instill less pity and more anxiety in the audience. Fear becomes the dominant theme of serious dramas in all playhouses, following cultural-political efforts—in connection with the suppression of royalist plans for a coup d'état in Vendémiaire 1795—to ban even allusions to the history of the Revolution from the stage.

For the last phase of the history of French theater during the Revolution (1796–99), it is necessary to distinguish between the repertoires of the various playhouses. While the Théâtre de l'Odéon (the former Comédie Française on the Left Bank) and the Théâtre de la République reconnected with the tradition of staging tragedies, more and more prototypes of the melodrama so characteristic of bourgeois theater in the early nineteenth century made their way into the playhouses in the center of the city, but especially in the popular stages of the boulevard du Temple. The needs of the public for materials exciting fear, as paradoxical as that might seem, quite obviously became all-encompassing: Lemercier's *Agamemnon* adaptation became the most successful tragedy of the time, probably not least of all because it drew on one of the most bloodthirsty myths of classical literature; the enthusiasm for Ducis's version of *Macbeth* would require a similar explanation. Now, the theme of adultery was no longer exploited to conceal a fascination with taboo-breaking sexuality under the guise of moral indignation, but rather the protagonists were afraid to confess to their spouses and feared the force of their own passions. Bonaparte caused Arnault, the author of the drama *Blanche et Montcassin* (1796), to change the happy ending of his play to a tragic one, because only then would "fear be able to follow him into his bed"—so the explanation of the general, already quite popular after his Italian campaign. The evidence for the attraction of theatrical fear could be extended indefinitely; but it is more important to understand that in the melodrama, in contrast to tragedy, the protagonists' and the audience's fears for the hero are bound together in a happy conclusion. So, for example, a colonial family is attacked by Negro rebels in *Adonis ou le bon nègre* (1798) and is in danger of their lives for a long time, only to be freed at the end with the aid of a faithful slave. The final words of this melodrama presented at one of the theaters on the boulevard du Temple ("virtue is always rewarded") makes it clear that the reception of this sort of piece by a popular audience had an ideological background. Such works assumed (which their authors, by the way, on no account passed over in silence) the psychosocial function of the Christian religion that had been publicly discredited in the revolutionary period.

As easy as it may be to understand the differences between tragedy and melodrama in the later years of the Revolution by taking into account the locations of their staging, it is equally as difficult to find a plausible explanation for the all-inclusive fixation on the motif of fear. Nonetheless, a glance at the comedies in those years enables the formulation of a hypothesis. Ever since Molière, this genre had been dominated by the plot of the opportunistic father, who wants to marry his lovely daughter off—of course, no longer to an aristocrat as in the seventeenth or early eighteenth centuries—but to a representative of the nouveau riche bourgeoisie, whether a stockbroker, the owner of a ballroom, or the publisher of British gothic novels, and who is set up as the target of the audience's mockery through the failure of his project. The change in the social membership of the son-in-law chosen by the father is decisive for a functional-historical explanation for the success of such pieces: that marriage with the parvenus is always doomed to failure seems to speak for the fact that such comedies offered the public the possibility of freeing themselves from accumulated aggressions against those contemporaries who had taken advantage of the Revolution's many political twists and their consequences for the economic and social structure. From this perspective, we can also understand why those comedies that first presented on the boulevard du Temple starring, as we would now say, "Madame Angot," a nouvelle riche fishmonger, a popular figure of identification like "Père Duchesne," were triumphant in all of the theaters of Paris. In *Madame Angot ou la poissarde parvenue* (1796), the heroine follows the plan of adding the touch of dignity her financial ascent lacks by marrying her daughter to an impoverished nobleman. She abandons this ambitious scheme only when it becomes clear in the concluding engagement scene that the desired son-in-law is not in fact noble but has merely pretended to be in order to profit from the fishmonger's wealth. This plot makes two kinds of reception possible. The laughter of the petit bourgeois public in the theaters on the northern periphery of Paris manifests sympathy with a heroine from their own class on whom it is possible to project their own desire for vertical mobility and who arrives at the insight, after some initial confusion, that any effort to suppress her own social background will be in vain. The denouement allows the upper middle-class and aristocratic audience on the stages at the center of the city a triumphant, aggressive laugh at the parvenus, whose attempt at social advancement has been successfully rejected—especially because the author has avoided putting the hereditary nobility in a compromising situation.

How then can this brief glance at the comedies during the late years of the Revolution help explain the fascination that the theme of fear held for the recipients of serious dramas? What the relatively stereotyped plots of the last-mentioned pieces sacrifice to laughter are the consequences of the previously unimaginable social mobility made possible by the Revolution. The experience of a changed social environment had not led most French people to expect their own social betterment but rather made them anxious about a wholly uncertain future, which threatened to endanger whatever status they had acquired. That there was no cause for such fear was one of the implications of the comedies, and that the open future as an object of anxiety was officially repressed by the various concrete forms of an optimistic historical philosophy has already been established. Yet there are any number of indications confirming that despite the comedies and the historical concretions, some collective disquiet was left over, a fear without an object, which in Freud's terminology is customarily referred to as "neurotic" or "free-floating anxiety." Now psychology tells us that this kind of neurotic fear is best pacified when it is provided with substitute objects and thus given the opportunity to develop "strategies of avoidance." Was this the reason for the boom in the theme of fear in the serious dramas of this period? That the development only set in after Thermidor 1794 would support our presupposition; for in the preceding years, a public faced with the Terror aroused by the guillotine and backed by the government with all of its power would have had little reason to attach a collective neurotic anxiety to fictional objects.

I close with an observation that acquires its meaning from the general shift in the function of literature from feudal to bourgeois societies but that also casts light on our central question about the realization or failure of ideal communication models coming from the Enlightenment. When we read the prefaces to serious dramas after Thermidor 1794, it is striking that, while every author, indeed, pursued the goal of inculcating in the audience "that feeling of painful joy" — "which it yearned for even while complaining about it," as Laya noted in the preface to his play *Falkland* (1798) — none of them provided information about the intended effect of such feelings on the action of the recipients as had been routinely the case in the Enlightenment. If this hypothesis is correct, then it also delivers a (simple) explanation for this phenomenon: the binding of collective neurotic fears in the medium of the serious drama could succeed only when it was carried out without the audience's knowledge — so to speak, "behind its back." This leads us to the conjecture that literature's partially deplored, partially programmatically postulated "lack of function" in bourgeois society is the necessary condition for the realization of its socially stabilizing effects.

Individual Readings

In designating this fourth communication context, we start with the attitudes that determine its production and reception, attitudes that are so familiar today it is difficult to think of them as a stage in historical development. In comparison to the conventions of speech acts we have been dealing with so far, they can be negatively defined in two ways. The reader experiences the text by him- or herself rather than in a group like the National Assembly, a theater audience, or a communal festival. The second criterion cannot be applied in the same way to all of the texts I will present here; but it embraces a general tendency in the literary history of the French Revolution: as reader, the author has less and less a "reasoning private person" in mind, someone who reads his or her text as a human being capable of common sense and pity and who thus experiences it with a receptive disposition Enlightenment anthropology would consider "common humanity." The tendency is rather to imagine a reader whose identity is constituted precisely by a deviation from "common humanity" or from the characteristics specific to a group.

Literary history has paid practically no attention to texts aimed at the individual reader between 1789 and 1799.[27] One can come up with a double explanation for these circumstances. For one thing, there seems to be no obvious relationship between the revolutionary period with its innovative cultural politics and the individual reader; for another, hardly any of the texts written and published during these years has been taken up into the canon of major literary testimonials of the past. It is characteristic that the Marquis de Sade, the only author here whose novels are still appreciated, admittedly with some misgiving, is frequently interpreted by looking away from the particular historical framework in which they originated and found their first audience, although he, as I will try to show, is surely one of the authors shaped by the revolutionary period. Moreover, the years of the Revolution mark much less of a caesura in the history of French lyric and the French novel in the eighteenth and nineteenth centuries than was the case for the theater. As the main characteristics of lyric and the novel during the 1790s, we could mention a tendency toward descriptive compositions on the natural and social environments, a predilection for melancholy or even horrifying material—as contemporary English literature had been presenting it for some decades. Admittedly, these tendencies had already been on the horizon in France sometime before 1789.

"With respect to lyric, the eighteenth century was undoubtedly the poorest period in our entire literary history, although rhymesters were more numerous than ever."[28] Anyone who goes to the trouble of acquiring a first impression of the poetry produced during the Revolution quickly realizes that this crushing judgment is quite justified. Nevertheless, a problem of historical understanding, which softens the edge of this verdict, should be pointed out: it is self-evident that the modern concept of poetry is confined to a relatively brief period in the history of the genre—namely, postromantic poetry. Therefore, literary historians are often seduced into interpretations that are completely inadequate historically, and it is precisely those texts of the past that admit such projections, like troubadour lyric or Renaissance sonnets, that have remained alive in today's literary consciousness—although based on a misunderstanding. The conventionalism and the erudite character of eighteenth-century lyric are inaccessible to such projections, which explains the general disdain for its texts. Thus it is less a matter of poor quality than the missing correspondence between our contemporary concept of poetry and the texts of the eighteenth century.

It is not unusual to undertake a kind of "apology" for this poetry by spicing it up with the songs of the Revolution. But at best this is legitimate only with respect to the classicistic repertoire of forms – and even then only with reservations. A functional-historical outline of the literary history of the French Revolution has to be able to distinguish between songs composed for republican festivals and poems intended for individual readers. In this section, we will pay as little attention to the songs of the Revolution as to the poetry of André Chénier (even if his work is frequently cited as an anticipation of romantic literature), as a way of "honorably" saving the late eighteenth century. Chénier's poems were written in prison, shortly before his execution, but – and this is the crucial factor here – were first published as late as 1819. The enthusiasm of their late reception was obviously more than just slightly urged on by the political interests of the Restoration.

What is most surprising when we read poems from the revolutionary period is the almost complete absence of thematic treatments or even allusions to political events and their social consequences. For instance, Nicolas-Germain Léonard (1744–93) had spent his life between Guadeloupe, where he was born, and France. It was political turmoil in the Antilles, ignited by the Revolution and the debates on slavery in almost every French colony, that had moved him to finally return to France in the fall of 1792. In the poem "Au bois de Romainville," he sings of his arrival in the traditional imagery of the bucolic. Today it would certainly not be worth taking the trouble to read these conventional stanzas, if, in the last analysis, they did not provide astonishing evidence for the experience of living through revolutionary France during the months after the declaration of the republic and the trials against Louis XVI. For Léonard, France remained a refuge of peace; if he feared the future, then only his own aging. All of this makes it clear that poetry did not play a part in the characteristic interests and cares of the period.

> O lovely place! O Happy Land!
> O France, sanctuary of the fine arts!
> I bewail the people whose fate
> distances them so far from you
>
> They will come, those Days of Darkness
> Where the heavy Finger of Age
> Will cover the Images of my Spring
> With the Veil of Death.

We have already mentioned Gabriel-Marie-Jean-Baptiste Legouvé as the author of the play *La mort d'Abel* (1792). When we now turn to his poem "La mélancholie" (1798), we do not claim that a shift from the literature of the late Enlightenment to romanticism had taken place between 1792 and 1798, between Legouvé's drama related to the Enlightenment question of the origins of human inequality and his reflection on melancholy. This turn cannot be as clearly located as many a literary historian would like to believe; but for all that, Léonard's and Legouvé's poems show that, when we include the revolutionary period in the literary histories, the cliché of "Romanticism as a countermovement to the Enlightenment" becomes problematic.

> Joy has its Pleasures; but Melancholy,
> Enamored of Silence and turned in on Itself,
> Despises these games, this loud Happiness,
> Where the Spirit is entangled,
> Where the Heart congeals.
> More than lively Cheer
> Does esteem the Sensitive Soul
> The heavy Spirit of Sweet Melancholy;
> He seeks it in the arts: let us follow him thither
>
> .   .   .   .
>
> Loneliness consumes his Soul,
> And a Tear has fallen on the Damp Page.
> Sweet Tear of the Heart, Darkened by Feeling,
> You are born in the Seclusion of a long Rapture:
> Happy he who knows you!
> Unhappy he who bewails you not.

Unlike the self-devotion of bourgeois drama, which was only supposed to be a preliminary step in an empathic process binding together all humankind and which is exactly the reason why it leads to a social criticism that strangles spontaneous feelings, lyric melancholy abided in the self-satisfied pleasure of the sensitive subject. Now it is no longer the fate of virtuous fellow humans exposed to a plethora of persecutions that, as it were, brings the observer to tears, but rather he reaches for literature in order to transport himself into the desired mood. This sort of effect is by no means ascribed by Legouvé solely to the popular *Werther*— the *Iliad*, the *Aeneid*, Rousseau's *Nouvelle Héloïse*, and Bernardin de Saint-Pierre's *Paul et Virginie* also belong to this literary horizon, all of them texts that in the contexts of other receptive dispositions might have wholly different functions.

From this viewpoint, melancholy seems like a late Enlightenment sentimentality from which the intersubjective dimension has been removed. This break in external relationships has to be seen in the context of a pathetic individualism originating in the late eighteenth century, which in turn points to the institutional crisis of class society. For it was precisely the disappearance of institutions that had supplied the people with orderly and self-contained existential contexts, which led to isolation in biographies, biographies that presented themselves as unique because they were not institutionally prescribed.[29] Surely the Revolution is simply the last dramatic stage in the crises of feudal society, which explains why, even though we can make out the symptoms of this new form of individualism long before 1789, we must nonetheless recognize a particularly accelerating factor of its development in the Revolution. When we take the psychological definition of melancholy as our point of departure, we also have such an indirect effect of the sociohistorical changeover on the origination of genres addressed to the individual reader. According to Freud, its characteristic narcissistic pleasure is a consequence of the loss of a loved object. This raises the question whether the theme of melancholy that was so clearly dominant in poetry at the end of the eighteenth century does not actually refer to the renunciation of a concern for one's fellow human beings, or as twentieth-century sociology would say, for the "generalized other," and whether this loss is not another symptom of the failure of the Enlightenment social models in the revolutionary period.

As far as the history of the novel is concerned, the same general ideas hold that were derived from our short treatment of the poetry. Surely there is no such thing as "the novel of the French Revolution." Instead, apart from a few isolated cases, the years 1789 to 1799 brought the end of the French Enlightenment novel and at the same time a few preliminary steps in the direction of the nineteenth-century novel, whereby we are thinking more of popular literary forms than of the works of the great French realists.

As the central theme of the sentimental novel, interest clearly slackens in the *vertu persécutée,* for which Richardson's *Pamela* had been the model. A sociohistorical explanation for this observation is quite obvious. The function of this theme was a strict dissociation of the reader's sympathies and antipathies. All of his aversion was steered toward the "persecutor of virtue," who, if not specifically aristocratic, was still always presented as representative of the feudal social order and its decadence. The reader's sympathies went completely to the protagonist, usually female, who was exposed to the machinations of the persecutor; her means for living (Diderot's *conditions*) were depicted in such a manner that they, along with the first-person narrative, invited the bourgeois reader to identify with her. In a society that could claim with a certain justification to have diminished class differences and which for a while successfully managed to repress the recognition of economic (that is, class-based) differences by incessantly referring to the achievement of legal equality, the dominant theme of the *vertu pérsecutée* may have lost part of its relevance. We will later return to its quite unconventional use in the novels of the Marquis de Sade, a use that points out a psychic ambivalence in the fascination of the topic that was not seen by other authors and the readers of the late eighteenth century—but which literary historians have not seemed to have grasped either.

In addition, Werner Krauss has pointed out that the utopian novel's historical moment ended with a revolution that conceived itself as a realized utopia.[30] A survey of the texts in this genre published in eighteenth-century France confirms such speculations and draws our attention, furthermore, to the astonishing affinity between political developments and the history of the genre.[31] So the number of utopian texts published before 1789 had been steadily increasing (indeed, between 1787 and 1789 there was even a collection in thirty-six volumes, which included literature of previous centuries) only to stagnate in the first years of the Revolution and rapidly decrease after 1794. Only two utopian novels published during the Revolution have been taken up by literary history — Bernardin de Saint-Pierre's *Chaumière indienne* (1791) and Diderot's *Supplément au voyage de Bougainville* (1796). In all likelihood the former, and definitely the latter text, was written before 1789. Both fit the late Enlightenment model for the genre in every respect: among peoples who have been arrogantly classified as "savage" by the feudal-aristocratic culture, traveling researchers discover social structures and a practical ethics that could be introduced as a positive counterpart to those found in eighteenth-century France.

While these texts are to be interpreted as if they were Enlightenment "laggards," then *La constitution de la lune, rêve politique et moral* (1793) by Louis-Abel Beffroy de Reigny shows that literary utopia reacquired a function only when hopes for realizing the model of the enlightened public had shrunk considerably in the course of the French Revolution. This utopian "constitution" was prefaced by a *Précis d'histoire de la révolution de la lune*. As could be expected, the history of the moon is similar to the course of the French Revolution down to the smallest detail and assumes a utopian character only where it is related how the Emperor of the moon, "a weak, but simple and naturally good man," instead of being tried and executed like Louis XVI, dies of grief over the bloodshed in his country. Also the constitution, as central part of Beffroy de Reigny's book, corresponds in every feature to that conception of the republic that the Girondistes, the political opponents of Robespierre and the Montagne, had championed from the trial of Louis XVI until May 1793: it forbade denunciations, repealed the *assemblées primaires* (which mainly referred to the sansculotte commune in Paris), and abolished the death penalty. For the history of the genre, it is interesting that here the use of the utopian form is conditioned once again, as in the ancien régime before, by political censorship and the author's fear of being persecuted by it.

Despite isolated instances like the *Constitution de la lune,* we may safely assume the end of the development of those forms of the novel whose themes directed the readers to changing perspectives of social structure. On the other hand, the question of personal identity was at the center of the successful novels of the revolutionary period, which helps us to understand their apparent tendency toward the structural forms of biography and autobiography. Already in our brief discussion of the poetry, it was pointed out that the thematic trend toward "personal identity" contains a reference to the sociohistorical process of evolution from feudal to bourgeois society. If the former society, which was frozen in the tightly organized life patterns dictated by classes, determined the people's biographies, bourgeois society seems to have left it up to the individual to formulate his life according to a battery of choices, which up until our present has been regularly praised as the opportunity of freedom. The successful novels of the revolutionary period try to cope with what—from the point of view of social history— seemed to be the new complication of freedom.

Charles-Antoine-Guillaume Pigault-Lebrun's novel *L'enfant du carnaval* (1792) takes recourse in the tradition of the picaresque novel, whose formulative possibilities, to be sure, no longer only (or even primarily) were used for social satire but function as a way of fictionally solving the knots of personal identity. The novel has clear autobiographical features. Born as the son of a newly rich bourgeois family in Calais, the author was soon drawn to Paris, where he disarranged his life according to all of the tactics of picaresque cunning. It is worth noting that precisely the obviously invented parts of the autobiography seem to compensate for the loss of personal identity shaped by outside pressures, especially the "true story of the hero's engendering" as the result of a slip committed by a vicar in his cups and a nun during carnival. Since he's "a child of the carnival," it is evident that the hero continually gets into conflict with society. But on the other hand, his parents have given him a *nature* that keeps him from experiencing his social uprootedness as loneliness; the "unity of his mood" that has been passed down guarantees his personal identity as the "carnival kid."

Quite similarly, the connections between narrative structure and communicative function, between the reconstruable biography of the author and the trajectory of the first-person narrator's life, go far to explain Nicolas Restif de la Bretonne's multivolume *Monsieur Nicolas* (1794–97). The hero moves out of the rural idyll of his youth to Paris, where he leads an irregular existence, mostly, but not always, in the demimonde of criminals and prostitutes. Even his identity is constituted out of a cluster of attitudes, which admittedly is far more pretentious than the picaresque identity of the "carnival kid." Strongly influenced by Rousseau, Restif de la Bretonne lets his heroes be motivated always and everywhere by natural goodness and pity. He tries to find these dispositions of an optimistic anthropology precisely in those protagonists who had been excluded from feudal society. That the parvenu Enlightenment figure Friedrich Melchior Grimm called Restif a "back-alley Rousseau" is interesting in several respects. This epithet is another confirmation of the hypothesis that the *philosophes* had nothing but contempt for the next generation of literati, who were denied entrance into the salons; it hints at how biography and fictional autobiography are mixed up in evaluating Restif; it explains for us why *Monsieur Nicolas,* which still has not completely disappeared from the literary histories, found so little response in the beginning. The lachrymose-philanthropic discourses, which the "back-alley Rousseau" attached to his descriptions, no longer suited public taste after Thermidor 1794. This detail of historical reception is all the more remarkable considering Restif de la Bretonne's great success before the Revolution with the far more obvious, moralizingly detailed descriptions of his biography. In *La vie de mon père* (1778) Restif chose his rural home as the location of the social idyll; in *Le paysan et la paysanne pervertis* (1787) this ideal world is confronted with the city's babel of sins, in which virtuous country folk succumb to the machinations of decadent sensualists. Despite his persistence, which had apparently become old-fashioned for the late years of the Revolution, in moralizing on such themes in *Monsieur Nicolas*, and despite the quite embarassing idea to present the hero's numerous female acquaintances as an appendix to the novel in the popular form of an almanac (*Mon calendrier*), Restif's most important work still looks ahead to the nineteenth-century novel in two respects. In a footnote to *Monsieur Nicolas*, he anticipates the insight of today's critics that the philanthropic interest of the reader of the bourgeois period in the "underworld" of his own society—we think, for example, of Eugène Sue's *Mystères de Paris* (1842–43) but also of Zola's early novel written in the same manner, *Les Mystères de Marseille* (1867)—replaces the need for escape in the Enlightenment period that utopian novels had satisfied by including reports of ethnological research trips:

> Fellow citizens, readers, . . . keep in mind that my story must interest you more than that of some lying traveler, who presents descriptions of distant countries, of which he only knows from hearsay and which you will never see, sticking Kaffirs and above all Hottentots in the robes of the old Romans. . . . On the contrary, I am only talking about your own country, how it looks fifty miles from the capital.[32]

Besides, there is a veritable obsession with detailed description. In places, the tableaux in *Monsieur Nicolas* are barely integrated in the narrative development. In *Les nuits de Paris ou le spectateur nocturne* (1788–94), Restif contributed to the establishment of a genre at the beginning of which stood Mercier's *Tableau de Paris* (1781). Undoubtedly, the genre of the tableau should be attributed to a need to save the homogeneity and the content of everyday reality—at a historical moment that was characterized by previously unheard of acceleration in social change and a multiplication of the perspectives for grasping reality—through the closure of literary description and the solidity of naming details that just a few decades earlier would have been unworthy of mention.[33] Thus we can delineate lines of development in the work of Restif de la Bretonne, which, with respect to the history of motives and functions on the one hand, leads to the popular novel and to the bourgeois novel of the nineteenth century, on the other.

What Pigault-Lebrun and Restif de la Bretonne share is the concern to solve the problem of personal identity by sustaining the protagonist's cluster of feelings. With François-Guillaume Ducray-Duminil, on the contrary, the unity of life's journey is guaranteed by the observance of certain behavioral norms. The great popularity of his novels among his contemporary readers is a telling contrast to

the difficulties Restif de la Bretonne had in finding readers for his fictional autobiography, which he finally had to publish himself. *Coelina ou l'enfant du mystère*
(1798) in contrast sold no fewer than 1,200,000 copies,[34] and *Victor ou l'enfant
de la forêt*, already in the year of its publication, 1796, was presented to a "well-
disposed public" in three editions. The titles show that Ducray-Duminil dug up
the traditional motif of the foundling in order to slip a concrete form over the
theme of problematic identity.

The opening scene in *Victor ou l'enfant de la forêt* corroborates at the same
time sociohistorical and psychoanalytic explanations for the fashion of literary
melancholy at the turn of the eighteenth to the nineteenth century. Looking out
of the window of a Bohemian castle in the bright moonlight, the hero abandons
himself to "sad reflections" because he does not dare to hold the hand of his beloved, who is, naturally, the daughter of the lord of the castle. He is forbidden
this by the commandments of decency and because a veil of secrecy is spread over
his origins – he was taken in by the lord of the castle as a foundling. Of course
the author construes a plot that makes it possible to quickly lift this veil. A band
of robbers threatens the castle, and only Victor is able to save the inhabitants from
this threat, for it turns out that he is the son of Roger, the dangerous captain of
the bandits. Through the four volumes of the novel, the reader experiences how
Roger, although plagued by a bad conscience, tries to convince his son to take
over his lucrative business of robbery; how Victor resists every temptation, must
witness his father's beheading (the pertinent chapter has the suggestive title,
"Which sensitive readers should pass over"); how the enlightened Bohemian lord
of the castle announces to him that the constancy of his virtue balances once and
for all the blemish of his birth, whereby the obstacle to his marriage with his beloved is finally removed. The function of this plot-scheme, "virtue as a compensation for birth" in a bourgeois society characterized by the opportunity for social
mobility and the threat of social instability, is obvious.

Admittedly, this plot gives the author a chance to satisfy several other needs
of the public. Hence he is unsparing with melodramatic effects designed to arouse
fear in the reader – for instance, at the climax of the hero's evasion of the bandit's
"subculture," during the visitation to the dungeon in which the prisoners languish
(chapter title, "A Trip through Hell"):

> "I'll probably," continued Roger with a smile, "have to amuse you with
> a funny scene. Come here, do you hear those screams, all those voices?
> That's the funniest thing in the world: a great cellar in which almost
> two hundred women are locked up."
> I would never come to an end if I wanted to report every sigh that
> Victor had to listen to in this place of horror, where every sort of tor-
> ment and torture had been united. There lay a person deep in mud and
> gnawed on daily by the most poisonous reptiles. Here a prisoner, who

lay on his back and in order to keep breathing had to continually lift a huge rock that threatened to crush his weakened chest.

Part of the success of the novels of Madame Sophie Cottin in the early nineteenth century might have come from the rumor that she had put an end to her own life at the age of thirty-seven. In her well-beloved novel, *Claire d'Albe* (1799), she took up the traditional textual pattern of the epistolary novel, using it as a framework for a plot that supposedly was a great favorite of the nineteenth-century reading public. The heroine, mother of two children, is married to a man who acts more like a benevolent father to her. Claire lives happily, even if she admits in numerous letters to a girlfriend that she does not hope to fulfill her ideal of passionate love from the marriage. Anyone who knows the nineteenth-century novel can guess that the plot picks up speed as soon as the unavoidable object of passionate love turns up (here in form of the husband's nephew), that, however, it is not so much this figure as the heroine's previously repressed wishes for love that assume the actant position of the "persecutor of her virtue." After the usual internal struggles, Claire succumbs to temptation only to die of the pyschosomatic disease of a "broken heart," which will become a regular epidemic among her literary successors. This novel also provides an answer *e negativo* to the question of the shaping of personal identity. The heroine understands that she has transgressed norms to which she has been enjoined by the typical plot framework of bourgeois society, the family. *Claire d'Albe* initiates the literary series of the bourgeois novel in two respects, and in a double difference from the sentimental novel: the threat to virtue can now no longer be blamed on the representatives of a dominant class to which one feels morally superior; instead of virtue preserving itself by fleeing from persecution, a renunciation of drives and devotion to the family as the refuge of true happiness are the command of the hour. This plot structure forms the basic pattern against which Stendhal's *Le rouge et le noir* (1830) and Flaubert's *Madame Bovary* (1857) have acquired their position in literary history.

Just as much as Pigault-Lebrun, Restif de la Bretonne, Ducray-Duminil, and Madame Cottin, Donatien-Alphonse-François de Sade drew on traditional motifs and structures from the genre history of the eighteenth century in his novels. He has become incomparably more famous and—understandably enough from the point of view of social history—infamous by arriving at a position through his productive assimilation of such models that is diametrically opposed to those ideologemes and behavioral norms the previously discussed novels served to legitimize. In his novels, he negates the norms of bourgeois society as a mode of shaping identity; therefore, the history of his reception during the past century is closely connected with the history of depth psychology, because it also questions the legitimation of such norms, although rather from a perspective of functional interpretation. The actuality of de Sade's work lets us forget all too easily that his origins are stamped in many respects by the late Enlightenment and the Revolution; indeed, it can even be maintained that he has remained so much more alive than the other novelists of his time because, in contrast to them, he stuck to the anthropology of the Enlightenment, albeit in a wholly new interpretation. The chronology of his publications alone makes de Sade into an author par excellence of the revolutionary period. With the exception of *Les 120 journées de Sodome,* which was first published in 1904 after the late discovery of the manuscript, all of the novels on which his fame rests appeared during the Revolution, even if they mostly go back to sketches de Sade had already conceived during his atonement for various sentences before 1789: *Justine ou les malheurs de la vertu* (1791), *Aline et Valcour ou le roman philosophique* (1793), *La philosophie dans le boudoir ou les instituteurs immoraux* (1795), and *La Nouvelle Justine ou les malheurs de la vertu* (1797).

Even more unequivocally than the complete title, the preface to the first version of *Justine* (1791) locates it within the tradition of the sentimental novel. Like his predecessors, de Sade feigns a concern with the scourging of vice. The path he chose for achieving this purpose, the unsparingly open depiction of perversion, was certainly far more effective than the customary glorification of virtue up until then. We know from de Sade's correspondence that countless obscene details were due to the publisher's wish for a "really spicy" text rather than to any immoral (or moral) intention on the part of the author. Nonetheless, the preface and the structure of the novel, which at regular intervals provide the first-person narrator, Justine, with the opportunity to express her loathing for her tormentors, conceal far more than a mere sales strategy adjusted to a pornography boom in the book business at the end of the eighteenth century.

The later novels published by de Sade make it evident that he exploited the fundamental ambivalence of the motif of *vertu persécutée.* If this plot constellation was suitable for arousing pity for persecuted virtue and disgust for its tormentors, it also made it possible for those readers who were prepared to identify with the persecutors to imaginarily live out aggressions against everything the virtuous heroes stood for — renunciation of drives, hypocrisy, and the self-image of the bourgeois class. And it is just as easy to conjecture that some recipients accepted the identification with the positive hero without giving themselves over to pity, thus satisfying masochistic desires in their imagination. That pity and sadism, sadism and masochism are not as fundamentally disassociated tendencies of the human psyche as bourgeois morality would like them to be has been well known since Freud. The productive reception of the sentimental novel by the Marquis de Sade seems like an anticipatory literary concretion of this scientific insight. In the first version of *Justine,* de Sade's innovative performance barely consists in the intensification of procedures that were involved long before 1789 in establishing the success of the sentimental novel (under the cover of the recipients' philanthropy). On the contrary, in *La Nouvelle Justine* (1797), de Sade not only takes a position on the philosophical discourses of his protagonists but by means of the novel structure also clearly opts for vice over virtue. In place of Justine, whose suffering is for the narrator nothing but a pretext for the elaboration of sexual tableaux, we have in her sister Juliette—whose adventurous life story in the plenitude of its episodes reminds us in turn of the picaresque novel[35]—a new approach to the question of the shaping of personal identity. Juliette unfolds individuality through a natural drive toward evil that is not inhibited by any sort of scruples whatsoever. The conclusion of the novel is also unexcelled for conceptual precision. At the apex of her power and wealth, evil Juliette delights in the death of her virtuous and chaste sister, who is punished by nature (she is struck by lightning) just like the despotic monarchs in Maréchal's *Jugement dernier des rois* were killed by the eruption of a volcano.

To be sure, it is not only the motif of *vertu persécutée* and the grounding of the plot line in the philosophy of nature in de Sade's novels that refer to the historical context in which they were generated. In the detailed depiction of Justine's fear of rape and "sadistic" tortures, and in the description of the dungeons, out of which her cries for help will never escape to the ear of a savior, de Sade was following the English gothic novel and its French imitations, which enjoyed so much popularity among readers of novels and theater audiences. His tableaux of sexual perversions have been interpreted by Michel Foucault as a last attempt to assure once again humankind's capability to comprehend reality by naming all of those phenomena whose thematic treatment had been banned from literature by numerous taboos up until the end of the eighteenth century.[36] Even someone who does not want to accept this interpretation will not be able to ignore the purely formal similarity of the tableaux in Mercier, Restif de la Bretonne, and de Sade.

The social history of the late eighteenth century and the affinities of de Sade's work to contemporary literature and philosophy provide us, to be sure, with important presuppositions for understanding the "de Sade phenomenon." Yet it is fairly evident that they still do not add up to a satisfactory interpretation, if only because we have claimed to explain historically those successful texts of the time, to which de Sade's work stands in a relationship of negation. Hence we must take recourse in the biography of the Marquis, despite his firm denials (quite in contrast to the other novelists of his period) of any connection whatsoever between his life and the vicious protagonists of his novels. Already before the Revolution, the Marquis belonged to the darlings of the scandal sheets; it was not for nothing that Théveneau de Morande dedicated many pages of the *Gazette noire* to his deviant tendencies. At any rate, it was in the political interests of the *Gazette noire* to diligently overlook the fact that the privileged of the ancien régime—although, or precisely *because* the Marquis belonged to the high nobility—had excluded him from their ranks. Like many imprisoned writers in the late eighteenth century, de Sade made use of natural philosophy—he was an enthusiastic reader of Rousseau—to justify himself. Like all natural philosophers, according to the simple but convincing hypothesis of Peter Bürger,[37] he projected whatever suited his own needs onto the semantically empty concept of nature. Seen so, de Sade proceeded in the apology of what we are accustomed to refer to as "sexually perverse" no differently than other Enlightenment spokesmen in their glorification of the intimacy of the family. We can therefore summarize: in de Sade's work the sheer unlimited freedom feudal society preserved for privileged individuals finds a philosophical justification in categories of bourgeois anthropology. Because this conjunction is as atypical of literary and philosophical history as were prison sentences for a nobleman condemned for sexual dissolution, we cannot regard de Sade's work as typical of the period; but on the other hand, it cannot be understood without the period's specific fields of action and thought.

Add to this that there were only a few years (those in which the revolutionary cultural politicians aspired to a radical realization of the ideal model of the enlightened public) that provided de Sade with the opportunity and inducement to publish his writings. Whether his short career as a revolutionary politician (he wrote a pamphlet against Louis XVI after his unsuccessful escape, a highly conventional funeral oration for Marat, and was commissioned by the departmental committee of that neighborhood in Paris where he had taken an apartment to make an effort, of all things, to reform the hospitals) was the result of a double misunderstanding (on the part of the Jacobins as well as de Sade) or simply hard-boiled opportunism cannot be decided with certainty. On the other hand, it seems unlikely that *Français, encore un effort si vous voulez être républicains* (the title of a philosophical tract de Sade published as inserted passages in *La philosophie dans le boudoir* [1795]) was meant ironically. Even if its propagation of unlimited egotism corresponded to the life forms of the *nouveaux riches* in the years after Thermidor and even if it cannot be interpreted as an "oppositional discourse" against an "official discourse" in the face of the apparent abstinence from ideology of the administrations following Robespierre, the carefully preserved incognito, the criticism of the contemporary scene, de Sade's internment in the madhouse of Charenton, and above all the history of the reception of his work all show that this philosophy hit a nerve in the bourgeois society that was in the process of being formulated. However repellent we might find the orgiastic tableaux of the Marquis, we have to admit that his damnation as an unrestrained pornographer had the function of repressing the ideological-critical force of his philosophy. It is for this reason that Horkheimer and Adorno in their *Dialektik der Aufklärung*, without valorizing his variant of an individualism exclusively determined by instincts, rediscovered de Sade's texts as a settling of accounts with the ideological bases of bourgeois society:

> Since nature prescribes vices and virtues to us on the basis of our constitution, or more philosophically formulated, on the basis of the ambivalent tendencies immanent in it, their inspirations would become a

very undependable means of deciding precisely between good and evil.[38]

Literary History of the French Revolution: Symptom of the Enlightenment's Double Failure

The literary-historical material that I have assembled and analyzed in the context of four communication situations during the years 1789 to 1799 allows for two different insights regarding the following historical developments. While the history of the political public and the revolutionary festivals, at least from the summer of 1793 on, demonstrated the impossibility of realizing the ideal Enlightenment models of communication, our analysis of the theater and of the genres aimed at individual reading helps us to understand functions of literature in nineteenth-century society. If it is clear that a consciousness of the aporias involved in establishing an enlightened public sphere and republican festivals first set in around 1793, a shift in the function of theater, poetry, and the novel had also taken place. The literary transition between the Enlightenment and the Revolution did not coincide with that of political history.

Now a materialistic literary historiography has obviously tended to play down the failure—so obvious from our point of view—of Enlightenment communication models in the years of the Jacobin dictatorship. Against that, it has stylized the art of the "revolutionary festivals" and the sansculotte party tabloids as forerunners of socialist cultural politics. Its special interests are also fairly obvious when it fails to mention in its history of revolutionary festivals the manifest withering of spontaneous enthusiasm by the participants, when it justifies measures of censorship, and when it sees in the development of political parties a crystallization of sansculotte consciousness rather than a deviation from the model of the enlightened public. Naturally, "bourgeois literary historiography" has no trouble accepting such symptoms for the *first* failures of the Enlightenment in the literary history of the French Revolution and it has no difficulty in simply overlooking any signs at the origins of modern literature that might contradict its exalted image of the social role of art, because it has scarcely been concerned with French texts from 1794 to 1799. To interpret the literature of this phase of the Revolution as a symptom for a *second* failure of the Enlightenment, however, means contradicting an interpretive schema that originated in political historiography. According to this schema, the French Revolution from 1794 on is supposed to have returned to its main course, which was the realization of central promises of eighteenth-century social philosophy—after an episode marked by "the excesses of Jacobin rule." The contrasts between the communication forms whose institutionalization begins in the years after Thermidor and the utopias of the enlighteners are manifold yet far more difficult to comprehend than with respect to the years 1793–94, simply because the historical actors were for the most part not conscious of them. Nonetheless, it is obvious that after the dispersion of science, religion, and art into self-enclosed partial systems, they no longer addressed themselves to a (theoretically) unlimited public, but to increasingly homogeneous groups of specialists, believers, and fans. It was in the Empire that such tendencies were first inscribed—even partially by law. Such a literature, "depoliticized" at the level of its explicit articulation, would still carry out important social functions by providing new models of identification and extolling the decline of action-oriented norms as an opportunity for the acquisition of individual freedom, by repressing fears of an open future and supporting a belief in the possibility of adequately comprehending reality. Not only does the socio-historical onset of recent history lie in the years 1794 to 1799, but it is also here that we find a first modernity of literature, in the early formulation of new functions of popular literary forms. The texts that have gone into the canon of literary history as evidence of post-Enlightenment periods almost look in this perspective like "second" and "third" modernisms. For the second modernism, it is the texts of literary romanticism that fulfill—very roughly speaking—a complementary role to those Enlightenment texts, which are still received today, insofar as they continue to be suitable for legitimizing individual norms of action in the same way that Enlightenment political philosophy served to establish the institutions that characterize our present public life. Baudelaire's poetry belongs to the "third" modernism just as much as Flaubert's novelistic work. Their implicit negation of the norms of bourgeois society has provided avant-garde literature with its direction up until the present. To these considerations we must add the insight that those reshufflings of political and social history, in which we are inclined today to see the beginnings of modernism, were not synchronized at their beginning with those literary traditions designated as "modern." Moreover, texts that can be historically ascribed to three subsequent literary traditions—the literature of the late years of the Revolution, the literature of romanticism, and mid-nineteenth-century "modern" literature—are presented today in a synchronic juxtaposition of three different reception levels: namely, as "popular literature" for media consumers, as "midclass" for the bourgeoisie, and as "avant-garde" for intellectuals.

If we grasp the literary history of the French Revolution as a symptom for the double failure of the Enlightenment, we do not even imply that there was a delayed realization of its ideal models of social communciation at all. Present-day sociology would have to reject as naive such a hope to institutionalize on a collective level communcation forms that have been formulated by unrepeatable historical conditions (and above all by the interaction of individual persons), and could support its position by precisely pointing to the history of the French Revolution. On the contrary, it would be well worth it to do further research on the literary history of the French Revolution as a contribution to the "adumbration of Enlightenment."[39]

Chapter 9
"Phoenix from the Ashes"; or, From Canon to Classic

To Bernard Cerquiglini,
Ancien Directeur des Ecoles,
Supporter of the Classics,
and yet friend of theory

Attempts to define the fundamental opposing concepts *canon/classic*[1] have revealed an important reason for the difficulties—aporias?—of drafting a metahistorical concept of canon as a basic category for a historical typology of culture. If it is indeed true that communication via the media of "art" and "literature" has, in the last two centuries, been subjected to a universal premise of *temporalization* (*Verzeitlichung*) and to a general postulate of *innovation*, it follows then that "canon" in the traditional sense of the term has long since disappeared, and this deductive conclusion corresponds entirely to a tendency to disqualify as "untimely" all attempts to establish an "aesthetic canon," in whatever form it might take.

That is why, in order to make "classic" acceptable, everything depends on the ability of the recipients to employ productively the state of tension between it and the premises of temporalization and innovation. If one tries, however, to define the concept "classic" as the concretization of the canon phenomenon in our time, the desired precision cannot be achieved, since the historical conditions delineated by "temporalization and innovation" exclude per se the possibility of the origination and perpetuation of a real canon. Stated more precisely: since in our present day, no "aesthetic canon" exists or can exist, theoretical preconsiderations for the historical and typological investigation of the canon phenomenon must first disregard our own nontheoretical experiences with the contemporary phenomenon of the classic.

Despite all the nostalgia and rationale by which the thought of a return to the "aesthetic canon" is made to seem palatable to us, we spontaneously assign to the

226

horizon of historical and cultural alterity any idea of a canon that normalizes artistic and literary activity. In the first of the following sections I will try to demonstrate that in this respect the Enlightenment in France was still a period of alterity. This will put us on a course of historical reconstruction that places the contrasting concepts *canon/classic* at opposite poles of a historical process.[2] At the beginning of the nineteenth century, when the aesthetic canon of the Enlightenment *sank into ashes* in the flames of enthusiasm for new modes of aesthetic experience (the subject of the second section), there arose *like a phoenix* a new attitude toward many texts and works of art of the past that we label "classic"—an attitude that has long since been institutionalized (third section).[3]

Yet the origin of the concept "classic" was by no means accompanied by an awareness that the reception of the classics would become possible only at the price of a confrontation with the premise of temporalization and the postulate of innovation. Rather, we notice—at least in France—a tendency simply to assign to "classical" authors and texts the place in the socialization process that had been occupied by the authors and texts of the canon until the Age of Enlightenment. Today it is becoming clear that the chances of actually attaining those goals of educational policy were no better than those for squaring the circle. Even in France, where the state has only in most recent times made an initial effort to revise the structure of the educational system,[4] which had relied on the effect of readings in Corneille, Racine, Molière, and La Fontaine, the impossibility of replacing "canon" with "classic" long ago led to a progressive weakening in the official justification for the reception of the "classics." This process had somehow arrived at its end point when Roland Barthes identified the tautology "Racine is Racine" as the secret maxim of the national reception of the classics and interpreted it as one of the "myths of everyday French life."[5] Certainly it is no accident that it was the student generation of the *Nouvelle Critique* that finally prompted a new conception of literary education, even in the ministries of government.

But what is the significance of the fact (true, of course, not only in France) that a repertory of names of literary figures and works continues to be a part of even the most modest educational knowledge, and that considerable financial resources and astonishingly large portions of the broadcast time of the media are still reserved, with practically no objection, to the "nurturing of the classics" (*Klassikerpflege*)? How can such matter of fact acceptance be reconciled with the "lack of function of the classics" (at least for any primary concern), a lack that seems to be objectified in tautologies of the type "Racine is Racine"? We can only begin to address such questions here—not least because it would take us too far away from the problematics of the canon. But I wish at least to predict at this early point that possible later studies on the functions of "classic" and "the classics" definitely will *not* lead to the legitimization of a continuity in their traditional social function.

The Persistence of the Canon

For some time now a useful convention of cultural history has been to have the epoch of the Enlightenment begin with the threshold event, the *Querelle des anciens et des modernes* – a debate that was carried on in the Académie Françiase and its intellectual milieu during the latter years of the reign of Louis XIV, and which questioned for the first time since the end of the Middle Ages the normative status granted exclusively to the art and literature of the ancients. Here we find the development of the earliest horizon of forms of historical thought, already remarkably well differentiated and extending from the schema of teleological progression to the consequence of historical relativization.[6] Although it has been correctly claimed that problems of literary evaluation were the original context of historical thought, this new intellectual climate had, in comparison with other aspects of the French Enlightenment, very little effect on literary production and reception, and the poetology (*Poetologie*) that accompanied them.[7] Of course we can note even here, from the retrospective of a "history of historical thought," symptoms of a first questioning of the normative effect of ancient culture and of its modern canon. But it would be a sign of "historiographical impatience" if one should attempt for that reason to push into the background the epoch-making fact that literature and art were seen by the French Enlightenment against the horizon of the traditional canon structure.

The most impressive and diverse documentation of this is Voltaire's *Temple du goût*, first published in 1733 and reprinted in 1784 with minor modifications. This is a *bagatelle* of scarcely a thousand lines, written in varying verse forms with prose insertions, originating, as the author himself explains in the foreword of 1784, from a *plaisanterie de société*.[8] Now the recollection of such a situation in itself scarcely suits the seriousness of the temple metaphor. One can therefore ask whether it is not true that this connection with the connotation of earlier literary and artistic canon horizons (far removed from all the significant questions associated in the preceding centuries with the images of such temples of fame as well as with scenes of "otherworldly literary criticism")[9] gives the title of the little work the pragmatic status of an oxymoron. It is true that Voltaire too raises the traditional question concerning the identity of "literature" (expressed in the allegory as a question about the appearance of the temple). However, he no longer answers it with a plethora of forms, norms, and values, but rather with a *je ne sais quoi*, as was typical of the epoch. His actual words are: "Il est plus aisé de dire ce que ce Temple n'est pas, que de faire connaître ce qu'il est" (It is easier to say what this temple is not than to explain what it is).

This feigned perplexity articulates the demand, heard in France and England since the late seventeenth century, that the *perfection of art be sought in the suppression of its artistic appearance*. On the other hand, art in which the artist's effort is apparent is regarded as "artificial" and rejected in the name of a concept of nature that, in its application, comes much closer to emphasizing "healthy common sense" than to accenting sentimentality. This is, in any case, the intent of the warning against the "God of Bad Taste" with which the "God of Taste" dismisses the visitors to the Temple:

> Il prend mon nom, mon étentard;
> Mais on voit assez l'imposture:
> Car il n'est que le fils de l'Art,
> Moi, je le suis de la Nature.

> (144)

> [He takes my name, my standard too;
> But his deceit is clear to all:
> For he is but the son of Art,
> While I . . . I am the son of Nature.]

This *Nature* was nothing but the viewpoint of a particular audience well known to the French authors of the seventeenth and eighteenth centuries. The "court and the city"[10] and "*Bon goût*" demanded of the recipient nothing more than the readiness to "submit circumspectly" to the dominance of the viewpoint of *Nature*.[11] Both *Nature* and *goût* were norms, specific codes of social behavior mediated by literature and constituted by literary communication. Their existence and continued validity required adherence to norms of literary production and reception in the narrow sense. Yet, in poetological discourse, confronted by the demand to suppress all signs of the "artificiality of art," the canon of *social behavior* norms replaced *aesthetic* norms.

Voltaire's desire is to exclude systematically from acceptance into the Temple all types of behavior he considers "excessive," such as those that parade or even subtly show pretensions to exclusivity and narrow, bookish knowledge. Among them are: "l'affectation de l'hôtel de Rambouillet," "le tumulte qui règne parmi nos jeunes étourdis," "Le précieux, le pédantisme, / L'air empesé du syllogisme," and "l'air fou de l'emportement" (135) ("the affectation of the *Hôtel de Rambouillet*," "the tumult prevailing among our young madcaps," "Preciosity, pedantry, / The stuffy air of syllogisms," and "the foolish pretense of passion"). How strictly the derogation of norms—in itself a norm—was observed is shown in its consequential application to the concepts opposed to preciosity, among which were— besides *Nature* and *goût—bon sens* and *esprit*: "Le bon sens, de peur d'ennuyer, / Se déguíse en plaisanterie" (136) (Common sense, for fear of being a bore, / Disguises itself as pleasantry). In short: the positive sociosymbolic value of the obligatory standards of behavior is transformed into "tastelessness" as soon as these standards are determined as established principles regardless of expectation.[12]

Even literature in which *Nature, goût, esprit,* and *bon sens* are supposed to be concretized must not become so fascinating that it goes beyond the expectable or is experienced as something of independent value. Therefore, in Voltaire's allegorical narration, the scholars hold themselves aloof from the realm of "taste," and at first do not want to take part at all in the pilgrimage to the Temple:

> Ce n'est pas là, grâce au Ciel, notre étude:
> Le goût n'est rien; nous avons l'habitude
> De rédiger au long de point en point
> Ce qu'on pensa; mais nous ne pensons point.

(114)

> [It is, thank God, not our concern:
> For taste is nothing; our habit is
> To edit long, from point to point,
> Another's thoughts, for we have none.]

The knowledge relevant to the praxis of literary production and literary reception should *not* become poetology or even philosophical aesthetics, but should rather remain as close as possible to social expectations, so that literature as a catalyst of socialization can stabilize and perpetuate these expectations.

Was it still possible for such requirements to be represented by and equated with the names of certain authors? Could there still be works worthy of being established as timeless models of *bon sens?* Or was the *Temple du goût* supposed to be a canon metaphor without a canon? In his text Voltaire preserved the *structure* of the canon, but he no longer dared to represent the works of the great figures of Latin antiquity as concretizations of his own (historically specific) guiding principles. In the *Temple* we meet, instead, the most popular authors of Voltaire's recent past, including Corneille, Racine, and Molière. It is clear that he at least sensed the problems that resulted from the connection of the traditional canon structure with very particular norms of social behavior and literary communication. For Voltaire was obliged to attribute to the prominent dramatists of the century of Louis XIV an impact that transcended their own present, and to set in contrast with it "the spirit of the time" as a bias against all noncanonized authors of the seventeenth century: "En effet, la plupart n'avaient guère que l'esprit de leur temps, et non cet esprit qui passe à la dernière postérité" (130f.) (Indeed, most of them possessed little but the spirit of their time, and not that spirit that is passed on to the latest generations). The ability to speak to "the latest generations" through their works is the attribute of the classical authors. Authors of the old canon did not have this characteristic because the canon as an institution did not concern itself with temporalization.

We should, of course, emphasize that Voltaire did not go the entire way from "canon" to "classic." The *Temple*, inhabited by the authors of his recent past, remains a thoroughly ambivalent structure. For although Voltaire speaks of the "timelessness" of the great authors and works, he is very critical of individual aspects of their writing – and his criticism does not follow any criteria of taste that are subject to historical relativization. The way in which he treats the great authors of the age of Louis XIV partly as classics, partly still as authors of the canon can probably not be reduced to a unified formula. Actually, the article "*Classique*" in the *Encyclopédie* of Diderot and d'Alembert certainly seems much stranger to us and much more paradigmatic for the concept of literature in the epoch of the Enlightenment in France than the *Temple du goût*. This confirms, by the way, a new perspective of cultural historians, namely, that the documentary value of the *Encyclopédie* is greatest for those who read it as a summation of the knowledge that was constitutive for the society of the ancien régime – and not as a vast reexamination and questioning of this knowledge:

CLASSIQUE, adj. (*Gramm.*) Ce mot ne se dit que des auteurs que l'on explique dans les collèges; les mots & les façons de parler de ces auteurs servent de modele aux jeunes gens. On donne particulierement ce nom aux auteurs qui ont vécu du tem[p]s de la république, & ceux qui ont été contemporains ou presque contemporains d'Auguste; tels sont Térence, César, Cornélius Népos, Cicéron, Salluste, Virgile, Horace, Phedre, Tite-Live, Ovide, Valere Maxime, Velleius-Paterculus, Quinte-Curce, Juvénal, Martial, & Frontin; auxquels on ajoûte Tacite, qui vivoit dans le second siécle, aussi bien que Pline le jeune, Florus, Suétone, & Justin. . . .
    On peut . . . donner le nom d'auteurs *classiques François* aux bons auteurs du siècle de Louis XIV & de celui-ci; mais on doit plus particulierement appliquer le nom de *classiques* aux auteurs qui ont écrit tout à la fois élégamment & correctement, tels que Despréaux, Racine, & c. Il seroit à souhaiter, comme le remarque M. de Voltaire, que l'Académie Françoise donnât une édition correcte des auteurs *classiques* avec des remarques de Grammaire.[13]

[CLASSICAL, adj. (*Gram.*) This word is used only for authors explicated in the *collèges*; the words and expression of these authors serve as a model for young people. The name is given in particular to authors who lived at the time of the Republic and those who were contemporaries or nearly so of Augustus, for example, Terence, Caesar, Cornelius Nepos, Cicero, Sallust, Virgil, Horace, Phaedrus, Titus Livius, Ovid, Valerius Maximus, Valleius Paterculus, Quintus Curtius, Juvenal, Martial, and Frontinus; to these are added Cornelius Tacitus, who lived in the second century, and Pliny the Younger, Florus, Suetonius, & Justinius. . . .
    The name "classical" can be given to the good authors of the century of Louis XIV and of the present century; but one should, more particularly, apply the name "classical" to authors who wrote both elegantly and correctly, such as Despréaux, Racine, etc. It would be desirable if,

as M. Voltaire notes, the French Academy would make a correct edition of the *classical* authors with grammatical notes.]

This is an almost ideal illustration of the canon concept *before* its restructuring under the pressure of "temporalization" and "innovation." As in antiquity (and later, in the *Temple du goût*) we still encounter *names* of authors rather than *titles of works*. The discursive constitution of the canon as a series of authors' names can be associated with the fact that the *imitation of exemplary action*, objectified in texts and constantly being reproduced in new texts, created the perspective of relevance that made the canon an element of education and socialization, for *structures of action* are bound to people. The author could only be left out of consideration (permitting a concentration on the works alone) when, after the early nineteenth century, *reception and interpretation*—instead of writing—as educative values moved into the foreground of attention. In the *Encyclopédie*, however, the function of the canon in the mediation of structures of action dominates even more clearly than in Voltaire. More precisely, it is a question of structures of action typical for the upper strata of society. The place of mediation was the *collège*, and what was taught there could not be relegated to the uncertainty of a *je ne sais quoi*. On the contrary, it was considered desirable to establish the "words and manner of speech" of the canonical authors in philological editions and to emphasize them by means of grammatical commentaries. This orientation to the "elegant and correct" style of upper-class communication determined the ranking of the "good authors" of the epoch of Louis XIV and of the eighteenth century according to the *Encyclopédie*. Although they are mentioned in the article "*Classique*," they function less as "classics" than they do in Voltaire. But their participation in the canon remains precarious because they lack the antiquity that determines the selection of the canonical from the mass of successful "concretizations of the obligatory." The article "*Ancien (vieux, antique)*" in the *Encyclopédie* states: "L'antiquité affoiblit les témoignages, & donne du prix aux monumens" (Antiquity weakens the testimonies and awards value to the monuments).

The elements that could refine the "elegant and correct" language of the upper classes into "literature" were to be found under the rubrics *art, poésie*, and *genre*; and the label *littérature* still designated, around the middle of the eighteenth century, *all* objectifications of elaborated erudition.[14] We read that art is unthinkable without "*spéculation*," and "*spéculation*" is defined as the induction and comprehension of the characteristic styles of authors of the canon. Insights gained through induction can be elevated to the status of rules for the praxis of literature. The rules, for their part, should function as prescriptive guides, with the help of which the simple imitation of nature can progress into the sublime *belle nature*, as realized in *poésie*. Because the canon, with poetic rules as its intermediary, governs only the constitution of the content (*matière*) of the work of art, the authors must, according to Voltaire in the article "*Genre*," have recourse to a second body of rules, namely, the conventions governing the attribution of stylistic levels to thematics. Yet, as he had already done in the *Temple du goût*, Voltaire permitted the elements of a new, evolving comprehension of literature to interfere with his representation of the traditional, artistically sanctioned, procedure: "La perfection consisteroit à savoir assortir toujours son style à la matière qu'on traite; mais qui peut être le maître de son habitude, et ployer à son gré son génie?" (Perfection would consist in knowing how to adapt each style to the content of the work; but who can be the master of one's habits and bend genius to will?)

It is precisely this juxtaposition of antique stylistics with the concept of genius, as well as the lack of desire (manifested by no less a figure than Voltaire) to "depragmatize" definitively the obligations imposed by canonical rules, that gives evidence of the continued validity of the canon in the Age of Enlightenment. The reproduction of the language and worldview of the authors of the canon remained for the time being, despite all strictures against "artificiality," *a requirement for the reproduction of the behavior and hierarchies of the social classes*. From this perspective it becomes clear that retaining the rule-governed dramas of Corneille, Racine, and Molière in the repertory of the *Comédiens du Roi* (the former name of the Comédie Française) did not yet initiate their rise to the status of "classics" but rather supplemented and intensified the goal of socialization entrusted primarily to the *collèges*. Whoever considers this assertion too bold (because of a belief in the timelessly superior "content" of the "classical" texts) may be convinced by the *Comédie's* performance statistics.[15] These show how the canon first represented by the *Comédiens du Roi* slowly but surely lost importance in the repertory during the second half of the eighteenth century and how, moreover, a discrepancy began to develop between the rule-governed repertory pieces and other enthusiastically received tragedies from the age of Louis XIV. This situation continued until, in the early nineteenth century, there appeared with astonishing speed the proportions that became institutionalized and have been maintained to the present day in the repertory of the Comédie Française. It was only this last shift that gave Corneille, Racine, and Molière *classical* status.

Such a clarification does not, however, have to contradict the observation that the presence of the *later* "classics" in the century of the Enlightenment, remarkable as it first may seem, also signaled the beginning of the dissolution of the canon of the authors of antiquity. And there is still one more reason for this presence, which I would at least like to mention. Voltaire presents in the *Temple du goût* a short history of literature and the fine arts that conforms completely to the schema of the *translatio studii*, and he ends it with their entrance into the kingdom of the "Great Louis" and his temple of the Muses. However, when he immediately makes the anxious remark, "Mais je ne sais s'il durera" (118) (But I do not know if it will last), he is not reacting, as one might first assume, to an open, undetermined horizon of the future. Rather, he is "writing himself into" a *laudatio temporis acti*, which was characteristic of the Enlightenment and entirely customary whenever the *philosophes* took a position toward the art of their time. An implication similar to that of Voltaire's "rhetorical" fear that the authors of the "age of Louis XIV" might be forgotten can be seen in the following words from the *Encyclopédie* article "*Littérature*," which depict (too pessimistically, we now know) the collapse of a scholarship oriented toward antiquity: " . . . plusieurs beaux-esprits prétendus ou véritables, ont introduit la coutume de condamner, comme une science de collège, les citations de passages grecs & latins, & toutes les remarques d'érudition" (. . . various beaux-esprits, whether pretended or real, have introduced the custom of condemning, as an affectation of the *collège*, the quoting of Greek and Latin passages, and all marks of erudition).

A history of literature and the arts bound to tradition as a principle was for the *philosophes*, consciously or unconsciously, a strategic counterbalance for the teleology of progress, especially as it was being articulated in the history of technics and science. I use the metaphor "strategic counterbalance" in alluding to a structure of mentality characteristic of the Enlightenment, a mentality that, on the one hand, spread confidence by means of the teleology of progress and, on the other, felt compelled to maintain, by means of the teleology of a menacing decadence, a motivation to engage in criticism of the present—a criticism that, for its part, was the starting point of efforts directed toward change in the future.

Canonical Ashes and Classical Phoenix

In the year 1810, Madame de Staël sent the voluminous manuscript of her book *De l'Allemagne* to her French publisher. Later, just before delivery, the entire printing was confiscated by the minister of police of the Empire, and the author received the order to leave the country within twenty-four hours. The letter in which this deadline was then extended to "seven or eight days at the most" reaches its climax in the sentence: "Il m'a paru que l'air de ce pays-ci ne vous convenait point, et nous n'en sommes pas encore réduits à chercher des modèles dans les peuples que vous admirez"[16] (It was apparent to me that you did not find the atmosphere of this country agreeable, and we do not yet feel ourselves reduced to searching for models among the peoples that you admire). A comment on this reproach offers us an excellent opportunity to illustrate the actual moment of transition from a still feudal understanding of literature to a bourgeois concept. Napoleon's minister of police was in error when he accused Madame de Staël of wanting to populate the literary canon of the French nation with German language authors as "models" for imitation. Her book is interesting not because it wished to negate and replace a traditional canon with a new one, but rather because *De l'Allemagne* belongs among those writings of the early nineteenth century that are situated between normative poetology and *philosophical aesthetics*, and concern themselves with, among other things, *the dissolution of basic structures of the canon as a social institution.* All those concepts which, in the *Temple du goût* or in the *Encyclopédie*, had been used to justify a mode of artistic and literary praxis based essentially upon the reproduction and stabilization of certain modes of behavior, appeared in *De l'Allemagne* as concepts counter to the new ideal of a *literary education* of the individual. *Goût* is contrasted with the ideal of *génie* and the intimacy of solitary reading; *raison* and *esprit* with dreamy contemplation, power of imagination, and individuality, *finesse* with truth; *imitation* with life:[17] "Il n'y a point de vie dans l'imitation; et l'on pourrait appliquer en général, à tous ces esprits, à tous ces ouvrages imités . . . l'éloge que Roland, dans l'Arioste, fait de sa jument qu'il traîne après lui: Elle réunit, dit-il, toutes les qualités imaginables; mais elle a pourtant un défaut, c'est qu'elle est morte" (97) (There is no . . . life at all in imitation; and one could apply, in general, to all these *esprits* . . . the elegy that Orlando, in Ariosto, spoke in praise of his mare, which he was dragging behind him: "She combines within her all imaginable virtues; but nevertheless she has one fault—she is dead").

The value of literature is now being measured less by the functions it performs for society than by its effect on *individual readers*. Such an effect is produced through the reception of singular literary works by individual readers; the reading of texts is no longer—or at least no longer primarily—seen in reference to the imitation and perpetuation of competence in writing.[18] At the same time, the first beginnings of a philosophical aesthetic are taking the place of normative poetology, an aesthetic that from the start gives primacy to the phenomenological aspect of the reader's experience. The liberation of the author from the hitherto obligatory orientation to social standards of behavior (*goût*), and from the reproduction of traditional norms (*imitation*) is paralleled by the transition of the work from the status of "exemplarity" to the aura of its "singularity" and to a freedom of reception in which the "solitary reader" can find his individual relationship with the work and so form his personality. Against the horizon of this threefold individualization (author/work/reader), there was no place left for a canon predicated on normativeness and on the reproduction of communicative behavior. But without a canon, without an institutionalized frame of reference for selection and negation, judgments of literature (together with their formerly so significant conceptual armament) also lost their *gesture* of authority, and even in those cases where a belief in their necessity persisted, they had to be justified on the basis of an idea (more or less meaningful) or "consensus by free agreement."

Let us return to *De l'Allemagne* (specifically to the chapter on Goethe's *Faust*) for a documentation of this relativization of literary criticism as we proceed to examine the various aspects of the new understanding of literature that dissolved the canon as an institution:

> Les critiques dont un tel ouvrage doit être l'objet sont faciles à prévoir d'avance, ou plutôt c'est le genre même de cet ouvrage qui peut en-

courir la censure plus encore que la manière dont il est traité; car une telle composition doit être jugée comme un rêve; et si le bon goût veillait toujours à la porte d'ivoire des songes pour les obliger à prendre la forme convenue, rarement ils frapperaient l'imagination. La pièce de Faust cependant n'est certes pas un bon modèle. Soit qu'elle puisse être considérée comme l'oeuvre du délire de l'esprit ou de la satiété de la raison, il est à désirer que de telles productions ne se renouvellent pas; mais quand un génie tel que celui de Goethe s'affranchit de toutes les entraves, la foule de ses pensées est si grande, que de toutes parts elles dépassent et renversent les bornes de l'art. (I, 367)

[The criticisms of such a work are easy to foresee. Or rather, it is the genre itself of this work that may incur censure more than the manner in which it is written. For such writing should be judged as a dream, and if good taste were always guarding the ivory gate of dreams, to force them to take the accepted form, they would rarely capture the imagination. However, the Faust play is certainly not a good model for others. Whether it be considered as the product of the delirium of the spirit or the satiety of reason, such a work should not be repeated. But when a genius such as that of Goethe frees itself from all fetters, it has such a multitude of thoughts that they pass and overturn the boundaries of art in all directions.]

Madame de Staël deserves our admiration for the accuracy of her observations and the ability to understand highly complex interdependencies. It is therefore all the more significant that she sees the contrasting concepts of literature in France and Germany (appearing like leitmotifs in her book) as a concretization of a difference in *"génies nationaux."* She traces these *"génies"* back to different original states of the national cultures, oriented on France's reception of antiquity and Germany's closeness to the spiritual world of the Christian Middle Ages. To be sure, we may assume that she was able, with a very good conscience, to reject the police minister's accusation that her cultural comparison (which clearly did not reflect an urge to evaluate or prejudice) had the ultimate intent of suggesting that French literature should imitate the German. But her outlook did not include what is self-evident to us as an explanation of the contrasting literary concepts — the linking of these different approaches to literature to the "before" and "after" of a profound historical change.

Why this change took place later in France than in Germany is a rather baffling question, since German culture of that time was so backward, both politically and sociologically. I shall content myself here with mentioning a conceivable solution to this self-posed problem. The tendency toward individualization or, better, toward the isolation and self-direction of the individual seems to have developed in many cases as the reverse side of the "bourgeois" revolutions and reforms, or, more simply, as a correlate of the "freedom" that the individual had been promised since the Enlightenment. In regard to this "isolation of the individual," the gradual and disappointing discovery was made, in France, for example, that the "*enlargissement*" of forms of interaction that had been effective in the small circles of followers of the Enlightenment was not operable on the overall social level (and such "enlargement" was exactly what the sociality of the new states and societies proposed).[19] The "retreat from society," however, had long since become a mode of self-characterization in those places—Germany, for example, where the rulers refused to yield to the demands of the Enlightenment. Formulated as a paradox this could be stated as follows: in Germany literature became "bourgeois" earlier than in France for the very reason that the "bourgeois" political forms in Germany were slower in coming.

But even the educated contemporaries of Madame de Staël first expected from art and literature a return to normativeness and the canon rather than to a gesture toward new liberties. Nor did the coronation of Napoleon Bonaparte, staged with such elaborate splendor, encourage those who were impatiently looking toward a new order: "Les modes qui, depuis plusieurs années, avaient l'inconvénient de se croiser sans cesse, d'être aussitôt remplacées que connues, et souvent de rester imparfaites, vont très probablement [i.e., after the emperor's coronation] prendre une marche régulière et redevenir belles et majestueuses"[20] (The fashions which for several years had the disadvantage of constant change, of being replaced as soon as they became well known, are very probably going to assume [i.e., after the emperor's coronation] a regular progression and become once more beautiful and majestic). On the other hand, someone who violated now and again the norms and the hierarchies of genres (as did the popular author Madame de Genlis in her prolific authorship over a period of several decades) did not by any means resort, for justification, to any premise of temporalization or historical consciousness, or even to arguments concerning the history of philosophy, but might have, rather, pointed out with equanimity how effective such transgressions were with the audience: "Il est à désirer que les auteurs dramatiques, en cherchant des sujets, ou en traîtant ceux qu'ils ont choisis, ne soient pas dominés par la crainte d'entendre comparées leur pièces à des mélodrames; car cette crainte gâteroit leur talent, et bientôt nous n'aurions plus que des tragédies sans effets et sans imagination. Tâchons de bien écrire, de n'être ni communs ni emphatiques, de tracer de grands caractères, de bien peindre les passions; mais tâchons aussi d'inventer des fictions théâtrales, et d'offrir un beau spectacle"[21] (It is desirable that dramatic authors, in seeking their themes or in dealing with those they have chosen, not be dominated by the fear of having their plays compared to melodramas; for this fear would harm or even destroy their talent, and soon nothing would be left but tragedies without effect and without imagination. Let us try to write well, to be neither common nor high-flown, to draw grand characters, to depict passion well, and let us try also to invent fictions that are theatrical and provide a handsome spectacle).

The Persistence of the Classics

What had happened between 1790 and 1810? Or to state the question with less artificial innocence: Do the sociohistorical changes of the revolutionary years and the Empire explain the shift in this period's relationship to literature?[22] Michel Foucault identifies this as the period in which the "classical *épistemé*" was replaced by the *épistemé* of the nineteenth and twentieth century (the "*Science de l'homme*"), and he mentions as the prerequisites of this process "the temporalization of experience" and the "crisis of representation." To be sure, both of the factors cited by Foucault help us to understand the dissolution of the canon that had been part of the old *épistemé*; but on the other hand it is clear that referring to the framework requirements for the dissolution of the canon cannot of itself solve the question of the requirements for elevation of the "classic."

This brings us to a discussion of the self-image of the French Revolution, an image that is usually taken much too seriously as a "picture of historical reality." The Revolution had sought to present itself as the fulfillment of the promises and desires of the Enlightenment. This characterization was—and still is—of considerable value for purposes of legitimation, but at the same time it exposed—and still exposes—the modern state to a very specific burden of expectation and a potential for criticism on the part of its citizens. Thus, after the occurrences of only the first year of the Revolution, there was already a tension developing between the self-image of the state and the citizens' everyday experience of its shortcomings, between the *sens voulu* and the *sens vécu*,[23] between the level of official perception and the contents of very divergent experiences corresponding to a multitude of new social situations and modes of existence. Instead of the ideologies of differing social classes, there was now *one* image of a "new society" that determined the locus of social self-reference. To be sure, this shift was by no means the result of a process of reduced differentiation. On the contrary, even the transformation of the society's self-reference was part of a complex drive toward differentiation, which led to a situation in which systems were becoming more and more specific in their functions, each of them taking over certain tasks for *all* other systems. This differentiation created a constitutive tension between the *one* social self-image and the *multiplicity* of perspectives of experience in a multiplicity of systems. On the basis of tension, the promised "freedom of the individual" was experienced in everyday terms largely as a lack of orientation or as isolation; the breaking of feudal power and repression was perceived as necessary for self-direction (and accordingly as an obligation of individuals to exercise their delegated power over themselves); and finally, legality before the law was experienced as the perpetuation of inequality of possession in ever new forms.

Since that time—and here will be found our answer to the question posed at the beginning of this section—forms of literary communication have no longer corresponded to different social classes or groups, but have, rather, constituted a *particular social subsystem* ("state of autonomy"), whose identity developed in connection with the performance of a new function for the total society. This function was to mediate between official perceptions (self-representations of the state) and forms of everyday experience (the citizen's specific experience of deficiencies). We certainly do not need to go into the different modes of these mediations and the compensations in the new "bourgeois" genres of literature that grew out of them. On the other hand, in order to understand the "classic," which was now rapidly becoming institutionalized, it is essential to note the otherwise trivial circumstance that such mediation and compensation between levels of social perception could become only effective when the mediation *was not disclosed* to the reader of literature.

At this point in the argument I must emphasize that my intention is not, in any all-inclusive way, to disparage literature and literary communication or to express suspicions of ideological bias in them—if only because it would be absurd to attribute "freedom from ideology" solely to my own perspective (as all "ideological criticism" must necessarily do). In proposing a thesis concerning the systematically concealed mediative (or conciliatory) function of literature, I by no means wish to exclude the possibility that individual processes of reception may produce completely different effects. My concern is nothing more than a necessarily general typological attribution of a function to a social subsystem, and for such an attribution I wish to call once more upon Madame de Staël as a witness for her time who was as innocent of scorn for literature as she was of opportunism in regard to the new nation. *De l'Allemagne* ends with a remarkable chapter entitled "Influence de l'enthousiasme sur le bonheur" (Influence of enthusiasm on happiness)—a topic, by the way, to which intellectuals of the late twentieth century might be especially receptive. The "enthusiasm" that promises happiness is prescribed here to the French nation as an alternative to the guiding values of the Enlightenment, *"raisonnement"* and *"calcul,"* which—as is actually stated in the final sentence of the work—might indeed bring mastery of the world, but would, in the end, leave this world as "desolate as the desert" for humankind.

"Enthousiasme"—a concept opposed to the cult of reason and concretized above all as the acceptance of and familiarity with literature and art—is of course not bound to a prognosis of "human happiness" in the style of the philosophy of the Enlightenment. Individual happiness—for example, the happiness of the solitary reader—is seen here as the only positive counterbalance to the fate of human existence. This existence, according to Mme. de Staël, can be experienced in no other way than in *suffering*: "L'enthousiasme est de tous les sentiments celui qui donne le plus de bonheur, le seul qui en donne véritablement, le seul qui sache nous faire supporter la destinée humaine dans toutes les situations où le sort peut nous placer" (Of all emotions, enthusiasm is the one that gives the most happiness, the only one that truly gives it, the only one that permits us to endure human destiny in all the situations where fate has placed us) (II, 309). This new attitude to-

ward literature and art makes possible a happiness that seems lost in everyday life; it is experienced by Madame de Staël (and this confirms our functionalist thesis) as the possibility of *mediation* between individual expectation of happiness and a social life spent in suffering.

Naturally she does not go beyond such descriptions of the experience of art and literature to pose, for example, any ideological or critical questions. On the contrary, Madame de Staël very rigorously separates "reconciliation" (with human and cosmic nature) from any intentionality or reflection. But, through her very adherence to a taboo that had been imposed since the beginning of the nineteenth century against questions concerning the function of literature, she indeed contributed to the securing of a compensatory effect (which was certainly not an exceptional case): "La nature peut-elle être sentie par des hommes sans enthousiasme? Ont-ils pu lui parler de leurs froids intérèts, de leurs misérables désirs? Que répondrait la mer et les étoiles aux vanités étroites de chaque homme pour chaque jour?" (Can nature be felt by human beings without enthusiasm? Have they been able to speak to her of their cold interests, their wretched desires? How would the sea and the stars respond to the narrow vanities of every human being every day?) (II, 312). Through *enthousiasme*, readers open themselves to the possibilites of experience offered by art and literature; they are ready to *transport themselves into these worlds*, instead of "enjoying" them. As the effect and as the reward for such submersion in the Other, they are given the prospect of an "elevated heart" (cf. II, 314). This is precisely the new ideal of literary education and formation of the individual (*Bildung*).

We could now ask whether, a few decades later, "national consciousness" as a referential horizon for literary communication in various European societies was not already replacing education of the individual, which for its part had replaced *explicitly* class-oriented norms of behavior after about 1800. If this question were pertinent to the consideration of canon and classic, we would have to continue our historical account of the function of literary communication on a sociohistorical level. But I would rather emphasize that, since romanticism, literature has been taken by its recipients as an appeal to their "unalienated individuality"—completely independent of the functions and results of this attitude in the social sphere. I regard the constituting of national consciousness as one of the many possible functions of individual reading in the social sphere.

The development, on the one hand, of the ideal of educating the individual (so staunchly defended to the present day), and the appearance, on the other hand, of the new mode of reception, the "worship of the classics" (which declares as persistently of the "classics" as of "literature" that "they always have something immediate to say to us"), do not coincide, although their chronological proximity alone suggests a functional relationship. In the search for such a connection one is first struck by the fact that the number of French authors whose works appeared in the curriculum of the educational institutions founded during the Revolution was considerably reduced after Thermidor 1794. Writings committed to the cause of the Enlightenment (regardless of partisan purpose or faction) were no longer compatible with a concept of literature that was rapidly being narrowed to the dimensions it has since maintained.[24]

The cultural bureaucrats of the Empire made a strong effort to maintain continuity in the theatrical repertories, but a French feuilleton critic or foreign visitor could scarcely overlook the fact that the contents of Corneille's and Racine's tragedies were less and less able to capture the interest of the audience. The performances degenerated into competitive clashes between prominent actors and their respective groups of followers. An especially impressive report of the situation is that by Ernst Moritz Arndt in *Pariser Sommer 1799*:

> Usually comedies and dramas were given, rarely tragedies, and the benches were usually empty for the tragedies, either because the taste for them has dulled as much as in Germany, or because they contain nothing new, and most people, after all, make the same claims on art as on their barber or tailor, so that "old" in regard to works of art means the same thing for them as "out of fashion" when they visit their barber or tailor. A tragedy can be seen only every three or four weeks, an insignificant proportion, since something was performed almost every day. I have seen Chénier's *Charles IX*, the *Cid, Mahomet*, and *Bérénice*. To judge from the tragedies I saw here, I must confess that most of the artists, who were otherwise not mediocre, had a very shallow conception of their roles and portrayed them just as shallowly.[25]

On the other hand, textbooks and anthologies directed toward pedagogical goals endowed the now "classical authors" of the French past with an aura of radiance such as had not graced even the prominent canonical poets of antiquity, and at the same time placed them at a distance untouched by criticism, a distance that has in no other country been so uninterruptedly characteristic of the textbooks to the present day. One question, to be sure, could not be avoided or suppressed, and the recommended curricula and seminar libraries are replete with answers to it, furnished by literary specialists. This is the question of the specific *value*, the *function* of those "classical" works preserved in safety from the barbs of criticism and from historical time. They were, and still are, praised as models of correctness and elegance of speech like the authors of the canon for centuries before them; as precious vessels for a certain "content" (which, one might add, always reflects those values of "humanity" and those traits of "national character" of which nations and governments represented themselves as the promoters and guardians); as the source of unbounded genius; and (as if this were the same thing) as arbiters of good taste. Among the truly innumerable documentations of that potpourri of values, recommendations, and functions, I shall cite only one example, which has been especially authoritative in the history of French education, from the *Leçons de littérature et de morale*, edited by Noël and Laplace—"an annotated collection of texts that constituted the standard work of literary instruction in the French secondary school system":[26] "Chaque morceau de ce recueil, en offrant un exercice de lecture soignée, de mémoire, de déclamation, d'analyse, de développement oratoire, est en même temps une leçon d'humanité et de justice, de religion, de philosophie, de désintéressement ou d'amour du bien public, *etc.* Tout dans ce recucil est le fruit du génie, du talent, de la vertu; tout y respire et le goût le plus exquis et la morale la plus pure"[27] (Each item in this collection offers an exercise in select reading, in memorization, declamation, analysis, oratorical development. At the same time it provides a lesson in humanity and justice, in religion, philosophy, in unselfishness or love for the public good, etc. Everything in this collection is the fruit of genius, of talent, of virtue; everything in it reflects both the most exquisite taste and the purest morality).

Almost all of the many different functions we have ascribed either to "canon" or to "classic" are found in those few lines – the development of particular competencies of communication, of morality (whether individual or collective), and of good taste. Therefore, taking out of context Odo Marquard's metaphor (originally applied to today's academic philosophers), we could say that the "classical authors" of the early nineteenth century were created as the "stuntmen of general pedagogy."

The profession of "stuntman" is, of course, a very useful institution – not only for filmmaking – and one can scarcely object to *uomini universali*, especially the dead ones. Yet I believe that the proliferation of values, roles, and functions attributed to the "classic authors" is the *expression of an embarrassment* for which rationalizations must be found. The most ponderous of these rationalizations is marked by discussion of the "eternal and immediate expressiveness" of the classics, while the most sympathetic refers to their "fruitful inherent tensions." What condition would French society be in if the majority of the French – or even only their elite – living today had actually molded their speech and writing, their thoughts and actions, after the classics by hearkening to their words or engaging in "fruitful interchange" with them? One can, however, quite easily observe the socializing effects of the "nurturing of the classics" in a secondary area: the reading of the classics makes available to the educated a common repertory of conversational topics and thereby assures for them the possibility of quick rapport with each other on the referential level of communication: "Racine *does remain* Racine."

Concerning the function of the "classics" I shall now present a last thesis *against* the rationalizations that go still further and have been represented and cherished above all by teachers of literature, university professors, and theater directors (whose own predecessors, not accidentally, had invented the rationalizations). This thesis is: *Only by means of the "classics" has literature, now transformed into an autonomous social subsystem, been able to demonstrate, since the nineteenth century, an identity noted beyond and within the boundaries of its system.*

I hope to have shown that literature can realize its primary function of mediation and compensation only under the condition that this function is concealed from society. Thus "literature," having become an autonomous social subsystem, will in fact not gain a *perceptible* identity by virtue of its function. Likewise, an identity configuration cannot be derived from recurrent contextual combinations and patterns, because the social subsystem "literature" — unlike preceding literary forms that were specific to certain social classes — must satisfy the expectations, needs, and dispositions of *different* groups of recipients, and, moreover (for reasons we shall not go into here), it has been subject in the last two centuries to an especially intensive pressure of temporalization, which leads to a constantly accelerating change of forms and contents.

From the fact that "literature as a social subsystem" needs "classics," it does *not* follow conversely that we also need "literature" as long as there are "classics."[28] The present situation prompts us nevertheless to ask why, among all the works of "literature," only the classics have been left over, from which we cannot separate (or free?) ourselves because we have protected them for such a long time, with astonishing circumspection, from all encroachments of temporalization. A West German publishing house that is having more and more difficulty finding a market for "contemporary literature" (but meanwhile subsists very well on "theory") is founding (as a self-replacement?) a *"Deutscher Klassiker-Verlag"* ("Library of German Classics"). Parallels here with the unanimous preference for classics editions on the part of the decision-making bodies of the German Research Association Deutsche Forschungsgemeinschaft cannot, in any case, be overlooked. But if this process of self-replacement continues, what will succeed the "Deutscher Klassiker-Verlag" and the editions of classics supported by the West German government? When will critics and culture politicians finally lose their astonishing fear of the question whether it is not true today that the functions and opportunities for experience that we still associate with the phenomenon "literature" are found in areas and media that, for one reason or another, we do not yet call "literature"?

These reflections are, of course, the expression of a not-unemotional plea for a long overdue change of direction and opening of literary studies to "nonliterary" forms of communication. In the process of such a reorientation, the "literature of the past," or better, "literature as a part of the past," should by no means disappear from the horizon of scholarly interest. An *archaeology of literary communication* is as legitimate and interesting as, for example, the excavation of pyramids, which, after all, has probably not prompted anyone to plead for the restitution of the Egyptian death cult. But this archaeology of literary communication would not include an academic and professional "nurturing of the classics" or a pedagogical demand for "literary education" perpetuated by means of the "classics."

Translated by Roger C. Norton

Part IV
After Literature?

Chapter 10
Pathologies in the System of Literature

Niklas Luhmann, in some of his essays, attempts to apply his concept of "system" to art and literature,[1] but these articles have barely been taken into account by literary critics. Ostensibly this is because he would seem to contribute very little that is new toward the solution of the specific (fundamental) problems of literary criticism. He determines the function of art as "the confrontation of a reality (familiar to everyone) with another version of the same reality," as "the production of contingency,"[2] and hence comes quite close to suggesting the kind of functional determination of literature with which Wolfgang Iser – probably the most competent German literary theoretician of Luhmann's generation – has already enjoyed some success, even among colleagues in his field: "Now all of the organizational forms of our world . . . are specific solutions to problems that, however, still tend to leave problematic fringes behind, even when they are successful. Literature concerns itself with such inheritances, which can be empty spaces, deficiencies, losses, destructions, but also missed opportunities. Thus literature is primarily involved with everything that has been turned away from our institutionally stabilized world."[3] Now the similarity of both of these functional determinations (in which Luhmann refers to "art" and Iser to "literature") by no means forces us to assume an identity between "literature" and "art." Rather the correspondence between their terminological recommendations means that the literary critic Iser was not induced to generalize (about "art") and the sociologist Luhmann saw no reason to be specific (about "literature").[4] Since in the following pages I do not wish to thematize the systemic problem of "delimitation," such imprecision is quite welcome. Like Iser, I will be talking about "literature" (as

247

system), where Luhmann until now has mostly talked about "art" (as system). To be sure, I do not suppose that his lack of a conceptual specification of "literature" has been a significant reason for the weak response of the literary critics to Luhmann's work on "the system of art."

Literary scholars normally "love" their subject and are therefore plainly directed toward "apologetics" or the establishment of those elements that make literature "sociologically necessary."[5] Anyone who cherishes such beautiful effects is bound to become defensive when the flight of his or her thoughts is sucked into the turbulence of Luhmann's commentaries on the contemporary aesthetic discussion: "So we could sign the death sentence. But we could also revise the theoretical foundations."[6] Of course it is not only from the point of view of literary studies that we get touchy about such commentaries on our own production. Undoubtedly, Luhmann's question whether the art system itself is going to be able to survive the ongoing process of social differentiation seems much more scandalous. He underlines the art system's difficulties in attaching itself to the past and operating into the future, and its problems in distinguishing between "code" and "program"—in short, he thematizes the stuttering in the autopoesis of the art system.[7] I would like to take off from these observations, hooking myself up to something that is manifesting itself in manifold ways and that I have—loosely and aggressively—provided with the title "Pathologies of the System of Literature." I am quite aware that with "pathologies," I have chosen a problematical metaphor; moreover, it is still unclear from this formulization on which level of the literary system the pathological is to be located. And yet I do not want to sacrifice the provocative value of the "pathology" metaphor for the philosophical purity and pragmatic innocence of other concepts that could conceivably be put in its place.

By attaching myself to Luhmann's diagnosis, I'm following two objectives. The first might be viewed as a survival question for literary studies. It is becoming increasingly difficult to locate and determine its field of objects, because the concept of literature that presided over the emergence of this discipline is hardly usable anymore. Today, whatever can be read in huge swaths and whoever ("simply") reads for pleasure—both the read and the reader find themselves, at best, at the edge of the literary system. *The Name of the Rose*—a sensational exception—merely confirms this observation. Now it does not have to follow from such change that literary critics will no longer continue to occupy themselves with Cervantes and Shakespeare, with Balzac and Dostoevski. But for all that, strong arguments indeed could be derived from such an insight to remobilize a certain discussion within literary studies—namely, to continue that reflection and discussion within the discipline whose fading away, for some time already, has been celebrated as a return to "business as usual."

My second objective is concerned with the path—perhaps we could even say, with the "method"—that must be followed in order to achieve some insight into the possible shift within the field of literary studies. Like Luhmann in his essay "The Work of Art and the Self-Reproduction of Art," I am going to make a rough sketch of the differentiating process within the *"art system"* ("literature system"), whereas—in contrast to Luhmann—I will stress the relationships between the *system function* and the development of *system codes/system programs*. More precisely, I suspect that those problems that leap into view stem from a problem in the differentiation between code and programs and are indirect consequences of its special function. If we should be successful here in bringing into view such a—so to speak, "pathological"—relationship between code and programs, then there might even be a (modest) gain for the theory of social systems. For since Luhmann himself—understandably—has until now illustrated the relationship between the differentiation of system and the emergence of code primarily through obviously successful instances, the parallel history of a development that at best was half successful, a development ending perhaps in an aporia, could help us to identify favorable conditions (negatively formulated, *risks*) for the differentiation of systems. Above all, I have in mind the difficulties already mentioned in coordinating system function and system code, but also those problems that arise as a consequence of the "unhappy" (in Austin's sense) differentiation between code and programs.

In the following pages, however, sociologically relevant insights will only turn up as by-products within the framework of a historical sketch "from the Middle Ages up to the present," which literary historians specialized in specific eras might want to disqualify as oversimplified. In the first section I will start out with a glance at the threshold of the eleventh to the twelfth century, when, in the so-called Provençal troubadour poetry, that *function*—still without a specific code—that would characterize the literature system up into the twentieth century could be observed for the first time (at least for the first time since antiquity). Next I will move chronologically up *to the change in medium from the manuscipt to the printed book.* I suspect that we will find there not only the origin of the phenomenon of "compact communication" that Luhmann has identified as the basic element of the literary system,[8] but also evidence for an especially narrow relationship between the function of the literary system and the new medium. Then, it seems—above all during the sixteenth and seventeenth centuries (third section)—once again to have been its specific function that left literature exposed to the undertow of *subjectivism and temporalization* and blocked the way to a differentiation of systems. This resulted, as I describe in the fourth section, in an *overlap of programs* and a peculiar obstruction in the normalization of system operations, which for its own part led to the mania of defining (the unity of) "literature" in paradoxical formulations. In the final section I demonstrate that such formulations (which, by the way, are reminiscent of Wittgenstein's aphorisms, according to which philosophy owes its existence to the infiltration of language confusions) have apparently been preserved with even greater fervor as the system *function of literature became more precarious in the twentieth century.* Precisely from this last conjecture we derive our opening hypothesis, namely, that today the code and the programs of the literary system direct the gaze of the literary critic and lover of literature toward phenomena that are—perhaps or at best—in the stage of their dissolution.

Function (without code)

Literary history has designated William IX (1071–1127), the ninth duke of Aquitaine and seventh count of Poitiers, as the first troubadour. This does not imply, as we now see it, that he was the "inventor" of the genre that today is called troubadour poetry and that is associated with the authorial role of troubadour. William of Poitiers is simply the oldest name to which single poems or cycles have been attached by the written tradition beginning in the thirteenth century. It is known that there must have been troubadours before William IX, and moreover it is well to be quite cautious in mutually assigning texts and authors' names from the medieval period (even when it is a matter of well-known protagonists out of "political" history). For academic medieval studies since its origins in the early nineteenth century, the name William IX has operated like a signal to search for affiliations with the discourses of his predecessors, and of course it has been (partially) successful: textual forms were discovered in Middle Latin hymns and textual content was identified in Arab-Andalusian culture, both of whose relationships to troubadour poetry are thoroughly plausible. But the tendency, on the one hand, to level the innovative character of late eleventh/early twelfth century troubadour poetry by researching the influences on it and, on the other, to canonize William IX as the first troubadour have run side by side unmediatedly up to the present. In fact, it cannot really be said that the search for a tradition of predecessors has been generated by a consciousness of the precarious status of textual and authorial ascription during the Middle Ages. More likely it is a consequence of literary critics' (diffuse) desire to regard the phenomenon "literature" (and if possible the "ur-forms" of some of its genres as well) as a metahistorical phenomenon.

At the outset of the passage through literary history that I will sketch out here, I would like to look at some of the texts attributed to William IX, for the simple reason that I need a point of departure for the history of a system (and its pathologies). Hence I maintain that—within the limits set by neophilological competence[9]—the texts attached to the name William IX are the earliest texts in which the function of literature described by Niklas Luhmann and Wolfgang Iser can be observed. At the turn of the eleventh to the twelfth century this was a function that was still completely imbedded in socially ranked communication forms— forms, by the way, that shaped, from case to case, those texts that have come down to us.[10] It is therefore that we find a consciousness of a specific competence that William IX—like all of the other early troubadours—often brings out in his few poems (especially in the introductory and concluding stanzas):[11]

> Ben vuelh que sapchon li pluzor
> D'est vers si's de bona color,
> Qu'ieu ai trag de mon obrador:
> Qu'ieu port d'ayselh mestier la flor,
> Et es vertaz,
> E puesc ne traire·l vers auctor
> Quant er lassatz.
>
> Ieu conosc ben sen e folhor,
> E conosc anta et honor,
> Et ai ardimen e paor;
> E si·m partez un juec d'amor
> No suy tan fatz
> No·n sapcha triar lo melhor
> D'entre·ls malvatz.[12]

The concept "obrador" (workshop) has received a lot of commentary. It opens up the semantic field of craftsmanship ("mestier"), which is applied here—certainly still metaphorically—to the making of songs ("vers" always refers to a text in bound language accompanied by music). The quality of the product (of the "song") is a demonstration of the craftsman's competence, as we learn at the end of the first stanza. Yet the following lines show that in this case, at least, a craft "like any other" cannot be meant. For it acquaints the "craftsman" with "sense and madness," "shame and honor," "boldness and anxiety." At the latest, we are at a point here where difficulties in comprehension can no longer be transmitted by interpretive certainty. For my part, I suspect that the contradictory concepts in this particular text are supposed to move song making into the light of the paradoxical and such a tendency could have something to do with the circumstance that the craftsmanship, which is the issue here, is a competence in play (the eleventh line refers to a "*juec* d'amor"). If we assume, along with Mikhail Bakhtin,[13] that games are always characterized by their "insularity," that they constitute themselves in everyday life as enclaves of "another sense," then the presumption suggests itself that the contradictory concepts yoke the inner and outer aspects, respectively, of play "craftsmanship." The completion of the game "from within" appears as sensible, honorable, and bold, "from without" as crazy, disgraceful, and cowardly. Yet this game is by no means consumed by versecraft. In the fourth stanza we read:

> Mas ben aya sel qui'm noyri,
> Que tan bo mestier m'eschari
> Que anc a negu non falhi;

> Qu'ieu sai jogar sobre coyssi
> A totz tocatz;
> Mais en say de nulh mo vezi,
> Qual que·m vejatz.[14]

Already here the metaphors of craft ("mestier") and the concept of the game ("jieu sai jogar") invest a common semantic level. But the concept of the game achieves a metaphorical horizon through an intentional ambiguity. One can play board games and shoot dice sitting on pillows, but "the game on the pillows" is also a metaphor for sexuality—which is why the "board" a few lines later becomes a metaphor for the woman's skirt and the "three dice" for the penis and testicles of the man. We can guess at the sort of competence this text is moving toward: the speaker brags about what an "infallible master" ("maiestre certa") he is considered to be, because he had never left a lady unsatisfied; even after a premature ejaculation ("Que·m fon trop bos al cap primier") he's ready for another coitus ("E leviey un pauc son taulier, / Ab ams mos bratz").[15]

Moving along the lines of this text, what can easily evade the modern reader's understanding—and what in any case is difficult to reconstruct—must be particularly emphasized here: the physical strength of the lover and the ability to make songs constitute a single competence; they are constituents of a single game. The game is completed outside of the explicit rules of morality, and this transgression has to have been intentional. In the famous rules of courtly love by Andreas Capellanus from the late twelfth century, the moral eccentricity of courtly love has already—ironically?—been so firmly codified that "marriage" and "courtly love" had become mutually exclusive: "non decet amare, quarum pudor est nuptias affectare."[16] That was certainly "an indication of the contingency of the normal view of reality, an indication that there are other possibilities."[17] Yet apparently the function of the game of courtly love was not only concerned with sexual morals. The song of William IX that is probably best known today exhausts itself in a veritable ecstasy of negations:

> Farai un vers de dreyt nien:
> Non er de mi ni d'autra gen,
> Non er d'amor ni de joven,
> Ni de ren au,
> Qu'enans fo trobatz en durmen
> Sobre chevau.[18]

Naturally such verses have become a virtual target for the projections of romantic and postromantic images of the poet William IX. The will to *creatio ex nihilo* has been attributed to him, and he has even been hastily stylized as a "nihilist." But it has been overlooked that, in succession, the negations do *not* converge. The basic semantic structure of the lines and stanzas reiterates an extremely simple (though apparently in texts, a quite rare) pattern: "not a, and/but also not b"; not courtly love, and/but also not conventional morality. In most of the stanzas, the final lines distance themselves from the sphere of everyday life where choosing between alternatives is necessary: "The song was composed as I rode sleeping on my horse"; "I was bewitched and spirited to a high mountain"; "all that worries me, by Holy Martial, less than a mouse"; "if someone can heal me, then he's a good doctor, and if he can't, then it also does not matter."

It is easy to be critical of previous interpretations here. In textual proximity, we can carry out ad absurdum all of those interpretations proffered by literary scholars that want to save a meaningful content for this text. But then it becomes difficult again as soon as we try to go beyond our colleagues' criticisms in order to formulate a view of the function of this song in its historical contexts. To be sure, the speaker's flippant distancing connotes once again the provocative distance of play from everyday life. But who/what is supposed to be provoked? It cannot be a matter of official sexual morality, for the suffering and joy of courtly love bother the speaker "as much as a mouse." I believe that it is a matter here of the provocative value of manuscript writing. A hundred years after William IX, the authors of the so-called courtly novels were still trying, in their prologues, to amply justify themselves for expending "so much effort" on worldly ("ostensibly worldly") material, and—even worse—for fixing common-language versions of secular material in manuscripts. It can thus be assumed that the significant threshold of the manuscript age, which the clerics had protected as their privilege, could have hardly been more ostentatiously called into question than by immortalizing a vulgate song (by a poet who was not even a member of the clergy) that opens with the line "I'll make up a song about nothing." This gesture also makes the contingency of the everyday norm (of the division of labor) transparent. Hence we are steering toward the hypothesis that the advent of the particular function of literature—at least in the Middle Ages—was bound up with a provocative relativization of that everyday world whose structures had been formulated, legitimized, and sanctioned by the clergy and had also served the interests of the nobility for so long (for instance, the complementarity of ecclesiatical sexual morality and the aristocratic interest in maintaining genealogical purity). Because the clergy was concerned with the monogamy (of the others) and (their own) writing privilege, courtly love poetry could at the same time talk about adultery and transgress the norms of the (nonsexual!) division of labor.

What we know from contemporary Latin historiography about the life of William IX of Aquitaine allows us to assume that the duke had sufficient "personal" motivation for provocation (or at least, that our knowledge of his biography urges us to make such an association between the texts we have just analyzed and his name). In this respect, the fact that William IX (according to the landed properties he inherited) was born the richest heir of his time *and* a bastard operates like a Romanesque leitmotif. Both of his parents belonged to the highest nobility, but it was still necessary—five years after his birth—for his father to make a journey to Rome in order to "clear away" the church's misgivings (because of too close sanguinity) about his marriage with Audearde of Burgundy. For political reasons and because of his scandalous life-style, William himself was excommunicated several times. Yet only in his later years was he moved by the threatening gestures of the church to give in. He had already become famous-infamous long before because of his counterprovocations in which he bearded the gravity of ecclesiastical punishment with mocking aloofness. My favorite anecdote culminates in William's answer to the bishop of Angoulême, who had demanded in the name of the pope that he give up his publicly exhibited love affair with the Baroness of Châtellerault: "'Antea, inquit, crispabis pectine refugum a fronte capillum, quam ego vicecomitissae indicam repudium', cavillatus in virum cuius pertenuis caesaries pectinem non desideraret."[19] His ability to confront "that reality (recognized by everyone) with another version of the same reality" was put to the test by William (in his role as a singer) for his astonished fellow combatants as they were returning from a disasterous crusade: "Pictavensis vero dux, peractis in Ierusalem orationibus, cum quibusdam aliis consortibus suis, est ad sua reversus; et miserias captivitatis suae, ut erat iocundus et lepidus, postmodum, prosperitate fultus, coram regibus et magnatis atque Christianis coetibus multotiens retulit rythmicis versibus, cum facetis modulationibus."[20] To derive material for comic songs from defeat and imprisonment (his listeners are supposed to have laughed "with chattering jaws"), to turn the holy solemnity of excommunication into raillery against the excommunicating prelate—these were, as the historiographical sources show, thoroughly extraordinary capabilities, even in the Middle Ages. But this is still no reason to stylize William IX, and other troubadours who were capable of similar acts, as "early modern subjects" *avant la lettre*. For what is inscribed in their songs probably still had very little to do with a consciousness of "autonomy or a strategy of action"; rather, it was the trace of a distancing from the suffocating pressure of ecclesiastical authority, a reaction, therefore, out of which the contours of a new discourse and a new life form only gradually formulated themselves.

Above all, however, it must be made perfectly clear that, at the time of William IX, such literary-like functions of speech could not be scooped out of an independent "literary" discourse or even out of a "literature system." What we find are functions similar to those of literature and pride in skill (comprising physical as well as mental knowledge)—without recourse to a communicative code of "literature." Where the qualities of this originating discourse and this new provocative gesture of distancing were supposed to enter into speech, it was necessary at first, as we have seen, to take refuge in metaphor: the songs have a "good color," originate in a "workshop," and test the mastery of a "craft." Moreover, the ability to participate in the new life form—whether as singer or listener (insofar as this allotment of roles, so familiar to us, is at all pertinent here)—was seen as a privilege of the nobility, of the court. What the adjective "courtly" implied – in its new sense around 1100 – could therefore still be described most easily by contrasting it with the clerical life form and, above all, with the behavior of the inhabitants of cities and villages (*"vilans"*):

> Obediensa deu portar
> A motas gens qui vol amar,
> E coven li que sapcha far
> Faigz avinens,
> E que's gart en cort de parlar
> Vilanamens.[21]

Let's summarize our observations and assumptions: what we have been able to identify, more or less constantly, in the century-long retrospection of the historians as "the function of literature" stands out for the first time around 1100 in a series of texts that seem to originate in gestures of distancing from the pressures of everyday norms. It is problematical, however, for at least two reasons, to characterize these texts through the predicate "literature": in the first place, because around 1100 such writing (?) and reading (singing and hearing) was still, as one element among many, meshed in a complex life form; second, because this life form, this play, was not simply removed from everyday life and from other "systems," but beyond that, was made up of only one class, the nobility (and most probably within the nobility itself, was limited to regional groups).

At the latest, after the middle of the twelfth century, when troubadour poetry, which had originated in southern France, had been picked up in northern France and in the areas of the Middle High German language (which was in the process of developing itself), moral seriousness caught up once again with the game of provocative distancing. In the courtly novels of a Chrétien de Troyes, the aggressivity in the protagonists' excesses of courtly love is depotentialized and becomes a transitional phase of the socialization process of the courtly Christian knight. In one of the songs ascribed to William IX – and it is not surprising that literary scholars believe that this was the last text he wrote – he could already say:

> Tot ai guerpit cant amar sueill,
> Cavalaria et orgeuill;
> E pos Dieu platz, tot o acueill,
> E prec li que'm reteng' am si.[22]

Compact Communication (and printing)

Already in the thirteenth century, urban Meistersinger guilds (in northern France they were called "Puys"; in Spain, "Gaya Ciencia") knew how to stage "courtly culture" on holidays and free evenings – almost as perfectly as the courtiers. The fact that such a detachment from the world of the nobility had become possible at all is symptomatic of an initial differentiation within "poetic" competence. To the extent, however, that courtly play became flexible and could be staged in various social contexts, the situational framework of its performance was no longer self-evident. For the literary historian, this development is accompanied by something like "a hermeneutical bonus." For while the attempt to localize, for instance, Provençal courtly love poetry in cultural history may generate a conflict with "philological responsibility," the textual traces of the courtly love revivals since the thirteenth century not uncommonly provide situational descriptions. This begins with the transmission of Provençal poetry regularly presenting (in all probability, highly fictional) biographies of authors (*vidas*) and *razos*, prose passages between stanzas in bound language, which spin narratives out of the limited situational patterns of the poetry. In the handwritten collections of songs, individual texts were configured into textual blocks through the compiler's commentaries, and it is easy to see that block formulation and commentary were determined far more by the thoughts about the possible situations in which they could be used than by any sort of "authentic knowledge" about the authors of the texts or even about the protagonists of the textual action.[23] All of this moves in the direction of compact communication, of the function of the work of art "as a communication program, in which the program can be so obvious that it makes every argument superfluous and establishes a secure feeling that everything is already understood."[24] To avoid any misunderstandings here of the concept of "compact communication," it must be kept in mind that it does not escape historicization: the phenomena drawn by Luhmann into the concept "compact communication" could appear only after a communication form had already dissociated itself from the initially concomitant framework of "its" life form.

Attention seems to have been paid to this relationship only after printing had given a veritable shove to the "differentiation of interaction and society" — and naturally all at once the difficulties of textual understanding also drastically increased for a while. In 1485, hardly twelve years after the appearance of the first printed book in the realm of the Catholic kings, Fernando del Pulgar, one of their historiographers, went to great pains to establish for the book readers the significance of the *Coplas de Mingo Revulgo*, a text from the closing years of the age of manuscripts.[25] The *Coplas,* which satirizes Henry IV, the unfortunate half brother and predecessor of Isabel of Castile, is a particularly interesting example; for in spite of the text's complete lack of ambiguity, outfitted as it is with all sorts of drastic late medieval amplifications, Fernando del Pulgar stakes his commentary on allegorization and subtleties out of the reservoir of biblical hermeneutics. So the shepherd, Mingo Revulgo, becomes — in this interpretation — an allegory of the common folk (as the name implies), and the shepherd's lampoon of the allegedly homosexual king is laboriously transformed by Fernando del Pulgar's commentary into the "moral" that such a bad lord — like Henry IV — could only expect to have the sort of subjects a better lord would not deserve. The "lesson," I suspect, had to be invented, because Pulgar was looking somewhat desperately for an "intención de esta obra," and he had to look for an "intención" to focus his interpretation, because the context presupposed by the text and consequently its meaning were no longer present to him. I have particularly emphasized the concept of "intention," which Fernando del Pulgar actually used, because it helps us to recognize that, in reaction to the establishment of a space-time distance between authors/reciters and recipients that was effected by the differentiation "interaction/society," it was increasingly necessary to build an authorial figure oriented toward understanding into the text, an innovation in which a conscious problem-solving strategy was objectivized. The proof of this tendency is given in Fernando de Rojas's prologue to his *Tragicomedia de Calisto e Melibea* (better know as *La Celestina*), which was first printed in Burgos in 1499. In a rhetorical gesture of resignation, Rojas speaks of his experience that ten different readers would read his text in ten different ways, each according to the *"differencia de condiciones,"* so that there could be no opportunity for the printer (and at the end of the fifteenth century this also meant the publisher) unequivocally to intercept potential divergences (through typography, commentaries, or summaries).[26]

We can probably risk the assertion that historical research is only now beginning to perceive[27] just how essential for the "origin of literature"—or, at least, for the origination of what, in textual typology, is called "literature"—were the manifold efforts to achieve that unambiguous understanding whose necessity was the immediate response to printing. There was suddenly an obsession with prefaces, it became standard practice to present didactical and other texts in dialogue form, and there was a completely new need for stability and a completely new attentiveness to the historicity of the textual forms. With regard to texts intended for scenic productions, one can perhaps go so far as to maintain that in the Middle Ages (that is, before the introduction of printing), it was extremely seldom that they provided even the barest presentiment of a plot—which is why the history of drama first installed itself as a history of topics at the point where dramatic texts began to organize understanding with the spectators themselves.[28]

For the novel, the course of this process was particularly complicated, at least in Spain. Between approximately 1450 and 1550, we come across a group of texts that literary historians have dubbed "novelas sentimentales."[29] Around a conventional plot, in which schemata from the late twelfth-century "courtly novel" are only slightly varied, frame stories are deployed, which, on the one hand, provide immediate understanding, yet on the other, show an obvious tendency to push the narrativity of the frame to the point where the fate of the frame's protagonists themselves can also be experienced as eccentric (a structural feature to which, undoubtedly, the name of the genre refers). Around 1550—directly before the replacement of the *novelas sentimentales* by the mode of the pastoral novel—the genre had developed into an extremely complex type of epistolary novel, which not only provided space for commentary directed at unequivocal understanding and a distancing of the lovers that created eccentricity but even opened up the possibility of discussing writing as an eccentric life form. For the context of our investigation, the phenomenon (which is otherwise thoroughly marginal) of the *novelas sentimentales* is particularly interesting, because it shows that, between the function of "literature" and "compact communication" as the solution to specific difficulties resulting from the differentiation of interaction and society produced by printing, a tension existed that was difficult to resolve. Because, however extensively the text itself organizes the possibility of being understood, it has to rely on a precognition of the communication situations among its readers, an understanding the readers—as substitution for the situation of direct interaction—are able to bring into play. If, however, it is supposed to be the function of "literature"—think of William IX—to stage situations and experiences that are not represented in the readers' knowledge, then the self-organization of the cognitive process through the text is actually not possible at all. To formulate it differently: under those conditions that make "compact communication" necessary, "literature" continually tends to substitute for itself a—potentially endless—discourse about literature (poetology). For it is its function to render the improbability of understanding experiential; yet in order to achieve this, it must nonetheless remain understandable.

And yet such a trend from literature to the discourse about literature does not seem to have been dominant at all in the beginning. The problem of compact communication, which was raised by the shift from script to print, became manageable by connecting what is (now) called "literature" up to less eccentric functions—in the prefaces, above all, to the function of moral instruction. And in fact, the centuries between 1500 and 1800 experienced the postantique boom in the topos *prodesse et delectare*,[30] with which, on the one hand, the reader's expectation of being instructed could be evoked out of the reader's knowledge but which, on the other, also kept open (indeed, even legitimized) a small claim to an "alternative program for reality."

Subjectivity/Temporalization (and too much poetology)

Communicative phenomena, as we have let them pass in review through the preceding pages, have been correctly seen by literary critics during the last decade as a supplement to the history of subjectivity in the early modern period—despite the discipline's tradition of saving the originating "literature" from its own eccentricity. We will not pursue the question that has become current in the meantime—namely, what, in this phenomenon, was still "mere reaction" to something else (like the courtly games of William IX) and what was already "consciousness of subjectivity"? It is more important for me that its function—which has been observable since the High Middle Ages—made literature particularly susceptible to the undertow of subjectivization and temporalization; why, then, subjectivization and temporalization have played such a significant and continually growing role for the autopoiesis of the social system since, let us say, the thirteenth century is again a problem that need not be gone into in the context of our reflections here. I only want to recall Luhmann once again, who registers the genesis of what we call "subjectivity" in the differentiating process between "social systems" and "psychic systems" and who sees temporalization as the consequence of increasing systemic complexity.[31] In what follows, it is for the moment sufficient to understand two reciprocal effects. First of all, at the level of everyday experience, temporalization ("historical consciousness") renders subjectivity more pregnant as a self-experiential form, and conversely, subjectivity (the consciousness of being different from others) can also be seen as an effect emphasized by temporality. Second, and this is more important, if it is the function of literature "to confront" its recipients "with other versions of the same reality," then it is plain that those who produce and take on such alternative versions of reality understand themselves as subjects par excellence and, moreover, that they stress the claim to eccentricity of the alternative realities by ascribing them to the past or to the future (in any case, not to the present). From the perspective of the history of mentalities, the framing conditions for subjectivization and temporalization—so much can already be anticipated—promote the literary function, but they also forbid literati to play "good literati" as an institutionalized role.

Pierre Corneille's ascension to literary fame can be exactly dated (namely, in 1637), and, as if it were already the nineteenth century, it happened because of a polemic scandal among specialists that literary historians have christened the *Querelle du Cid.* That the *Querelle du Cid* actually "took place" belongs to the information crammed for exams by undergraduates in French literature; otherwise the event is taken as a demonstration that Corneille, "like all great authors," had shocked the rule-ridden decorum of his contemporary world through his innovative power. From the perspective of our main question as to the stages in the history of the differentiation of the literary system, however, the pertinent documents become surprisingly interesting. It all began with the *Excuse à Ariste,* an epistolary poem in which Corneille explained in detail to a friend why he had declined the friend's entreaty to write a song-poem to a certain melody. It is worth noting that text and music were already then completely distinguished. But what nonplussed his contemporaries was Corneille's central argument. To give it a modern conceptual formulation: because of the pregiven musical structure the unfolding of his poetic subjectivity would be inadmissibly impaired. And in the original:

> Ce n'est donc pas assez, et de la part des Muses,
> Ariste, c'est en vers qu'il vous faut des excuses,

Et la mienne pour vous n'en plaint pas la façon,
Cent vers luy coustent moins que deux mot de chanson:
Son feu ne peut agir quand il faut qu'il s'applique
Sur les fantasques airs un resveur de Musique,
Et que pour donner lieu de paroistre á sa voix
De sa bigearre quinte il se fasse des loix,
Qu'il ait sur chaque ton ses rimes ajustées
Sur chaque tremblement ses syllabes contées,
Et qu'une froide pointe à la fin d'un couplet
en dépit de Phebus donne à l'art un soufflet:
En fin ceste prison desplaist à son genie,
Il ne peut rendre hommage à cette tyrannie . . .[32]

To talk about "self-esteem" on the basis of these lines truly does not require any interpretive projection. I would like to quote Corneille at length once more in order to show that he no longer bet on the products, of which he was so proud, according to traditional odds, but solely on the basis of the public's applause, whose composition, by the way, began at that time to—cautiously—break through the limitations of social rank:

Le prix que nous valons qui le sçait mieux que nous?
Et puis la mode en est et la Cour l'authorise,
Nous parlons de nous mesme avec toute franchise,
La fausse humilité ne met plus en credit,
Je sçay ce que je vaux, et croy ce qu'on m'en dit:
Pour me faire admirer je ne fas point de ligue,
J'ay peu de voix pour moy, mais je les ay sans brigue,
Et mon ambition pour faire plus de bruit
Ne les va point quester de Reduit en Reduit,
Mon travail sans appuy monte sur le Théâtre,
Chacun en liberté l'y blasme ou l'idolâtre,
Là sans que mes amis preschent leurs sentiments
J'arrache quelque fois trop d'applaudissments,
Là content du succès que le merite donne
Par d'illustres advis je n'eblous personne
Je satisfaits ensemble et peuple et courtisans
Et mes vers en tous lieux sont mes seuls partisans
Par leur seule beauté ma plume est estimée
Je ne dois qu'à moy seul toute ma Renommée . . .[33]

So much *sang froid*—we will see later how well this metaphor fits—drove the seventeenth century Parisian poetic milieu up the wall. The poetological critic Mairet forked up the *vers* "Je ne dois qu'à moy seul toute ma Renommée" in order to disqualify—quite unjustifiably—Pierre Corneille's successful play as a plagiarism of the *Mocedades del Cid* by Guillén de Castro. The aristocrat Scudéry (on whose pamphlet literary historians have mainly concentrated) reproached Corneille for having broken too many poetological rules. And even the almighty Cardinal Richelieu is supposed—from a distance suitable to his rank—to have poured a few drops of oil onto the fire of the polemic.[34] It is also in the *Querelle du Cid,* at the very latest, that we encounter initial signs of the formation of a binary code for "literature." Checking over the passages quoted from *Excuse à Ariste,* we find, on the one hand, "feu," "génie," "franchise," "sans brigue," "beauté." These predicates are opposed to "loix," "rimes ajustées," "syllabes contées," "froide pointe," "tyrannie," "fausse humilité." We have no difficulty identifying a semantics of the autonomous subject caught up in a polarizing process with a semantics of external determination and negation of inspiration. And I would like to go one step further (as the text itself suggests): Corneille also declined to write verse to order because he believed (or pretended to believe) that he owed the "fire" of his inspiration to the state of being in love (which, naturally, could not be delegated!):

> J'ay bruslé fort long temps d'une amour assez grande,
> Et que jusqu'au tombeau je dois bien estimer,
> Puisque ce fut par là que j'appris à rimer . . .
> Charmé de deux beaux yeux, mon vers charma la Cour,
> Et ce que j'ay de nom je le dois à l'amour.
> J'adoray donc Philis, et la secrette estime
> Que ce divin esprit faisoit de nostre rime
> Me fit devenir Poete aussi tost qu'amoureux,
> Elle eut mes permiers Vers, elle eut mes derniers feux . . .
> Aprés beaucoup de voeux et de submissions
> Un malheur rompt le cours de nos affections;
> Mais toute mon amour en elle consommé,
> Je ne voy rien d'aimable après l'avoir aimée,
> Aussi n'aymay-je plus, et nul objet vainqueur
> N'a possedé depuis ma veine ny mon coeur.
> Vous le diray-je, amy? tant qu'ont duré nos flames
> Ma Muse egallement chatoüilloit nos deux ames . . .[35]

Just how sincere Corneille is in these lines interests me very little. On the other hand, I consider it paradigmatic that the semantics of the literary system nourishes itself in the first instance on the semantics of love. Considering the eccentric function of literature, this borrowing was rather unsurprising, insofar as love had become, ever since the invention of the game of courtly love, a general metaphor for any kind of attempt to evade social determination. To be sure, for the differentiation of the literary system, this semantic proximity between "literature" and "love"—along with the moral conjunction "prodesse et delectare"—amounted to a second disadvantageous starting condition.

Nicolas Boileau's *Art poétique,* which was published for the first time in 1674, has been registered in the ledgers of literary history as a "poetics of rules and codes." Yet in the four *Chants* of that text, we cannot find anything resembling a set of "writing instructions." Rather, Boileau continues, so to speak, Corneille's program of subjectivity ("consultez long-temps vostre esprit et vos forces," I.12), but he already has concepts at his disposal ("raison," "bon sens") that he can use to designate the consensus between "good authors" and the influential public ("la Cour et la Ville"). What is new with respect to Corneille are those indications binding subjectivization to temporalization. Boileau sketches (I.113ff.) a teleological path from station to station beginning in the "siècles grossiers" and leading up to the literary summits of his own time, along which the names of individual authors (Villon, Marot, Ronsard) are associated with particular "advances." In a famous sentence (with an even more famous *passé simple*), the name "Malherbe" marks the entrance into the glorious present:

> Enfin Malherbe vînt, et le premier en France,
> Fit sentir dans les vers une juste cadence:
> D'un mot mis en sa place enseigna le pouvoir,
> Et reduisit la Muse aux regles du devoir:
> Par ce sage écrivain la Langue reparée
> N'offrit plus rien de rude l'oreille épurée.[36]

To simplify narratively the historical situation, it can be said that, after Boileau's *Art poétique,* a redetermination of the relationship between classical-antique literature and the literature of the "Age of Louis the Great" (as one said at the time) was on the agenda. On the one hand, Boileau had left the premises of the fundamental superiority of antique culture intact, yet on the other, he had also celebrated works from his own time in tones that could hardly be intensified. The debate—which from our perspective was "inevitable"—took place at the end of the seventeenth century and continued into the eighteenth in the forum of the Académie française; it was called the "Querelle des anciens et des modernes." In the course of our historical survey, I would like to use this *Querelle* to mark the literary system's temporalizing shift, just as the *Querelle du Cid* was related to the undertow of subjectivization.[37] Quite early historically (and moreover on one of the first pages of Charles Perrault's *Parallèle des anciens et des modernes*), an insertion of the Abbé stakes out the argumentative latitude of the disputation invented by Perrault:

> Nous verrons tout cela sur les lieux, mais je soustiens par avance qu'on fait tous les jours des choses tres-excellentes sans le secours de l'imitation, & que comme il y a encore quelque distance entre l'idée de la per-

fection & les plus beaux ouvrages des Anciens, il n'est pas impossible que quelques ouvrages des Modernes ne se mettent entre deux, & n'approchent plus près de cette idée.[38]

We will set to one side the concept of "perfection" (as well as the concept *perfectibilité*), which is so exceedingly important for the development of "historical thought," in order to stress that, with the idea of artistic production "without imitation" (which was still quite unusual at the end of the seventeenth century and could not be thought without the prerequisite of subjectivization), temporalization in the sense of a performance surpassing tradition first became possible. And, in fact, artistic praxis and aesthetic reflection in the eighteenth century fluctuated between the goals of being responsive "to the ancients" and at the same time surpassing them by trying to achieve "perfection." But the dialectical play of the *Querelle* generated a position that already projected beyond Enlightenment classicism and for which the designation "beau relatif" was later invented: the beauty of the artistic products from various ages and nations, as we read toward the end of Perrault's *Parallèle,* could not be comparatively evaluated; they had "to be appreciated according to distinctions of taste at different times."[39]

Luhmann has analyzed this argumentative field, which at first glance is extremely involved, on the basis of other documents (and in a much more microscopic manner).[40] For him, the historization of the concept of style (certainly more adequate from the standpoint of historical causation), which was so significant for Winckelmann's studies in art history, occupies the place of the historicism anticipated by the *Querelle des anciens et des modernes.* But at this point I want to return once again to our leitmotiv, the reciprocal action between the function of literature and the problems of differentiation in the literary system. In this context so far, we have only discussed the paradoxical circumstance that the literary system, in order to arrive at the primary levels of differentiation, needed support from other systems ("morality"/"love"). If we agree with the hypothesis that the dominant effect of subjectivization and temporalization on literature was tied to its function of presenting "other versions of reality," then we can now draw the conclusion as well that the early separation of literature from the principle of the *imitatio* (and ultimately its prohibition by the aesthetics of genius) was connected, indirectly, to this function. To be sure, it was not just a matter of separating the respective contemporary literary production from the reception of the past and the future; it was also a consequence of the function of literature that the past, which could be accessed through the principle of the *beau relatif,* remained present as an alternative version of the present reality. Hence one consequence of subjectivization and temporalization for the literary system was an "excess of literature." The other consequence of subjectivization and temporalization, an "excess of poetology," has already been pointed out. It looks as if the impossibility of affirming an operational program for the literary system (maintaining norms for literary production and reception) had intensified the efforts to be able to say something programmatic at least about the unity (the concept) of "literature."[41] This would be a way of explaining the genesis of aesthetics as a branch of philosophy in the second half of the eighteenth century. The "excess of literature" and the "excess of poetology," which aesthetic reflection could take as its starting point, seem on their part to have impeded the differentiation between program(s) and codes. On the basis of texts from the second half of the eighteenth and the nineteenth century, I would like, in the next section, to take a closer look at this context.

Paradoxical World Formulas (instead of programs and codes)

Combining Michel Foucault's history of the "crisis of the classical episteme"[42] with Luhmann's historiographical hypothesis of the "differentiation of social subsystems," we are able to regard d'Alembert's and Diderot's *Encyclopédie* as a gigantic attempt – and an equally gigantic failure – to maintain cosmological unity in an era of galloping differentiation. This miscarriage becomes particularly evident when we look at its synoptic table Systéme figuré des connoissances humaines, where the editors arranged the areas of human knowledge according to their relative nearness to or distance from one another – still unable to understand that the possibility of global representation had already faded away as social subsystems became independent and the stocks of knowledge constituting them in each case had been specified. However, as long as the belief in the possibility of *représentabilité* (as Foucault would have said) still existed, authors desperately tried to define and referentialize even those predicates that today we can identify as elements of system-specific communication codes. In other words, the effect of the Enlightenment project to save the unity of knowledge was to block the uncoupling of the codes from the programs. This "disturbance" (if we consider "smooth differentiation" in all directions as "normal") was particularly glaring in the fields of art and literature, where the excess of works that remained "hermeneutically present" and the excess of aesthetic reflection brought to a standstill not only the differentiation of codes and programs but also the making of definitions. It is not by accident that the Enlightenment is the literary-historical era in which the prologues are often longer – and more important for authors as well as readers – than the works themselves.

How literary specialists dealt with this situation is drastically exemplified by Diderot's item in the *Encyclopédie* on *beau*, a text that would be a logical first reading, given the context of our investigation, even for someone outside of the concerns of literary history:

> BEAU, adj. (Métaphysique.) Avant que d'entrer dans la recherche
> difficile de l'origine du *beau* je remarquerai d'abord, avec tous les au-

teurs qui en ont écrit, que par une sorte de fatalité, les choses dont on
parle le plus parmi les hommes, sont assez ordinairement celles qu'on
connoît le moins; & et que telle est entre beaucoup d'autres, la nature
du *beau*. Tout le monde raisonne du *beau*: on l'admire dans les
ouvrages de la nature; on l'exige dans les productions des Arts: on accorde ou l'on refuse cette qualité à tout moment; cependant si l'on
demande aux hommes du goût le plus sûr & et plus exquis, quelle est
son origine, sa nature, sa notion précise, sa véritable idée, son exacte
définition; si c'est quelque chose d'absolu ou de relatif; s'il y a un *beau*
essentiel, éternel, immuable, reglé & modelé du *beau* subalterne; ou s'il
en est de la *beauté* comme des modes; on voit aussitôt les sentiments
partagés; & et les uns avoüent leur ignorance, les autres se jettent dans
le scepticisme. Comment se fait-il que presque tous les hommes soient
d'accord qu'il y a un *beau;* qu'il y en ait tant entr'eux qui le sentent
vivement où il est, & que si peu sachent ce que c'est?

Diderot's difficulties are not only related to an excess of definitions but also reveal
the aporia that resulted from the attempt to define a predicate whose successful
career in the eighteenth century was precisely due to its functionalization as a
code value within a social subsystem, all of which becomes evident when we consider the finding in the *Encyclopédie* that *laid,* the other code value of the art system, could actually already be considered to be sufficiently determined through
its reference to *beau:*

LAID . . . se dit des hommes, des femmes, des animaux, qui man-
quent des proportions et des couleurs dont nous formons l'idée de
beauté. . . . Les idées de la laideur varient comme celles de la
beauté . . . ; . . . Si le contraire de beau ne s'exprime pas toujours
par *laid,* & si on donne ce dernier mot bien moins d'acceptions qu'au
premier, c'est qu'en général toutes les langues ont plus d'expression
pour les défauts ou pour les douleurs, que pour les perfections ou pour
les plaisirs.

But let's return to Diderot's Laocoönian struggle with the store of definitions of
beauty. In the first place, his procedure is "encyclopedic" in the truest sense of
the word: he presents a meticulous survey of the pertinent discussions during his
century (the discursive charms of which remind me of "exhaustive research
reports" or of certain obligatory passages in applications for research grants). Yet
Diderot would not be "our Diderot" if the threads of his patience spun endlessly
forth. So after, at any rate, fourteen *Encyclopédie* columns, he climbs down from
his lectern in order to stow away in various pragmatic contexts, as best he can,
the fundamental antinomy of his stock of definitions, the classicistic and the temporalized (one could also say, "preromantic") concept of the beautiful:

Il faut bien distinguer les formes qui sont dans les objets, & la notion
que j'en ai. Mon entendement ne met rien dans les choses, & n'en ôte

rien. Que je pense ou ne pense point à la façade du Louvre, toutes les parties qui la composent n'en ont pas moins telle ou telle forme, & tel & tel arrangement entr'elles: qu'il y eût des hommes ou qu'il n'y en eût point, elle n'en seroit pas moins *belle,* mais seulement pour des êtres possibles constitués de corps & d'esprit comme nous; car pour d'autres, elle pourroit n'être ni *belle* ni laide, ou même être *laide.* D'où il s'ensuit que, quoiqu'il n'y ait point de *beau absolu,* il y a deux sortes de *beau* par rapport à nous, un *beau réel,* & un *beau aperçû.*

The ambivalence of this reflection—Diderot would like to avoid the substantialism of the *beau absolu,* only to find himself (on the path of sensualism, no doubt) confronted by it (*beau réel*) again and again—would be worth a separate study, which I will leave aside here. What interests me is his strategy for dealing with the "excess of poetology," which, as we will see, is repeated in other texts. Definitions of art and literature, which originated in different historical situations and which could differ to the point of being mutually exclusive, Diderot made compatible with each other by relocating them within the synchronism of the communication process. The classicistic *beau absolu* (camouflaged as the *beau réel*) was assigned to the artistic product, the temporalized *beau relatif* (masked as the *beau aperçû)* to the consumer.

From these observations, our expectation that such a unification of mutually exclusive principles could end up in paradox is actually realized in Diderot's work—especially in the posthumous *Paradoxe sur le comédien.* Though in this case, it is not so much a matter of the opposition between a metahistorical and a historicized concept of beauty as of a rationalistic and sensualistic concept of the theater. Diderot is renewing here his attempt to unite these mutually exclusive principles by distributing them between the artistic product and its consumption. According to the *Paradoxe,* an actor's quality depends on his ability, based on systematic observation and with a cerebral distance to the scene being played, to employ his own body in such a manner and to excite the senses of the audience to such an extent that it can follow the play with empathy and no distance whatsoever—as if the play were its own reality. Reduced to a formula: "Ce n'est pas l'homme violent qui est hors de lui-même qui dispose de nous; c'est un avantage réservé l'homme qui se possède."[43] Moreover, Diderot wanted this paradox and had fun with it. On November 14, 1769, he wrote to the Baron de Grimm: "C'est un beau paradoxe. Je prétends que c'est la sensibilité qui fait les comédiens médiocres; l'extrême sensibilité les comédiens bornés; le sens froid et la tête, les comédiens sublimes."[44]

Naturally, the (really) "beautiful paradox" ought to be comprehensible within the context of our historical sketch of the "pathologies in the literature system" as a problematicizing solution. But that was certainly not the way Diderot's contemporaries understood it. They—and even more so the literary specialists of the nineteenth century—were enthusiastic about a play that generated highly pretentious formulas to define art and literature out of the semantic extension that necessarily resulted from the unification of polar concepts. If theater—as we could speculate in connection to (but not with) Diderot—unified the flow of affects and the acuity of understanding, *sensibilité* and *raison,* then it was a true copy of humankind (at least a copy of humankind as the eighteenth century wanted to see it). This position is somewhat reminiscent of Buffon's famous dictum, "Le style est l'homme même."[45]

The pertinent definitions by Goethe and Hegel have the same pattern. They demand that literature mirror the truth (no longer just "humankind"), because it unifies a total submission to the thematisized object ("imitation") with an appropriative subjectivity ("mannerism").[46] Since, in any case, names like Goethe and Hegel easily induce literary critics to abandon historical as well as analytic distance, I would like to call to mind once again the central thesis of these observations: with respect to the "excess of poetology," the greater those difficulties became that located themselves at the level of definitions of literature in order to avoid the formulation of rules at the level of work, production, and consumption, the more "philosophical" and "substantialistic" the programs turned out to be. In the end, they answered the question of what "literature" must be and said less and less about what authors and readers could do.

Perhaps the poetics and aesthetics of the nineteenth century were less productive than those of the Enlightenment. At any rate, it is hard to overlook the increasing fascination the juggling of paradoxes exerted on authors and literary specialists after 1800. A nineteenth-century creation, for instance, is the concept of *klassisch,* so familiar in German-speaking countries.[47] Fundamentally, it is a question of a synthesis of *beau éternel* and *beau relatif,* except that now the polar concepts were no longer distributed between the production and the reception of literary communication (as with Diderot), but were both ascribed to the work—so that the concept of classicism seemed like an emblem of a nineteenth-century ambivalence, in which authentic historical experience clashed with the need to maintain the belief in a stable reality.[48] When Sainte-Beuve talked about the classical authors of French literature from this perspective, it sounded like this: "Nous croyons faire preuve d'un respect mieux entendu en déclarant le style de Racine, comme celui de La Fontaine et de Bossuet, digne sans doute d'une éternelle étude mais impossible, mais inutile à imiter, et surtout d'une forme peu applicable aux drames nouveaux, précisamment parce qu'il nous paraît si bien approprié à un genre de tragédie qui n'est plus."[49]

Within the nineteenth-century production of poetological definitions, Victor Hugo, who tended toward hyperbole in every respect, hit the bull's-eye in 1827, if I see it correctly, with his famous, somewhat notorious (and today, barely readable) preface to the drama *Cromwell.* He no longer merely forced the unification of aesthetic principles or mutually exclusive concepts of time but also bluntly amalgamated the weary code values of the literary system:

La muse purement épique des anciens n'avait étudié la nature que sous une seule face, rejetant sans pitié de l'art presque tout ce qui, dans le monde soumis à son imitation, ne se rapportait pas à un certain type de beau. Type d'abord magnifique, mais, comme il arrive toujours de ce qui est systématique, devenu dans les derniers temps faux, mesquin et conventionnel. Le christianisme amène la poésie à la vérité. Comme lui, la muse moderne verra les choses d'un coup d'oeuil plus haut et plus large. Elle sentira que tout dans la création n'est pas humainement *beau*, que le laid existe à côté du beau, le difforme pèrs du gracieux, le grotesque au revers du sublime, le mal avec le bien, l'ombre avec la lumière.[50]

The *Préface de Cromwell* has achieved its fame as the manifesto of French romanticism. What Hugo formulated, however, also anticipated the legitimization of the *realism* that later on dominated the art and literature of the nineteenth century. For after "humankind" and after "truth," reality had become the goal to which literature was supposed to accommodate itself. Having reached this point, Hugo did not quit by simply juxtaposing "beautiful" and "ugly"; caught in the discursive flight of the preface and duty bound by an expectation to provide definitions, he soon allowed poetry to mix its poles into a paradoxical unity: "Elle (sc. la poésie) se mettra à faire comme la nature, à mêler dans ses créations, sans pourtant les confondre, l'ombre à la lumière, le grotesque au sublime, en d'autres termes, le corps à l'âme, la bête à l'esprit; car le point de départ de la religion est toujours le point de départ de la poésie. Tout se tient." And finally too, Hugo kept in reserve a deparadoxization instrument, to which the literati began to recur in the course of the nineteenth century. This instrument could be called "poetology rejection," to which, however, it must then be immediately added that it was, more precisely, just a question of "preface rejection." A thorough "invisibilization" could hardly succeed, because literature was naturally constrained, on the basis of its function and as compact communication, to go on writing about itself. For this reason, Hugo ultimately renounced the renunciation of prefaces and still got a good printed page of prefacing out of his metarenunciation:

Ce n'est pas du reste sans quelque hésitation que l'auteur de ce drame s'est déterminé à le charger de notes et d'avant-propos. Ces choses sont d'ordinaire fort indifférentes aux lecteurs. Ils s'informent plutôt du talent d'un écrivain que de ses façons de voir; et, qu'un ouvrage soit bon ou mauvais, peu leur importe sur quelles idées il est assis, dans quel esprit il a germè. On ne visite guère les caves d'un édifice dont on a parcouru les salles, et quand on mange le fruit de l'arbre, on se soucie peu de la racine. D'un autre côté, notes et préfaces sont quelquefois un moyen commode d'augmenter le poids d'un livre et d'accroître, en apparence du moins, l'importance d'un travail. . . . Des considérations d'un autre ordre ont influé sur l'auteur. Il lui a semblé que si, en effet, on ne visite guère par plaisir les caves d'un édifice, on n'est pas fâché quelquefois d'en examiner les fondements. Il se livrera donc, encore une fois, avec une préface, à la colère des feuilletons. *Che sara, sara.*[51]

Why is it that, in nineteenth-century poetology and aesthetics, even attempts at deparadoxization—paradoxically—turned into *mises-en-relief* of their paradoxes? For the moment, it can be established that, after 1800, the problem of leftover programs and still actual literary works of the past could certainly not be checked, but—on the contrary—only aggravated by the historicism of the time and probably too by the new academic discipline of "literary history." But maybe even then poetology and aesthetics only continued writing what had been the function of the literary discourse itself for centuries—namely, the production of other versions of the given dominant "reality." If it is true that something like a "centrifugality of the world" belonged to the fundamental experiences of everyday life during the nineteenth century and that the hope of preserving a unified cosmology became increasingly remote, then the adjuration of the unity of what was different—indeed, mutually exclusive—would have to have been experienced as such an alternative to everyday reality.[52] Except that the works did not always turn out like the poetologists' preformulations.

Exhaustion of the Function (and paralysis of the code)

In many respects, the nineteenth century was "the great age of literature." Why in the twentieth century it has turned into a crisis that threatens the survival of the literary system incomparably more radically than all of the previously described problems of its differentiation and autopoesis can be easily understood, I feel, from the fin-de-siècle perspective of the late 1980s. That we live in a "world of multiple realities"—generated out by social differentiation—is an experience that, in the meantime, readily convinces even those contemporaries who, to begin with, have continued to regard their own reality as the sole "reality current for everybody." But if there is no longer *one* such reality, then literature can also no longer fulfill the function of providing "other versions of the same reality." To experience "overall contingency" today, it is not necessary to have a specific system generating this experience; for many contemporaries, it is sufficient to make the daily run through the various social systems (or, in the meantime, even through cable TV, continually changing stations, zapping).[53] Faced with this drop in the price of the experience of contingency, it is a fair question whether mass movements such as cultural tourism (which is still in an upward trend) and cheap historicism ("everything that's old is beautiful")[54] still serve to make the everday worlds of tourists and antique collectors contingent. Perhaps it has long since become a search for the "authentic" or for things not created in the present, a search for the feeling that at least the contingency of the world of the late twentieth century is not contingent.

Artists and literati had already begun to react to this exhaustion of the function of art and literature when the idea of a world of multiple realities had still barely been concreticized in concepts. A respectable attempt was painting's step into nonfigurality; for, of course, it could not lead to a world of meaning beyond the manifold meanings of the manifold realities, although it nourished the illusion—at least for a while—with "mere" forms, colors, and materials, that it had left behind itself everything that was constituted by meaning. Since the early twentieth century, however, the human body and extrahuman nature have also been discovered—(too) many times—as a point beyond the multiple realities created by humankind, and for the discoverers it seems to have been important that body and nature can be experienced, not only as instances opposed to "meaning," but also as counterpoints to "plurality." This is probably why the "dismembered body" is almost as good for discursive compassion as the body that is "suppressed" or even "violated" (by intentions and functions).[55] For my part, I can (and will) scarcely try to evade such a longing for a sensibility not mediated by meaning— even less, the scenarios imagined for us in a future with a body totally plugged into television and a radically functionalized nature. But I also have (unfortunately, in many respects) a philosophical sympathy for that gesture of postmodern life-style that keeps the cafés as cool as the offices and fixates all affectivity in videoclips. For if we only want to, we can surely attribute to the cool-white walls of the cafés and the image simulations of the clips the insight—in their own style, stoic insight—that the body and nature, *without* the mediating instances of our respectively different "knowledge of the body and nature" (i.e., pure) can never be had anyway. That in spite of everything it could be somehow philosophical (at least not naive) to show how to avoid abandoning ourselves to any illusions.

Today there are high-grade theories of art and literature for what could be called "the wish for immediate sensibility (as opposed to meaning) and for unity (as opposed to manifold realities) in the consciousness of their impossibility." When Jacques Derrida writes about "Architrace" and "Différance" or Jean-François Lyotard about "Sublime," they engage themselves in the "deconstruction" of forms of meaning and the "destabilization" of unifying discourses, because they have become melancholic in the search for a noncontingent absolute. The fact that in doing so they inevitably evoke names from the "classic moderns" brings us to a set of circumstances I would like to call "the paralysis of the codes." Millions of human beings in the late twentieth century are looking for something beyond the manifold realities of their everyday worlds—in body culture and enthusiasm for nature (or, to put it ironically, in beauty farms and community organizations for the preservation of the "last" tree). But who is concerned with Cage Barnett Newmann—unless he or she is formally trained in art or has an investment interest?[56] Naturally such a quantitative drop in participation speaks neither for the Greens nor against contemporary American art. For those concerned, however, it is an uncomfortable but indisputable fact that, as a rule, specialists in literature and art pay attention to the twentieth century Sublime only when it is printed in a book or hanging in a museum.

In everyday language, it has been possible for some time now to find synthetic music and ads "beautiful" (or "ugly"), as was possible with trees and bodies for centuries. A doctoral text about similar objects, which, in their late twentieth-century stylization, want to be "other versions of reality" and also experienced as such, still implies a considerable existential risk for the candidate. This rigidness of the academic institutional gaze seems to be connected to the fact that – for the historical reasons I have tried to work out in this essay – the differentiation of codes and programs has not been successful in the systems of art and literature. When we say "beautiful" (or "ugly") more than just incidentally, we feel immediately obliged simultaneously to reflect what the beautiful (or the ugly) might be. And even "literary authors" write literary and art theory (on the whole, rather more explicitly than immanently) instead of poems and novels.

From a sociological standpoint, such a rigid gaze may not be of any further significance, and, to question it from the standpoint of social philosophy, it would be worth debating whether a society of manifold realities actually requires "another version of the realities" at all. On the other hand, for a discipline like literary studies, the paralysis in the use of the code can be "a death sentence." Already now it is often sufficient grounds for deadly boredom. Which is why many literary critics prefer to read outside of their field – for example, Niklas Luhmann.

Chapter 11
It's Just A Game:
On the History of Media,
Sport, and the Public

Late Breakthrough

The Olympic Games in 1988 would have been a breakthrough even if no records had been broken.[1] For on the one hand, it turned out that the best professional athletes in the world no longer had to act like they had simply taken a vacation without pay from their civilian employer in order to participate. And on the other, the scheduling of the events—however detailed the organization might have ultimately made them—was generally adjusted to the playtime/sleeptime rhythm of the financially powerful TV stations representing the North American and European audiences. The good old motto "It's just a game" can finally no longer be understood as a negation of the athletes' drive to win and to earn (because there is simply no place in twentieth-century morals for the encouragement of employees to forgo justly earned emoluments). With regard to Seoul, "It's just a game" can at best refer to the spectators, around whom practically "everything" is supposed to revolve.

Now surely no spectator or commentator at the 1984 Los Angeles or the 1980 Moscow Olympics actually believed that anybody won a medal without receiving financial compensation; and it is just as absurd today to imagine that any country engages in international sports merely to strengthen the bonds of friendship among "the world's youth"—without giving a thought to the spectators and their willingness to pay. But why then was there such a tenacious opposition to going professional and adjusting the structure of the events to the needs of the media audience? Why do so many reporters speak and write about sport spectacles in phrases that sound as if, during a Sunday walk, one were accidentally to come across a group of boys and girls playing games? To put it more exactly (more theoretically?): why is so much of the interest in sport concerned with preserving the appearance of "purity" in the sport event, to protect it against "contamination" by money and media?

In order to stave off any false hopes—I will not and cannot provide a satisfactory answer to these questions. But it might be useful to point out that the intense resistance to the "contamination of sport by money and media" is especially strong in western Germany.[2] Where else would an anti-Becker Club have been founded after his astounding victory at Wimbledon? Where else would the one-time American Soccer League have been called "operetta league" with bitter scorn mainly because its sponsors dropped the offside rule that has been straining the patience of soccer fans for decades? To be sure, the German Soccer Association has concluded in the meantime, with "pitiless realism," that the support of the paying fans had sunk to such a low level that the existence of *all* of the professional clubs represented by it had become questionable. But the resulting investigation ended by demanding that a particular "German virtue" should be kept in mind: namely, if the teams were *really* performing well, then the stadiums would fill up again. Equally "romantic"—and the term should signify here a "melancholy fixation on the past"—was the course of a West German colloquium on "sport and literature" at the end of 1985 in which I had the honor of participating. One kite-flying professor and a literary man, as haggard as he was famous, who regularly tortured himself through extreme jogging marathons, reported to the amazed listeners the extent to which their consciousnesses could be expanded by repressing and forgetting their bodies. About those forms of sport, which are "mass sports" simply because millions of viewers watch them on TV, only the American participants at that colloquium, if my memory is correct, had anything to say.

In reply to the question why criticism of spectator sports particularly in (West) Germany strikes such a rabid tone and why only a limited number (if any) of sports are considered worthy of being thematized in literature, I hope in this essay to provide some historical material—even if this will not be my central concern. The problem is rather, from a *historical perspective*, to contribute arguments toward the thesis that participatory sport and spectator sport do not necessarily have to be seen as a concurrence and consequently that the (perpetual) adjustment of the techniques in professional sport to the technical requirements of media and the needs of the viewers can be accepted as legitimate without further ado. Moreover, within the frame of our historical flashback we will see that precisely literature, which is so often welcomed as the intellectual antipole to modern spectator sports, played a quite substanial role in generating them. In more detail, I would like to postulate three theses.

1. Spectator sports, regarded sociologically and functionally, are a substantial area of everyday life in the late twentieth century. Like all forms of communication and participation from which the body has been screened out, they contribute to the habitualization of a dichotomy between "body" and "mind," to every adult's ability (at least in the industrialized countries) to continue his or her actions despite the fact that the body and corporeal presence are largely excluded. The functional peculiarity of spectator sports fulfills itself in its offer to compensate (even if it is an imaginary, illusionary compensation) for this corporeal screening.

2. With the introduction of the printed book, at the very latest, it has been literature, more than any other form of communication, that has contributed to the institutionalization of the body/mind dichotomy. Hence without literature, the habit that spectator sports compensate for today would not even exist. As an emblem for an *authentic* experience on the part of the subject that can be opposed to "mere passive watching," literature has only been recognized since the early nineteenth century.

3. The history of the body/mind split, like the history of the bipolarity of "authentic experience" and "passive watching," passed through a phase of intensive acceleration in the first decades of the twentieth century following the introduction of new media techniques (for example, film, radio, the phonograph). This "historical thrust" objectified itself—in particular around 1930—in a series of specific sense configurations legitimizing the body/mind dichotomy, but also in collective gestures and oppositional intellectual movements in the name of the norm of a "holistic image of humanity." Here the (alleged) competition between spectator sports on the one hand and literature on the other seems to have reached the level that still holds today.[3]

Naturally, there is a plan buried in the histor(iograph)ical plausibility of these theses, which no one could seriously hope to resolve in such a short essay. Hence it will be necessary (and probably somewhat unsatisfying for the reader) to include in the following attempts at reconstruction very condensed arguments from other investigations from time to time. Yet if I see it correctly, theoretical work on the problems introduced here is, at best, just beginning. And such a beginning requires "strong hypotheses."

Also, in the following sketch, I would gladly abstain from value judgments. But, of course, as someone whose "intellectual socialization" took place within the German tradition, I am bound to regard any hope of fulfilling this wish as naive. Yet for all that, I am going to resist the temptation to provide well-meant advice "to humanity" to the extent that I am going to replace it with straightforward references to those (subjective) experiences in which my own interest in this theme has originated: I'm a literary historian (but not an *unconditional* lover of literature); I'm an enthusiastic sports fan (but *exclusively* as a spectator).

Emerging Structures

When we search for a feature, a concept, by means of which it would become possible to narrate the relationship between literature and sport as the history of a differentiation of forms of action and (later historically) as the history of an (indirect) functional relationship, it is a good idea to take recourse in the concept of play.[4] In particular, two elements of the play concept, which Johan Huizinga above all has recommended, can be recovered from literature as well as sports in numerous, historically concrete forms. On the one hand, there is a distance to the everyday world of intentions and goals that can be experienced from a number of different points of view: for instance, as the "insularity" of play or also as the vagueness of the motive that induced the participant to start playing. Second, games are characterized by rules (either worked out during the game or determined ahead of time). What "rules" in athletic games are and can be requires no special illustration. The objective spectrum of "literary rules" is considerable, reaching from poetologically codified language forms to particular habits of communicative behavior up to that "pact" between author and reader in which Jean-Paul Sartre wanted to ground his concept of "engaged literature." It is evident that games need rules because they don't provide the players with clear motives to guide their behavior.

But since we are concerned with the history of the relationships between literature and sport, it is not just a matter of finding perspectives that mediate between the two phenomenal spheres but also of determining criteria that can historically distinguish between the individual forms of sport and literature. We will concentrate on three such criteria: first of all, on the respective proportions of "body" and "mind" involved — obviously there cannot be any games that completely screen out the one or the other; second, on the degree of distance of a given game from the everyday world of goals; and third, on the relationships between players and spectators — also including, of course, the possibility of games wholly without spectators.

We will start this minihistory of the relationships between literature and sport, which leads to a polarization of sport between "authentic subjective experience" and "mere passive spectator sports" (which, by the way, is synchronized with the dichotomy between "trivial literature" and *belles lettres*), in the Middle Ages (simply because of inadequate competence in ancient culture). Now whether we concentrate on the court festival or on the popular milieu of the carnival, in the Middle Ages the protoforms of literature and sport are inextricably interwoven, making it scarcely possible to determine, in a modern sense, the ratio of (im)balance between the share of the body and that of the mind. A demonstration of the ethos of a particular social rank was expected from a warrior in a courtly tournament; the troubadour performed his songs with his own voice (his own, his entire body), thus surely contributing to the intensification, indeed, to the actualization of a latent erotic tension. The blasphemous body gestures of the carnival were bound up with an institutionalized transcendental meaning. The court festival and carnival stood as ensembles of medieval forms of play distinct from everyday life: especially the court festival because of its social exclusivity, but also because it was limited to the short space of "late spring"(if we can read the courtly novels of the Middle Ages as historical documents, then we have the impression that they were only celebrated during the weeks around Whitsuntide; carnival, which included all classes, had the much more rigid boundaries set by the church calendar that are still traditional today). Up into the late Middle Ages, there would have hardly have been spectators for such games. Anyone who remembers contemporary representations of festively clad ladies peeking at the knights' combat out of the alcove of a castle or from specially constructed tribunes should not forget that their favors (if not their bodies) went only to the victors.

The dissemination of the printed book as a medium of communication since the end of the fifteenth century ushered in a structural shift through which it became the norm of communicative forms to screen out the body as much as possible.[5] It was only then that those kinds of speech acts were formulated that today are subsumed (more or less) under the concept "literature." Even a brief glance at contemporary medieval tournaments shows that, here, the scene was dominated by a veritable "professionalization" of prominent combatants, and that, consequently, this physical praxis ceased to be a privilege of nobility. In these beginnings, "literature" as well as "sport" moved nearer to the functions and needs of everyday life. It is no accident that there was an astounding boom in the classical topos *prodesse et delectare*. While in the thirteenth century it still had to be emphasized that knightly tournaments belonged to the catalogue of aristocratic games *although* they also contributed to military toughening, some "types of sports" (for example, archery) were only considered legitimate in the early modern period, when they clearly furthered martial competence. At the same time, a differentiation between participants and spectators became constitutive of intellectual as well as physical games. A direct symbol of this development (for literature) was the theater curtain, which was unknown in the Middle Ages. It corresponded to a marked differentiation between the roles of author and reader whose actions would be experienced less and less frequently as exchangeable.

It is symptomatic that those reforms and revolutions that led to the so-called bourgeois democracies—in the sense usual today, as a fulfillment of the Enlightenment—have regularly stylized Gutenberg as one of their most important "forerunners" and "benefactors of humanity." Such a canonization was more or less considered an obvious honor given that the printed book was regarded—surely with justice—as the single most significant instrument in the proliferation of new knowledge. Yet from the retrospective of the late twentieth century, we can and must add another dimension to this obviousness. Seen from the viewpoint of the theory of the state, the "bourgeois" parliamentary democracies are characterized by the principle of representation, which also means, by a conception of political action and political exercise of power that screens out body presence by making it a problem of delegation. To this extent, what Gutenberg had made possible was made obligatory by the reforms and revolutions of the eighteenth and nineteenth centuries.

To be sure, the everyday existence that was marked by the new political systems did not correspond in every aspect to the Enlightenment's dreams or the official collective self-image. Hence, Niklas Luhmann has called our attention to the fact that the enlargement ("Enlargierung") of the ideal of consensus-creating communication by extending it from the familiar circles of the *philosophes* to the entire social space was doomed to failure from the very beginning. Michel Foucault reconstructed how the citizen's "self-control" grew out of the physical exercise of state power in feudal society: the mastery and restraint (of numerous) corporeal needs through the strict maintenance of "civil morality." Under these conditions, all of the specific forms of body- and mind-accentuated games, which had previously functioned (at least since the early modern period) as the respective dispositions of class-specific socializations, now came together into a new sphere of "leisure time."[6] Its (internally highly complicated) unity becomes visible the moment it is recognized that the (at least today) infinitely differentiated forms of behavior and action in leisure time are always focused in order to perform just *one* thing: to compensate for the deficits that the experience of everyday existence in the new societies has incurred in opposition to their claims of self-representation. Because such compensation only becomes viable where it is not recognized as compensation, ever since the early nineteenth century it has been considered "philistine" to ask sport and literature questions about their goals. Once again, they therefore seem to be keeping a safe distance from the everyday world of goals.

Now there are two basic modes of leisure-time behavior in bourgeois society, one regarded as "demanding" and one as "trivial," and this evaluative dichotomy is accompanied by a further differentiation that, since the early modern period at least, can be observed between games emphasizing the body and games emphasizing the mind, between sport and literature. At the "demanding" level, literature and sport are experienced as forms of "authentic" subjective experience; at the "trivial" level, the spectator participates in literature and sport "from a distance." Since the beginning of the nineteenth century, "cultivated education" has been increasingly constituted by a certain dabbling in literature (or at least in the development of special literary tastes) and by actively cultivating certain sports (which can be nicely illustrated by the history of the first climbs and climbers in the Alps). On the other hand, a potential legitimation for the nonactive mode of leisure-time behavior was carried over from the eighteenth century. It was the premise, bound up with the figure of the "cognitive subject" that distance furthered cognition. Yet not every nineteenth-century novel came from Flaubert &

Cie, no more than Richard Wagner's *Gesamtkunstwerk* was the only musical theater of that period. What we still today (more or less condescendingly) call "trivial
literature" was (and is) a stock of texts and plays that made it possible for the spectator to experience in his imagination everything that he could not experience
authentically—at "first hand," so to speak.

Already in the nineteenth century,[7] actively practiced sport and literary con-
noisseurship began to converge in the life form of "education" just like (from the
standpoint of the spectator) trivial literature and sport spectacles. Lord Byron
learned to box, while, on the other hand, melodramas could be enjoyed on the
stages of Paris ever since 1795 (that is, since the French Revolution, as the
historians say today, "had gotten into its bourgeois rut") and (at least once a year,
namely, on July 14) on the Champs de Mars monumental chariot races were held.
There is a great deal of evidence for the conjecture that it was precisely such spectacular shows that compensated the spectators for their state of disembodied action. Thus playwrights and critics complained time and again about spectators
who were more fascinated by the beautiful bodies of the actors and actresses than
by the dramatic "content." Here we have the prototype of the film star or TV star
for whom individual pieces are written so that his or her body could be staged
in a particularly effective way. Complementary phenomena can be seen in the
professionalization of boxing, of horse racing, and—at the very end of the nineteenth century—of soccer.

When the two basic modes of leisure time—the forms of "authentic" experience
for the subject and the forms of "trivial" spectacles for the passive viewer—are
confronted with one another, then it is the former that throughout the nineteenth
and twentieth centuries has proved more resistant to historical change. On the
other hand, we cannot even imagine something like a "classic trivial spectacle"—
except where they have been stylized as "high culture" or as "national symbolic
figures" and thus withdrawn from the world of trivial spectacles. This is what happened to the heroes of the silent films and to some sports heroes, and it seems
to be going on today with the automobile races of the early twentieth century and
with the novels of Karl May. But normally a ceaseless turnover in the media and
their contents is taking place in the sphere of "trivial" leisure-time amusements.
A number of individual developments within this dynamic up until the present
suggest that, taken altogether, it has been characterized by a growing distance
from the traditional stock of literary forms and by an intensification of an (illusory) presence of the body. Colette, perhaps France's most successful woman
novelist in the twentieth century,[7] made her début around the turn of the century
with an epoch-making novel series starring the (more or less) autobiographical
heroine, Claudine. At first, these books appeared under the pen name "Willy,"
the literary pseudonym of Colette's first husband, a genial businessman in the
genre of the trivial entertainment industry. However, apparently once Colette
realized the erotic attraction that the Claudine series exercised on hetero- and

homosexual target groups, she not only began to publish new editions of her novels under her own (artistic) name (in the meantime she was for the most part separated from Willy) but also rarely missed any chance to publicly stage her nonfictional biography – and above all her own body – as the "actual reality" behind the Claudine novels. With a repertoire of the most undemanding pantomimes imaginable, she traveled through French provincial cities and made history in 1906 when she bared her breasts (still worth looking at today) night after night in such a *mimodrame*. Yet only in 1907 did Colette's calculated stage scandal reach its high point: in a *Rêve d'Egypte,* for which the Moulin Rouge pulled out all the stops, Colette incarnated (if that can be said) a mummy that was kissed back to life by an archaeologist. The role of the archaeologist was played – under the oddly inventive name, "Yssim" – by Colette's new lover, the Marquise de Belbeuf, better known as "Missy" by her girl friends.

To be sure, Colette was not definitively lost for the male world. In the 1920s, she turned once again (and permanently) to the more serious muse of writing. At the end of this minihistory, it should not go unmentioned that around 1930, possibly due to a slackening in the sales of her novels, Colette put her body at the disposal of the cosmetics industry and even sold cosmetics in her own boutique.

Experiencing and Resisting the Mind/Body Split

The social functions during the nineteenth century and up to the present that were fulfilled by so-called trivial literature and by certain forms of theater (at which we have hinted in our glance at Colette's career) were increasingly taken over after the turn of the century by various forms of staging in Variétés, music halls, films, and stadium sports, that pushed the actors' bodies into the foreground of entertainment repertoires. It was exactly during those years that the entertainment branch of the sport spectacle began its triumphal march. We call to memory the Olympic Games, the great bicycle tours, national soccer contests, automobile rallies, six day races, and the truly epic history of the heavyweight championship boxing matches. Admittedly, Madison Square Garden and the Palais d'Hiver, Berlin's Sportpalast and the Westfalenhalle in Dortmund, were not only "sports arenas," for it was by no means exclusively sport spectacles that contributed to the habitualization – and at the same time to the compensations – of the mind/body dichotomy. An enormously differentiated store of entertainments was elaborated, stretching from the programs of the sports arena to the variety shows and new dance halls (where homage was paid to the charleston and the tango) and on to the silent film theaters. It is through the example of one of the great film stars of the 1920s that we can understand just exactly what spectator identification meant. In a special edition for September 1926, the French magazine *Mon Ciné* wrote on the death of Rudolf Valentino:

Rudolphe Valentino plaisait par ses qualités physiques et aussi par son jeu qui était d'une rare maîtrise. . . . Rudolphe Valentino meurt avec l'auréole d'un grand séducteur et de nombreuse jolies spectatrices de salles obscures le pleureront longtemps. Si ses aventures sentimentales furent contés avec un luxe de détails qui lui déplaisait souverainement, par la presse cinématographique de tous les pays, il s'énervait de lire de telles indiscrétions, réclamant pour lui le droit de vivre à sa guise comme les autres hommes. A vrai dire, il n'avait guère été heureux en amour. Son premier mariage avec Jean Acker, une artiste qui n'est pas parvenue à la notoriété, ne dura guère, et le divorce fut prononcé à la demande de la femme qui l'accusait de "Cruauté mentale" en 1922. Sans doute cette accusation n'avait pas la moindre valeur, car deux jours avant l'issue fatale de la maladie de Valentino, sa première femme lui fit parvenir une couverture luxeuse d'un coussin de soie parfumé sur lequel avait été brodée cette inscription: "A Rudy, Jean." . . . Et ce sera peut-être une légère consolation pour toutes les admiratrices de Rudy de savoir que, malheureux en amour, il fut tout de même pleuré à sa mort par les yeux d'une femme qui l'amait.

Valentino's body, these lines leave no doubt, was offered up in film to his female admirers as an (illusory) possession. If "identification" means "to put yourself in the place of another," then the target of the identification here is not the space occupied by Valentino's body but the space at his side. Ideally, therefore, the space at the side of the star must fulfill two conditions at the same time: it has to remain free for the projections of the fans and it has to provide a pattern for how one should behave "at the side of the star." Jean Acker, Valentino's ex-wife, no longer appears in the quotation from *Mon Ciné* as a rival of the identifying fans, yet her final greeting is a kind of behavior well suited to stimulate the imagination of Valentino fans.

When Rudolf Valentino died, it had already long been a modernist duty for intellectuals—even in Germany—to be enthusiastic about sport spectacles, especially boxing. Bertolt Brecht had written part of the autobiography of the middleweight champion Paul Samson-Körner and provoked the cultivated theater public by wishing to have the same kinds of audiences for his plays as those found at boxing matches. To be sure, when we take a closer look, we get the impression that Brecht and his ideal audience remain just as far from the type of spectator found in trivial entertainment as all of his intellectual forerunners in the nineteenth century. For his "epic theater" demands distance and habitualizes a thoroughly cerebral attitude of reception; what is Brecht likely to have written about female theater viewers, who, like the fans of Rudolf Valentino, would have fainted in the lobby? His famous axiomatic declaration about boxing was in any case never formulated from the perspective of the spectator greedy for identification, but negated the "educational value" of sport in favor of an "authentic" subjective experience, which, indeed—more radically than ever—was supposed to be corporeal experience:

> Sometime back I bought me a punching bag, mainly because it looked pretty neat hanging over a whiskey bottle with shattered nerves, and because it gave my visitors the chance to carp at my tendency towards exotic things and because, at the same time, it kept them from talking about my plays. Now I had come to realize that whenever I had, in my opinion, done some good work (by the way, even after reading the critics) I'd throw a couple of moody punches into the bag, whereas during periods of laziness and physical deterioration I never even thought about improving myself with some decent exercise. Sport as hygiene is abominable. I know that the poet Hannes Küpper, whose work is really fairly decent so that no one will publish it, is a racing driver and that George Grosz, who there is also nothing to complain about, boxes, but they do it, as I know perfectly well, because they have fun and would do it even if it would ruin them physically.[8]

When Brecht explains that such "pleasure in sport" is "the pleasure in taking risks,"[9] then it should—finally—be clear that the subject experience sought by the intellectuals in literature and sport is no less a function of compensation than the identification of the "broad public" with the heroes of screen and stadium. Now at first it might be surprising to find a positive statement about the body/mind split in a German Olympics album from 1936, which, aside from the verbal gesture, looks very much like the comment just quoted from Brecht:

> The leap of a panther is something complete and self-contained. Everything in the leaping panther, every hair bends into the leap, there is nothing left in the animal that resists the leap, neither corporeal nor soul-like. The same pantherlike completeness manifests itself when Cornelius Johnson, the Negro from the U.S.A., springs across the bar in the high jump. The entire beauty of his leap can only be finally judged when we see it frame for frame in slow motion—a brown man climbing high, slowly, stretching himself horizontally, slow and soft, and then diving down, slow and loose, as we only know it from animals. But even so, even with bare eyes, we recognize already that Johnson's jumps are something special. He's a Negro, he's still closer to nature than the white man; he still has animalic capabilities at his disposal, to really yield himself with skin and hair to the movement of the leap; he still possesses that indescribable something that brings victory over and beyond technique.[10]

Anyone who would find *intentional* discrimination—over and beyond the factual discrimination against black athletes in 1936—in these lines is mistaken. On the contrary, the admiration for Cornelius Johnson has almost completely the same motivation as the satisfaction at the medals won by the German boxing team: "We sent a fighting team into the ring that was selected less for technical skill than for sheer toughness and a fighting spirit that would never give up."[11] To be sure, in the fascist sport and political spectacles, the hypostasis of corporeality – by screening out the intellect – was not aimed at compensation. The athletic star as muscle man was supposed to function as a model of physical fitness of the individual (taken here in the biological sense) and as a model of physical training, which was a matter of human material potentialized for the military. Already in 1933, a Spanish Fascist was full of admiration for the new German youth: "La inmensa pista del Stadium, el mismo sitio que ha de mostrar a los atletas del mundo la Olimpiada mundial de 1936, está repleta ya con la muchadada de ciento cincuento mil entusiastas y viriles mozos de la nueva Alemania."[12] Here the body/mind split was motivated and functionalized in a completely different way than in the liberal social forms of the nineteenth and twentieth centuries, but it was carried through at the individual level with relentless consequence. The old ideal of a "unity of body and mind" was reserved for *das Volk,* or more precisely, for the fascist discourse about *das Volk:* "Unrivaled and unique were the space and echo in the newly flowering happiness of the nation. The joy and jubilation at winning back youth beat against the young envoys of all nations with unreserved candor. Nowhere in the world was there a place in which space and mankind were so filled with the Olympic Spirit as in Berlin."[13]

We are all familiar with the astounding perfection with which national socialism employed the most advanced media of the time in order to extend the audience horizon of such games far beyond the number of spectators present in the stadium. It is no accident that the 1936 Olympic album quoted from above artfully depicts a monumental painting of "the closing festivities in the Olympic stadium," including two radio reporters with their microphones, a film cameraman and, in the middle, an overlarge "television cannon." Be that as it may, there seems to have been a certain sluggishness, indeed even certain forms of resistance – which are difficult for us to understand today – to the intensification of the body/mind dichotomy the broadcasting of sport spectacles brought with itself; nor was it a matter of educated privileges nor (unfortunately) even less a question of political resistence. In a cable on the heavyweight match between Max Schmeling and the American, Steve Hamas, which took place in Hamburg on March 10, 1935, the correspondent from the *Frankfurter Zeitung* commented, not without astonishment:

> There must have been a lot more people in the Hanseatenhalle than it can actually hold. In a special train from Berlin, two young men were sitting who had scrounged up the money for the train tickets at the last minute. Otherwise they didn't have a penny in their pockets and they certainly didn't expect the waves to wash up a couple of free tickets for the fight as flotsam on the bank of the Alster. The only important thing was to be in the city of the match, which in the course of a few days

had become the center of the world, as is the case in New York City during such events.

Presumably it was the same inertia—or to phrase it positively, the same need for a corporeal experience of the environment—against which a pioneer of television criticism clashed in the fall of 1939 when he asked himself why the enthusiasm for the new medium (in which in any case the National Socialists never invested very much hope) had fallen so far behind expectations after only a good four years of "programming service":

> At first it seemed as if television was a "winter" art, as if it had to be reserved for those hours ruled by darkness or at least twilight. In the first place, there were technical and practical reasons for this. It is only in the dark that the television picture really becomes good; in fall or winter one stays at home, and "in the evening one appreciates the house." On a beautiful summer afternoon, to be sure, one is glad to listen to radio music on the balcony, but one is not happy to leave the warmth and light in order to go inside, in order to look at pictures in the oppressive humidity of the closed room.[14]

As has already been pointed out, such corporeal persistence has nothing to do with political resistance, and it surely would not manifest itself solely in front of the screen. At any rate, fascism and new media—together with other factors—have contributed, since the end of the 1920s, to the conscious experiencing of certain consequences of the body/mind dichotomy, whose historical roots—as we have tried to show—go much further back. To these "other factors" the introduction of sound films probably belongs, which—since approximately the death of Rudolf Valentino—fundamentally changed the film audience's receptive habits that had been first of all imprinted by the silent film. In 1928, the internationally famous magazine, *Révue du Cinéma,* initiated a lengthy and for us highly interesting dialogue with its readers with the—quite serious—question, "Avez-vous peur du cinéma?" The answers give us the impression that "fear of the movies" was a fear of the superabundance of bodily presence offered by the sound film on the screen:

> Avez-vous pensé à ce que toute une salle ressent quand une Greta Garbo, une Clara Bow, un John Gilbert, un George O'Brian (par exemple) prend tout d'un coup possession de l'écran? A toutes les ondes d'amour, de jalousie, de regret, de haine, de pitié, de renonciation, de complaisance qui circulent aussitôt et se mélangent parmi les spectateurs?

When we talk about the surfeit of bodily presence on the screen that sound films made possible, then this formulation is not primarily related to the new audio dimension that moved film experience closer to everyday life. Comparing stills from silent films with stills from (early) sound films, we become aware of the contrast in the "desemantisizing of the actor's body." Since mime and movement no longer had to take over the functions of language as a communicative medium, the erotic fascination, indeed the physical violence of the actor's body (which appeared on the screen in gigantic dimensions), was enhanced. Perhaps "fear of the movies" was nothing but the spectator's even more intense frustration at never possessing, not even touching, those bodies that were so near.

We are much more familar with the reactions of intellectuals to this dichotomy than with the feelings of anonymous moviegoers in the 1920s and 1930s. Brecht's emphatic rejection of "sport as hygiene" and "sport as spiritual creativity" belongs to these reactions, because it was undoubtedly a symptom of a lack of direct experience. Michel Leiris, who in 1930 in the *Révue du Cinéma* had vehemently supported the films of the African-American director, King Vidor, was one of the leaders of an ethnological field-research project that has gone down in the history of science as the Dakar-Djibouti Expedition. In order to finance the project, a public spectacle was organized, which from our perspective today seems emblematic for the consciousness of Western intellectuals around 1930. Al Brown, the black welterweight world champion (without jeopardizing his title), fought ten rounds against the featherweight champion of France, Roger Simendé, and put the purse at the disposal of the scientific project, which for its part had been motivated by an intellectual weariness with civilization.[15]

In the late 1930s, the same Leiris was active in the foundation of the now famous Collège de Sociologie. The Collège de Sociologie never achieved, nor sought, the status of an official academic institution; rather it stayed an informal discussion group that organized, over a period of two academic years between 1937 and 1939, a series of thematically centered lectures.[16] The interests that unified this circle become clear as soon as we see that among its founders was Georges Bataille, who had estranged himself from the (in his opinion, far too disciplined and intellectualized) surrealist circle around André Breton and who had, together with Roger Caillois, called into life a magazine with the significant title *Acéphale*. In July 1938, along with three other manifestos by Caillois and Leiris, Bataille published in *Acéphale* his text "L'apprenti sorcier," which provided the initial impulse for the work at the Collège de Sociologie and at the same time formulated its program. Bataille accused European civilization not only of having left the corporeal needs of humankind unsatisfied, but, through the permanence of such frustration, of having repressed them—at the collective level:

On emporte avec lui [sc. le malheur] un grand nombre de besoins auxquels il faut satisfaire pour éviter la détresse. Mais le malheur peut le [sc: l'homme] frapper même à l'heure qu'il n'éprouve pas de souffrances. Le mauvais sort peut le priver des moyens de subvenir à ces besoins: mais il n'est pas moins atteint quand tel de ses besoins élémentaires lui fait défaut. L'absence de virilité n'entraîne le plus souvent ni souffrance ni détresse; ce n'est pas la satisfaction qui manque à celui qui diminue: elle est pourtant redoutée comme un malheur. Il est donc un premier mal qui n'est pas ressenti par ceux qu'il frappe: il n'est mal que pour celui qui doit envisager la menace d'une mutilation à venir.[17]

These words help us to understand why the discussions that soon followed at the Collège always began with the representation of archaic rites in prehistorical times or with social forms in the present that had not as yet, as Bataille would say, consummated the sin of civilization. Later Bataille went on to stylize the dream of an eroticism whose physical intensity would necessarily lead to death. He discovered a smile on the faces of executed or tortured victims that he took to be the expression of a physical fulfillment denied by civilization.

And finally, it was also in the Paris of the 1930s that the *chansonnière* Edith Piaf began her rocky career, in whose end the entire French nation participated. She is not only a striking example because the entertainment industry made such a great effort (quite similar to what we have seen with Colette) to present her chansons as condensed expressions of her life (above all, of her suffering). Most of her texts have the effect of seeming to be pop versions of Bataille's pan-erotic philosophy — "heureux / se à s'en mourir." Even though we can exclude any direct influence, there is something to the hypothesis that Piaf's chansons were a media-tailored production of a new life feeling for intellectuals — that is, their reaction to the experience of the body/mind dichotomy. Hence, it was then also no surprise that the French and American press went into raptures over Piaf's affair with Marcel Cerdan, who became the welterweight champion of the world in New York on September 21, 1948, lost the title on June 16, 1949, and was killed in a Super Constellation crash over the Azores on the morning of October 28, 1949.[18] In her despair, the rainbow press reported, Piaf accused herself of having killed Cerdan for love, for her lover was on his way to meet her in New York.

Here, just before the middle of the century, central myths and fascinations from one of the great eras of entertainment are assembled in a single story — the boxer Cerdan, whose life had been dominated by physical violence to such an extent that it seemed to leave only little space for a sympathetic childish disposition; a new eroticism (for the time), sung by Piaf in concerts and records, whose intensity took on a particular pathos through the implicit risk of corporeal destruction; the plane, in which technologically materialized human intellect and physis — all these elements were once again reunited in a symbolic but always dangerous unity. What has remained present today — physically present — is the voice of Piaf. For the physical effect of recordings of this voice, as an objectification of her body, on listeners is more material, more "real" than the image of a body could ever be.[19]

It is one of the conventions of film critics to devalue music films of the 1930s as a decline from the art of the silent film in the 1920s; they are looked down on as "mere fiddling" with new technical possibilities. But perhaps the boom in records and the enthusiasm for music films during this era, precisely because of the corporeal presence of the voices they brought closer and retained, was something more (or at least, something different) than merely a loss of aesthetic quality – namely, the least frustrating reaction to the experience of corporeal loss. At any rate, music films were flourishing again by the 1980s – along with the body, which in body-building studios and graduate seminars of philosophy has once again moved into the center of interest.

The Structural Mutation of the Dichotomies

In the third quarter of the twentieth century, the history of the leisure-time industry has been dominated by the transfer to the television medium of the functions that had been fulfilled and imprinted by film and radio since 1900; and we can observe in this process astonishingly scant phasal fluctuations between different countries and cultural regions. This cannot be merely a consequence of technical innovations and productive optimizations; the triumph of television presupposes, to pick up a quotation from a previous paragraph, a new willingness on balmy summer evenings to forgo fresh air in favor of the "evening programs." And along with that, the argument that a visit to the stadium as a spectator experience could never achieve the plethora of details and the overview of "sports reporting" has become steadily more convincing. Does this mean that we have finally come to terms with the screening out of the body and the forms of its compensation? Yet on the other hand, active sport has steadily found new adherents, as can be seen above all in sports like tennis or horseback riding, which formerly had been virtually reserved for the rich (and in part, for intellectuals). In the meantime, these sports have largely lost their "philosophy" and social prestige – for instance (among other things), specific clothing rules have become obsolete.

The enormous quantitative expansion of the realm of "free time" should be mentioned first of all as a prerequisite for the obvious double development. Today, people simply have more time at their disposal for play than in 1950 or even 1930. But is the host of new skiers recruited out of the mass of viewers of sports programs? Do the participants of tennis courses sold in supermarkets read modern poetry? Given the contemporary situation, it is considerably more difficult to recognize typical configurations of leisure-time behavior than in the first half of the century, which certainly has something to do with the fact that the structures of the various life forms have become more contingent. Maybe someone who still needs his body in his working existence would rather watch a soccer game in the stadium or on TV, while someone who sits day after day at a desk producing one or another kind of "head work" prescribes herself a vacation of horseback riding.

Taken altogether in any case, the situation is far less perspicuous than we would have dreamed of only twenty years ago.

But let's pose the question one last time: who reads contemporary literature, and what do its (few remaining) readers—typically—do with their bodies? For a moment, the question can be sidestepped by pointing out that movies or the choice of programs on educational TV have approximately the same value today as reading a novel half a century ago. But that just defers the problem; we have to ask further: what do the viewers of films by Fellini or Wenders do with their bodies? In any case, they do not normally take boxing lessons and also they only occasionally watch a soccer game. As "authentic" subjective experiences of the body, today's intellectuals stick to those body experiences that "go the limit," or more exactly, to those limits where the experiencing of the body turns into an "expansion of consciousness." Perhaps this obsession with "experiencing limits" is an indication of how difficult (impossible) it has become for them to be in their bodies at all.

Notes

1. The Consequences of an Aesthetics of Reception: A Deferred Overature

For many of the considerations in this chapter I am indebted to innumerable discussions with Karl-heinz Stierle before and after the Congress of the German Romance Philology Association at Mann-heim (1975), but also to the criticisms of the students in my graduate seminar at Bochum in the summer semester of 1975.

1. *Poetica* 7 (1975), pp. 325–44, here p. 327.

2. *The Structure of Scientific Revolutions* (Chicago, 1962). Kuhn did not expressly order the following three phases as a temporal sequence, and it is quite conceivable that, in individual instances, the development of the critical questions I have designated as phase 1 is only effected by the appearance of an exemplary answer as phase 2. The systematization suggested here is not to be understood as a historicotheoretical attempt to make Kuhn's model more precise, but serves rather as a comparative screen on which to project a systematic discussion about the condition of the interests and methodological reorientation of literary criticism.

3. See Jauss, "Der Leser," pp. 325–27.

4. See Iser, *Der implizite Leser: Kommunikationsformen des Romans von Bunyan bis Beckett* (Munich, 1972), p. 9.

5. For a criticism of Gadamer's distinction between "false" and "true" cognition, which is based on the belief in the classical, see Rainer Warning, "Rezeptionsästhetik als literarturwissenschaftliche Pragmatik," in *Rezeptionsästhetik: Theorie und Praxis* (Munich, 1975), pp. 9–41, here pp. 21f.

6. Stierle, "Was heisst Rezeption bei fiktionalen Texten?" *Poetica* 7 (1975), pp. 345–87, especially pp. 361ff., where the development of a normative model for the reception of fictional texts is postulated—i.e., the development of forms of reception adequate to the "specific status of fiction," as well as pp. 371ff. for the criticism of the concept of the "implicit reader."

7. In his lecture, "Formen des Lesens" (held at the Congress of the German Romance Philology Association, 1975, in Mannheim), p. 6, Karl Maurer pointed out that the reconstruction of the "im-

plicit reader" at its present stage of development "principally has the same difficulties as the older style of interpretation—even if Iser tries to set up an essential differentiation between subjectively actualizing interpretation and the objective proof of the possibilities of meaning built into the 'structure of the work.' "

8. See Thomas Luckmann, "Aspekte einer Theorie der Sozialkommunikation," in *Lexikon der germanistischen Linguistik*, ed. H. P. Althaus, H. Henne, and H. E. Wiegand (Tübingen, 1973), pp. 1-13, here p. 4. The sociology of communication (grounded in a theory of action), a subdiscipline of which literary criticism will be considered from here on, must be clearly distinguished from every information-theoretical model of communication, whose physicalistic terminologies do not take into account the phenomenon of human communicative actions. Cf. the thoroughgoing criticism by Franz Koppe in his review of Umberto Eco's *Einführung in die Semiotik* (1972), *Poetica* 6 (1974), pp. 110-17.

9. Niklas Luhmann in *Historisches Wörterbuch der Philosophie*, vol. 2, ed. J. Ritter (Basel, 1972), col. 1142f., "Funktion IV," here col. 1142.

10. For the concept of meaning that is assumed here, see Luckmann, "Aspekte einer Theorie der Sozialkommunikation": "Meaning is first constituted when the ego later turns to its experiences and puts them in a context that transcends the mere actuality of the original experience" (p. 6).

11. Alfred Schütz, *Der sinnhafte Aufbau der sozialen Welt: Eine Einleitung in die verstehende Soziologie* (Vienna, 1960), p. 59.

12. Ibid., p. 58.

13. Max Weber, *Wirtschaft und Gesellschaft* (Tübingen, 1956), p. 1, quoted from *Historisches Wörterbuch der Philosophie*, vol. 3, ed. J. Ritter, (Basel, 1974), col. 994-96, here col. 994.

14. "The sense of social action includes not only the directly experienced social environment but also the social milieu, historical world, and future world, which are accessible only through ideal constructions" (ibid.).

15. See Schütz, *Der sinnhafte Aufbau*, pp. 150f.

16. This follows the interpretation of Schütz by Stierle, "Text und Kontext" (ms) (Bochum, 1974), pp. 39f.

17. See ibid.: "Understanding an unfamiliar action means . . . comprehending the complete action as a sign of a project through which it first becomes possible to talk about completed action at all" (p. 40).

18. See Schütz, *Der sinnhafte Aufbau:* "If I ask about the 'because motive,' then I have presented the subjective meaning context of the 'in-order-to motive' as an already constituted objective being and from it I ask about the constitution of the lower strata on which this meaning context is based" (p. 147). For a narrower determination of the term "Um-zu-motiv," see Schütz, ibid., p. 146.

19. See Hans Robert Jauss, "Literaturgeschichte als Provokation der Literaturwissenschaft," in *Literaturgeschichte als Provokation* (Frankfurt, 1970), pp. 144-207, here pp. 162 and 199ff. On methods for investigating the "social function of literature" see Hans Ulrich Gumbrecht, "Soziologie und Rezeptionsästhetik: Der Gegenstand und Chancen interdisziplinärer Zusammenarbeit," in *Neue Ansichten einer künftigen Germanistik*, ed. Jürgen Kolbe (Munich, 1973), pp. 48-74. The continuation here is intended as a further development and partial correction of this essay.

20. Jauss, "Der Leser als Instanz einer neuen Geschichte der Literatur," pp. 334f.

21. D. Richter, "Geschichte und Dialektik in der materialistischen Literaturtheorie" in *Alternative* 82 (Jan. 1972), pp. 2-14, here p. 3.

22. Robert Weimann, "Gegenwart und Vergangenheit in der materialistischen Literaturtheorie," in *Methoden der deutschen Literaturwissenschaft*, ed. Victor Zmegác (Frankfurt, 1974) pp. 291-323, here p. 322.

23. For instance, Jan Mukařovský, "Ästhetische Funktion, Norm, und ästhetischer Wert als soziale Fakten," in *Kapitel aus der Ästhetik* (Frankfurt, 1970), pp. 7-112; Hans Robert Jauss, *Kleine Apologie der ästhetischen Erfahrung* (Constance, 1972); Franz Koppe, "Thesen zu einer Literatur-

wissenschaft in handlungsorientiernder Absicht," in *Zum normativen Fundament der Wissenschaft*, ed. Friedrich Kambartel and Jürgen Mittelstrass (Frankfurt, 1973), pp. 318-30; Wolfgang Iser, "Vorwort" to *Der implizite Leser*, pp. 7-12.

24. Schütz, *Der Sinnhafte Aufbau*, p. 193; for this problem see in particular the important chapter, "Das Verstehen der Vorwelt und das Problem der Geschichte," pp. 236-46.

25. See Pierre Macherey, *Pour une théorie de la production littéraire* (1966; rpt. Paris, 1970), especially pp. 159-80, "L'analyse littéraire, tombeau des structures," here, e.g.: "Cette condition sans laquelle l'oeuvre ne pourrait exister, et qu'il est pourtant impossible de trouver en elle tant elle la précède radicalement" (p. 174).

26. I understand Stierle's essay as an example of such a theory, which, in order to describe "the possibility of the relatively stable structures of reception establishing the work itself, . . . is bound to the identity of the work in the process of its reception" (p. 346); here especially, "acts of reception" will be analyzed with respect to the superimposed interest of orienting action by the communicative partner (in pragmatic texts) or to the specific epistemological opportunities opened up by fictional texts.

27. Paul Valéry, *Eupalinos ou L'Architect*, in *Oeuvres* (Bibliothèque de la Pléiade), vol. 2 (Paris, 1960), p. 118.

28. For this see my review of Bernhard Badura and Klaus Gloy, eds., *Soziologie der Kommunikation* (Stuttgart, 1974), in *Poetica* 6 (1974), pp. 103-10, here pp. 106f.

29. One of the "kinds of literary reception that is not keyed to the work" that Jauss has thematicized (*Poetica* 7 [1975], pp. 340ff.) also shows up in those cases where readers establish hypotheses about the author's project developed during the reading of one text as a prerequisite for the reception of other texts by the same author. Of course this sort of information about the author, as the cases of Böll and Grass show, can also influence the reception that is available to the public outside of literary texts. My hypothesis about the primarily author-related character of reception should also not be misunderstood as a variant of the concept of necessarily text-oriented reception, which Jauss has criticized.

30. For instances of this medieval variant of the aesthetics of reception, see Christoph Cormeau, *Wigalois und Diu Crône, Zwei Kapitel zur Gattungsgeschichte des nachklassischen Aventiure-romans* (Munich, 1976); and my "Literary Translation and Its Social Conditioning in the Middle Ages: Four Spanish Romance Texts of the Thirteenth Century," *Yale French Studies* 51 (1974), pp. 205-22.

31. Jauss, "Der Leser," pp. 339f.

32. Jauss, "Literaturgeschichte als Provokation der Literaturwissenschaft," p. 119.

33. Schütz, *Das Problem der Relevanz* (Frankfurt, 1971), p. 100.

34. For the difference between the forms of reception related to pragmatic and fictional texts, see Stierle, *Poetica* 7 (1975), especially sections 2 and 3. A criticism of the Marxist theory of the autonomy of art is in my review of Peter Bürger's *Theorie der Avantgarde* (1975), *Poetica* 7 (1975), pp. 223-33, especially pp. 227-30.

35. The criticisms of the proposal I presented at the Romance Philology Congress in Mannheim have led me to stress, first of all, that I do not want to deny the possibility that literary reception influences the action of the recipients but feel it is fitting to point out the difficulties of critically describing such effects, and second, that the example of *Love Story* does not implicitly recommend limiting research on the sociology of reception to the effects of trivial literary texts.

36. Cf. Max Weber, "Soziologische Grundbegriffe," in *Gesammelte Aufsätze zur Wissenschaftslehre*, ed. J. Winckelmann (Tübingen, 1968): "When confronted with given situations, human beings in action are quite often exposed to contradictory, combative impulses that we 'understand' collectively. But the magnitude to which the various relationships of meaning, caught up in a 'battle of motives' and immediately comprehensible among themselves, are accustomed to express themselves in action is shown by experience to be utterly regular but not certain; in very many cases they cannot even be approximately evaluated" (pp. 548f.).

37. In this sense, Friedrich Engels pointed out in a letter to Joseph Blöch on September 21-22, 1890, that the theory of the priority of the base over the superstructure can also be established as a

heuristic necessity. He acknowledges an active role of the superstructure in the historical process, which he, however, considers as "so impossible to demonstrate that we can neglect it as nonexistent" (*Marx-Engels Werke*, vol. 37, p. 463).

38. My warning against exaggerated optimism about research on the history of reception is naturally valid only when the "historicoformative function of literature" is understood as a modification or stabilization of social structures through literary reception across the communicative strata of individual and collective changes in motivation and action. In another, quite concrete sense (surely not implied by Jauss), literature has a "historically formulative" effect in those cases where fictional interactive models serve as a means of organization, of (mostly polemical) interpretation, and of generally understandable quoting of recurrent phenomena in (political) reality. Helmut Kessler, in *Terreur: Ideologie und Nomenklatur der revolutionären Gewaltanwendung in Frankreich von 1770 bis 1794* (Munich, 1973), pp. 85f., has shown that, for instance, with Robespierre's representation of the "people" as "vertu persécutée" (which was frozen into a lexeme by Jacobin rhetoric) there was a demonstrable "transfer of a literary model," (i.e., Richardson's Clarissa Harlowe) "to the field of politics." An approximate analogy could be seen in the relationship between the literary model and Mohammed Ali's put-down of his opponent, Joe Frazier, as an "Uncle Tom."

2. Metahistorical Historiography?

1. See A. Schütz, *Der sinnhafte Aufbau der sozialen Welt: Eine Einleitung in die verstehende Soziologie* (Vienna, 1932); and *On Phenomenology and Social Relations* (Chicago, 1970); with T. Luckmann, *Strukturen der Lebenswelt* (Neuwied, 1975); for the no longer surveyable literature on Schütz, see W. M. Sprondel and R. Grathoff, eds., *Alfred Schütz und die Idee des Alltags in den Sozialwissenschaften* (Stuttgart, 1979).

2. [It is difficult to know what to do with the useful distinction between *erleben* and *erfahren* (and all of their derivatives) in English. We (the author and the translator) decided on "experience" and "practical experience," respectively, which seem to come closest to the commonly used contents of the two expressions in everyday German. – Trans.]

3. [See note 21 in "The Role of Narration in Narrative Genres." – Trans.]

4. [Sometimes "presentification" is used to translate *Vergegenwärtigung*, but it is by no means an attractive solution. – Trans.]

5. For more detail on this theoretical problem, see Hans Ulrich Gumbrecht, "Erzählen in der Literatur/Erzählen im Alltag," in *Erzählen im Alltag*, ed. K. Ehlich (Frankfurt, 1980), pp. 403-19; and "Über den Ort der Narration in narrativen Gattungen," in *Erzählforschung*, ed. E. Lämmert (Stuttgart, 1982), pp. 202-17. See chapter 3, this volume.

3. The Role of Narration in Narrative Genres

1. See Eberhard Lämmert, *Bauformen des Erzählens* (Stuttgart, 1967), p. 17.

2. See Wolf-Dieter Stempel, "Gibt es Textsorten?" In *Textsorten*, ed. Elisabeth Gülich and Wolfgang Raible (Frankfurt, 1972), pp. 175-79.

3. See Eugenio Coseriu, "Sprache, Norm, und Rede" in his *Sprachtheorie und allgemeine Sprachwissenschaft* (Munich, 1975), pp. 11-101.

4. See Gérard Genette, "Genres, 'types,' modes," in *Poétique* 32 (1977), pp. 389-421, here p. 420.

5. Rainer Warning, "Pour une pragmatique du discours fictionnel," *Poétique* 39 (1979), pp. 321-37, here p. 325.

6. For the theory of genre's interest in the sociological concept of the institution, see Wilhelm Vosskamp, "Gattungen als literarisch-soziale Institutionen," in *Textsortenlehre – Gattungsgeschichte*, ed. Walter Hinck (Heidelberg, 1977), pp. 27ff.; the third paragraph of Warning's article quoted in n. 5, this chapter; Hans Ulrich Gumbrecht, "Faszinationstyp Hagiographie: Ein historisches Experi-

ment zur Gattungstheorie," in *Deutsche Literatur im Mittelalter—Kontakte und Perspektiven*, ed. Christoph Cormeau (Stuttgart, 1979), pp. 39–84; and the informative study "Soziologische Fundierung literarischer Kategorien (I)—Diskursformen, Genres, und Genre-Systeme," in Jürgen Link and Ulla Link-Heer, *Literatursoziologisches Propädeutikum* (Munich, 1980), pp. 377–415.

7. Peter L. Berger and Thomas Luckmann, *Die gesellschaftliche Konstruktion der Wirklichkeit: Eine Theorie der Wissenssoziologie* (Frankfurt, 1971), p. 88.

8. Algirdas Julien Greimas and Joseph Courthès, *Sémiotique—dictionnaire raisonné de la théorie du langage* (Paris, 1979), pp. 250f. (*Narrativité*).

9. Karlheinz Stierle, "Die Struktur narrativer Texte: Am Beispiel von J. P. Hebels Kalendergeschichte 'Unverhofftes Wiedersehen,' " in *Funk-Kolleg Literatur I*, ed. Helmut Brackert and Eberhard Lämmert (Frankfurt, 1977), pp. 210–33, here p. 217.

10. Lämmert, *Bauformen*, p. 21.

11. Genette, "Genres," p. 420.

12. Luckmann, "Philosophie, Sozialwissenschaft, und Alltagsleben," in *Soziale Welt* 24 (1973), pp. 137–68, here p. 164.

13. Schütz and Luckmann, eds., *Strukturen der Lebenswelt* (Neuwied, 1975), pp. 44–46.

14. For the distinction between polythetic and monothetic reproduction of past experiences, see Alfred Schütz, *Der sinnhafte Aufbau der sozialen Welt* (Vienna, 1960), pp. 68f. See also Husserl, *Zur Phänomenologie des inneren Zeitbewusstseins*: "By moving back into the past, the temporal object contracts" (p. 26).

15. See Schütz and Luckmann, *Strukturen*, pp. 44–46.

16. Most recently in "Les temps et les personnes," *Poétique* 39 (1979), pp. 338–52, here p. 340: "Si les temps verbaux du monde commenté sont pour l'auditeur/lecteur des signaux d'attention et d'alerte, ceux du monde raconté sont pour lui des signaux de repos et de la fin d'alerte."

17. See the chapter, "Aktive und passive Genese," in Edmund Husserl, *Cartesianische Meditationen und Pariser Vorträge* (The Hague, 1973), pp. 111–13.

18. Karl Bühler, *Sprachtheorie* (Stuttgart, 1965), p. 28.

19. Wolfgang Iser, *Der Akt des Lesens: Theorie ästhetischer Wirkung* (Munich, 1976).

20. See Hans Ulrich Gumbrecht, "Faszinationstyp Hagiographie" (see n. 6), and "'Narrating the Past Just as if It Were Your Own Time': An Essay on the Anthropology of Historiography," chapter 4 in this volume.

21. The term "fascination" is taken over from various works by the medievalist Hugo Kuhn (more bibliographical details are available in my essay "Faszinationstyp Hagiographie"), who, however, uses it to designate a concept of norms of communication that can be located merely on a historical level. As a recurrent attention that the experiencing subject does not reflect, "fascination" should be set off from "interest."

22. A particularly impressive example of biographies drawn from the American worlds of the media, the underground, and the intellect was pointed out to me by Jann Matlock: Katinka Matson, *Short Lives: Portraits in Creativity and Self-Destruction* (New York, 1980).

23. Wolf-Dieter Stempel, "Aspects génériques de la réception," in *Poétique* 39 (1979), pp. 353–62, here pp. 359f.

24. Genette, "Genres," p. 421, n. 78.

25. Friederike Hassauer-Roos, "Die Philosophie der Tiere: Von der theoretischen zur praktischen Vernunft; Untersuchungen zu Funktions- und Strukturwandel in der Fabel der französischen Aufklärung" (dissertation, Bochum University, 1980); Marion Wedegärtner, "Staatspolitische Programmschriften und die utopischen Romane in der französischen Literatur des XVIII. Jahrhunderts: Studien zu ihrer funktionsgeschichtlichen Komplementarität" (Master's thesis, Bochum University, 1980).

26. Hassauer-Roos, "Die Philosophie der Tiere," p. 344.

27. Wedegärtner, "Staatspolitische Programmschriften," p. 47.

28. Moutonnet de Clairfons, *Les isles fortunées ou les aventures de Barthylle et de Cléobule* (Paris, 1778), pp. viif. (Quoted from Wedegärtner, pp. 70f.)

4. "Narrating the Past Just as if It Were Your Own Time": An Essay on the Anthropology of Historiography

1. The title of this chapter is quoted from the prologue to the *Primera crónica general de España* (which Alfonso the Wise commissioned and which was continued under Sancho IV in 1289); ed. Ramón Menéndez Pidal (Madrid, 1955), p. 3. The complete passage reads as follows: "And by looking for this [an instrument for the preservation and transmission of their experiences], they invented the forms of letters; and by putting them together, they made syllables, and out of the combinations of syllables, they made parts of sentences (*partes*) and by combining sentence parts in the same way, they created meaning (*razon*) and to the purpose that they would understand knowledge and make it useful and to be able to narrate what had been in times past as if it were in their own world."

2. See Hugo Kuhn, "Versuch über das fünfzehnte Jahrhundert in der deutschen Literatur," in *Literatur in der Gesellschaft des Spätmittelalters*, ed. Hans Ulrich Gumbrecht (Heidelberg, 1981). For the category "fascination type" see Hans Ulrich Gumbrecht, "Faszinationstyp Hagiographie: Ein historisches Experiment zur Gattungstheorie," in *Deutsche Literatur im Mittelalter: Kontakte und Perspektiven*, ed. C. Cormeau (Stuttgart, 1979); Hans Ulrich Gumbrecht, J. Rüsen, and J. J. Duggan, "Préliminaires théoriques, analytiques et hermeneutiques," in *Grundriss der romanischen Literaturen des Mittelalters*, vol. 11, ed. Gumbrecht, U. Link-Heer, P. M. Spangenberg (Heidelberg, 1982).

3. See E. Le Roy Ladurie, *Histoire du climat depuis l'an mille* (Paris, 1967). On the jacket it is stated: "Pour l'auteur, l'histoire climatique doit d'abord être définie comme une recherche autonome par son objet. . . . C'est seulement si l'on respecte cette autonomie initiale que l'on peut déterminer s'il y a eu un lien réel entre telle fluctuation du climat et telle épisode de l'histoire des homme." The indication that in a second phase of the investigation will the perspective of climate as the condition of human action be taken up makes it clear that it is assumed that the primary interest for the reader of historiographic texts is past *actions*.

4. See Alfred Schütz's explication of the concept *reine Vorwelt* in *Der sinnhafte Aufbau der sozialen Welt*, 2nd ed. (Vienna, 1960), p. 238.

5. For the determination of the concepts, *Faktenobjektivität (Begründungsobjektivität)* and *Konsensobjektivität*, see Lübbe, *Geschichtsbegriff und Geschichtsinteresse* (Basel, 1977), pp. 18ff.

6. For the differentiation between a *konzeptuelle Tiefenschicht*, which in discussions of fictional texts is also often predicated on reality, and the semantic textual surface, see Hans Ulrich Gumbrecht, "Wirklichkeit als Fiktion/Sprachspiele als Antifiktion," in *Funktionen des Fiktiven*, ed. D. Henrich and W. Iser (Munich, 1982).

7. For the concept of Neohistoricism see J. Rüsen's review of Lübbe's *Geschichtsbegriff und Geschichtsinteresse*, "Zur Kritik des Neohistorismus" in *Zeitschrift für philosophische Forschung*, 33 (1979).

8. See K. Stierle, "Erfahrung und narrative Form: Bemerkungen zu ihrem Zusammenhang in Fiktion und Historiographie," in *Theorie und Erzählung in der Geschichte*, ed. J. Kocka and F. Nipperdey (Munich, 1979).

9. I. Srubar's determination of the *sinnhafte Erlebniss*, which he develops according to Schütz's pertinent analyses, can be related to processes as well as to longer-lasting constant structures: "A meaningful experience is . . . one that can be lifted out of the continuous flow of experiences with clear contours and can be reflexively grasped in its unity"; "Die Theorie der Typenbildung bei Alfred Schütz: Ihre Bedeutung und ihre Grenzen," in *Alfred Schütz und die Idee des Alltags in den Sozialwissenschaften*, ed. W. M. Sprondel and R. Grathoff (Stuttgart, 1979), p. 49.

10. A. C. Danto, *Analytische Philosophie der Geschichte* (Frankfurt, 1974), p. 232.

11. See J. Rüsen, "Geschichte und Norm: Wahrheitskriterien der historischen Erkenntnis," in *Normen und Geschichte*, ed. W. Oelmüller (Paderborn, 1979), p. 117.

12. Along with chapters 558 and 559 of the edition of the *Crónica general* cited in note 1 of this chapter, the following texts have been drawn on for my analysis: *Das altfranzösische Rolandslied nach der Oxforder Handschrift*, 6th ed., ed. A. Hilka and G. Rohlfs (Tübingen, 1965); the chapter "Prise de la Bastille, 14 juillet 1789," in J. Michelet's *Histoire de la Révolution Française*, vol. 1 of the Paris edition from 1869, pp. 56–70; W. Dettelbacher, *Würzburg: Die Jahre nach 1945* (Würzburg, 1974); E. Le Roy Ladurie, *Montaillou, village occitan de 1294 à 1324* (Paris, 1975).

13. What is meant is the "world in potential extension"; for this concept see A. Schütz and T. Luckmann, *Strukturen der Lebenswelt* (Neuwied, 1975), pp. 55ff.

14. Dettelbacher, *Würzburg*, p. 115.

15. Dettelbacher states in his epilogue: "Twenty years after the catastrophe of March 16, 1945, visitors found barely a trace of destruction left. The younger people, born during the war and postwar period, only knew Würzburg as growing. Older folks forgot the hardship and want of the beginning years, found Würzburg cleaner and more comfortable than before" (p. 123)

16. For the distinction between "polythetic" and "monothetic" reproduction of past experiences see Schütz, *Der sinnhafte Aufbau*, p. 236, and Schütz and Luckmann, *Strukturen der Lebenswelt*, pp. 68f.

17. Following the usage of W. Iser, *Der Akt des Lesens* (Munich, 1976), pp. 143ff., the termin "textual strategy" is used to designate those speech acts (and their textual concretizations) through which individual elements of the evoked recipient's knowledge are integrated into complex configurations of meaning.

18. N. Luhmann, "Sinn als Grundbegriff der Soziologie" in *Theorie der Gesellschaft oder Sozialtechnologie*, ed. J. Habermas and N. Luhmann (Frankfurt, 1971), p. 58.

19. M. Halbwachs, *La mémoire collective*, 2nd ed. (Paris, 1968), p. 68.

20. H. White, *Metahistory* (Baltimore, 1973), in particular the section in the introduction dedicated to tropes, pp. 31ff.; for the concept of the "historical field," see pp. 5ff.

21. First used in February 1977 in preparation for a graduate seminar that we gave together in the summer semester of 1977. See for now Luckmann, "Lebensweltliche Zeitkategorien, Zeitstrukturen des Alltags, und der Ort des historischen Bewusstseins," in *Der Diskurs der Literatur- und Sprachhistorie*, ed. B. Cerquiglini and Hans Ulrich Gumbrecht (Frankfurt, 1982).

22. M. Kossok, "Für Walter Markov," in W. Markov, *Kognak und Königsmöder: Historischliterarische Miniaturen* (Berlin, [DDR],1979), p. 5.

23. Edmund Husserl, *Vorlesungen zur Phänomenologie des inneren Zeitbewusstseins* (Halle, 1928), quoted from Schütz and Luckmann, *Strukturen der Lebenswelt*, p. 67.

24. For the difference between, on the one hand, "routinemässiger Deckung zwischen Thema und Wissenselementen" and, on the other, "Problemauslegung," see Schütz and Luckmann, *Strukturen der Lebenswelt*, pp. 200ff.

25. In this regard, see Stierle, "Erfahrung und narrative Form," pp. 85ff., who ties onto Benjamin's essay "Der Erzähler: Betrachtungen zum Werk Nicolai Lesskows."

26. For the concept *Weltzeit* see Schütz and Luckmann, *Strukturen der Lebenswelt*, pp. 61ff.

27. For the experience of the social preworld as the prerequisite for the impression of the irreversible character of world time, see Schütz and Luckmann, *Strukturen der Lebenswelt*, p. 65.

28. Le Roy Ladurie, *Montaillou*, p. 467, n. 2.

29. See in particular the chapter "Outillage mental: Le temps et l'espace," in Montaillou, ibid., pp. 419ff.

30. R. Koselleck in his foreword to *Vergangene Zukunft: Zur Semantik geschichtlicher Zeiten* (Frankfurt, 1979), p. 11.

31. M. Fuhrmann in a discussion of Koselleck's presentation "Terror und Traum: Methodologische Anmerkungen zu Zeiterfahrungen im Dritten Reich," at the tenth colloquium of the

research group "Poetik und Hermeneutik" (September 1979); Koselleck's essay is published in *Vergangene Zukunft*.

32. See G. Devereux, "Zeit–Geschichte versus Chronik: Sozialisation als kulturelles Vor-Erleben," in Devereux, *Ethnopsychoanalyse* (Frankfurt, 1978), especially p. 283.

5. A History of the Concept "Modern"

1. Hans Robert Jauss, "Literarische Tradition und gegenwärtiges Bewusstsein der Modernität" (1965), in *Literaturgeschichte als Provokation*, 5th ed. (Frankfurt, 1974), pp. 11ff.; Jauss, "Antiqui/moderni (*Querelle des Anciens et des Modernes*)," *Historisches Wörterbuch der Philosophie* 1 (1971), pp. 410ff.; Fritz Martini, "Modern, die Moderne," in *Reallexikon der deutschen Literaturgeschichte*, founded by Paul Merker and Wolfgang Stammler, 2nd ed., ed. Werner Kohlschmidt and Wolfgang Mohr, vol. 2 (Berlin, 1958), pp. 391ff.; Jost Schneider, "Ein Beitrag zu dem Problem der Modernität," *Der Deutschunterricht* 23 (1971), pp. 58ff.; Marie Dominique Chenu, "Antiqui, moderni," in *Revue des sciences philosophiques et théologiques* 17 (1928), pp. 82ff.; Ernst Robert Curtius, *Europäisches Literatur und lateinisches Mittelalter*, 6th ed. (Bern, Munich, 1967), pp. 257ff.; Walter Freund, *Modernus und andere Zeitbegriffe des Mittelalters* (Cologne, Graz, 1957); Elisabeth Gössmann, *Antiqui und Moderni im Mittelalter: Eine geschichtliche Standortbestimmung* (Paderborn, 1974); Johannes Spörl, "Das Alte und das Neue im Mittelalter," *Historisches Jahrbuch* 50 (1930), pp. 297ff., 498ff.; Jochen Schlobach, *Zyklentheorie und Periodenmetaphorik: Studien zur bildlichen Sprache der Geschichtsreflexion in Frankreich von der Renaissance bis zur Frühaufklärung* (Munich, 1976); Siegrun Bielfeldt, *Die čechische Moderne im Frühwerk Saldas: Zur synchronen Darstellung einer Periodenschwelle* (Munich, 1975). For the period dealt with in the third section, the following treatises are relevant for conceptual history: H. R. Jauss, "Schlegels und Schillers Replik auf die 'Querelle des Anciens et des Modernes,' " in his *Literaturgeschichte als Provokation*, pp. 67ff.; for the fourth section, see his "Das Ende der Kunstperiode: Aspekte der literarischen Revolution bei Heine, Hugo, und Stendhal," ibid., pp. 107ff.; for the fifth section, see *Die literarische Moderne: Dokumente zum Selbstverständnis der Literatur um die Jahrhundertwende*, ed. Gotthart Wunberg (Frankfurt, 1971).

2. For their encouragement and assistance in the study of sources, I would like to thank the participants in my seminars "Einführung in die begriffsgeschichtliche Methode" and "Literarische Avantgarden zwischen 1880 und 1920" at the University of Constance in the summer semesters of 1973 and 1974.

3. The history and present status of the discussion about a method for conceptual history are summarized by Helmut G. Meier, "Begriffsgeschichte," *Historisches Wörterbuch der Philosophie* 1 (1971), pp. 788ff.; see the same source, p. 789, "Eine Theorie der Begriffsgeschichte ist zur Zeit noch Desiderat."

4. Hans Ulrich Gumbrecht, "Für eine phänomenologische Fundierung der sozial historischen Begriffsgeschichte," in *Historische Semantik und Begriffsgeschichte*, ed. Reinhart Koselleck (Stuttgart, 1978), pp. 75–101. The ideas developed there go back to my lecture to the Habilitation Colloquium in Constance, July 1974, and to contributions to the colloquia on historical semantics at Bielefeld in the spring of 1975 and 1976.

5. See, e.g., Hermann Lübbe, "Zur Theorie der Begriffsgeschichte," in *Säkularisierung: Geschichte eines ideen-politischen Begriffs* (Freiburg, Munich, 1965), pp. 9ff., especially p. 14.

6. Eugenio Coseriu, "Sistema, norma y habla" (1952), in *Teoría de lenguaje y lingüística general* (Madrid, 1962), pp. 11ff., and *Sincronía, diacronía, e historia* (Montevideo, 1958).

7. After Hansfried Kellner, "On the Cognitive Significance of the System of a Language in Communication" (Darmstadt, 1974; MS).

8. Ludwig Wittgenstein, *Philosophische Untersuchungen*, especially sections 19ff. (Frankfurt, 1967), pp. 20ff.

9. Systematic considerations on the possible meanings of "modern" have also been made by Franz Overbeck in *Christentum und Kultur: Gedanken und Anmerkungen zur modernen Theologie*, ed. Carl Albrecht Bernoulli (1919; rpt. Darmstadt, 1963), pp. 243ff.

10. See Johann Christoph Nehring, *Historisch-politisch-juristisches Lexikon*, 10th ed. (1756), pp. 344f., entry "Modern, modernus."

11. See the entry "Epoche" (by Manfred Riedel), in *Historisches Wörterbuch der Philosophie* 2 (1972), pp. 596ff.

12. My description of the third meaning of "modern" profits from Jauss's interpretation of Baudelaire, in "Literarische Tradition," pp. 53ff.

13. Gelasius, *Epistolae*, 20 and 22, in *Epistolae Romanorum pontificum genuinae*, Andreas Thiel (Brunsberg, 1868), pp. 386 and 389.

14. Cassiodorus, "Letter to Symmachus," *Monumenta Germaniae AA*, vol. 12 (1894), p. 138.

15. Quoted from Freund, *Modernus*, pp. 67, 83.

16. For the twelfth-century Renaissance in the vernacular, see Jauss, "Literarische Tradition," pp. 21ff.

17. Walter Map, *De nugis curialium*, 4, 5, ed. Montague Rhodes James (Oxford, 1914).

18. See the quotations in Hans Schulz, *Deutsches Fremdwörterbuch*, vol. 2, fortgeführt von Otto Basler (Berlin, 1942), pp. 134f.

19. Francesco Petrarca, "Epistolae de rebus familiaribus 3, 30," *Le Familiari*, ed. Vittorio Rossi, vol. 4 (Florence, 1942), p. 29.

20. Giovanni Boccaccio, *Trattatello in laude di Dante* (1357-59), in *Opere*, ed. Vittore Branca, vol. 3 (Verona), 1974), p. 442.

21. Marsilio Ficino, *Opera* (Basel, 1561), p. 778.

22. Nathan Edelmann, "The Early Uses of 'Medium Aevum,' 'Middle Ages,' " in *Romanic Review* 29 (1938), pp. 4ff.; see also Adalbert Klempt, *Die Säkularisierung der universalhistorischen Auffassung* (Göttingen, 1960).

23. Du Bellay, *La deffence et illustration de la langue françoyse*, I, 3 (Paris, 1549), ed. Louis Humbert (Paris, n.d.), p. 48.

24. Estienne (1549), p. 388.

25. See Jauss, "Schlegels und Schillers Replik," pp. 71ff.

26. *Parallèle des Anciens et des Modernes en ce qui regarde les arts et les sciences*, rpt. ed. H. R. Jauss (Munich, 1964). My interpretation draws on the editor's introduction, "Ästhetische Normen und geschichtliche Reflexion in der 'Querelle des Anciens et des Modernes,' " pp. 8ff.

27. *Parallèle*, p. 49 (p. 113 of the reprint).

28. Jean de La Bruyère, "Discours sur Théophraste," introduction to his *Les caractères, ou les moeurs de ce siècle, Oeuvres complètes*, nouvelle edition Julien Benda (Paris, 1951), p. 11.

29. François de Fénelon, quoted in Jauss, "Literarische Tradition," p. 41.

30. Louis Antoine de Bougainville, Avertissement to *Jean Baptiste de la Curne de Saint-Palaye: Memoires sur l'ancienne chevalerie considérée comme un etablissement politique et militaire*, 2nd ed. (Paris, 1759), p. ix.

31. Voltaire, *Dictionnaire philosophique, Oeuvres complètes*, vol. 17 (Paris, 1878), pp. 228, 240.

32. *Encyclopédie*, vol. 10 (1765), p. 601.

33. Montesquieu, "Essai sur le goût" (1765), in *Mes pensées, Oeuvres complètes*, vol. 1 (1949), pp. 1016ff., esp. 1020.

34. Jean Jacques Rousseau, *Du contrat social* 3, 15, in *Oeuvres complètes*, vol. 3. (Paris, 1964), p. 430.

35. See Hans Ulrich Gumbrecht, *Funktionen politischer Rhetorik in der französischen Revolution* (Munich, 1978).

36. Antoine Saint-Just, speech on November 13, 1792, *Archives parlementaires 1787 à 1860*, 1st ser., vol. 53 (Paris, 1898), p. 390. In the extremely rare examples of "modern" from revolutionary

speeches, the first meaning always appears: for the most part, "modern" designates institutions and roles in the revolutionary politics that, as "today's," were opposed to the paradigms of antiquity also quoted by Saint-Just (and not "ancien régime"). So, for example, Lafayette was called *moderne Catilina* at a discussion of the Jacobin Club on July 25, 1792; *La société des Jacobins*, vol. 4., ed. François-Alphonse Auland (Paris, 1892), p. 142.

37. Gaspar Melchor de Jovellanos, *Obras escogidas*, ed. Angel del Río, vol. 3 (Madrid, 1965), p. 100.

38. "The entire generation abominates the generations that have preceded it. I don't understand it." José Cadalso, *Cartas marruecas* (Madrid, 1935), pp. 55ff., 68.

39. Entry "Modern" (see n. 1), pp. 393ff.

40. *Adelung*, vol. 3 (1777), p. 552; *Sperander* (1728), p. 384.

41. Johann Joachim Winckelmann, *Kunsttheoretische Schriften*, vol. 1 (Baden-Baden, Strasbourg, 1962), p. 3. For Winckelmann's work on the *Querelle*, see Jauss, "Schlegels und Schillers Replik," pp. 80ff.

42. Herder, *Über die neuere deutsche Literatur* (1767), *Sämtliche Werke*, vol. 1 (1877), p. 383.

43. Herder, "Briefe zur Beförderung der Humanität," *Sämtliche Werke*, vol. 18 (1883), p. 6.

44. Schiller, "Über naive und sentimentalische Dichtung," *National-Ausgabe*, vol. 20 (1962), p. 438; *Über das Studium der griechischen Poesie*, ed. Paul Hankamer (Godesberg, 1947), pp. 208, 203, 53, 45; quoted from Jauss, "Schlegels und Schillers Replik," pp. 85, 75, 96, 95, 87, 97.

45. W. von Humboldt, *Ansichten über Ästhetik und Literatur: Seine Briefe an Christian Gottfried Körner*, ed. Fritz Jonas (Berlin, 1880), letter from April 30, 1803.

46. August Wilhelm Schlegel, *Vorlesungen über dramatische Kunst und Literatur*, ed. Giovanni Vittorio Amoretti, vol. 1 (Bonn, Leipzig, 1923), p. 8.

47. For the history of the meanings of "romantic" and its use as a designation of "contemporary art" at the beginning of the nineteenth century, see Jauss, "Literarische Tradition," pp. 44ff.

48. Anne-Louise-Germaine de Staël, *De l'Allemagne 2* (1810), *Oeuvres complètes*, vol. 2 (Paris, 1838), p. 62.

49. *Brockhaus*, 4th ed., vol. 6 (1817), pp. 451f.

50. *Konversations-Lexikon oder encyclopädisches Handwörterbuch für gebildete Stände*, new expanded ed., vol. 4 (Stuttgart 1818), p. 708.

51. *Eberhard/Maass*, 3rd ed., vol. 4 (1827), p. 419; *Heinsius* (1828), p. 185.

52. *Rees*, vol. 23 (1819), entry "Modern."

53. F. Schlegel, *Geschichte der alten und neuen Litteratur*, vol. 2 (Vienna, 1815), p. 130.

54. Hegel, *Vorlesungen über die Ästhetik*, *Sämtliche Werke*, vol. 13 (1928), p. 198.

55. Ibid., vol. 14, p. 416.

56. Goethe, *Klassiker und Romantiker in Italien, sich heftig bekämpfend* (1820), *Weimarer Ausgabe*, vol. 42/1 (1902), p. 137.

57. A. von Arnim, "Owen Tudor" (1821), *Sämtliche Werke*, vol. 2, ed. Wilhelm Grimm (Berlin, 1839), p. 261.

58. Victor Hugo, "Préface d'Hernani," *Théâtre complet*, ed J. J. Thierry and Josette Mélèze, vol. 1 (Paris, 1963), p. 1147.

59. "In Nordamerikas Freistaaten herrscht schon viel Sinn für das Moderne, aber man wendet den Gebrauch des Neuen und Verbesserten mehr auf das Nützliche im Mobiliar als auf dessen Luxus." *Hübner*, 31st ed., vol. 3 (1826), p. 179.

60. Schelling, *Vorlesungen über die Methode des akademischen Studiums, Werke*, vol. 3 (1927; rpt. 1965), p. 330. A collection of descriptions of cities and landscapes from around 1840 by Gustav von Heeringen, *Wanderungen durch Franken* (Leipzig, 1839; rpt. Hildesheim, 1973), shows in many places that a romantic appreciation continued to be applied to subjects the predicate "modern" in the new, pragmatic sense did not fit. For instance, it was admittedly "not possible to call Würzburg a beautiful city in the modern sense, but quite possible to call it a magnificent one. Few of its streets

are broad and long, but lively, noisy, formed by high stone houses, and a quantity of churches with towers, the great number of official buildings, canonical courts, former cloisters, the grandiose palace, the residence with its surrounding grounds—the leftover traces of a long series of rulers, who were at the same time princes of the Empire, endow it with something imposing, noble, and with the stamp of historical greatness" (pp. 115f.).

61. Reinhart Koselleck in Koselleck, L. Bergeron, and F. Furet, *Das Zeitalter der europäischen Revolutionen 1780–1848* (Frankfurt, 1969), p. 296.

62. According to these main interests, the Pre-March period was characterized retrospectively by Julian Schmidt in 1880: "Alles wollte modern und praktisch sein, die Romantik was ein förmliches Scheltwort geworden; von Poesie und Geschichte wollte man nicht viel mehr wissen, Naturwissenschaft und Nationalökonomie war das einzige, was man gelten liess." In "Der russische Nihilismus und Iwan Turgenjew," *Preussische Jahrbücher* 45 (1880), p. 315.

63. Koselleck, Bergeron, and Furet, *Zeitalter*, p. 303.

64. Stendhal, *Souvenirs d'égotisme*, new ed. Henri Martineau (Paris, 1950), 57. The experience of a new type of acceleration of time had already been articulated by Stendhal almost a decade earlier in the first part of the essay "Racine et Shakespeare" (1823): "De mémoire d'historien, jamais peuple n'a éprouvé, dans ses plaisirs, de changement plus rapide et plus total que celui de 1780 à 1823." *Oeuvres complètes,* ed. Henri Martineau (Paris, 1928), p. 50.

65. Stendhal, *Souvenirs*, p. 38.

66. Baudelaire, *Le peintre de la vie moderne* in *Oeuvres complètes*, ed. Yves-Gérard la Dantec and Claude Pichois (Paris, 1961), p. 1163. I follow here the interpretation by Jauss, "Literarische Tradition," pp. 54ff.

67. For "Historisierung der Zeit," see Niklas Luhmann, "Weltzeit und Systemgeschichte: Über Beziehungen zwischen Zeithorizonten und sozialen Strukturen gesellschaftlicher Systeme," in *Soziologie und Sozialgeschichte: Aspekte und Probleme*, ed. Peter Christian Ludz, *Kölner Zeitschrift für Soziologie und Sozialpsychologie*, Sonderheft 16 (1972), p. 91.

68. L. von Stein, *Die Municipalverfassung Frankreichs* (Leipzig, 1843), p. 68. Cf. Reinhart Koselleck, "Geschichtliche Prognose in Lorenz v. Steins Schrift zur preussischen Verfassung," in *Der Staat* 4 (1965), p. 472.

69. Alphonse de Lamartine, *Histoire de la restoration, Oeuvres complétes*, vol. 17 (Paris, 1861), p. 3. To this problem, compare the contemporary Spanish evidence in José F. Montesinos, *Costumbrismo y novela*, 3rd ed. (Madrid, 1972), pp. 44ff.

70. Heinrich Heine, review of Wolfgang Menzel, *Die deutsche Literatur, Sämtliche Schriften*, vol. 1 (1965), p. 455; *Zur Geschichte der Religion und Philosophie in Deutschland*, vol. 3 (1971), p. 636. Selections from the most important programmatic pre-1848 writings in *Der literarische Vormärz*, ed. Wolfgang W. Behrens, Gerhard Bott, et al. (Munich, 1973).

71. Heine, *Französische Maler, Sämtliche Schriften*, vol. 3, p. 72. The argument for this historical localization of his own present shows that Heine regarded the history of politics and art as indivisible: "Present-day art is going to have to perish, because its principles are still rooted in old abandoned regimes, in the past of the Holy Roman Empire—because like all of the withered remains of this past it is in the most pleasant contradiction to the present."

72. See W. Oehmüller, "Hegels Satz vom Ende der Kunst und das Problem der Philosophie der Kunst nach Hegel," *Philosophisches Jahrbuch* 73 (1965), pp. 75ff.

73. See Heine, *Französische Maler*; Hugo, "Préface d'Hernani."

74. Laube, "Moderne Charakteristiken," *Gesammelte Werke*, ed. Heinr. Hubert Houben, vol. 49 (Leipzig, 1909), p. 17.

75. Theodor Mundt, "Zeitperspective 1834," in *Schriften in bunter Reihe, zur Anregung und Unterhaltung*, 1, (Leipzig, 1834; rpt. Frankfurt, 1971), p. 4.

76. Mundt, *Allgemeine Literaturgeschichte*, vol. 3 (Berlin, 1846), p. 452.

77. Heine, "Die romantische Schule," *Sämtliche Schriften*, vol. 3, p. 468.

78. Laube, "Moderne Charakteristiken," pp. 313, 17.

79. "Die Mode und das Moderne," *Werke*, ed. R. Gensel, vol. 11 (Berlin and Leipzig, n.d.), pp. 16, 21, 24.

80. Marx, *Marx-Engels Werke*, vol. 1 (1956), p. 279.

81. Tocqueville, *L'Ancien Régime et la Révolution* 4 (1856), *Oeuvres complètes*, 2nd ed., vol. 2, (1952), p. 94.

82. The sudden increase in the quantity of editions of single lexica during the first half of the nineteenth century permits the conjecture that already in this period they were no longer only mirrors of the language norm, but could themselves have a normative effect. Whereas for the initial edition of *Brockhaus's Konversations-Lexikon* (1809) only 2,000 copies were printed, the eighth edition reached 32,000 copies; Johann Gold-Friedrich, *Geschichte des deutschen Buchhandels*, vol. 4 (Leipzig, 1913), pp. 202f.

83. *Brüggemann*, vol. 5 (1836), pp. 224f.; *Heyse*, 8th ed., vol. 2 (1838), p. 345.

84. *Pierer*, 2nd ed., vol. 19 (1843), p. 369; also the 4th ed., vol. 11 (1860), p. 345.

85. *Manz*, vol. 7 (1848), p. 282.

86. *Brockhaus*, 10th ed., vol. 10 (1853), p. 555.

87. Paul Valéry, "Propros sur le progrès" (1929), *Oeuvres*, ed. Jean Hytier, vol. 2 (Paris, 1960), p. 1022.

88. Bogumil Goltz, "Zur Geschichte des Tages," in *Die Bildung und die Gebildeten: Eine Beleuchtung der modernen Zustände*, vol. 1 (Berlin, 1864), p. 47.

89. Theodor Fontane, "Unsere lyrische und epische Poesie seit 1848" (1853), *Sämtliche Werke*, ed. Edgar Gross, Kurt Schreinert, et al., vol. 21/1 (Munich, 1963), p. 9.

90. Letter from April 1, 1852; in Kurt Gehard Fischer, "Noch einmal: Adalbert Stifter und Johann Rint," *Vierteljahrschrift der Adalbert-Stifter-Instituts des Landes Oberösterreich* 9 (1960), p. 29.

91. Reichensperger, 3rd ed. (1872), pp. 94f.

92. Richard Wagner, "Modern," *Gesammelte Schriften und Dichtungen*, vol. 10 (Leipzig, 1883), pp. 78, 80.

93. Wilhelm Scherer, *Geschichte der deutschen Literatur*, 5th ed. (Berlin, 1889), pp. 19f. For the historical models for German studies in Germany (above all, in the nineteenth century), see Hans Ulrich Gumbrecht, "Mittelhochdeutsche Klassik: Über falsche und berechtigte Aktualität mittelalterlicher Literatur," *Zeitschrift für Literaturwissenschaft und Linguistik* 3 (1973), book 11, pp. 97ff.

94. Nietzsche, *Die Geburt der Tragödie oder Griechentum und Pessimismus* (1872), *Werke*, vol. 1 (1954), p. 16.

95. Nietzsche, *Die fröhliche Wissenschaft* (1881–82), *Werke*, vol. 2 (1955): "But it was first of all the French Revolution that solemnly and ceremoniously pressed the scepter into the hands of 'the good man' (the sheep, the donkey, the goose, and everything that is hopelessly shallow . . . and ripe for the madhouse of 'modern ideas')" (p. 216).

96. Nietzsche, *Jenseits von Gut und Böse* (1888), *Werke*, p. 1141. Cf. the preceding sentence: "This book is . . . in all essentials, a criticism of modernity . . . as well as pointing out an opposite type, who is as little modern as possible, an affirmative type."

97. Nietzsche, *Von Nutzen und Nachteil der Historie für das Leben* (1874), *Werke*, vol. 1, p. 267.

98. Nietzsche, *Jenseits von Gut und Böse*, *Werke*, vol. 2, p. 708.

99. Wagener, *Lexikon*, vol. 13 (1863), p. 497.

100. *Meyer*, 4th ed., vol. 11 (1888), p. 703.

101. *La familia de Léon Roch* (1878; new ed. Madrid, 1972), p. 26.

102. "La sociedad moderna tiene en su favor el don del olvido, y se borran con prontitud los orígenes oscuros plebeyos. El mérito personal unas veces, y otras la fortuna, nivelan . . . y nuestra sociedad camina con pasos de gigante a la igualdad de apellidos" (Modern society has the gift of for-

getting, and obscure, plebeian origins are promptly forgotten. Sometimes the leveling comes about through individual merit, sometimes through wealth . . . and our society is taking giant steps toward a condition where all family names are equal) (ibid., p. 55). Galdós felt that the task of the modern novel was to provide expression for the life-style of the bourgeois class, which was from then on determined fashion; cf. his "Observaciones sobre la novela contemporánea en España" (1870), in *Ideología y política en la nove la española del siglo XIX*, ed. I. M. Zavala (Salamanca, 1971), p. 323.

103. *Larousse*, vol. 11 (1865), p. 362.

104. Edmond and Jules Goncourt, "Préface de *Renée Mauperin*" (1875), in *Préfaces et manifestes littéraires* (Paris, 1888), p. 18.

105. This presumption for modern literature, which was self-evident for Zola and apparently for that reason was not argued separately in his manifesto "Roman expérimental," is clear in his judgments of other writers of the time, for example, as a criticism in his letter to Bourget on April 22, 1878: "Vous, poète moderne, vous détestez la vie moderne. . . . Vous n'acceptez pas franchement votre âge. . . . Pourquoi trouver une gare laide? C'est très beau une gare. Pourquoi vouloir vous envoler continuellement loin de nos rues, vers les pays romantiques? Elles sont tragiques et charmantes, nos rues" (*Correspondance: Les lettres et les arts*, ed. Eugène Fasquelle [Paris, 1908], p. 156); as a criterion for including Alphonse Daudet in the naturalist school: "Il appartient au groupe des naturalistes. . . . Toutes ses oeuvres sont prises en pleine vie moderne" (*Les romanciers naturalistes* [Paris, 1881], p. 261).

106. Zola, *Le roman expérimental* (1880; rpt. Paris, 1905), p. 53. For the theoretical bases of naturalism, see Hans Ulrich Gumbrecht, *Emile Zola im historischen Kontext* (Frankfurt, 1977).

107. Niklas Luhmann, "Sinn als Grundbegriff der Soziologie," in Luhmann and Habermas, *Theorie der Gesellschaft oder Sozialtechnologie: Was leistet die Systemforschung?* (Frankfurt, 1971), pp. 57f.

108. In the controversy over the authorship of this "first" manifesto, I have followed Martini: "Modern die Moderne." (see n. 1), p. 408.

109. Eugen Wolff, "Thesen zur literarischen Moderne," in *Allgemeinen deutschen Universitätszeitung* (1887), rpt. in Wunberg, ed., *Literarische Moderne*, pp. 1f.

110. Otto Brahm, "Zum Beginn" (1898), *Freie Bühne für modernes Leben*, p. 57.

111. Michael Georg Conrad, "Die Sozialdemokratie und die Moderne" (1891), ibid., p. 99.

112. Curt Grottewitz, "Wie kann sich die moderne Literaturrichtung weiter entwickeln?" ibid., p. 61; Leo Berg, *Der Übermensch in der modernen Litteratur* (Munich, 1897), p. 88.

113. Heinrich Hart, "Die Moderne" (1890), rpt. in Wunberg, ed., *Literarische Moderne*, p. 72.

114. Friedrich Michael Fels, "Die Moderne" (1891), ibid., p. 73.

115. *Brockhaus*, 14th ed., vol. 11 (1902), p. 952. cf. *Herder*, 3rd ed., vol. 6 (1906), p. 48.

116. Antoine Albalat, *Le mal d'écrire et le roman contemporain* (Paris, 1895): "Voilá la consigne, le but, la condition actuelle de la littérature: être dans-le-mouvement, c'est-à-dire adopter l'esprit parisien, copier le boulevard, publier, écrire!" (p. 26).

117. Entry "Avanguardia" in *Grande dizionario enciclopedico*, vol. 2 (Turin, 1968), p. 493. Cf. John Weightman, *The Concept of the Avant-Garde: Explorations in Modernism* (Bradford, 1973), p. 20, who, along with materials for conceptual history, also provides a sagacious criticism of different uses of "avant-garde" in the twentieth century, pp. 13ff.

118. E. and J. Goncourt, *Preface of Les frères Zemgano* (1879) in *Préfaces*, p. 53. For further evidence in the nineteenth century, see Renato Poggioli, *The Theory of the Avant-Garde* (Cambridge, Mass., 1968); Peter Bürger's book *Theorie der Avantgarde* (Frankfurt, 1974), a West German attempt to describe and explain historically the phenomenon of the avant-garde, does not involve itself in conceptual history at all.

119. See the sources cited in n. 115.

120. Hermann Bahr, "Das junge Oesterreich," in *Studien zur Kritik der Moderne* (Frankfurt, 1894), p. 78.

121. Cäsar Flaischlen, "Vorbemerkung" to *Neuland: Ein Sammelbuch moderner Prosadichtung* (1894); rpt. in Wunberg, *Literarische Moderne*, p. 127.

122. M. G. Conrad, *Von Emile Zola bis Gerhart Hauptmann: Erinnerungen zur Geschichte der Moderne* (Leipzig, 1902), p. 135.

123. Quoted by Paul Goldmann, "Der Rückgang" (1908); rpt. in Wunberg, *Literarische Moderne*, p. 237.

124. Rudolf Borchardt, "Rede über Hofmannsthal" (1905-7), ibid., p. 141.

125. *Mauthner*, vol. 2 (1910), p. 95.

126. "Since time does not stand still for any element of present-day life, it is insane to maintain that something that looks modern and young today will also still look like that in a few years." *Enciclopedia universal ilustrada*, vol. 35 (Barcelona, n.d. [1907ff.]), p. 1230.

127. The conception of the following section (on nineteenth-century church history) was worked out by F. J. Hassauer-Roos.

128. Robert Scherer, "Modernismus," *Lexikon für Theologie und Kirche*, 2nd ed., vol. 7 (1962), p. 513.

129. Roger Aubert, "Modernismus," *Staatslexikon*, 6th ed., vol. 5 (1960), p. 794.

130. Scherer, "Modernismus," p. 513.

131. Robert Scherer, "Modernismus," in *Philosophisches Wörterbuch*, 7th ed., vol. 2 (1970), p. 735.

132. Aubert, "Modernismus," pp. 800f.

133. Oswald von Nell-Breuning, "Integralismus," *Lexikon für Theologie und Kirche*, 2nd ed., vol. 5 (1960), p. 717.

134. Günther Böing, "Liberalismus," ibid., 2nd ed., vol. 6 (1961), p. 1008.

135. Erik Ernst Schwabach, "Über einen Charakter der kommenden Literatur," in *Die weissen Blätter* 1 (1913), p. 5; cf. the correction in ibid., p. 202.

136. Azorín [José Martinez Ruez], "Clásicos y modernos," *Obras completas*, ed. Angel Cruz Rueda, vol. 2 (Madrid, 1947), pp. 737, 932.

137. The hypothesis of a transfer from a diachrony of stylistic periods to a synchrony of stylistic possibilites is argued in Hans Ulrich Gumbrecht, "Zum Wandel des Modernitätsbegriffs in Literatur und Kunst," in *Studien zum Beginn der modernen Welt*, ed. Reinhart Koselleck (Stuttgart, 1978).

138. *Encyclopaedia universalis*, 4th ed., vol. 11 (Paris, 1972), p. 139.

139. "Salon de 1859" in *Oeuvres complètes*, pp. 1025ff. See too the discussion "Kunst und Kunstphilosophie der Gegenwart," in *Immanente Ästhetik, ästhetische Reflexion: Lyrik als Paradigma der Moderne*, ed. Wolfgang Iser (Munich, 1966), pp. 524ff.

140. Roland Barthes, *Le plaisir du texte* (Paris, 1973), p. 66. See p. 40, where this hypothesis of the negativity of modern art as a flight from alienation is argued in more detail.

141. André Breton, "Picasso dans son élément" (1933), in *Point du jour* (1934; rpt. Paris, 1970), pp. 151f.

142. Cf. Jost Hermand, *Pop International: Eine kritische Analyse* (Frankfurt, 1971), p. 46. My hypotheses about pop art also draw on Rainer Crone and Wilfried Wiegand, *Die revolutionäre Ästhetik Andy Warhols* (Darmstadt, 1972).

143. H. Szeemann, "Attituden" (Constance, 1972; MS), p. 4.

144. Oswald Spengler, *Der Untergang des Abendlandes* (1917; rpt. Munich, 1972), pp. x, 21f.

145. *Larousse du XXe siècle*, vol. 4 (Paris, 1931), p. 913.

146. For the representation of the largely parallel development in the history of the concept "modern state," see Stefan Skalwiet, *Der moderne Staat: Ein historischer Begriff und seine Problematik* (Opladen, 1975).

147. Niklas Luhmann, "Der politische Code: 'Konservativ' und 'progressiv' in systemtheoretischer Sicht," in *Zeitschrift für Politik* 21 (1947), pp. 253ff.

148. *Südkurier* (Constance), April 6, 1974.

149. M. Rainer Lepsius, "Soziologische Theoreme über die Sozialstruktur der 'Moderne' und die 'Modernisierung' " (1972, MS). Cf. Hans-Ulrich Wehler, *Modernisierungstheorie und Geschichte* (Göttingen, 1975).

150. Paul Valéry, "Avant-propos de 'Regards sur le monde actuel et autres essais,' " in *Oeuvres*, vol. 2, p. 922.

151. Reinhard Koselleck, "Geschichte, Geschichten und formale Zeitstrukturen," in *Geschichte: Ereignis und Erzählung*, ed. Koselleck and Wolf-Dieter Stempel (Munich, 1973), p. 221.

152. *Weltzeit und Systemgeschichte*, p. 104.

6. Laughter and Arbitrariness, Subjectivity and Seriousness: The *Libro de buen Amor*, the *Celestina*, and the Style of Sense Production in Early Modern Times

1. Cf. the title of one of the most significant comparative interpretations: María Rosa Lida de Malkiel, *Two Spanish Masterpieces: The Book of Good Love and The Celestina* (Urbana, Ill., 1961).

2. Cf. D. Poirion's foreword and the contributions in the first volume of the companion series to *Grundriss der romanischen Literaturen des Mittelalters: Literatur in der Gesellschaft des Spätmittelalters* (Heidelberg, 1980).

3. Jochim Ritter, "Über das Lachen," in *Blätter für deutsche Philosophie* 14 (1940–41), pp. 1–21; Helmut Plessner, "Der Ursprung von Lachen und Weinen," in Plessner, *Lachen und Weinen* (Frankfurt, 1970), pp. 149–71; and the various perspectives for the further development of these approaches in *Das Komische*, ed. Wolfgang Preisendanz and Rainer Warning (Munich, 1976).

4. For the pre- and early history of the sociology of knowledge, see Karl Mannheim, *Wissenssoziologie: Auswahl aus dem Werk* (Neuwied, 1964); Alfred Schütz, *Der sinnhafte Aufbau der sozialen Welt: Eine Einleitung in die verstehende Soziologie*, 2nd ed. (Vienna, 1960); Peter Berger and Thomas Luckmann, *Die gesellschaftliche Konstruktion der Wirklichkeit: Eine Theorie der Wissenssoziologie* (Frankfurt, 1971); Alfred Schütz and Thomas Luckmann, *Strukturen der Lebenswelt* (Neuwied, 1975); Walter Sprondel and Richard Grathoff, eds., *Alfred Schütz und die Idee des Alltags in den Sozialwissenschaften* (Stuttgart, 1979); and finally—with a series of examples worked out for historical application—Luckmann, *Lebenswelt und Gesellschaft: Grundstrukturen und geschichtliche Wandlungen* (Paderborn, 1980). As far as the systematic foundations of Luhmann's theory of social systems are concerned, I would like to mention his discussion with Jürgen Habermas that has been canonized as a classic in Germany: *Theorie der Gesellschaft oder Sozialtechnologie* (Frankfurt, 1971). The concept of the "style of meaning constitution" (*Stil der Sinnbildung*) was introduced by Luhmann in his contribution, "Über die Funktion der Negation in sinnkonstituierenden Systemen," in *Positionen der Negativität*, ed. H. Weinrich (Munich, 1975), pp. 101–18.

5. For a more extensive deduction of three negation types from the premises of the theory of social systems, see my "Literarische Gegenwelten, Karnevalskultur und die Epochenschwelle vom Spätmittelalter zur Renaissance," in *Literatur in der Gesellschaft des Spätmittelalters*, pp. 98ff.

6. Mikhail Bakhtin, *Rabelais and His World* (Cambridge, Mass., 1965); in addition, my attempts at systematization in "Literarische Gegenwelten," pp. 96ff.

7. The terms "text repertoire" and "text strategy" are used in W. Iser's sense in *Der Akt des Lesens: Theorie ästhetischer Wirkung* (Munich, 1976).

8. Cf. the documentation of this text (no. 4556) in *Grundriss der romanischen Literaturen des Mittelalters*, vol. 6 (Heidelberg, 1972).

9. E. Leube, *Die "Celestina"* (Munich, 1971), p. 6.

10. For this aspect, see C. Real de la Riva, "Notas a la Celestina," in *Strenae: Estudios de filología e historia dedicados al professor Manuel García Blanco* (Salamanca, 1962), pp. 1–10.

11. C. Real de la Riva, *Libro de buen amor: Estudio histórico-crítico y transcripción textual del Códice de Salamanca* (Madrid, 1975), p. 1.

12. M. R. Lida de Malkiel, *La originalidad artística de la Celestina* (Buenos Aires, 1962), p. 513.

13. Leube, *Die "Celestina,"* p. 32.

14. For the problem of the connection between identity types and the structures of (auto)biographical texts, see the statements in W. Marquard and K. Stierle, eds. *Identität* (Munich, 1979), pp. 685ff.

15. See my sketch of the problem, "Lebensläufe/Literatur/Alltagswelten," in *Biographie aus soziologischer Perspektive*, ed. J. Matthes (Nuremberg, 1982).

16. For the history of the reception of the *Libro de buen amor* (with particular attention to the interpretations of medieval philology), see my introduction to the bilingual (Spanish-German) edition, "Literarische Technik und Schichten der Bedeutung im *Libro de buen amor*," in Juan Ruiz, Arcipreste de Hita, *Libro de buen amor*, trans. Hans Ulrich Gumbrecht (Munich, 1972), pp. 9-19.

17. Huizinga's *Homo Ludens: Vom Ursprung der Kultur in Spiel* (Hamburg, 1956).

18. The studies were reedited in R. Menéndez Pidal, *Poesía juglaresca y juglares: Aspectos de la historia literaria y cultural de España* (Madrid, 1956), in particular pp. 140ff.

19. See, e.g., A. Haverkamp, "Illusion und Empathie—die Transferstruktur der teilnehmende Lektüre (The Rhetoric of Empathy)" in *Erzähltheorie und Geschichte des Erzählens*, ed. E. Lämmert (Stuttgart, 1983).

20. For the term, *Weil-Motiv*, see Schütz, *Der sinnhafte Aufbau der sozialen Welt*, pp. 99ff.

21. Kuhn, "Soziale Realität und dichterische Fiktion am Beispiel der mittelalterlichen Ritterdichtung Deutschlands," in *Dichtung und Welt im Mittelalter* (Stuttgart, 1969), pp. 22-40.

22. Hugo Kuhn, "Versuch einer Theorie der deutschen Literatur im Mittelalter," in his *Text und Theorie* (Stuttgart, 1969), pp. 3-9.

23. Real de la Riva in the introduction to *Libro de buen amor*, pp. ii ff.

24. Jacques LeGoff, *Les intellectuels au moyen âge* (Paris, 1957).

25. R. Menéndez Pidal, *Poesía árabe y poesía europea: Con otros estudios de literatura medieval* (Madrid, 1963), pp. 145ff.

26. For the drolleries, see O. Mazal, *Buchkunst der Gotik* (Graz, 1975), pp. 52ff. Our observations and their interpretation can be checked on the basis of the detailed facsimile reproduction of manuscript S, which accompanies Real de la Riva's edition.

27. "The Grotesque Image of the Body and its Sources," in Bakhtin, *Rabelais and His World*, pp. 303ff.

28. Cf. Leube, *Die "Celestina,"* p. 19.

29. Ibid., p. 8. The sum of the research on Rojas's biography is presented by Lida de Malkiel, *La originalidad artística de la Celestina*, pp. 11ff.

30. "Lettre à M. d'Alembert sur son article 'Genève,' " quoted from the edition by M. Launay (Paris, 1967), pp. 233ff.

7. Who Were the *Philosophes*?

1. The first manuscript of the original German version of this essay was substantially enriched, in its documentary part, by the suggestions of my colleague and friend Rolf Reichardt. It was therefore published under his and my coauthorship.

2. J. Balcou, *Fréron contre les philosophes* (Geneva, 1975); T. Barling, "La guerre des brochures autour des 'Philosophes' de Palissot de Montenoy," in *Modèles et moyens de réflexion politique au XVIIIe siècle*, vol. 1 (Lille, 1977), pp. 241-66; C. W. Byrd, "The 'Philosophes' and 'Anti-philosophes' in 1760: A Literary Struggle" (Ph.D. dissertation, Vanderbilt University, 1973); R. Desné, "Apparition du mot 'philosophe' dans l'oeuvre de Diderot," *Annales d'Histoire de la Révolution française* 35 (1963), pp. 287-94; Herbert Dieckmann, *"Le Philosophe": Texts and Interpretation* (St. Louis, 1948); C. Duckworth, "Voltaire's 'L'Ecossaise' and Palissot's 'Les philosophes': A Strategic Battle in a Major

War," *Studies on Voltaire and the Eighteenth Century* 87 (1972), pp. 333–51; A. W. Fairbairn, "Dumarsais and 'Le Philosophe,' " *Studies on Voltaire and the Eighteenth Century* 87 (1972), pp. 375–92; H. H. Freud, *Palissot and 'Les philosophes"* (Geneva, 1967); Rolf Reichardt, *Reform und Revolution bei Condorcet* (Bonn, 1973); P. S. Robinove, "The Reputation of the 'Philosophes,' 1789–1799") (Ph.D. dissertation, New York University, 1955); F. Rocquain, "Le parti des philosophes, 1762–1770," *Séances et travaux de l'Académie des sciences morales et politiques* (Institut de France), n.s. 14 (1880), pp. 102–46; C. G. Stricklen, "The 'Philosophe's' Political Mission: The Creation of an Idea, 1750–1789," *Studies on Voltaire and the Eighteenth Century* 86 (1971), pp. 137–228; A. Thomson, "Les philosophes et la société," *Studies on Voltaire and the Eighteenth Century* 90 (1980), pp. 273–84; Ira O. Wade, *The "Philosophe" in the French Drama of the Eighteenth Century* (Princeton, N.J., 1926).

3. Such an attempt has been undertaken by J. Lough, "Who were the 'Philosophes'?", in *Studies in Eighteenth-Century French Literature Presented to Robert Niklaus* (Exeter, 1975), pp. 139–50.

4. Dieckmann, *'Le Philosophe,"* p. 68.

5. N. Elias, *Über den Prozess der Zivilisation* (1937), 3rd ed. (Frankfurt, 1977); Niklas Luhmann, *Gesellschaft und Semantik*, vol. 1 (Frankfurt, 1980), pp. 72–161; R. Galle, *'Honnêteté und Sincérité,"* in *Die französische Klassik,* ed. F. Nies and Karlheinz Stierle (Munich, 1984).

6. "Celuy qui veut estre de bonne compagnie doit faire en sorte, que plus on connoist son coeur et sa façon de proceder, plus on le souhaite; et qu'il est beau d'estre humain, de n'avoir rien d'injuste! que la sincérité donne bon air, et que la fausseté me paroist desagreable!" Chev. de Méré, "De la Conversation" [1671], in *Oeuvres complètes,* 2 vols., ed. C. H. Boudhors (Paris, 1930), p. 115.

7. Rémond des Cours, *La véritable politique des personnes de qualité* [1692] (Jena, 1750), p. 66.

8. Jean Starobinski, "Sur la flatterie," *Nouvelle Revue de Psychoanalyse* (1971), p. 132.

9. Molière, *Oeuvres complètes,* vol. 2 (Paris, 1965), pp. 43–46, with indications on its reception; for example, Alceste's tirade in 1.I:

> Non, je ne puis souffrir cette lâche méthode
> Qu'affectent la plupart de vos gens à la mode;
> Et je ne haïs rien tant que les contorsions
> De tous ces grands faiseurs de protestations,
> Ces affables donneurs d'embrassades frivoles,
> Ces obligeants diseurs d'inutiles paroles,
> Qui de civilités avec tous font combat,
> Et traitent de même aire l'honnête homme et le fat.

10. La Rochefoucauld, *Oeuvres* (Paris, 1969), p. 409.

11. See Reinhart Koselleck, *Kritik und Krise* (Freiburg, 1959), p. 91 passim.

12. *Richelet* (1680,) vol. 2, p. 157.

13. *Furetière* (1690), vol. 3, entry Philosophe.

14. *Dictionnaire de l'Académie française* (1694), vol. 2, p. 140.

15. Ibid.

16. Ibid., repeated in the fourth edition (1764), vol. 2, p. 238; taken over in *Richelet,* 5th ed. (1732), vol. 2, p. 388.

17. D. Richet, "Autour des origines intellectuelles de la Révolution française," *Annales Economies Societés, Civilisations* 24 (1969), pp. 1–23.

18. Saint-Simon, *Memoires* (1712; Paris, 1977–79), vol. 9, p. 316.

19. Ibid.

20. Mathien Marais, *Journal et Mémoires,* vol. 2, p. 375 (Dec. 4, 1732) (Paris, 1863–68).

21. Ibid., vol. 3, p. 331 (May 25, 1725).

22. "La théologie qui resemble à la Philosophie comme une fille à sa mère . . . " F. de la Dillonnire, *L'athésime découvert par le R. P. Hardouin, jésuite* (Paris, 1715), p. 5.

23. "Cet Auteur . . . veut instruire, tantôt en Philosophe." *Journal de Trévoux* 21, (1721), p. 440.

24. Quoted in the discussion by the Abbé Budet in the *Mercure de France* (June 1720), pp. 66–115, here p. 110. Precisely this verse drew a great deal of attention: Marais, vol. 1, p. 319 (July 10, 1720). See also the interpretation of the satire in Wade, *The "Philosophe" in the French Drama of the Eighteenth Century*, pp. 16–29.

25. *Mercure de France*, June 1720, p. 68.

26. Ibid., Aug. 1734, p. 1893.

27. Voltaire, *Lettres philosophiques*, ed. Raymond Naves (Paris, 1962), p. 54.

28. Ibid., pp. 54–57, 68f., 129ff. Addison, Newton, Pope, and Swift appear here as *gens de lettres*. Soon afterward Voltaire continued his propagation of the new English philosophy with a popularization of Newton's experimental physics, protesting reassuringly: "Toute la philosophie de Newton conduit nécessairement à la connaissance d'un être suprême, qui a tout créé . . . mais elle reste impuissante à nous apprendre ce qu'il est, ce qu'il fait, comment et pourquoi il le fait." *Eléments de la philosophie de Newton, mis à portée de tout le monde* [1738], in *Oeuvres*, ed. Moland (Paris, 1883–85), vol. 20, pp. 403, 407.

29. *Dictionnaire de Trévoux*, 3rd ed. (1732), vol. 4, pp. 801f.; taken over in ibid., (41740, ed. 1743), vol. 5, pp. 168–70.

30. In his translation of an English-language history of Greece, Diderot did not call Prometheus a "wise man" as in the original but freely translated: "Ce philosophe travailla toute sa vie à ramener à la raison les humains attachés à l'ignorance et à la stupidité." Cf. T. Styan, *The Graecian History* (1707), 2nd ed., vols. 1–2 (London, 1739), with Diderot's translation, *Histoire de Grèce*, vol. 1 (Paris, 1943), p. 29. For further data, see Desné, "Apparition du mot 'philosophe' dans l'oeuvre de Diderot."

31. According to Panckoucke, *Essais sur les philosophes* (Amsterdam, n.d.).

32. According to R. de Bonneval, *Progrés de l'éducation* (Paris, 1743), "Du titre de philosophe," pp. 158–60.

33. Dieckmann, "Le Philosophe," pp. 1–26.

34. C. Dumarsais, *Le Philosophe*. In *Nouvelles Libertés de penser* (Amsterdam, 1743), pp. 187f.

35. Ibid., pp. 174–76.

36. Ibid., pp. 173, 183.

37. Ibid., pp. 114, 194f.

38. Ibid., 194, 197: "Séparez pour un moment le Philosophe de l'honnête homme. Qui lui reste-t-il? . . . l'idée de malhonnête homme est autant opposée à l'idée de Philosophe, que l'est l'idée de stupide; et l'expérience fait voir tous les jours que plus on a de raison, et de lumière, plus on est sûr et propre pour le commerce de la vie."

39. This is confirmed by La Metrie's introduction to his *Oeuvres philosophiques* (London, 1751), pp. iii-lvi, which is directly attached to Dumarsais; cf. Thomson, *Les philosophes et la société*, pp. 279–81. For the related problem of Enlightenment "hypocrisy," see Koselleck, *Kritik und Krise*.

40. "Il y a bien de gens dans le monde à qui le mot de Philosophe fait peur, parce qu'il y en a bien peu qui entendent ce terme dans sa véritable signification. . . . Demandez au peuple ce que c'est qu'un Philosophe . . . ? C'est, vous dira-t-il, un fantasque, qui contrôle toutes les action, qui traite de préjugés les trois quarts de nos opinions, qui ne croit ni aux esprits ni aux Sorciers, & qui peut-être ne croit même en Dieu. – Mais faites la même question à un homme de bon sens: Un Philosophe, vous répondra-t-il, est un homme qui examine avant que de croire, & réfléchit avant que d'agir, et quit conséquemment, quand il est décidé, ne peut manquex d'être ferme dans sa croyance & constant dans ses démarches.–C'est sans doute dans des hommes de ce caractère que se rencontre la vraie & solide piété." François-Vincent Toussaint, *Les moeurs* [Amsterdam, 1748]; ed. 1760, pp. 18f.

41. "Cependant le Roi est très-mal conseillé; il se donne toujours tort et donne toujours raison

au parlement. On le dégrade peu à peu, surtout dans le siècle lumineux et philosophique où nous vivons. Si Henri III fut obligé de se mettre à la tête de la Ligue, Louis XV devrait se mettre à la tête de la philosophie, de la justice et de la raison pour établir son pouvoir et son bonheur." Argenson, *Journal et Mémoires* (Paris, 1859-61), IX 222, 5.III 1756.

42. Ibid., VII 224 (May 5, 1752).

43. Rolf Reichardt, "Bastille," in *Handbuch politisch-sozialer Grundbegriffe in Frankreich, 1680-1820, book 9* (Munich, 1988).

44. Robert Darnton, *The Great Cat Massacre and Other Episodes in French Cultural History* (New York, 1984), pp. 145-89, 276f.

45. *Encyclopédie*, vol. 1 (1751), p. xxx; also pp. xix-xxxi.

46. Ibid., after p. xlvi.

47. Entry "*Encyclopédie*," ibid., vol. 5 (1755), p. 636b.

48. Ibid., vol. 12 (1765), pp. 509-11. The sentence is missing: "Or ce qui fait l'honnête homme, ce n'est point d'agir par amour ou par haine, par experance ou par crainte." Dumarsais, *Le philosophe*, p. 190. Also missing is the passage quoted in n. 38, this chapter. See too the concordance in Dieckmann, "*Le Philosophe*," pp. 46, 52.

49. *Encyclopédie*, vol. 12 (1765), pp. 511-15; today Diderot is no longer considered to be the author of this entry.

50. *Journal encyclopédique* 1769, II/2, (March 1, 1769), pp. 167f.

51. François Furet, *Penser la Révolution française* (Paris, 1978), p. 57.

52. For more particulars, see *Sozialgeschichte der Aufklärung,* ed. Hans Ulrich Gumbrecht, Rolf Reichardt, and Thomas Schleich (Munich, 1981), vol. 1, pp. 11-16, 91-106, and vol. 2, pp. 26-31.

53. Argenson, vol. 7, pp. 58 and 68 (Dec. 31, 1751, and Jan. 12, 1752).

54. *La Religion vengée ou Refutation des auteurs. Por une société de gens de lettres* (Paris, 1757-63), vol. 10 (1760), pp. 38f.

55. E.g., *Le Manon des Granges:* "Le Christianisme ne condamne & ne réprouve cette philosophie déraisonnable qui s'acharne à abolir tout culte de la divinité, à combattre & à rendre incertaine l'existence de la Divinité même; cette Philosophie désespérante qui cherche à dépouiller l'homme de ses plus beaux droits. . . . Cette Philosophie arrogante qui n'oppose aux légitimes raison, que d'indécentes railleries & de grossieres injures" (p. 227).

56. Louis Petit de Bachaumont, *Mémoires secrets pour servir à l'histoire de la république des lettres* (London, 1777-89), vol. 5, pp. 152f. (Aug. 17, 1770; also ibid., vol. 19, Aug. 28, 1770). The pastoral letter was called *Avertissement du clergé de France, assemblé à Paris par permission du Roi, aux fidéles du royaume, sur les dangers de l'incrédulité* (Paris, 1770).

57. Paul-Henri d'Holbach, *Théologie* (London, 1768). This entry he slipped into Palissot and J.-N. Moreau. The latter was the author of the spectacular "antiphilosophical" pamphlet, *Nouveau Mémoire pour servir à l'historie des Cacouacs* ([Paris], 1757).

58. Cf. Argenson, vol. 8, p. 290 (May 9, 1754); *Espion Anglois,* vol. 1, p. 219 (Dec. 1, 1773).

59. Grimm, *Correspondance littéraire*, vol. 1, p. 384 (Dec. 1749) to Maupertuis. Similarly, *Journal Encyclopédie.* 1756, vol. 3 (Aug. 1, 1756), pp. 11-14; Bachaumont, *Mémoires*, vol. 5, pp. 18f. (Nov. 26, 1769) on Holbach's *Essai sur les préjugés:* "On parle de l'antipathie qui subsistera toujours entre la Philosophie & la Superstition." The French Academy attempted a conservative determination of *philosophie* by offering a prize to whoever answered the question "En quoi consiste l'esprit philosophique, conformément à ses paroles de L'Ecriture: 'Non plus sapere, quam oportet sapere?' " The prize went to the Jesuit father, A. Guénard, for his *Discours qui a remporté le prix de l'éloquence de L'Academie française en l'année 1755* (Paris, 1755). See, in addition, *Irréligion dévoilée . . .* (1774), pp. 2f.: "La Philosophie est . . . une Théologie naturelle qui rapproache l'homme de Dieu"; also Flexier de Reval, *Catéchisme philosophique . . . propre à défendre la Religion chrétienne (Liège, Brussels, 1773): "Quelque abus qu'on a fait du mot de Philosophie, . . . nous donnons le

titre de *Philosophique* à la chose la plus simple et la plus négligée par les Philosophes, qui est le Catéchisme des Chrétiens" (p. vii).

60. La Père Aimé-Henri Paulian, *Dictionnaire philosophico-théologico* . . . (Nîmes, 1770): "On appelle *Philosophes* de préntendus esprits forts, qui surtout en matière de Religion se donnent la liberté de tout penser, de tout écrire" (p. 248).

61. The liberal *Konversation-Lexikon* of Alletz (1761) states that "de Philosophes, qui ont été par conséquent appellés à bon droit Athés" (p. 43). On the death of the Duchesse D'Aiguillon we read in Bachaumont, *Mémoires*, vol. 6, June 16, 1772: "C'étoit une femme . . . fort entichée de la philosophie moderne, c'est-à-dire, de Matérialisme et d'Athéisme" (p. 148).

62. *Dictionnaire de Trévoux*, (6th ed. 1771), vol. 6, p. 738.

63. "Ceux qui ne sont que Philosophes, et qui croient de bonne foi le patriotisme offensé par les droits du clergé, verront avec plaisir, que loin d'être nuisible au bien public, ils font, en les réduisant à leurs justes bornes, öun des plus sûrs garants de la prospérité publique" (Ephémérides 13, Dec. 16, 1765, vol. 1, pp. 201f.).

64. Delisle de Sales, *Philosophie* (1770), vol. 1, p. 108.

65. *Dictionnaire* (1765), p. 346. Grimm, *Correspondance littéraire*, vol. 4, p. 135 (Aug. 15, 1759), complained that the antiphilosophical pamphlet of Guyon simply amounted to the demand that "il faut exterminer tous ceux qui ne sont pas bons catholiques." See too ibid., vol. 4, p. 305 (Oct. 15, 1760); and Argenson, vol. 7, p. 106 (Feb. 12, 1752).

66. Palissot, *Petites lettres,* is quoted in agreement in *Année littéraire,* vol. 8/11 (Dec. 1757), p. 239.

67. J. Mirasson, *Le philosophe rechersé* (1765), pp. 67f.; in this connection, see Grimm, *Correspondance littéraire*, vol. 6, p. 338 (Aug. 1, 1765). See too Diderot's discussion of Morellet's pamphlet, which was immediately interdicted, copied, and traded at black-market prices (ibid., vol. 4, pp. 108–11, May 15, 1759).

68. S. Linguet, *Le fanatisme des philosophes* (London, 1964); also Grimm, *Correspondance littéraire,* vol. 6, pp. 55f. (Aug. 15, 1764).

69. *Année littéraire.* 7/7 (Nov. 18, 1764), pp. 173, 178. See also ibid. 1/1 (Jan. 3, 1768), p. 19. Other examples of the reproach of fanaticism by Fréron are provided by J. Balcou, *Fréron contre les philosophes*, pp. 134f., 186f., 448.

70. Nonnotte, *Dictionnaire philosophique de la religion* (Paris, 1774), vol. 4, p. 362.

71. *Année littéraire,* vol. 7/7 (Nov. 28, 1764), p. 66; ibid., vol. 2/13 (April 15, 1772), p. 291.

72. Le Père Joseph-Romaine Joly, *Dictionnaire de morale philosophique* (Paris, 1771), vol. 1, p. iv. Similarly against the Encyclopedists, Palissot et al., *Lettre,* p. 5; also *Conseil de Lanternes.*

73. Bachaumont, *Mémoires,* vol. 4, p. 109 (Nov. 22, 1768); also Charles Colle, *Journal et Mémoires sur les hommes de lettres,* vol. 3, p. 353 (April, May 1772).

74. Grimm, *Correspondance littéraire,* vol. 9, pp. 308f. (May 15, 1771).

75. "Les philosophes du jour vulgairement appelés 'Encyclopédistes' " (Bachaumont *Mémoires,* vol. 6, p. 249, Jan. 8, 1773). See n. 72 as well as Collé, vol. 2, pp. 290f. (March 1763).

76. *Espion anglois,* vol. 1, pp. 276–78 (June 6, 1775). Also *Ephémérides,* vol. 6/7 (Sept. 22, 1766), p. 97. For more on this, see the entry "Economie politique."

77. "Quand les philosophes seraient en état de découvrir la vérité, qui d'entre eux prendrait intérêt en elle? . . . Il n'y en a pas un seul, qui, venant à connaître le vrai et le faux, ne préférât le mensonge qu'il a trouvé la vérité découverte par un autre." *Emile ou de l'éducation* [1762], ed. M. Launay (Paris, 1966). See the parallel statements in the preface to the *Nouvelle Héloïse* and its analysis by Hans Robert Jauss in *Ästhetische Erfahrung und literarische Hermeneutik* (Frankfurt, 1982), pp. 585–653, as well as Darnton, *The Great Cat Massacre,* pp. 215–56, 279–82.

78. Bachaumont, *Mémoires,* vol. 1, p. 61 (March 30, 1762).

79. To D'Alembert, June 26, 1766 (Bestermann Document 13374, vol. 30, p. 282).

80. To Thieriot on Aug. 20, 1760 (ibid., 9159, vol. 22, p. 65); also his letter of Aug. 20, 1760,

to Damilaville (ibid., 11227, vol. 26, p. 148), Jan. 4, 1764 to Marmontel (ibid., 11618, vol. 27, p. 148), and Oct. 27, 1766, to Helvétius (ibid., 13626, vol. 31, p. 44).

81. R. Noack, "Zur Rolle der Korrespondenz in der französischen Aufklärung," in *Beiträge zur romanischen Philologie* 16 (1977), pp. 33–38.

82. *La vraie philosophie, ou l'art d'être heureux: Epître en vers libres* (Paris, 1760); see the discussion of the *Journal encyclopédique* 5/2 (July 15, 1760), pp. 105–11.

83. Entry "Philosophie" in *Encyclopédie*, vol. 12 (1765), p. 515a.

84. Grimm, *Correspondance littéraire*, vol. 3, pp. 113f. (Nov. 1, 1775).

85. "Les Philosophes . . . renversent toutes les loix de la nature et les fondements de la religion; ils autorisent les débauches vagues, l'adultere même; enfin les vices les plus opposés au bien de la société, et cela par humanité." Joly, *Dictionnaire*, vol. 1, pp. 462f. Also Nonnotte, *Dictionnaire*, vol. 1, p. ix.

86. *Journal encyclopédique* 5/1 (April 1, 1756), pp. 32f. Grimm, *Correspondance littéraire*, vol. 5, p. 375 (Sept. 1, 1763): "Le philosophe est le précepteur du peuple. Dès qu'il quitte les mystères de sa science, ou plutôt de la nature . . . c'est toujours pour l'instruction publique qu'il doit écrire." That most of the Enlightenment spokesmen did not take up the consequences of such explanations is shown by, among others, H. Chisick in *The Limits of Reform in the Enlightenment* (Princeton, N.J., 1981).

87. Boncerf, especially pp. vf., 1–6, and 35ff. For the active dedication to society, which now completely determines the self-image, Voltaire's letter to Cramer from Jan. 20, 1767, is also quite suggestive (*Bestermann Document* 13871, vol. 31, p. 279), as well as [Holbach:] *Essai sur les préjugés* (Amsterdam, 1770), p. 348.

88. *Le Sage, ou Le Philosophe du jour* . . . (The Hague, 1760): "Plus de mortels dans ces cachots affreux" (p. 36); "je ne sers point les rois" (p. 48); "l'homme est né pour n'avoir point de maître" (p. 84). Palissot, *Les Philosophes* (Paris, 1760): "Les hommes sont égaux par le droit de la nature" (p. 40); "Le Sage est le seul monarque et son Législateur"; "je ne m'occupe pas des Rois, de leur querelle" (p. 88). A. Poinsinet, *Le petit Philosophe* (Paris, 1760): "Les hommes sont égaux malgré leur vanité"; "un sage ne connaît, ni coutume, ni loi, ni dignité, ni rang, ni préséance" (p. 19). Duval, *La nouvelle Philosophie veau l'eau* (Amsterdam, 1775): "Voulez-vous vivre heureux, vivez toujours sans maître" (p. 4). All of these quotes from Wade's tables: *The "Philosophe" in the French Drama of the Eighteenth Century*, pp. 78–81.

89. Mirasson, *Le philosophe recherché*, pp. 163–65. Also Grimm, *Correspondance littéraire*, vol. 7, p. 122 (Feb. 25, 1752): "Le sieur Diderot est celui des auteurs de *l'Encyclopédie* qu'on accusait le plus de travailler contre la religion, l'autorité royale et les moeurs"; *Année littéraire* 8/5 (Oct. 10, 1770), p. 109; Fréron also provided a detailed report on the frequently published anonymous novel *Confidence philosophique* [by J. Vernes], the eighth "letter" of which sketched the portrait of a state-threatening *philosophe*, ibid., 4/9 (July 20, 1771), pp. 194–209.

90. See Robert Darnton, *Bohème littéraire et Révolution* (Paris, 1983), pp. 7, 128, passim.; also Bachaumont, *Mémoires*, 3/73 (Sept. 4, 1766).

91. Speech for court order by the attorney general Séguier, on the Parisian Parliament's blockage of Holbach's and others' writings (Aug. 18, 1770), quoted from F. Rocquain, "Le parti des philosophes, 1762–1770," in *Séances et travaux de l'Académie des sciences morales et politiques* (1880), pp. 102–46.

92. "Le philosophe au contraire, quelque liberté qu'il mette dans ses écrits, ne cherchant que la réputation d'esprit, ne peut jamais faire ombrage au gouvernement." Grimm, ed., Kölving, vol. 1, pp. 114f. Also Voltaire to Helvétius on Oct. 27, 1760: "C'est l'intérest du roy que le nombre des philosophes augmente, et que celuy des fanatiques diminue. Nous somme tranquiles, et tous ce gens là sont perturbateurs. Nous sommes citoiens, et ils sont sédietieux" (Bestermann Document 9354, vol. 22, p. 248).

93. Delisle de Sales, *Philosophie* (1770), vol. 1, pp. 111-13, from the chapter "Apologie du Philosophe."

94. For a semantic typology of negations, see Hans Ulrich Gumbrecht, "Literarische Gegenwelten, Karnevalskultur und die Epochenschwelle vom Spätmittelalter zur Renaissance," in *Literatur und Gesellschaft des Spätmittelalters*, ed. Hans Ulrich Gumbrecht (Heidelberg, 1980), pp. 95-149.

95. For the following, in general Wade, *The "Philosophe" in the French Drama of the Eighteenth Century*, pp. 41-45; Freud, especially pp. 125-87; and to a lesser extent Duckworth, Byrd, and Barling (see n.1).

96. D. Gembicki, *Histoire et politique à la fin de l'Ancien Régime: J.-N. Moreau, 1717-1803* (Paris, 1979), pp. 71-84.

97. Grimm (ed. Dafgård), vol. 1, pp. 110f. (June 1, 1760). See also Diderot's obvious play on Palissot in his entry "Menace": "Lorsque le gouvernement d'un peuple se déclare contre la philosophie, c'est qu'il est mauvais: il *menace* le peuple d'une stupidité prochaine. Lorsque les honnêtes gens sont traduit sur la scène, c'est qu'ils sont *menacés* d'une persécution plus violente: on cherche d'abord à les avilir aux yeux du peuple." *Encyclopédie* (1765), vol. 10, p. 331a.

98. "Le sort de l'Encyclopédie intéresse tant les Sciences & les Arts, qu'il n'est pas possible de laisser ignorer tout ce qu'on fait pour anéantir cet ouvrage immense, & livrer les Auteurs à la haine publique." *Journal encyclopédique* 5/3 (Aug. 1, 1760), p. 103; also ibid., 3/3 (May 1, 1760), pp. 118-30.

99. "Elle est critiquée quant à la pièce et fort condamnée pour la méchanceté." Edmond Jean François Barbier, *Journal historique et anecdotique du règne de Louis XV* (Paris, 1947-56), vol. 4 (May 2, 1760).

100. *Année littéraire* 3/9 (May 6, 1760), pp. 214-16; also ibid., 4/9 (June 16, 1760).

101. Cf. Duckworth's "Voltaire's 'L'Ecossaise," p. 347. For the first performance, see J. M. B Clément's report, et al., *Anecdotes dramatiques*, vol. 2 (Paris, 1775): "Depuis la fondation du Théâtre, on n'avoit peut-être jamais vu, à la Comédie Française, un concours de monde aussi prodigieux . . . Le sujet de la Pièce avoit excité dans Paris une fermentation générale de curiosité etc." (pp. 67f.).

102. Voltaire's letter to Thieriot on Aug. 20, 1760: "La philosophie ne peut que gagner à toute cette guerre. Le Public voit d'un côté Palissot, Fréron, et Pompignan à la tête de la religion, et de l'autre les hommes les plus éclairez qui respectent cette religion encore plus que le Fréron ne la deshonorent" (Bestermann Document 11418, 22/64).

103. Voltaire to Helvétius, Sept. 15, 1763 (ibid., 11418, vol. 26, p. 404); also Grimm, vol. 7, p. 194 (April 15, 1764).

104. *Année littéraire* 1/1 (Feb. 3, 1752), p. 1; thereto Balcou, *Fréron contre les philosophes*, p. 80. See also Grimm, vol. 2 (Sept. 15, 1754): "L'esprit philosophique . . . continuant de se répandre de plus en plus, on en trouve le germe, ou dur moins le simulacre, jusque dans nos auteurs les plus minces et les plus mauvais" (p. 407)

105. A. Guénard, *Discours qui a remporté le prix de l'éloquence à l'Academie française en l'année 1755* (Paris, 1755), p. 3.

106. *Année littéraire* 1/1 (Jan. 4, 1772), p. 4; also Balcou, *Fréron contre les philosophes*, pp. 297-331.

107. Letter to d'Alembert, June 26, 1766 (Bestermann Document 13374, vol. 30, p. 208).

108. To d'Alembert, Aug. 8, 1765 (ibid. 12790, vol. 29, p. 208).

109. Grimm, *Correspondance littéraire*, vol. 3, p. 334 (Jan. 15, 1757), vol. 7, p. 201 (Feb. 1767).

110. Darnton, *Bohème*, pp. 8-41.

111. Le Manon des Granges, *Le philosophe moderne* (Paris, 1769), pp. 227f.; also *Année littéraire* 7/12 (Nov. 24, 1764), pp. 279-81.

112. Nonnotte, *Dictionnaire*, vol. 1, pp. 5, 8.

113. *Année littéraire* 2/1 (Feb. 24, 1767), pp. 9-26.

114. L. Brunel, *Les Philosophes et l'Académie française au XVIIIe siècle* (Paris, 1884); K.

Racewskis, "Le règne des philosophes à l'Académie française," *Studies on Voltaire and the Eighteenth Century* 154 (1976), pp. 1801–12.

115. *Discours prononcez dans l'Académie française le jeudi 4 août 1774, à la réception de M. Suard* (Paris, 1774); quoted here according to Grimm, *Correspondance littéraire*, vol. 10, p. 465 (Aug. 1774). See also Bachaumont, *Mémoires*, vol. 7, p. 201 (Aug. 13, 1774).

116. S. Fiette, "La 'Correspondance' de Grimm et la condition des écrivains dans la seconde moitié du XVIIIe," *Revue d'histoire économique et sociale* 47 (1969) pp. 473–505; L. Schwarz, "M. Grimm, the Correspondance littéraire and the Philosophic Spirit" (Ph.D. diss., Los Angeles, 1962), pp. 321–84.

117. Grimm, *Correspondance littéraire*, vol. 8, p. 213 (Dec. 15, 1768).

118. Ibid., pp. 216f.

119. "Etat et description de la ville de Montpellier, fait en 1768," in *Montpellier en 1768 et en 1836 d'après deux manuscrits inédits*, ed. J. Berthelé (Montpellier, 1909), p. 57.

120. "La Mandrinade . . . "(Saint Geoirs, 1755), rpt. in *Histoires curieuses et véritables de Cartouche et de Mandrin*, ed. Hans-Jürgen Lüsebrink (Paris, 1984), p. 233.

121. D'Alembert, "Sur la Destruction des Jésuites en France" (1765), in *Oeuvres*, vol. 2 (Paris, 1821), p. 64. Mirasson's refutation, which has also been partly attributed to L. A. LePaige, received much less attention. For the larger context, see D. van Kley, *The Jansenists and the Expulsion of the Jesuits from France, 1757–1765* (New Haven, Conn., 1975).

122. Voltaire, "Avis au public sur les parricides imputés aux Calas et aux Sirven" (1766), in *Oeuvres*, ed. Moland, 1883–85, vol. 25, p. 536. See too Voltaire's letter to Marmontel from March 25, 1765 (Bestermann Document 12500, vol. 28, p. 480) and Bachaumont, *Mémoires*, vol. 2, p. 190 and vol. 3, pp. 77f. (May 5, 1765, and Sept. 15, 1766). For the general significance of the affair, see D. D. Bien, *The Calas Affair* (Princeton, N.J., 1961) and W. D. Howarth, "Tragedy into Melodrama: The Fortunes of the Calas Affair on the Stage," *Studies on Voltaire and the Eighteenth Century* 174 (1978), pp. 121–50.

123. *Vie de M. Turgot* (1786), in Condorcet, *Oeuvres*, vol. 5, p. iii; also Bachaumont, *Mémoires*, vol. 33, p. 84 (Oct. 3, 1786). For an analysis of Turgot's ministry see Reichardt, *Reform und Revolution bei Condorcet*, pp. 129–53; C. C. Gillespie, *Science and Polity in France at the End of the Old Regime* (Princeton, N.J., 1980), pp. 21–50.

124. Bestermann Document 20134, vol. 43, p. 157; also his letter to the Count of Hessen-Kassel on May 18, 1776 (ibid., 20179, vol. 48, p. 153).

125. Reichardt, *Reform und Revolution bei Condorcet*, p. 99.

126. "Nous venons d'apprendre que M. de Voltaire, le Poëte & le Philosophe de l'Europe, est mort. Il n'est plus exposé à mille ennemis, qui, tant qu'il a vécu, hont dégradé ses Ouvrages & diffamé son charatère" ("Lettre d'un philosophe chinois sur la mort supposé de M. de Voltaire," n. d. [1778], pp. 1f., rpt. in *Les Voltairiens*. Collection preparé par Jeroom Vercruysse. Vol. 1, p. 127.

127. Ximénez, p. 18.

128. Grimm, *Correspondance littéraire*, vol. 20, pp. 105f. (May 1778) occasioned by J. B. M Clément's *Satire sur la fausse philosophie* (n.d. 1778), where he wrote:

'Se dire philosophe est la mode aujourd'hui;
L'on n'entend que ce mot: mais, bon Dieu! quel ennui
De voir des charlatans nous étaler sans cesse
Tant de philosophie & si peu de sagesse!
. . . .
Le sage qui m'est cher, & que seul je respecte,
. . . .
Il n'eniera jamais un poste ambitieux,
Pour réformer l'état, qui n'en iroit pas mieux.'

Quoted from the advertisement for the *Journal encyclopédique* 7/3 (Nov. 1, 1778), pp. 499–504.

129. [Abbé A. B. de Crillon], *Mémoires philosophiques du baron de********. . . , vols. 1 & 2 (Vienna and Paris, 1777–78; 2nd ed. 1779); quoted here from the review in Grimm, *Correspondance littéraire*, vol. 11, p. 494 (July 1777).

130. See comprehensively the praising review in *Année littéraire* 4/2 (May 1777): "Tous les philosophes s'y rendent avec empressement. L'assemblée commence par s'entretenir des nouvelles politiques de l'Europe, on y juge avec liberté les Rois & leurs Ministres, & l'on dîne gaiement; . . . c'est dans ces grandes comices qu'on venge solennellement la mémoire des philosophes, insultés par les suppôts du fanatisme; qu'on accorde des gratifications & des encouragements aux jeunes auteurs, qui témoignent du zèle pour la propagation des lumières & l'extinction des préjugés; . . . qu'on dénonce les ennemis de la philosophie, & qu'on note, *dans le livre rouge des persécutions*, les noms de ceux dont on a résolu de tirer une vengeance éclatante, &c." (pp. 46f.). In contrast, the *Journal encyclopédique* 4/2 (June 1778) interceded: "Quand on songe que la philosophie exerce sur les esprits l'empire que la religion exerce sur les consciences, on est forcé de respecter l'une & l'autre . . . On voit des deux côtés, les passions prendre le nom des vertus & les excès d'un parti justifiés par les excès du parti contraire . . . ; on se croit dévot, quand on hait les philosophes; on se croit philosophe, quand on hait les dévots; tandis que la véritable philosophie & la véritable religion, faites pour être d'accord, rapprochent les hommes, & leur ordonnent de s'aimer au milieu de ce choc d'opinions ennemies" (pp. 271f.).

131. [C. F. C. le Roy de Lozembrune], *Tableau des Moeurs d'un siècle philosophique: Histoire de Justine de Saint-Val* . . . (Mannheim, 1786). See too, *Année littéraire* 5/22 (July 1778), pp. 347–49; and *Journal de Paris* 209 (July 28, 1786), pp. 3–24.

132. Grimm, *Correspondance littéraire*, vol. 15, p. 46 (April 1787); see too the ambivalent review in the *Journal encyclopédique* 4/1 (May 15, 1787), pp. 3–24.

133. Mme. de Genlis, pp. 218, 230; also ibid., pp. 188, 224ff., 290ff., and the chapter entitled "Si l'on a une idée précise de ce que c'est qu'un Philosophe," pp. 328–58. In its discussion, the *Année littéraire* found its old aggressivity again: "Les Philosophes se piquent sur-tout d'être supérieurs aux préjugés . . . ; cependant ils sont eux-mêmes entêtés d'une foule d'opinions aussi fausses que dangereuses; & voici les principales. Parce qu'ils n'ont point eux-mêmes de vertu; parce que l'intérêt personnel est leur unique principe . . . ; ils on un souverain mépris pour l'espèce humaine; ils font des peinture horribles de la Cour & du monde; . . . ils se regardent comme des êtres privilégiés, supérieurs aux autres hommes."

134. Wade, *The "Philosophe" in the French Drama of the Eighteenth Century*, pp. 46, 63f., 83–96.

135. Doray de Longrais, *Faustin ou le siècle Philosophique* (Amsterdam, 1784), p. 12.

136. So the *Journal encyclopédique* 2/2 (March 1, 1786), p. 233.

137. For Maury's Easter sermon, see the report of Louis-François Metra ("Mettra"), *Correspondance secrète* (London, 1787–90), vol. 6, p. 182 (April 25, 1778).

138. *Procès-verbale de l'Assemblée du Clergé de France, tenue en 1785* (Paris, 1787), entry of July 2, 1785. See also Charon, *Lettre ou Mémoire historique sur les troubles populaires à Paris en août et septembre 1788* (London, 1788): "La philosophie, celle qu'on enseigne aujourd'hui, fera-t-elle beaucoup d'honnêtes gens dans les dernières classes? . . . cette philosophie funeste que les hommes les plus grossiers même affectent de substituer à la simple morale religieuse."

139. Letter to the editor, *Journal de Paris* 336 (Dec. 2, 1786), p. 1400.

140. Grimm, *Correspondance littéraire*, vol. 11, p. 496 (July 1777) on Holbach's *Système de la nature*: "Il a gâté à tout jamais le métier de philosophe." See also ibid., vol. 12, p. 200 (Jan. 1779).

141. Advertisement for the *Journal de Languedoc*, rpt. in *Journal de Paris* 324, suppl. (Nov. 20, 1786), p. 1341. The *Affiches du Poitou* wrote on Nov. 16, 1786: "Grâce à la philosophie les esprits désabusés rougissent de la longue ignorance dans laquelle ils ont croupi."

142. "Les persécutions auxquelles ce parti fut d'abord en butte, loin de diminuer son crédit, ne firent qu'augmenter encore sa force et sa célébrité. Pour se défendre et se soutenir contre ses ennemis, on n'en

eut que plus de zèle et plus d'union, on fut plus empressé à faire des prosélytes et à se ménager des protections sûres et puissantes. . . . . La cour, qui dans d'autres temps semblait redouter l'influence des philosophes, ne paraît aujourd'hui ni les craindre ni les aimer. Elle protège sans aucun esprit de parti tous les talents qui contribuent à son amusement ou se distinguent par des ouvrages utiles; elle ne témoigne aux derniers soutiens de l'*Encyclopédie* que la plus parfaite indifférence. Est-il donc nécessaire qu'il y ait dans la littérature un parti dominant? et si les philosophes avaient su conserver le degré de considération dont ils ont joui pendant quelque temps, est-il bien sûr qu'ils n'en eussent jamais abusé, et qu'en prenant la consistance d'une secte quelconque, ils n'en eussent pris bientôt tous les vices et tous les inconvénients? Rien de plus nuisible à la société que l'abus des honneurs rendus à l'oisiveté spéculative. Que chaque individu ait une desination fixe et déterminée, que tout le monde soit occupé, et nous n'aurons aucun besoin ni de prêtres ni de philosophes." Grimm, *Correspondance littéraire*, vol. 12, pp. 204–7 (Jan. 1779).

143. Ibid., pp. 201–7; Bachaumont, *Mémoires*, vol. 1 (1780), pp. 3–4; for similar statements by Condorcet, see Reichardt, *Reform und Revolution bei Condorcet*, p. 127.

144. Grimm, *Correspondance littéraire*, vol. 15, p. 84 (June 1787).

145. P. F. N. Fabre D'Eglantine, *Inscription en style lapidaire, pour mettre sous le buse de J. J. Rousseau* [Geneva, 1781]. As a fellow worker of Prudhomme, Fabre d'Eglantine had this "inscription" reprinted with slight changes in *Révue de Paris* 78 (Jan. 1–8, 1791), pp. 699f.

146. *Année littéraire* 4/1 (May 8, 1787), pp. 20f.

147. Hans-Jürgen Lüsebrink, "Stratégies d'intervention, identité sociale et présentation de soi d'un 'défenseur de l'humanité': La carrière de l'abbé Raynal, 1713–1796," in *Bulletin du Centre d'Analyse du discours* 5 (1981), pp. 28–64.

148. These were the ones celebrated in Ximénes's 1786 poem, "Les philosophes."

149. D. Bleitrach, *Le Music-Hall des âmes nobles: Essai sur les intellectuels* (Paris, 1984). The concept *les intellectuels* first originated in the context of the Dreyfus affair; see D. Bering, *Die Intellektuellen: Geschichte eines Schimpfwortes* (Stuttgart, 1978), pp. 39–52; also *Les écrivains et l'affaire Dreyfus: Actes du Colloque . . .* , ed. G. Leroy (Paris, 1984).

150. Darnton, *Bohème*, pp. 8–69.

151. Louis-Sebastien Mercier, *Tableau*, vol. 1 (1783), p. 23.

152. Ibid., vol. 7 (1783), pp. 259f.

153. At the same time, there were tendencies toward an elitist, illusionary, playful life form of the "philosophical idyll" in which the old gesture of maintaining a distance from society was connected with the bucolic tradition. Examples are Rousseau's *Nouvelle Héloïse* (1761), whose basic constellation is the relationship between a young private tutor and his [female] pupil, and a series of articles, *Soirées d'hiver d'une femme retirée à la campagne,* which has to do with conversations and romantic situations between this refined lady and a "philosophe"; see *Journal de Paris,* no. 312 (Nov. 8, 1786), pp. 1289–91; no. 315 (Nov. 11, 1786), pp. 1297–99; no. 318 (Nov. 14, 1786), pp. 1314f.; no. 321 (Nov. 17, 1786), pp. 1325–27.

154. Diderot, "Essai sur les règnes de Claude et de Néron et sur la vie et les écrits de Sénèque" (1778), book 2/25 in *Oeuvres* (Paris, 1875–77), vol. 3, p. 248; quoted here from Mettra's review, vol. 7, p. 302 (Feb. 25, 1779).

155. "Sages de la terre, philosophes de toutes les nations, c'est à vous seuls à faire de loix, en les indiquant à vos concitoyens. Ayez le courage d'éclairer vos freres . . . Faites rougir ces milliers d'esclaves soudoyés, qui sont prêts à exterminer leurs concitoyens, aux ordres de leurs maîtres. . . . Apprenez-leur que la liberté vient de Dieu, l'authorité des hommes." Raynal, *Histoire*, vol. 1 (1780), pp. 132f.

156. "Les princes eux-mêmes partageront la sagesse de leur siècle. La voix de la philosophie ira réveiller au fond de leurs âmes des sentimens trop long-temps assoupis, & leur inspirera de l'horreur et du mépris pour une gloire singuinaires." Ibid., vol. 10, p. 183.

157. "Si jamais, en effet, la philosophie peut s'insinuer dans l'ame des Souverains ou de leurs

ministres, . . . le bien public entrera dans les négociations, non comme un mot, mais comme une chose utile, même aux rois." Ibid., vol. 10, p. 444.

158. Ibid., vol. 9, p. 364.

159. "Recherche du vrai, désir d'être utile, voilà les caractères de l'écrivain philosophe"; "Le charlatan pérore, le philosophe agit; le charlatan parle d'humanité, le philosophe est homme, aime les hommes." J.-B. Brissot, *De la vérité* (Neufchâtel, 1782), pp. 20, 200f.

160. Ibid., pp. 222–47.

161. Ibid., pp. 96, 204. For the reception of this text, cf. *Journal encyclopédique* 4/1 (May 15, 1783), pp. 3–22; *Année littéraire* 2/19 (April 1783), pp. 391–415 and 3/2 (May 1783), pp. 36–68.

162. [J.-L. Carra], *Système de la raison ou le prophète philosophe* (London, 1782), pp. 51, 55f. Mettra noticed the radicality of this text; vol. 13, pp. 409–11 (Nov. 2, 1782).

163. J. E. D. Bernardi, *Principes des loix criminelles* (Paris, 1788) (awarded a prize in 1780 by the Academie à Châlons-sur-Marne), p. 216; quoted from Hans-Jürgen Lüsebrink, *Kriminalität und Literatur im Frankreich des 18. Jahrhunderts* (Munich, 1983), p. 200; ibid., pp. 205, 181.

164. Hence Bachaumont, *Mémoires*, vol. 33, p. 45 (Sept. 17, 1786) in his review of C. M. J. B. M. Dupaty, *Mémoire justificatif pour trois hommes condamnés à la roue* (Paris, 1786).

165. Salviat, *La jurisprudence du parlement de Bordeaux* (Paris, 1787), p. 115.

166. *Réflexions sur le projet d'éloigner du milieu de Paris les tueries des bestiaux* . . . (London, 1787); cf. the review in *Journal de Paris* 75 (March 15, 1788), p. 329.

167. Letter to the editor, *Journal de Paris* 84 (March 24, 1788), p. 366.

168. Bachaumont, *Mémoires*, vol. 35, pp. 156f. (May 28, 1787).

169. Grimm, *Correspondance littéraire*, vol. 13, p. 132 (May 1782); similar to two letters to the editor in *Journal de Paris*: "Un des plus grands bienfaits de la Philosophie est de concourir à perfectionner les institutions sociales" (no. 105 from April 14, 1788, p. 465); the Abbé Fauchet wrote about "les actes bienfaisans que la vraie philosophie multiplie si heureusement de nos jours" (no. 167 from June 15, 1788, p. 370).

170. Féraud, vol. 3 (1788), pp. 153f.; the definition of *philosophe* there is "incrédule, libertin d'esprit, qui, sous prétexte de s'affranchir de préjugés, se met au-dessus des devoirs de la Religion et des bienséances, s'élève même, quand il le peut sans danger, contre les lois divines et humaines et contre le Gouvernement. Cette espèce de *Philosophes* s'est extrêmement accrue."

171. This was especially the case with *philosophisme*: Mettra, vol. 8, p. 185 (July 14, 1779); *Journal encyclopédique* 8/3 (Dec. 15, 1780), p. 438; Bachaumont, *Mémoires*, vol. 34, p. 318 (April 4, 1787). For *philosophistes*, ibid., vol. 35, p. 230 (June 16, 1787). For an anonymous drama, *La Philoso-manie* (1787), see Wade, *The "Philosophe" in the French Drama of the Eighteenth Century*, p. 102.

172. Féraud, *Dictionnaire critique de la langue française* (Marseille, 1787–88), vol. 3 (1788), p. 154.

173. Année littéraire 4/1 (May 8, 1787), p. 20.

174. Mercier, *Tableau*, vol. 10 (1788), pp. 23f.

175. This section's title is taken from *Ami du Peuple* 142 (June 23, 1790), p. 3.

176. Letter to the editor from Aug. 17, 1789, in *Journal de Paris*, 233 (Aug. 21, 1789), p. 1052, in justification of his political sermon in Notre-Dame on August 5.

177. *Ami du Peuple* 274 (Nov. 8, 1790), p. 3. See too J.-P. Marat, *Appel à la Nation* (March/April, 1790), p. 5; *Père Duchesne* 4 (Jan. 8, 1791), pp. 5f.: "Grâces aux écrits de nos phylosophes, les lumières se répandirent progressivement. . . . La révolution s'est ainsi opérée."

178. Speech by C. Villette in the Parisian Jacobin Club on Nov. 10, 1790 (François-Alphonse Aulard, ed., *La société des Jacobins* [Paris, 1898–1902], vol. 1, p. 368).

179. *Ami du Peuple* 421 (April 6, 1791), pp. 6f.; as well as the petition signed by about 160 members of the Parisian sections, *Pétition à l'Assemblée Nationale*, Paris, June 1791, p. 2; rpt. in *Les Voltairiens* (see n. 126, this chapter), vol. 5, p. 22.

180. The representative Gosin substantiated the law for the Pantheonizing of Voltaire on March 30, 1791, in the name of the constitutional committee: "Oui, Messieurs, la philosophie et la justice réclament pour l'époque de leur triomphe, celle où le fanatisme presécuteur a tanté de proscrire sa [Voltaire] mémoire" (*Les Voltairiens*, vol. 5, p. 1). P. P. Gudin de la Brenellerie, in *Réponse d'un ami des grands hommes, envieux de la gloire de Voltaire* (Paris, 1791), replied to this text: "Voltaire est le premier Philosophe qui ait attaqué courageusement et de front les préjugés, la superstition, le fanatisme, la féodalité et tous les genres de la tyrannie . . . Il a fait comme le Peuple française; il a pris la Bastille avant de poser les fondemens de la Constitution"(p. 3). It was exactly this text that was taken over as an editorial in the *Journal de Paris* 199 (July 18, 1791), p. 4.

181. Quoted from the *Chronique de Paris* 193 (July 17, 1791), p. 781. For the Pantheonizing of Voltaire and its general reception, see J. A. Leith, "Les trois Apothéoses de Voltaires," *Annales de l'Histoire de la Révolution française* 51 (1979), pp. 161–209, especially pp. 199ff; also R. Rockwood, "The Legend of Voltaire and the Cult of Revolution," in *Ideas in History: Essays Presented to L. Gottschalk*, ed. R. Herr and H. Parker (Durham, 1965), pp. 135–56.

182. In a petition of the canton Montmorency, which had attached itself to the citizens of Paris, presented to the National Assembly on Aug. 27, 1791: *Pétition à l'Assemblée nationale, contenant demande de la translation des cendres de J.J. Rousseau, au Panthéon français* (Paris, 1791), p. 10; rpt. in *J.-J. Rousseau dans la Révolution française, 1789–1801* (Paris, 1977, no. 13). See also L. S. Mercier, *J.J. Rousseau considéré comme l'un des premiers auteurs de la Révolution*, vols. 1–2 (Paris, 1791), as well as n. 146.

183. J. Lakanal, "Rapport sur J.J. Rousseau, fait au nom du Comité d'instruction publique, dans la séance du 29 Fructidor, Paris" (Sept. 14, 1794): "Honorez en lui le génie bienfaiteur de l'humanité; honorez l'ami, le défenseur, l'apôtre de la liberté et des moeurs, le promoteur des droits de l'homme, l'éloquent precurseur de cette révolution . . . ; honorez en lui le malheur . . . ; car il est douloureux et il est peut-être inévitable que le génie et la vertu soient en butte à la calomnie et à la persecution" (p. 9). For the whole context, see J. Higgins, "Rousseau and the Pantheon" in *Modern Language Review* 50 (1955), pp. 272–80. For the gradual admission of Diderot into the ranks of the precursors of the Revolution, see Hans-Jürgen Lüsebrink, "'Le livre qui fait naître des Brutus . . . ': Zur Verhüllung und sukzessiven Aufdeckung der Autorschaft Diderots an der 'Histoire des Deux Indes,' " in *Diderot: Vorträge des Erlanger Kolloquiums*, ed. F. J. Hausmann, T. Heydenreich, and H. Hudde (Erlangen, 1985).

184. So the speaker Joly apostrophized Franklin, Rousseau, Voltaire, and Mirabeau at the dedication of their busts as "ces philosophes, premiers dieux de la liberté." *Société fraternelle des patriotes des sexes . . . à Paris. Extrait du Procés-verbal de la Séance du Dimanche, 12 Février 1792* (Paris, 1792), p. 9. See also Douneau-Démophile, *Couplets civiques pour l'inauguration des bustes de Franklin, Voltaire, Buffon, J.-J. Rousseau, Marat et le Pellitier* (Paris, an II).

185. *Alphabet des sans-culottes* (1793), p. 11.

186. Sédillez on Dec. 5, 1791, in the "Legislative" looking back on the "Constituante," *Moniteur* 340 (Dec. 6, 1790), p. 550. See also *Correspondance secrète* (July 23, 1790), vol. 2, p. 461; the poster in Metz, *Paix aux Chaumières, Guerre aux Châteaux* from June 2, 1793 (Bibliothèque historique de la Ville de Paris 8192); as well as the song "A la philosophie" by T. Rousseau in *Chansonnier de la République pour l'an III* (Bordeaux and Paris, 1794), pp. 104f.

187. See in sequence, the *Cahier* of the community Saint-Just-sur-Loire from March 8, 1789, in *Etats Généraux de 1789. Cahiers de doleánces de la province de Forez* (St. Etienne, 1975), vol. 2, p. 348; *La résurrection des bons François et la mort civile des aristocrates* (1789), p. 4.

188. P. Manuel, "Lettre sur le jugement de Louis," in *Journal de Paris* 16 (Jan. 16, 1793), p. 3.

189. Report of the commissioner of the "convention" Pérès from Valenciennes from Feb. 8, 1795 (Aulard, *Recueil des actes du Comité de salut public* [Paris, 1889–1932], vol. 20, p. 153).

190. According to the commissioner of the convention Clauzel from Toulouse on Sept. 5, 1795, about the welfare commission (ibid., vol. 27, p. 196).

191. Report of the commissioner of the convention Carrier to the welfare commission of Angers on Nov. 12, 1793 (ibid., vol. 8, p. 381). See also his report from Nov. 17, 1793 (ibid., p. 505); letter of commissioner Fouché to the convention from Nevers on Oct. 29, 1793 (ibid., p. 114); text of the welfare committee of Oct. 11, 1793, to the commissioner of the convention Laplanche to Orléans (ibid., vol. 7, pp. 363f.).

192. Letter to the editor of the *Journal de Paris* from Aug. 17, 1789; see also his *De la religion nationale* (Paris, 1789), pp. 36–38.

193. Report of commissioner Lequino and Laignelot from Oct. 21, 1793, from Rouen (Aulard, *Comité*, vol. 7, p. 551).

194. "Ils ont juré de n'enseigner désormais que les grands principes de la morale et de la saine philosophie" (report from Nov. 2, 1793, ibid., vol. 8, p. 189).

195. "Une acte de philosophie est extraordinaire dans un pays où l'erreur est encore en butte contre la raison" (report of commissioner le Carpentier from Jan. 29, 1794, ibid., vol. 10, p. 519).

196. "Partout dans ce département la philosophie fait des progrès. Beaucoup de communes ne veulent plus de prêtres. D'autres ont pris pour l'exercice du culte des maîtres d'école . . . d'autres ne veulent que l'instruction publique . . . ; d'autres enfin ne veulent plus de cérémonies religieuses" (report of the commissioner Godefroy of Jan. 10, 1794, from Courtalin, ibid., vol. 10, p. 169). See also the report of commissioner Reynaud of Nov. 22, 1793, from the Département Haute-Loire to the welfare commission (ibid., vol. 8, p. 642).

197. *Journal du vrai Jacobin* 7 (Sedan, March 13, 1794), p. 25.

198. Robespierre's speech to the club on Nov. 21, 1793, and his plan for an address to the commissioner of Dec. 5, 1793 (*Oeuvres*, vol. 10, pp. 194–201 and 229).

199. *Gazette française*, Mar. 8, 1795 (Aulard, *Paris pendant la Réaction thermidorienne et sons le Directoire* [Paris, 1898–1902], vol. 1, p. 542).

200. So was the chapter "De la religion et de la philosophie," in Lacretelle, *Où faut-il s'arrêter?* (1797), pp. 71–75.

201. *Moniteur*, July 27, 1802 (Aulard, *Paris sons le Consulat* [Paris, 1903–9], vol. 3, p. 179).

202. See the police report of Oct. 12, 1797 (Aulard, *Réaction*, vol. 4, p. 390).

203. "C'est la philosophie que a préparé et commencé la grande révolution qui s'opère; malheureusement ce n'est pas la philosophie qui en dirige tous les mouvements." Advertisement for Suard's newspaper *Les indépendants* 86 (March 27, 1791), suppl. p. 1.

204. "Chez tout peuple . . . il n'est pas un homme sensé qui n'eut senti qu'aucune révolution ne peut se consoler sans qu'un parti ait écrasé l'autre: il étoit réservé aux français de prétendre renverser toutes leurs institutions politiques, pour établir un nouvel ordre de choses par la seule force de la philosophie: comme si les passions les plus impérieuses étoient soumises à voix de la raison!" *Ami du peuple*, 2nd. ser., no. 211 (May 8, 1793), p. 2; ibid. (Nov. 26, 1792), p. 8.

205. In his report to the convention of May 7, 1794, Robespierre distanced himself from the "secte" of Encyclopedists and their "espèce de philosophie pratique" (*Oeuvres*, vol. 10, pp. 454f.).

206. "Philantropes, amis vrais de la liberté, rassurez-vous sur les destinés du peuple français, la philosophie a reconquis la révolution. C'est elle qui a donné la première impulsion au char de la liberté, c'est elle qui le conduira dans la carrière." Letter to the editor, *Journal de Paris* 122 (Jan. 21, 1795), p. 493.

207. "Tableau analytique de la situation du Départment de la Seine" (10/11, 1798), in Aulard, *Réaction*, vol. 5, p. 216.

208. Cf. the biographical survey by F. A. Kafker, "Les encyclopédistes et la Terreur," *Révue d'histoire moderne et contemporaine* 14 (1967), pp. 284–95; R. Mortier, "Les héritiers des philosophes devant l'expérience révolutionnaire," *Dix-huitième siècle* 6 (1974), pp. 45–57.

209. *Adresse* to the National Assembly, read there and vigorously discussed (*Archives parlementaires de la France*, vol. 26, pp. 650 and 652).

210. On April 25, 1792, Brissot spoke at the Parisian Jacobin Club: "Vous déchirez Condorcet,

lorsque sa vie révolutionnaire n'est qu'une suite de sacrifices pour le peuple: philosophe, il s'est fait politique; académicien, il s'est fait journaliste; noble, il s'est fait jacobin; placé par la cour dans un poste éminent, il l'a quitté pour le peuple. . . . Le monument le plus ferme de votre République, c'est la philosophie. . . . Le patriote par excellence est philosophe" (Aulard, *Jacobins*, vol. 3, p. 529).

211. P. J. B. Chaussard, *Lettre d'un homme libre à l'esclave Raynal* (Paris, [1791]), p. 4; for an analysis of the whole affair, see Lüsebrink, "Stratégies d'intervention," pp. 46–55.

212. Reichardt, *Reform und Revolution bei Condorcet*, pp. 241ff.

213. Official speech of the president of the commission of elders for July 14, 1798, in *Moniteur* 298 (July 16, 1798), vol. 39, pp. 314f.

214. "Il [i.e., Dillon] appelle une société composée de *philosophes* tous connus par leurs talens, leurs lumières, leur réputation pour les meilleurs amis de la justice, de l'humanité et de la vérité, et pour les plus grands propagateurs de la raison universelle, *une société de soi-disant philosophes*," in *Annales patriotiques* 133 (March 19, 1791), p. 1190. In reality, Dillon spoke to the National Assembly about "prétendus philanthropes"; *Archives parlementaires* 23, p. 665.

215. "Et vous citoyens éclairés, philosophes (j'appelle ainsi tout homme qui ayant de la justesse dans l'esprit, de la droiture dans le coeuer, et de la fermeté dans l'âme, a pris soin d'éclairer sa raison, et sait en faire un légitime usage), vous donc vrais philosophes," in *Le triomphe des communes* (1789), p. 5; repeated literally in *Manifeste de la souveraine raison,* ibid.

216. "L'Assemblée Nationale n'est autre chose qu'une Secte de *menus* Philosophes, que les ignorans admirent." *De la décadence de l'Empire français, fruit de la philosophie moderne* (1790). See n. 214.

217. Dasseau made the following suggestion on Oct. 12, 1792, in the Jacobin Club: "Une adresse rédigée par des philosophes, c'est-à-dire des patriotes, car il n'est pas de philosophie sans patriotisme," in Aulard's *Jacobins*, vol. 3, p. 195. See also the song "Définition d'un vrai philosophe" by Auguste (1792), in Pierre Barbier and France Vernillat, *Histoire de France par ses chansons* (Paris, 1956–61), vol. 3, pp. 199–201; as well as the confrontation in an anecdote: "Le maître est philosophe, par conséquent dans les principes de la révolution, tandis que sa femme au contraire est aristocrate et royaliste au superlatif," in *Journal des sans-culottes* 3 (Nov. 16, 1792), pp. 3f.

218. *Journal de Paris* 258 (June 16, 1800), p. 1202; see also Mercier, *Nouveau Paris* (1798), vol. 2, pp. 110f.

219. Marat protested against his legal persecution with the following comment: "Me faire un crime de la liberté de philosopher," in *Ami du Peuple*, 2nd ser., no. 180 (April 28, 1793), p. 3.

220. See the entry "Conspiracy," in Reichardt and Schmitt, eds., *Handbuch politisch-sozialer Grundbegriffe in Frankreich, 1680–1820.*

221. Roux, "Les moyens de sauver la France" (1792), in *Scripta*, p. 57. See also *Publiciste* 246 (July 23, 1793), ibid., p. 182; and against it, ironically, *Quotidienne* 108 (Dec. 14, 1793): "Qu'est-ce qu'un philosophe? . . . Un homme qui aime la sagesse, la justice, la liberté, l'égalité; or, les sans-culottes aiment tout cela, donc les sans-culottes sont philosophes" (p. 2).

222. "*Un paysan.* Voulez-vous bien, citoyen, commencer dès aujourd'hui à nous donner des leçons de philosophie . . . et qui sait si nous ne deviendrons pas aussi nous philosophes?—*Le Philosophe.* Hé pourquoi ne deviendrez-vous pas philosophes ainsi que moi? Suis-je fait autrement que vous?" Lequinio, *Philosophie du peuple* (1796), pp. 11f.

223. The *Affiches de la Commune* declared in no. 168 (Dec. 14, 1793): "Il est urgent de porter chez nos bons frères de la compagne le flambeau étincelant de cette philosophie simple et naturelle, à la portée de tous les sans-culottes."

224. Commissioner of the convention Boisset on Feb. 16, 1794, from Montpellier: "La philosophie a fait de progrès rapides dans nos climats. Le jeune enfant pense et raisonne." Aulard, *Comité*, vol. 11, pp. 204f. Parisian police report from May 4, 1797: "Dans le public éclairé . . . l'on fronde avec beaucoup de chaleur les chauds partisans de la philosophie moderne; on en veut surtout à ceux qui supposent parmi le peuple le progrès des lumières assez rapide." Aulard, *Réaction*, vol. 4, p. 96. The newspaper *Citoyen français* on May 8, 1801: "Nos braves, si longtemps appelés des

bleus dans la Vendée, des *terroristes* ailleurs, sont maintenant des philosophes, mais de *philosophes à moustaches.*" Aulard, *Consulat*, vol. 2, p. 189.

225. Furet, *Penser la Révolution*, p. 73.

226. Basire on Nov. 18, 1792, in the Paris Jacobin Club (Aulard, *Jacobins*, vol. 4, p. 490).

227. For the use of the predicate "bourgeois" in the revolutionary and postrevolutionary eras, see Hans Ulrich Gumbrecht, "Klassik ist Klassik: Eine bewundernswerte Sicherheit des Nichts?" in Fritz Nies and Karlheinz Stierle, eds., *Französische Klassik* (Munich, 1985), pp 441-94.

228. *Quotidienne* 413 (June 14, 1797), pp. 1f. The last phrases play on the Jacobin dictatorship's prisons of the reaction following on the *maisons d'arrêt*. The *Almanach des honnêtes gens* (1801) took over the article with some changes, pp. 71-78.

229. A. Barruel, *Le Patriote véridique ou Discours sur les vraies causes de la révolution actuelle* (Paris, 1789): "Les causes de la révolution actuelle sont toutes dans la dépravation des moeurs publiques, et dans les progrès du philosophisme. . . . Mais en nous retrouvant François . . . , souvenons-nous qu'encore un pas vers le philosophisme, et nous cessions de l'être" (pp. 6, 35). See also A. Barruel, *Remarques et anecdotes sur le château de la Bastille* (Paris, 1789), p. 106.

230. Buée (1792), pp. 97f. See also *Des factions en France* (1792), pp. 5, 8f.

231. Léonard Snetlage, *Nouveau dictionnaire français* (Göttingen, 1795), p. 173; Charles-Frédéric Reinhard, *Le néologiste français* (Nürnberg, 1796), p. 256.

232. See also the anonymous article against the *philosophes* in *Accusateur public* 9/11 (1795), pp. 19-24; as well as Dières, *Philosophomanie, poëme, ou la maladie des têtes à systèmes. . .* (Rouen, 1795).

233. La Harpe, *Fanatisme* (1797), pp. 7, 33.

234. "En un mot, la philosophie divise les hommes par les opinions, la religion les unit dans les mêmes dogmes, et la politique dans les mêmes principes; il y a donc un contrat éternel entre la politique et la religion." Antoine de Rivarol, *De la philosophie moderne* (Paris, 1797), pp. 35f.

235. Abbé Barruel, *Mémoires pour servir à l'histoire du jacobinisme* (1797-98), rpt. vols. 1-2 (Paris, 1973), here vol. 1, p. 46.

236. Ibid., vol. 2, pp. 524 passim.

237. Ibid., vol. 1, pp. 49ff.

238. Ibid., vol. 1, p. 251. Similarly the allegedly antimonarchistic "rebellion" of the Girondistes under Brissot: "Il voudrait lui [la rébellion] donner l'apparence d'une révolution tout philosophique, toute sollicitée par un peuple philosophe, lassé de ses Monarques, et ne voulant enfin avoir d'autre Roi que lui-même" (ibid., vol. 2, p. 457). Barruel's position here is close to that of J. Mallet du Pan in "Du degré d'influence qu'a eu la philosophie française sur la Révolution," *Mercure Britannique* (March 10, 1799), pp. 342-70.

239. J. E. M. Portalis, *De l'usage et de l'abus de l'esprit philosophique durant le dix-huitième siècle*, 2 vols. (Paris, 1820), vol. 2, p. 435.

240. "Soyons justes: ce ne sont pas les philosophes qui ont corrompu le siècle, c'est la corruption du siècle qui a influé sur les philosophes." Ibid., vol. 2, p. 469.

241. "La manie de se montrer philosophe et esprit fort, et poussée à un tel point, que l'on rougit presque de paroître sensible." Ibid., vol. 1, pp. 438-50.

242. Ibid., vol. 1, pp. 16-50; vol. 2, pp. 284-87.

243. Ibid., vol. 1, pp. 147-80, 247f; vol. 2., 71ff., 116ff.

244. André Morellet, "Apologie de la philosophie contre ceux qui l'accusent des maux de la Révolution" (1796), in his *Mélanges de littérature et de philosophie du 18e siècle*, vol. 4 (Paris, 1818), pp. 308-32.

245. "Cet écrivain [La Harpe] connaît trop bien sa langue pour ignorer que les mots *philosophes, athées, impies, irréligieux, factieux*, ne sont point synonymes dans la langue française, . . . il a trouvé plus commode de changer l'épithète honorable de *Philosophes* en une flétrissure infamante:

donc il est de mauvaise foi." *De la persécution suscitée par J.-F. Laharpe, contre la Philosophie* (n.p., 1800), p. vi; see also pp. vii f., 37, 47.

246. Ibid., p. 11; see also p. 61.

247. J. J. Mounier, *De l'influence attribuée aux philosophes, aux francs-maçons et aux illuminés sur la révolution de France* (Tübingen, 1801), p. 15.

248. "Malgré toutes les déclarations actuelles sur l'influence des philosophes modernes, on peut dire qu'avant la révolution, elle étoit diminuée en France depuis quelques années." Ibid., p. 72.

249. Ibid., p. 134. See also M. de Cubières-Palmézeaux, *Le défenseur de la philosophie, ou Réponse à quelques satires dirigées contre la fin du XVIIIe siècle* (Paris, 1800); for the reading of this satire in the club "Le portique républicain," see *Journal des Hommes Libres* (Jan. 6, 1800), Aulard, *Consulat*, vol. 1, p. 82.

250. So went the writing by the Abbé L. B. Proyart, which ran through six printings by 1803, *Louis XVI détrôné avant d'être roi, ou Tableau des causes nécessitantes de la Révolution française et de l'ébranlement de tous les trônes* (Hamburg, 1800); a police report from May 16, 1801, summarized the content as follows: "Le *philosophisme*, voilà ce que combat l'auteur, voilà ce qu'il indique pour cause des événements politiques qu'il déplore: 1x Le philosophisme conspirateur et protégé répand impunément les semences de l'anarchie; 2x il détermine la Révolution du règne de Louis XVI; 3x il prépare cette tragédie révolutionnaire dont la France est devenue le thèâtre sous Louis XVI" (Aulard, *Consulat*, vol. 2, p. 304). A. J. de Barruel-Beauvert, *Actes des philosophes et des républicains recueillis et remis en évidence* (Paris, 1807). There is another police report on this: "L'auteur consacre quarante pages à l'histoire de sa détention au Temple, où le *Philosophisme athée et républicain a rivé ses fers et tiré ses verrous, pendant plus de quatre ans*; où il a été emprisonné de vert-de-gri, par l'incurie *philosophique* du traiteur, et où il était servi par des *tigres à visage humain*, par des *Philosophes républicains*, c'est ainsi qu'il appelle un des guichetiers" (Aulard, *Paris son le Premier Empire* [Paris, 1912–23], vol. 3, p. 350). See also Gourju, *La philosophie du XVIIIe siècle dévoilée par elle-même*, vols. 1–2 (Paris, 1816).

251. *Citoyen français* (May 1, 1801) on a Viennese library edict against the books of Bayle, Helvétius, and Rousseau (Aulard, *Consulat*, vol. 3, p. 460).

252. The number from July 15, 1803 (Aulard, *Consulat*, vol. 4, p. 245). See also the newspaper *Clef du Cabinet* from Feb. 17, 1801: "Les fanatiques, les intrigants et les radoteurs continuent à se déchaîner contre la *philosophie*. . . . Eh, mon Dieu! que vous a fait cette pauvre philosophie qui vous conseille de répondre par des vérités à vos mensonges, à vos calomnies par des bienfaits?" (Aulard, *Empire*, vol. 1, p. 495).

253. *Journal des Hommes Libres* (May 4, 1800), ibid., vol. 1, pp. 392f.

254. J. L. Piestre, *Les crimes de la philosophie, ou Tableau succinct des effets qu'elle a opérés dans la plupart des sciences, des arts et dans le régime des associations politiques* (Lyon, 1804); see also the Fouché's police report on it from Dec. 28, 1804 (Aulard, *Empire*, vol. 1, p. 495).

255. *Citoyen français* (May 1, 1801): "Apprenons à ceux qui suent sang et eau pour tuer, à coups d'épingle, ce qu'ils appellent la *coterie philosophique*, qu'il existe vraiment une coterie philosophique bien difficile à renverser. . . . En effet quelle immense coterie philosophique forment les Montaigne, les Bacon, les Descartes, les Newton, les Locke, les Leibnitz [*sic*], les Shaftesbury, les Maupertuis, les Diderot, les d'Alembert, les Buffon, les Montesquieu, les Raynal, les d'Holbach, les Helvétius, les Mably, les Thomas, les Boulanger, les Condillac, les d'Argens, les La Fontaine, les Molière, les Rousseau, les Fréret, les Malesherbes, les Voltaire, les Condorcet, les Bailly, les Mirabeau, les Franklin, etc., qui respirent encore. . . . Leur génie plane sur l'horizon qu'il embrase des plus beaux feux. Leurs écrits . . . vivent et circulent dans toutes les mains" (Aulard, *Empire*, vol. 2, p. 274).

256. *Vite, Soufflons Morbleu! Eteignons les lumières* . . . Bibiliothèque nationale, Département des Stampes. Collection de Vinck, 10303.

257. "Le *Français né malin*, continua, par ironie, d'appeler du nom de *philosophes* ces esprits faux,

professeurs de cette morale absurde et dangereuse. . . . Depuis, ce titre dérisoire leur a toujours été conservé; cependant ils s'enorgueillirent d'un nom qu'on leur avait laissé par mépris. . . . Ce jeu . . . eut l'inconvénient de laisser confondus ensemble ces apôtres fanatiques de l'erreur et les défenseurs de la vérité; ces pédagogues infâmes . . . et les sages précepteurs . . . ; ces corrupteurs des coeurs et les sévères censeurs des moeurs . . . ; enfin, cette foule impie de sophistes et les vrais amis de la philosophie" (*De l'Abus des mots*, pp. 12f.).

258. "PHILOSOPHIE. Les ultra ne pardonnent pas aux grands rois de les avoir faits asseoir avec eux sur le trône" (Saint-Maurice, 1823, p. 71). Even more parenthetic is the entry in the *Petit Dictionnaire de la Cour* (1826), p. 60.

259. "Dans les sens familiers à la *Gazette de France*, philosophie n'est autre chose que le mépris de tout ce qu'il y a de sacré sur la terre; elle n'est qu'une métaphysique dangereuse pour la morale publique et la tranquillité des Etats" (report from Aug. 31, 1804, Aulard, *Empire*, vol. 1, p. 229). "*La Gazette de France*, qui, quant à la politique, est toujours dans un assez bon esprit, ne modifie nullement ses opinions antiphilosophiques" (report from Oct. 15, 1804, ibid., vol. 1, p. 321).

260. Report of the police prefect from Oct. 27, 1801 (Aulard, *Consulat*, vol. 2, p. 590).

261. See the entry "Sciences et Arts" in Reichardt and Schmitt, eds., *Handbuch politisch-sozialer Grundbegriffe*.

262. [J. Frey], *Philosophie sociale dédiée au peuple françois*, by the section "République française" (Paris, 1793), pp. iii–vi. A reviewer remarked: "L'auteur y débute par convenir que ce sont les ouvrages de J.J. Rousseau & surtout son Contrat Social qui ont amené la révolution française." *Journal encyclopédique* 9/33 (Nov. 30, 1793), p. 43.

263. For the history of the *Idéologues* see the entry in Reichardt and Schmitt, eds., *Handbuch politisch-sozialer Grundbegriffe* as well as S. Moravia's *Il pensiero degli Idéologues* (Florence, 1974), and his "Les Idéologues et l'âge des Lumières," *Studies on Voltaire and the Eighteenth Century* 154 (1976); Marc Régaldo, "Lumières, élite, démocratie: La difficile position des Idéologues," *Dix-huitième siècle* 6 (1974), pp. 193–207; *Les Idéologues*, ed. W. Busse and J. Trabant (Amsterdam, 1984).

264. Moravia, *Il Pensiero*, p. 371. From the perspective of the history of linguistics, see W. Oesterreicher, "'Historizität' und Variation in der Sprachforschung der französichen Spätaufklärung," in *Der Diskurs in der Sprach- und Literaturhistorie*, ed. Hans Ulrich Gumbrecht and Bernard Cerquiglini (Frankfurt, 1983), pp. 167–205; B. Schlieben-Lange, "Die französiche Revolution und die Sprache," in *Zeitschrift für Literaturwissenschaft und Linguistik* 41 (1981), pp. 90–123.

265. Quoted from Marc Régaldo, *Un milieu intellectuel: La "Décade philosophique," 1794–1807*, vol. 4 (Lille and Paris, 1976), p. 612.

266. *Décade philosophique* from 30 Fructidor an VII (Sept. 16, 1799), p. 533.

267. "Science qui a pour objet la connaissance des chose physiques et morales par leurs causes et par leurs effets; étude de la nature et de la morale." *Dictionnaire de l'Académie française*, 6th ed. (1835), vol. 2, p. 407.

268. Ibid., p. 406

269. Ibid., p. 407.

270. Hugo said the following on the one hundreth anniversary of the death of Voltaire, the "philosophe courroucé": "Combattre le pharaîsme, démasquer l'imposture, terrasser les tyrannies, les usurpations, les préjugés, les mensonges, les superstitions, démolir le temple, . . . attaquer la magistrature féroce, attaquer le sacerdoce sanguinaire, . . . réclamer l'héritage des déshérités, protéger les faibles, les pauvres, les souffrants, les accadblés, lutter pour les persécutés et pour les opprimés, c'est la guerre de Jésus-Christ. Et quel est l'homme qui fait cette guerre? c'est Voltaire." *Oeuvres*, ed. J. Lemonnyer and E. Testard, 7/3 (Paris, 1940), pp. 302f.

271. The first discussions on the basic conception of this presentation and the interpretation of central sources took place in a seminar I gave at the Ecole des Hautes Etudes des Sciences Sociales

in Paris in February 1982. I would like to thank a number of colleagues, above all Roger Chartier, and the participants at the seminar for important suggestions and stimulating comments.

8. Outline of a Literary History of the French Revolution

1. For the final version of this essay, I have profited from suggestions formulated by Hans Robert Jauss, Fritz Nies, Rita Orgel, César Real de la Riva, and Rolf Reichardt.

2. See the detailed case study by Thomas Schleich, "Die Wirkungsgeschichte Mablys in Frankreich (1740–1797)" (Ph.D. diss., Bochum University, 1979).

3. All quotes like these statements by Mirabeau from parliamentary speeches during the revolutionary period can be found under their respective dates in the *Archives Parlementaires de la France, 1st series 1787–1799* (Paris, 1899; rpt. Liechtenstein, 1969).

4. A. Thibaudet, *Histoire de la littérature française de 1789 à nos jours* (Paris, 1936), p. 13. Quite understandably, M.-J. Chénier attempted to refute this kind of judgment current among his contemporaries in *Tableau historique de l'état et des progrès de la littérature française depuis 1789* (Paris, 1816), when he was commissioned by the Institut Français to write a literary history of the years around the turn of the nineteenth century. See p. xxviii: "On no account has France stopped producing talent as its power has grown."

5. On the literary history of the revolutionary period there have only been a few individual studies up to now (1980) and no overall representation at the level of current standard works of period history. Thus our sketch here does not present a synthesis of available investigations but only a preliminary framework, which will have to be filled in and modified by future studies.

6. See Niklas Luhmann, "Interaktion in Oberschichten: Zur Transformation ihrer Semantik im 17. und 18. Jahrhundert,"in *Gesellschaftsstruktur und Semantik*, ed. N. Luhmann (Frankfurt, 1980), vol. 1, pp. 72–161.

7. Among the countless historical presentations of the revolutionary period, François Furet's and Denis Richet's *La Révolution française* (Paris, 1965), which has already become a classic, has best combined a lucid presentation with information about contrary research directions. For a bibliographical survey of individual fields of research, see above all Eberhard Schmitt, *Einführung in die Geschichte der französosischen Revolution* (Munich, 1976).

8. See Rolf Reichardt, "Zu einer Sozialgeschichte der französischen Aufklärung," *Francia* 5 (1977), pp. 231–49, here pp. 234–36.

9. "Du dégré d'influence qu'a eu la philosophie françoise sur la Révolution," *Mercure britannique* 14 (March 10, 1799), pp. 342–70, here p. 367.

10. See for instance Robert Darnton, "The High Enlightenment and Low Life of Literature in Prerevolutionary France," *Past and Present* 51 (1971), pp. 81–115.

11. For Rousseau's concept of the "republican festival," see Jean Starobinski, *Jean-Jacques Rousseau: La transparence et l'obstacle* (Paris, 1971), pp. 116–21.

12. Joachim Campe, *Briefe aus Paris während der französischen Revolution geschrieben*, ed. H. König (Berlin [GDR], 1961), p. 250.

13. On the history of reading and writing competence in France, see the comprehensive empirical study by François Furet and Jacques Ozouf, *Lire et écrire: L'Alphabétisation de Français de Calvin à Jules Ferry* (Paris, 1977).

14. The texts mentioned in the following section are quoted—when not according to the *Archives Parlementaires de la France* or from contemporary publications—from facsimile editions of the *Editions d'Histoire Sociale (EdHis)*, which provides a good survey of the political literature of the revolutionary period—at least up until 1794.

15. In the meantime a monograph oriented to the functional history of the animal fable in the French Enlightenment—including the revolutionary decade—has become available; Frederike Hassauer-Roos, "Die Philosophie der Tiere—von der theoretischen zur praktischen Vernunft: Unter-

suchungen zu Funktions- und Strukturwandel in der Fabel der französischen Aufklärung" (Ph.D. diss., Bochum University, 1979).

16. The numbers 1–247 of the *Affiches de la Commune de Paris* have been edited by Albert Soboul (Paris, 1975).

17. Campe, *Briefe aus Paris*, pp. 147f.

18. The title already, but even more so the individual articles of this "constitution" and the project of an air force developed in the afterword, makes the reader suspect that it could be a parody of the recommendations for a constitution that were so popular in 1793–94, all the more so since the facsimile of the decree with L'Ange's death sentence by the Revolutionary Tribunal is included in the edition of the *Editions d'Histoire Sociale*. In any case, Irmgard Hartig and Albert Soboul consider the text for the expression of an effort to develop institutions for a "truly direct democracy" that should be taken seriously in their *Pour une histoire de l'utopie en France au XVIIIe siècle* (Paris, 1977), p. 78.

19. ["Je suis le véritable Père Duchesne, foutre!" The literal translation of "foutre" (fuck) distorts the meaning; on the other hand, "dammit" would not make it sufficiently clear how decisively the style of Père Duchesne broke with the conventions of printed speech. The author uses "Verdammt" because "ficken" is simply too strong in German, but English usage is much closer to French in this respect. – Trans.]

20. The formula, "sens vécu/sens voulu" comes from M. Ozouf, "La fête – sous la Révolution française" in *Faire de l'histoire*, ed. J. Le Goff and P. Nora, vol. 3 (Paris, 1974), pp. 256–77, here p. 266.

21. The appellation of Louis XVI as "Monsieur Véto," from which the formula "Véto femelle" is derived, goes back to the constitutional debates in 1789 in the course of which the king for the first time openly claimed the right to veto parliamentary decisions.

22. *Literatur im Epochenumbruch: Funktionen europäischer Literaturen im 18. und beginnenden 19. Jahrhundert*, ed. G. Klotz et al. (Berlin [GDR], 1977), p. 306. The texts of songs sung at revolutionary festivals are presented in the collection *Ça ira: 50 Chansons, Couplets und Vaudevilles aus der Französischen Revolution, 1789–1795*, ed. G. Semmer (Berlin [GDR], 1977).

23. My comments on the ideal model of republican festivals refer back once again to Starobinski, *Jean-Jacques Rousseau*, pp. 116–121.

24. Quoted from J.-L. Jam, "Fonction des hymnes révolutionnaires," in *Les fêtes de la Révolution: Colloque de Clermond-Ferrand* (June, 1974), ed. Jean Ehrard and Pierre Viallaneix (Paris, 1977), pp. 433–41, here p. 439.

25. Quoted from A. Mathiez, *La Théophilanthropie et le culte decadaire: Essai sur l'histoire religieuse de la Révolution, 1796–1801* (Paris, 1903; rpt. Geneva, 1975), p. 96.

26. A comprehensive though incomplete microfiche collection of texts on the theater of the revolutionary period has been presented by Marc Régaldo, *Le théâtre de la Révolution française* (Paris, 1975). The anthology *Théâtre du XVIIIe siècle*, ed. J. Truchet, vol. 2 (Paris: Pléiade, 1974), includes six plays from 1789–99. A first impression of the theater of the revolutionary period is facilitated by the richly annotated editions of M.-J. Chénier's *Charles IX* and Sylvain Maréchal's *Jugement dernier des rois*, which have been prepared by David Hamiche in *Le théâtre et la Révolution: La lutte des classes au théâtre 1789 et 1793* (Paris, 1973).

27. There are no pertinent anthologies of the poetry and novels of the revolutionary period discussed in this section, and apart from the works of Retif de la Bretonne and de Sade there are no reprints. Only the *Anthologie poétique française, XVIIIe siècle* (Paris, 1966), ed. M. Allem, presents some poems, for the most part inexactly dated.

28. *Anthologie poétique française*, Introduction, p. 5.

29. Cf. Roland Galle, "Sozialpsychologische überlegungen zu Rousseaus Autobiographie" (University of Constance, 1979, MS). I have also made use of some of the central hypotheses of this study in my analysis of the novel of the revolutionary period in the following pages.

30. Cf. Werner Krauss, "Quelques remarques sur le roman utopique au XVIIIe siècle," in *Roman et lumières au XVIIIe siècle* (Paris, 1970).

31. Irmagard Hartig, "Essai de bibliographie," in Hartig and Soboul, *Pour une histoire de l'utopie en France an XVIIIe siècle*.

32. Quoted from Restif de la Bretonne, *Oeuvres*, ed. H. Bachelin (Paris, 1930-31; rpt. Geneva, 1971), vols. 7-8, p. 69.

33. The crisis of denominating and comprehending reality at the turn of the nineteenth century is one of Michel Foucault's central themes under the key word "représentabilité des êtres," in *Les mots et les choses* (Paris, 1966).

34. See R. D. Mayo, "Ann Radcliffe and Ducray-Duminil," *Modern Language Review* 36 (1941), pp. 501-5, here p. 505.

35. Is it by accident that a famous Spanish picaresque novel from the early seventeenth century, which represents the life of a female "pícara," just happens to be called *La pícara Justina*?

36. Foucault, *Les mots et les choses*, pp. 221-24.

37. Peter Bürger, "Moral und Gesellschaft bei Diderot und Sade," in *Literatur der bürgerlichen Emanzipation im 18. Jahrhundert*, ed. Gert Mattenklott and Klaus Scherpe (Kronberg, 1973), pp. 77-104, here p. 97.

38. Their Sade quotation is from *La philosophie dans le boudoir*, in *Oeuvres complètes*, vol. 10 (Paris, 1966), p. 490.

39. "Abklärung des Aufklärung": This formulation was coined by Niklas Luhmann, *Soziologische Aufklärung: Aufsätze zur Theorie sozialer Systeme*, vol. 1 (Opladen, 1972).

9. "Phoenix from the Ashes"; or, From Canon to Classic

1. See, eg., Aleida and Jan Assmann, "Kanon und Zensur," in *Kanon und Zensur*, ed. Aleida and Jan Assmann (Munich, 1987), pp. 7-27.

2. Special aspects of this extremely complex process are traced in my essays "Skizze einer Literaturgeschichte der französischen Revolution," in *Die europäsche Aufklärung III*, ed. Jürgen Stackelberg, vol. 13 of *Neues Handbuch der Literaturwissenschaft* (Wiesbaden, 1980), pp. 269-328; "Chants révolutionnaires, maîtrise de l'avenir et niveau du sens collectif," *Revue d'histoire moderne et contemporaine* 30 (1983), pp. 235-56; " 'Ce divan étoilé d'or.' Empire als Stilepoche / Epochenstil / Stil / Epoche?" In *Zum Problem der Geschichtlichkeit ästhetischer Normen: Die Antike im Wandel des Urteils im 19. Jahrhunderts* (Berlin, 1987), pp. 269-94; and (with special attention to the classic/canon problem) " 'Klassik ist Klassik—eine bewundernswerte Sicherheit des Nichts'? oder: Funktionen der französischen Literatur des siebzehnten Jahrhunderts nach Siebzehnhundert," in *Französische Klassik: Theorie, Literatur, Malerei*, ed. Fritz Nies and Karlheinz Stierle (Munich, 1985), pp. 441-94. The following pages refer to these studies, even when not specifically indicated.

3. Relevant symptoms of this historical situation are the neologisms *classicisme* and the German equivalent *Klassik (Klassizismus)*. See Fontius, " 'Classique' im 18. Jahrhundert," in *Beiträge zur französischen Aufklärung und zur spanischen Literatur: Festgabe für Werner Krauss zum 70, Geburtstag*, ed. Werner Bahner (Berlin, 1971), pp. 87-120.

4. Cf. Ministère de l'Education Nationale, *École élémentaire. Programmes et instructions* (Paris, 1985), p. 37, where reception of the "Classics" and instruction in poetic composition are no longer connected: *"Usage poétique de la langue*: Mémorisation de poémes empruntés a l'ensemble de la poésie française. / Création poétique, après adoption libre de contraintes" (*Poetic usage of language*: Memorization of poems taken from the entire body of French poetry. / Poetic creation, after an adoption free of constraints). The text comes from Bernard Cerquiglini, former *Directeur des Écoles* in the French Ministry of Education.

5. Roland Barthes, "Racine est Racine," in his *Mythologies* (Paris, 1957), pp. 109-11.

6. Concerning the *Querelle* as the starting point of historical thought, see Hans Robert Jauss's study, which has long since been deservedly canonized, "Ästhetische Normen und geschichtliche

Reflexion in der 'Querelle des Anciens et des Modernes,' " in his edition of Ch. Perrault, *Parallèle des anciens et des modernes en ce qui regarde les Arts et les Sciences* (Munich, 1964), pp. 8–64.

7. This hiatus in the history of the reception and institutionalization of "historical thought" is documented in the sources noted by Hans Ulrich Gumbrecht, "Modern, Modernität, Moderne," in *Geschichtliche Grundbegriffe: Historisches Lexikon zur politischsozialen Sprache in Deutschland,* ed. Otto Brunner, Werner Conze, and Reinhart Koselleck (Stuttgart, 1978), IV, 93–131.

8. François-Marie Aronet Voltaire, *Le Temple du goût,* ed. E. Carcassonne (Geneva, 1938), p. 105; hereafter cited in text. All translations are my own, unless otherwise noted.

9. See, e.g., the Chaucer documentation in Aleida and Jan Assmann's *Kanon und Zensur.* Karl Maurer provides profound typological and historical insights into this thematic horizon in "Jenseitige Literaturkritik in Dantes *Divina Commedia* und anderweit," in *Literatur in der Gesellschaft des Spätmittelalters,* ed. Hans Ulrich Gumbrecht, vol. 1 of Begleitreihe zum Grundriss der romanischen Literaturen des Mittelalters (Heidelberg, 1980), pp. 205–52.

10. Concerning the origin, social structure, and mentality of the French (Parisian) theater public in the century of classicism, see Erich Auerbach, " 'La cour et la ville' " (1951), trans. by Ralph Manheim, in Erich Auerbach, *Scenes from the Drama of European Literature* (1959; rpt. Gloucester, Mass., 1973), pp. 133–79. This is a pioneering work in the sociology of literature and *histoire des mentalités.*

11. See Niklas Luhmann, "Das Kunstwerk und die Selbstreproduktion der Kunst," *Delfin* 3 (1984), p. 53.

12. See historical examples for the imperative of orienting behavior to social expectations in Niklas Luhmann, "Interaktion in Oberschichten: Zur Transformation ihrer Semantik im 17. und 18. Jahrhundert," in *Gesellschaftsstruktur und Semantik: Studien zur Wissenssoziologie der modernen Gesellschaft,* ed. Niklas Luhmann (Frankfurt, 1980), vol. 1, pp. 72–161, and Roland Galle, *Geständnis und Subjektivität: Untersuchungen zum französischen Roman zwischen Klassik und Romantik* (Munich, 1986).

13. Denis Diderot, "Classique," in *Encyclopédie, ou Dictionnaire raisonné des sciences, des arts et des métiers* (Paris, 1753), vol. 3, p. 507.

14. See Burkhard Steinwachs, "Epistemologie und Kunsthistorie: Zum Verhältnis von 'arts et sciences' im aufklärerischen und positivistischen Enzyklopädismus," in *Der Diskurs der Literatur- und Sprachhistorie: Wissenschaftsgeschichte als Innovationsvorgabe,* ed. Bernard Cerquiglini and Hans Ulrich Gumbrecht (Frankfurt, 1983), pp. 73–110.

15. See Gumbrecht, " 'Klassik ist Klassik.' "

16. Anne Louis Germaine de Staël, *De l'Allemagne,* ed. Simone Balayé (Paris, 1968), vol. 1, p. 39; hereafter cited in text. The full text of the minister's letter was reproduced by Madame de Staël in her preface to the first edition of *De l'Allemagne* (printed in London, 1813). It is well known that Madame de Staël's understanding of literature, with which we are concerned, profited greatly from the aesthetics of the early romantic movement in Germany, despite a few significant distortions.

17. Individual documentation of the pairs of opposed concepts is found in volume 1 of *De l'Allemagne*: pp. 160, 247f. (*goût* vs. *génie* and *lecteur solitaire*); pp. 106, 108, 110, 159 (*raison* and *esprit* vs. *imagination* and *songe*); p. 95 (*finesse* vs. *vérité*); p. 97 (*imitation* vs. *vie*).

18. Cf. Niklas Luhmann, "Das Kunstwerk und die Selbstreproduktion der Kunst": "Only now can the work of art lay full claim to its own singularity, since the uniqueness of each work of art is the surest guarantee that art will always produce something new. Only now will there be a theoretical aesthetic that employs specifically focused conceptualizations" (p. 60).

19. Concerning this "enlargement" (and its failure after the "bourgeois revolutions") see Niklas Luhmann, "Interaktion in Oberschichten," and his "Frühneuzeitliche Anthropologie: Theoretische Lösungen für ein Evolutionsproblem der Gesellschaft," in *Gesellschaftsstruktur und Semantik,* pp. 162–234, and Gumbrecht, "Skizze einer Literaturgeschichte."

20. Cited from the documentation in *Paris sous le Premier Empire: Recueil de documents pour*

l'histoire de l'esprit public à Paris, ed. François-Alphonse Aulard (Paris, 1912; rpt. New York, 1974), vol. 1, p. 326.

21. Stéphanie Félicité de Genlis, *La feuille des gens du monde, ou, Journal imaginaire* (Paris, 1813), pp. 51ff.

22. For more details on the following, see Gumbrecht, "Chants révolutionnaires" and " 'Klassik ist Klassik.' "

23. Cf. Mona Ozouf, "La fête – sous la Révolution française," in *Faire de l'historie*, ed. Jacques Le Goff and Pierre Nora (Paris, 1974), vol. 3, p. 266.

24. Concerning the structural changes in the normative canon after 1794 and the early history of the literary and educational "nurturing of the classics," see Heinz Thoma, *Aufklärung und nachrevolutionäres Bürgertum in Frankreich – zur Aufklärungsrezeption in der französischen Literaturgeschichte des 19. Jahrhunderts (1794-1914)* (Heidelberg, 1976), and Hans-Jürgen Lüsebrink, " 'Cours de littérature' und 'education nationale.' Zur Genese und Konzeption von Literaturunterricht und Literaturwissenschaft in Institutionen der Spätaufklärung, der Französischen Revolution und der napoleonischen Ära," in *Der Diskurs der Literatur- und Sprachhistorie*, pp. 111-34.

25. Ernst Mortiz Arndt, in *Pariser Sommer 1799*, ed. W. Gerlach (Munich, 1982), p. 199.

26. Lüsebrink, " 'Cours de littérature,' " p. 126.

27. François Noël and Guislain de Laplace, *Leçons de littérature et de morale* (1804), vol. 1, 4, as quoted in Lüsebrink, p. 127.

28. I discuss this problem in more detail in "Pathologien im Literatursystem," in *Theorie als Passion: Niklas Luhmann zum 60. Geburtstag*, ed. Dirk Baeker et al. (Frankfurt, 1987), pp. 137-80.

10. Pathologies in the System of Literature

Much of this discussion was worked out in a graduate seminar at the University of Siegen during summer semester 1986 on the history of code and programs in the literary system. For texts, ideas, and intellectual generosity I would like to thank Andreas Bahr, Paco Caudet from Madrid, Monika Elsner, Anja Görzel, Claudia Krülls-Hepermann, Thomas Müller, Juan-José Sánchez, Peter-Michael Spangenberg, and Dagmar Tillmann-Bartylla. Finally I would especially like to compliment Dirk Baecker for his share in a particularly pleasurable editor-author dialogue.

1. In particular I draw on the essay "Ist Kunst codierbar?", which is quoted from *Soziologische Aufklärung*, vol. 3 (Opladen, 1981), pp. 245-66. We will have to wait and see the reaction of the literary critics to "Das Kunstwerk und die Selbstreproduktion der Kunst," in *Stil: Geschichten und Funktionen eines kulturwissenschaftlichen Diskurselements* (Frankfurt, 1986), ed. Hans Ulrich Gumbrecht and K. Ludwig Pfeiffer, pp. 620-72; and to "Das Medium der Kunst," *Delfin* 4 (1986), pp. 6-15.

2. "Das Kunstwerk und die Selbstreproduktion der Kunst," pp. 624ff.

3. Wolfgang Iser, *Das Literaturverständnis zwischen Geschichte und Zukunft* (Saint Gall, 1981), p. 20.

4. See "Ist Kunst codierbar?", p. 249.

5. Symptomatic are titles like Hans Robert Jauss, *Kleine Apologie der ästhetischen Erfahrung: Mit Kunstgeschichtlichen Bemerkungen von Max Imadahl* (Constance, 1972).

6. "Das Kunstwerk und die Selbstreproduktion der Kunst," p. 661.

7. Here too I draw on "Ist Kunst codierbar?" and "Das Kunstwerk und die Selbstreproduktion der Kunst."

8. "Das Kunstwerk und die Selbstreproduktion der Kunst," pp. 626ff.

9. A well-thought-out synthesis of the research on William IX is Michel Zink's "Troubadours et trouvères," in *Précis de littérature française du moyen âge*, ed. Daniel Poirion (Paris, 1983), esp. pp. 129ff.

10. In this regard, see my essay "Beginn von 'Literatur'/Abschied vom Körper?" In *Der Ursprung*

von Literatur, ed. Gisela Smolka-Koerdt, Peter-Michael Spangenberg, and Dagmar Tillmann-Bartylla (Munich, 1988), pp. 15-50.

11. For the sake of simplicity, I deal with the name William IX as if it were a modern author's name, although this is problematic because the relationship between the self-referential gestures in the text and the identities of the text's creator/performer remains much more unclear than in modern communicative phenomena.

12. That would have to mean approximately (the translation problems of the early Provençal courtly-love lyric are still far from consensual solutions): "I would be very glad if it were known that this song, which I bring out of my workshop, is of a good color; that I carry the crown (flower) of this craft. And it is true, and I can present the song as proof, when it has been knit (finished up). // I know sense and madness, and I know shame and honor, and I'm daring and afraid. And if you suggest a love game to me, then I'm not so, that wouldn't know how to make the best of a bad situation." Quoted from the edition of Alfred Jeanroy, *Les chansons de Guillaume IX, Duc d'Aquitaine – 1071-1127* (Paris, 1964), pp.13ff.

13. I have suggested connecting Huizinga's concept of "play" (as interaction form) with Bakhtin's concept of "carnival" (as situational frame) and attaching them to a concept for the reconstruction of courtly culture in "Literarische Gegenwelten, Karnevalskultur und die Epochenschwelle vom Spätmittelalter zur Renaissance" in *Literatur in der Gesellschaft des Spätmittelalters,* ed. Hans Ulrich Gumbrecht (Heidelberg, 1980), pp. 95-145.

14. Jeanroy, *Chansons:* "Blessed may he be who raised me so that I choose a good craft, which I have never denied and in which I never failed; for I know how to play all of the (dice) games on the pillow; as you can see, I know more about it than any of my neighbors" (p. 14).

15. For the stanzas quoted here, VII and VIII, the editor refused to attempt a translation (the first printing appeared in 1926), although they are relatively easy to understand: "It all went good for me the first time" / "And I raised her playing board with my arms a little bit."

16. E. Trojel, ed., *Andreae Capellani Regii Francorum De Amore Libri Tres* (Munich, 1964), p. 310.

17. "Das Kunstwerk und die Selbstreproduktion der Kunst," p. 624.

18. Jeanroy, *Chansons:* "I will make up a song about nothing at all: it will be neither about me nor about other people, it will be neither about love nor youth, nor about anything else. I just made it up (found it) while I was sleeping on my horse" (p. 6).

19. Quoted from Martín de Riquer, *Los trovadores: Historia literaria y textos,* vol. 1 (Barcelona, 1983), p. 107.

20. Ibid., p. 108.

21. Jeanroy, *Chansons:* "Whoever will love, must show himself obedient to many people. And it is fitting that he behave in a pleasant way, and that he watches out in court not to talk in an uncourtly manner" (p. 18).

22. Ibid.: "Everything that I used to love I have given up: the courtly life and pride; and because it pleases God, I resign everything and bid him to take me up in his presence" (p. 28).

23. See Gisela Smolka-Koerdt's excellent study of the structure and pragmatics of Spanish-Portuguese song manuscripts (*cancioneros*): *Die iberischen Liedersammlungen von 1450-1600* (Siegen, 1987).

24. Luhmann, "Das Kunstwerk und die Selbstreproduktion der Kunst," p. 628. In this historical context, Dante's *Vita Nuova* is paradigmatic.

25. I am summarizing here a detailed analysis from my *Eine Geschichte der spanischen Literatur* (Frankfurt, 1990), the chapter entitled "1474-1556."

26. Cf. Fernando de Rojas, *La Celestina,* ed. Julio Cejador y Frauca, vol. 1 (Madrid, 1968), pp. 24ff.

27. A proof is Smolka-Koerdt, Spangenberg, and Tillmann-Bartylla, *Der Ursprung von Literatur.*

28. This highly significant insight, from the point of view of literary history, belongs to Dagmar Tillmann-Bartylla.

29. To my advantage, Claudia Krülls-Hepermann is particularly well informed about them.

30. Luiz Costa Lima has studied the consequences of this attachment to morality for the fictionality of literature in *O controle do imaginário, Razão e imaginação no Occidente* (São Paulo, 1984), and *Sociedade e discurso ficcional* (Rio de Janeiro, 1986).

31. Cf. Luhmann, *Soziale Systeme: Grundriss einer allgemeinen Theorie* (Frankfurt, 1984), pp. 70ff.

32. Armand Gasté, ed., *La Querelle du Cid: Pièces et pamphlets publiés d'apres les originaux avec une introduction* (Hildesheim, 1974), p. 63.

33. Corneille, *Excuse à Ariste*, p. 65.

34. Cf. the texts by Mairet and Scudéry in Gasté's anthology. The editor talks about Richelieu in the foreword, p. 14.

35. Corneille, *Excuse à Ariste*, p. 65.

36. Quoted from Boileau, *Oeuvres*, ed. G. Mongrédien (Paris, 1961), p. 163.

37. On the *Querelle des anciens et des modernes*, Hans Robert Jauss's "Introductory Treatise" is still quite indispensable: "Ästhetische Normen und geschichtliche Reflexion in der 'Querelle des anciens et des modernes,' " new edition of Perrault's *Parallèle des anciens et des modernes en ce qui regarde les arts et les sciences* (Munich, 1964), pp. 8–81.

38. *Parallèle*, I, 11.

39. Jauss, "Ästhetische Normen und geschichtliche Reflexion," p. 57.

40. Cf. "Das Kunstwerk und die Selbstreproduktion der Kunst," pp. 640ff.

41. I am orienting myself to a schema that Luhmann (much more successfully) applied to the analysis of similar restructuring processes in the legal system; *Ökologische Kommunikation* (Opladen, 1986), p. 95.

42. The first part of Michel Foucault's *Les mots et les choses* (Paris, 1966) is nothing else.

43. Diderot, *Oeuvres esthétiques*, ed. P. Vernière (Paris, 1965), p. 309.

44. Quoted from Vernière's commentary, ibid., p. 292.

45. Cf. Buffon's concept of style with Hans Ulrich Gumbrecht, "Schwindende Stabilität der Wirklichkeit: Eine Geschichte des Stilbegriffs," in *Stil*, pp. 728–88, here 754ff.

46. Ibid., pp. 757ff.

47. On its origin, see Hans Ulrich Gumbrecht, " 'Klassik ist Klassik—eine bewundernswerte Sicherheit des Nichts'? oder: Funktionen der französischen Literatur des siebzehnten Jahrhunderts nach Siebzehnhundert," in *Französische Klassik: Theorie, Literatur, Malerei*, ed. Fritz Nies and Karlheinz Stierle (Munich, 1985), pp. 441–94; and "Phönix aus der Asche, oder: Vom Kanon zur Klassik" in *Kanon und Zensur: Archäologie der literarischen Kommunikation*, ed. A. Assman and J. Assman, vol. 2 (Munich, 1987), pp. 284–99.

48. The tenacity with which the nineteenth century held on to metahistorical categories (and the belief in "originating forms") was called to my attention by Siegfried J. Schmidt in a seminar we did together at Siegen on the history of genre theory.

49. Sainte-Beuve, "*Portraits littéraires*," in *Oeuvres*, vol. 1, ed. M. Leroy (Paris, 1966), p. 758.

50. Victor Hugo, *Théâtre*, vol. 1, ed. J. J. Thierry and J. Mélèze (Paris, 1966), p. 416.

51. Ibid., p. 409ff. I will not go into Baudelaire's definition of modernity and art here; it is sufficiently well known and has been interpreted to the point of supersaturation.

52. For more text-analytical detail on this hypothesis, see Hans Ulrich Gumbrecht and Jürgen E. Müller, "Sinnbildung als Sicherung der Lebenswelt—ein Beitrag zur funktionsgeschichtlichen Situierung der realistischen Literatur am Beispiel von Balzacs Erzählung 'La Bourse,' " in *Honoré de Balzac*, ed. Hans Ulrich Gumbrecht, Karlheinz Stierle, and Rainer Warning (Munich, 1980), pp. 339–89.

53. This useful (and for me, welcome) concept I heard for the first time from Helmut Kreuzer.

54. Luhmann has dedicated two ironic (and brilliant) pages to this in "Das Kunstwerk und die Selbstreproduktion der Kunst," pp. 657ff.

55. A veritable lexicon of syntagmata of this kind could be compiled from the table of contents of books like Dietmar Kamper and Christoph Wulf, eds., *Die Wiederkehr des Körpers* (Frankfurt, 1982), and their *Der andere Körper* (Berlin, 1984); the second was published in the series "Editio Corpus" by the publisher "Mensch und Leben" (Berlin).

56. Luhmann formulates it so: "In the result, the intensification of the requirements for inclusion has the effect of exclusion." "Das Kunstwerk und die Selbstreproduktion der Kunst," p. 650.

11. It's Just a Game: On the History of Media, Sport, and the Public

1. Various passages of this essay go back to discussions in the project on the "Prehistory and Early History of Television" within the Siegen University Special Research Project *Aesthetics, Pragmatics, and History of Screen and Television Media*, which I held together with Monika Elsner, Thomas Müller, and Peter-Michael Spangenberg.

2. A poster on a Catholic church in Bochum (April 1986) declared "God is not a spectator sport."

3. See Niklas Luhmann, *Soziale Systeme: Grundriss einer allgemeinen Theorie* (Frankfurt, 1984), pp. 331ff., especially p. 337: "Rather, the body seems perfectly suited to be a focus of senselessness, when it doesn't persist in pure actuality but serves, from the point of view of sport, as the level of departure for its own sphere of meaning. Sport neither needs nor tolerates any ideology (which by no means excludes its political misuse). It presents the body which nowhere else is so intensely claimed. It legitimizes the attitude towards one's own body by the meaning of the body itself—not free of asceticism, to be sure, but basically as its exact opposite, that is, not negative but positive. And it does this, without having to attach itself to the domains of meaning of other antecedents. Certainly, sport is considered healthy; but also this context of sense only refers back again to the body itself."

4. For the concept of play see Hans Ulrich Gumbrecht, "'Mens sana' und 'Körperloses Spiel'/'Sinnloses Treten' und 'In corpore sano,' " *Sprache im technischen Zeitalter*, 92 (1984), pp. 262–78.

5. Cf. Luhmann, *Soziale Systeme*, pp. 323ff., and Hans Ulrich Gumbrecht, "The Body vs. the Printing Press: Media in the Early Modern Period, Mentalities in the Reign of Castile, and Another History of Literary Forms," *Poetics* 14 (1985), pp. 209–27.

6. See Hans Ulrich Gumbrecht, "Chants révolutionnaires, maîtrise de l'avenir et les niveaux de sens collectif," *Revue d'Histoire Moderne et Contemporaine* 30 (1983), pp. 235–56.

7. For Colette, see the biography—and above all, the pictures that are so important for the arguments raised here—by Geneviève Dormann, *Amoureuse Colette* (Paris, 1984).

8. Bertolt Brecht, *Schriften zur Politik und zur Gesellschaft*, vol. 20 of the *Gesammelte Werke* in 20 vols. (Frankfurt, 1967), pp. 90ff.

9. Ibid., p. 28.

10. *Die Olympischen Spiele 1936 in Berlin und Garmisch-Partenkirchen*, 2 vols. (Altona-Bahrenfeld, 1936), vol. 2, p. 18.

11. *Die Olympischen Spiele*, vol. 2, p. 101.

12. Miguel Cruchaga Ossa, *El Tercen [sic] Reich* (Berlin, 1933), p. 145.

13. *Die Olympischen Spiele*, vol. 2, p. 5.

14. Kurt Wagenführ, *Anmerkungen zum Fernsehen 1938 bis 1980* (Mainz/Stuttgart, 1983), p. 23.

15. The original texts and posters in the brochure, *Al Brown boxt für die Soziologen*, ed. Wolf-Dieter Gericke (Frankfurt, 1980).

16. For a more differentiated view of this institution, see the excellent study *Le Collège de Sociologie: 1937–1939*, ed. Denis Hollier (Paris, 1979).

17. *Le Collège de Sociologie*, p. 18.

18. This is according to a book, formatted in the style of a society tabloid, by Dominique Grimault and Patrick Mahé, *Eine Hymne an die Liebe: Edith Piaf und Marcel Cerdan* (Hamburg, 1984).

19. For the hypothesis of the special potential of the voice in actualizing corporality, see Paul Zumthor, *Introduction à la poésie orale* (Paris, 1983).

Index

Compiled by Eileen Quam and Theresa Wolner

Theory and History of Literature

Hans Ulrich Gumbrecht is professor of comparative literature and romance literatures and chair of the comparative literature department at Stanford University. He has published numerous books and essays on medieval literature, cultural history between the 18th and the 20th century, the history of literary criticism, and the theoretical problems of the social history of literature.

Glen Burns is a lecturer in English and a free-lance translator in Germany.

Wlad Godzich is professor of emergent literatures at the University of Geneva and coeditor, with Jochen Schulte-Sasse, of the Theory and History of Literature series.